Eyes Open 4

TEACHER'S BOOK

Garan Holcombe

CAMBRIDGE
UNIVERSITY PRESS

Discovery
EDUCATION™

CAMBRIDGE
UNIVERSITY PRESS

University Printing House, Cambridge CB2 8BS, United Kingdom

Cambridge University Press is part of the University of Cambridge.

It furthers the University's mission by disseminating knowledge in the pursuit of education, learning and research at the highest international levels of excellence.

www.cambridge.org
Information on this title: www.cambridge.org/9781107467835

© Cambridge University Press 2015

First published 2015

Printed and bound in Italy by Rotolito Lombarda S.p.A.

A catalogue record for this publication is available from the British Library

ISBN 978-1-107-46781-1 Student's Book with Online Workbook and Online Practice
ISBN 978-1-107-46780-4 Student's Book
ISBN 978-1-107-46782-8 Workbook with Online Practice
ISBN 978-1-107-46783-5 Teacher's Book
ISBN 978-1-107-46786-6 Audio CDs (3)
ISBN 978-1-107-46787-3 Video DVD
ISBN 978-1-107-49052-9 Presentation Plus DVD-ROM

Additional resources for this publication at www.cambridgelms.org/eyesopen

Contents

Welcome to *Eyes Open*

Eyes Open is a four-level course for lower-secondary students, which will give you and your students all the tools you need for successful and enjoyable language teaching and learning. Teaching secondary students can be challenging, even for the most experienced of teachers. It is a period of great change in young teenagers' lives, and it sometimes seems that their interests lie anywhere but in the classroom. It is the teacher's demanding task to engage students in the learning process, and *Eyes Open*'s mission is to help them as much as possible to achieve this. After extensive research and investigation involving teachers and students at secondary school level, we've come to a clear conclusion: sparking students' curiosity and desire to learn is one of the main driving forces which can enhance and facilitate the learning process. The aim of *Eyes Open* is to stimulate curiosity through interesting content via impactful video, visual images and 'real world' content on global themes.

How *Eyes Open* will benefit you and your students

Engaging real world content

Eyes Open contains a wealth of fascinating reading texts and informative Discovery Education™ video clips. The two-page *Discover Culture* sections bring global cultures to the classroom, greatly enhancing the students' learning experience whilst simultaneously reinforcing target language. The texts and three Discovery Education™ video clips per unit often revolve around teenage protagonists. The wide variety of themes, such as natural history, inspiring personal stories, unusual lifestyles, international festivals and customs teach students about the world around them through the medium of English, whilst also promoting values such as cultural awareness and social responsibility. Each unit also has an accompanying *CLIL* lesson (with accompanying Discovery Education™ video) which contains a reading text and activities. Each unit's texts, together with the videos, encourage the students to reflect on, discuss and explore the themes further. For more information on culture in *Eyes Open* go to page 19. For more information on the CLIL lessons please go to page 25. For specific extension activity ideas please see the relevant video lesson pages of the Teacher's Book.

Easier lesson preparation

Everything you need to prepare your lessons is available on the *Presentation Plus* discs which, once installed, allow you to access everything easily and from one place. The package contains digital versions of the Student's Book and Workbook, with interactive activities for class presentation, all audio (Student's Book, Workbook and tests), video clips, tests and additional practice activities, which include video worksheets, grammar, vocabulary, communication activities and a link to the Cambridge Learning Management System for the Online Workbook and Online Extra.

Clear goals to build confidence

Eyes Open has been designed to provide a balance between exciting, real-world content and carefully guided and structured language practice to build both confidence and fluency.

Students of this age also need to know exactly what their learning goals are if they are to become successful learners. In *Eyes Open,* this is addressed in the following ways:

- The unit presentation page at the beginning of each unit clearly lays out the contents and objectives of the unit, so students know from the beginning what they will be studying in the coming lessons. More detailed objectives, together with CEFR relevance, are given in the relevant opening page of the Teacher's Book notes.
- Clear headings guide students to key content. Target language is displayed in easy-to-identify tables or boxes.
- Each page builds to a carefully controlled productive stage, where students are asked to use relevant language and often expand on the topics and themes of the lesson.

Extra support for speaking and writing

Most learners find speaking and writing particularly challenging, and so the Speaking and Writing pages in the Student's Book and the Workbook are structured in such a way as to lead the students step by step through the tasks necessary to reach the final goal of that page. This approach has been designed to help build students' confidence and fluency. In addition, the guided *Your turn* sections at the end of lessons give students the opportunity to activate new language. For more information, see page 20.

Visual impact

Youth culture today is visually oriented and teenagers are easily bored by material that is not visually attractive. In addition to the video content, images in *Eyes Open* have been chosen to appeal to young students. Each unit begins with a large impactful image designed to attract the students' attention and encourage them to engage with the content of the unit. Reading texts are accompanied by artwork which draws the students into the page and stimulates them to want to know what the text is about. For more information on use of visuals in *Eyes Open* see page 18.

A personalised approach

Secondary students also need to see how the world they are reading about, watching or listening to relates to them and their own world in some way. They also need ample opportunity to practise new language in a safe environment. *Eyes Open* offers multiple opportunities for students to personalise the topics via the carefully structured *Your turn* activities which appear at the end of lessons. These sections add a relevance to the subjects and themes which is central to their successful learning. In *Eyes Open* students are encouraged to talk about themselves and their opinions and interests, but care is taken to avoid them having to reveal personal information which they may be uncomfortable discussing.

Graded practice for mixed abilities

Teaching mixed-ability classes creates more challenges for the busy teacher, and with this in mind we've provided a wealth of additional practice activities, including:

- Two pages of grammar and vocabulary activities per unit available to download from *Presentation Plus*. These are graded to cater for mixed abilities, 'standard' for the majority of students and 'extra' for those students who need or want more challenging practice.
- Graded unit progress and end- and mid-year tests ('standard' and 'extra' as above). Available from *Presentation Plus*.
- Graded exercises in the Workbook, with a clear one- to three-star system.
- Additional grammar and vocabulary practice in the *Vocabulary Bank* and *Grammar reference* section at the back of the Student's Book.
- Suggestions for alternative approaches or activities in the Teacher's Book notes for stronger / weaker students.

Common European Framework compatibility

The content in *Eyes Open* has also been created with both the Common European Framework (CEFR) and Key Competences in mind. Themes, topics and activity types help students achieve the specific objectives set out by The Council of Europe. These have been mapped and cross-referenced to the relevant parts of the course material. More information on this can be found on pages 32–36, and on the first page of each unit in the Teacher's Notes.

Relevant content

For *Eyes Open*, research was carried out on the language syllabus using the Cambridge Learner Corpus. The results of this research became the starting point for the selection of each error to be focused on. By using the Cambridge Learner Corpus, we can ensure that the areas chosen are based on real errors made by learners of English at the relevant levels. In addition, the authors of *Eyes Open* have made extensive use of the English Vocabulary Profile to check the level of tasks and texts and to provide a starting point for vocabulary exercises. For more information on the Cambridge Learner Corpus and English Profile please see pages 23 and 32.

Thorough recycling and language reinforcement

New language is systematically recycled and revised throughout the course with:

- A two-page *Review* section every two units in the Student's Book,
- A two-page *Review* after every unit in the Workbook, plus a Cambridge Learner Corpus informed *Get it Right* page, with exercises focusing on common errors,
- Unit progress tests,
- Mid and End of Year progress tests.

In addition, the *Vocabulary Bank* at the back of the Student's Book provides further practice of the core vocabulary.

For more information on the review sections, including ideas for exploitation please go to page 30.

Flexibility for busy teachers

Eyes Open is designed to be flexible in that it can meet the needs of teachers with up to 150 hours of class time per school year, but is also suitable for those with fewer than 90 hours. (There are also split combo editions with half of the Student's Books and Workbooks for those with fewer than 80 hours of class time, please see www.cambridge.org/eyesopen for a full list of components).

If you're short of time, the following sections can be left out of the Student's Books if necessary, without affecting the input of core grammar and vocabulary which students will encounter in the tests. However, it's important to note the video activities in particular are designed to reinforce new language and provide a motivating and enjoyable learning experience:

- The Starter Unit (the diagnostic test will allow you to assess your students' level of English before the start of term, please see page 31 for more information).
- *Review* pages: these could be set for homework if need be.
- The *Discover Culture* video pages: though we believe this is one of the most engaging features of the course, no new grammar is presented and the content of these pages doesn't inform the tests.
- The *CLIL* pages at the back of the Student's Book.
- The *Project* pages at the back of the Student's Book, and on the Cambridge Learner Management System (please see page 26 for more information).
- The *Vocabulary Bank* at the back of the Student's Book: many of the activities can be set for homework, or can be done by 'fast finishers' in class.
- The video clips on the *Language Focus* and *Speaking* pages: though these are short and there are time-saving 'instant' video activities available in the Teacher's Book (see pages 122–137).
- The additional exercises in the *Grammar reference*: these can be set for homework if need be.

Course Components

Eyes Open provides a range of print and digital learning tools designed to help you and your students.

Student's Book

The Student's Book contains eight units, plus a Starter section to revise basic grammar and vocabulary. High interest topics, including 24 Discovery Education™ video clips and additional vox pop-style videos motivate learners and spark their curiosity. Each lesson is accompanied by guided, step-by-step activities and personalised activities that lead to greater fluency and confidence.

Workbook with Online Practice

The Workbook provides additional practice activities for all the skills presented in the Student's Book. The Workbook also includes free online access to the Cambridge Learning Management System for Workbook audio, wordlists, extra writing practice, vocabulary games and interactive video activities.

Student's Book with Online Workbook and Online Practice

The Student's Book with Online Workbook provides access to full workbook content online, with all audio content. It also provides online access to the Cambridge Learning Management System so teachers can track students' progress.

Digital Student's Book with complete video and audio programme

Digital Student's Books and Workbooks are available for iOS and Android devices and include activities in interactive format, as well as full video and audio content for each level. The Digital Books can be downloaded to a computer, tablet or other mobile device for use offline, anytime.

Combo A and B Student's Books with Online Workbooks and Online Practice

Student's Books are available as split combos, with the entire contents of the combined Student's Book and Workbook for Units 1–4 (Combo A) and 5–8 (Combo B). The Combos include access to the Cambridge Learning Management System with Online Workbooks, embedded audio and video content and access to Online Practice.

Teacher's Resources

Teacher's Book

The Teacher's Book includes full CEFR mapping, complete lesson plans, audio scripts, answer keys, video activities, optional activities, tips for mixed ability classes and a *Games Bank*.

Cambridge/Discovery Education™ Video DVD

Compelling, high interest Discovery Education™ video clips spark students' interest and help develop language abilities. 32 videos per level, including 24 Discovery Education™ clips, reinforce each unit's target language through a variety of video types:

- Engaging explorations of cultures, people, and locations from around the globe
- Interviews with native language speakers discussing topics of interest to teens
- CLIL-based content to accompany the eight-page *CLIL* section.

Presentation Plus Digital Classroom Pack

Presentation Plus is a complete planning and presentation tool for teachers. It includes class presentation software, fully interactive Student's Book and Workbook, answer keys and full video and audio content, with scripts for each level. The digital Teacher's Book and Teacher's Resources, including the Test Centre, and additional graded practice activities, allow easy and fast lesson planning. A link to the online learning management platform enables teachers to track pupils' progress.

Cambridge Learning Management System

The CLMS is a simple, easy-to-use platform that hosts the Online Workbook, extra Online Practice resources for students and teachers, and progress monitoring in one user-friendly system. Students can access their online workbooks and extra online practice and receive instant feedback, while teachers can track student progress and manage content. There is also a free online Professional Development module to help teachers take advantage of the latest classroom techniques.

Class Audio CDs

The Class Audio CDs include the complete audio programme of the Student's Book and Workbook to support listening comprehension and build fluency.

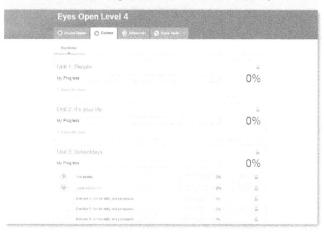

Unit tour
Student's Book

Each unit starts with an impactful image designed to spark curiosity and discussion, and introduce the unit topic.

The four unit video clips are summarised on this page.

The second page of each unit focuses on vocabulary, which is presented in a memorable way.

Vocabulary, grammar and unit aims are clearly identified so that students and teachers can easily follow the syllabus progression.

A short *Be Curious* task encourages students to speak and engage with both the image and with the theme of the unit.

Through the listen, check and repeat task, students are given the opportunity to hear how the target vocabulary is pronounced and to practise it themselves.

Your turn activities at the end of every lesson give students the opportunity to practise new language in a personalised, communicative way.

The third page of each unit features a reading text which provides a natural context for the new grammar. All reading texts are recorded.

The *Language Focus* pages in *Eyes Open* highlight examples that are contextualised in the preceding reading and listening passages. Students are encouraged to find the examples for themselves.

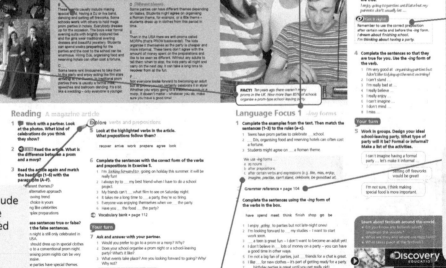

A short *Fact Box* imparts a snippet of interesting information related to the topic of the reading text.

The *Reading* pages include *Explore* features where students are encouraged to notice vocabulary from the text. Often the focus is on lexico-grammatical sets. Other times, collocation or word formation is focused on. In levels 3 & 4, students are also encouraged to understand the meaning of above-level words.

The grammar is presented in a clear, easy-to-read format.

Many of the *Language Focus* pages include a *Get it Right* feature, where corpus-informed common learner errors are highlighted.

The *Grammar reference* at the back of the book contains more detailed examples and explanations, plus additional practice exercises.

A Discovery Education™ video complements the reading topic, and provides further exposure to the target grammar, in the context of a fascinating insight into different cultures around the world.

The next page focuses on Listening and Vocabulary from the Listening. Sometimes this second Vocabulary section pre teaches vocabulary before the students listen.

The *Language Focus 2* page features examples from the preceding listening passage.

The listening passage provides a natural context for the new grammar and vocabulary items.

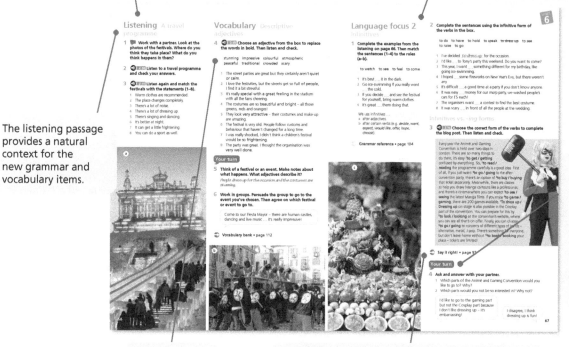

Your turn sections at the end of every lesson provide speaking practice and enable students to revise, personalise and activate the language taught, for more effective learning.

New language is clearly highlighted.

Many *Language Focus* pages contain a *Say it Right* feature, where common pronunciation difficulties associated with the *Language Focus* are dealt with. In levels 2–4, these appear at the back of the book.

The *Discover Culture* spread expands on the unit topic and provides a motivating insight into a variety of cultures around the world.

In levels 3 & 4, students are also encouraged to understand the meaning of above-level words.

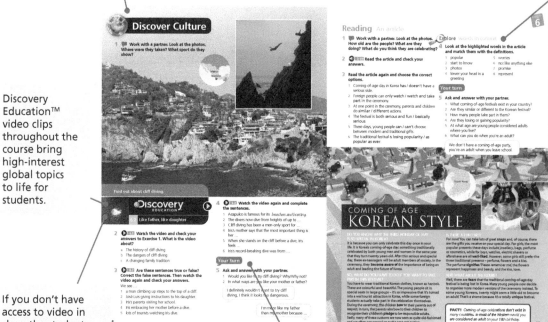

Discovery Education™ video clips throughout the course bring high-interest global topics to life for students.

The second lesson in the *Discover Culture* spread focuses on a reading text which is thematically linked to the cultural angle of the video.

If you don't have access to video in class, the students can access this video, together with the interactive activities, via the Online Practice.

The *Your turn* sections on these pages encourage learners to compare their lives with the lives of the people featured in the reading texts and video clips.

Speaking and writing skills are carefully developed through a progression of easy-to-follow activities which guide students towards written and spoken fluency.

The optional *Real Talk* video features English and American teenagers answering a specific question linked to the language or unit topic.

All *Writing* pages include a model text from the featured genre.

After a short comprehension activity, students are encouraged to answer the same question as the teenagers in the clip.

Writing lessons broadly follow a Process Writing methodology, where students are encouraged to plan and check their writing.

Both Speaking and Writing lessons present Useful Language in chunks to develop fluency.

A clear model is provided for the speaking task.

Useful Language sections on these pages highlight specific linguistic features from the model writing text and dialogue which will help build students' writing and speaking skills.

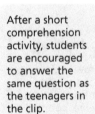

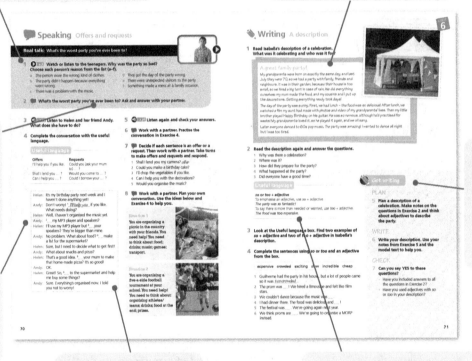

There are two pages of *Review* after every two units. The exercises are grouped under *Vocabulary* and *Language focus* (grammar). These can be set for homework if time is short in class.

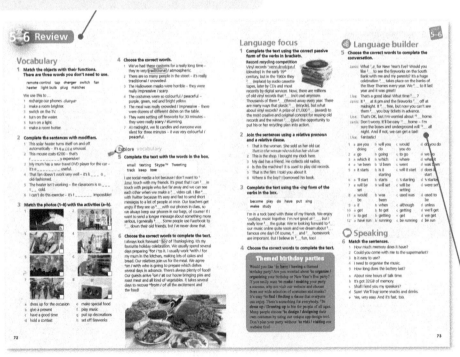

Language builder sections revise the target grammar from all the previous units.

Each *CLIL* lesson is linked to the topic of the corresponding unit. They give students the opportunity to study other subjects through the medium of English.

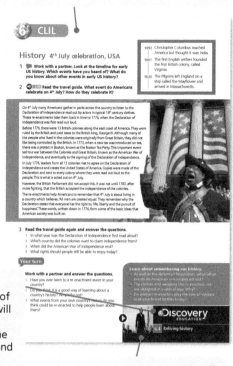

The *Grammar reference* provides more detailed explanations with clear examples.

If you want to make fuller use of the video, you will find a complete lesson plan at the back of the TB and photocopiable worksheets on the Presentation Plus software.

The third Discovery Education™ video clip brings high-interest global topics to life for students.

Additional grammar exercises provide even more practice.

The *Vocabulary Bank* contains all the new vocabulary from each unit. Activities revise and consolidate the language.

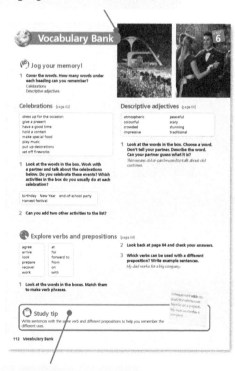

There are three optional projects in the Student's Book, and more ideas for additional projects available via *Presentation Plus*.

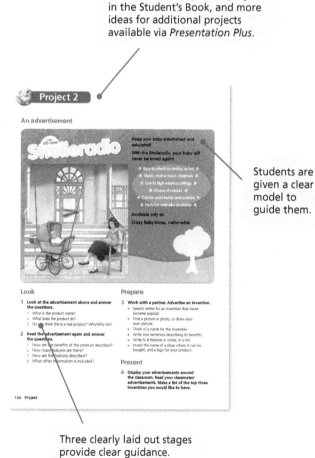

Students are given a clear model to guide them.

Each page includes a study tip to help students record and remember new words and encourage autonomy.

Three clearly laid out stages provide clear guidance.

Workbook

The first page of each unit practises the vocabulary from the opening pages of the unit in the Student's Book.

The second page practises the first *Language Focus* section.

Every unit contains a listening activity.

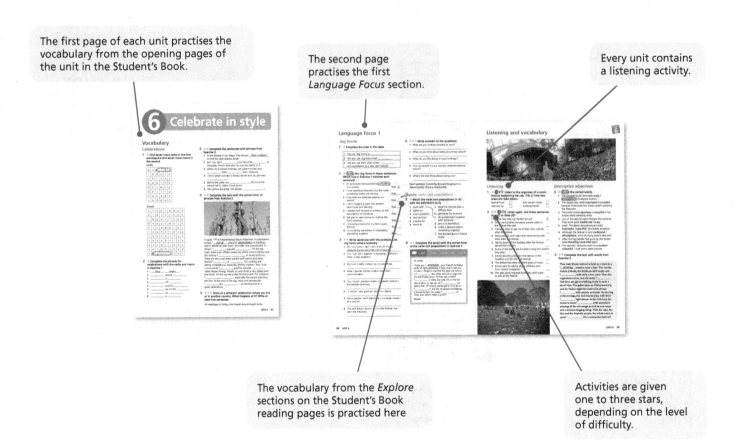

The vocabulary from the *Explore* sections on the Student's Book reading pages is practised here

Activities are given one to three stars, depending on the level of difficulty.

Language Focus 2 provides further practice of the target grammar from the Student's Book.

The model writing text includes more useful language, which is extended from the Student's Book.

There is a double-page *Writing* section in every unit.

The organisation and contents of the model text are highlighted.

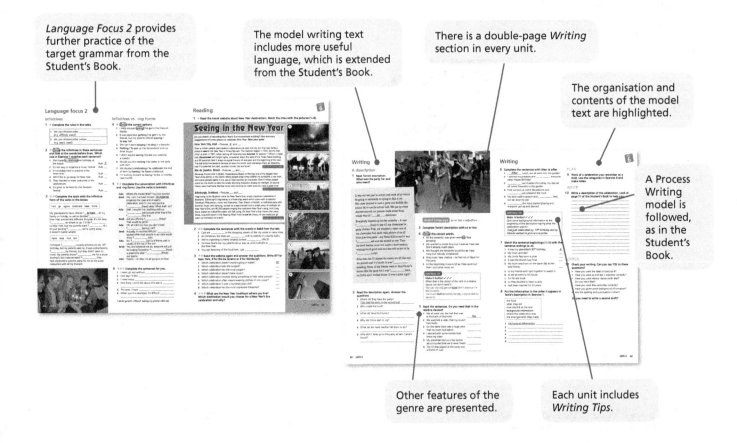

A Process Writing model is followed, as in the Student's Book.

Other features of the genre are presented.

Each unit includes *Writing Tips*.

The first page of the *Review* section focuses on the grammar and vocabulary of the unit.

Each unit is followed by a two-page *Review* section.

The second page revises the grammar, vocabulary and functional language from all units to this point.

Each unit finishes with a *Get it Right* page where common learner errors are focused on, including spelling errors. The errors are informed by the Cambridge Learner Corpus.

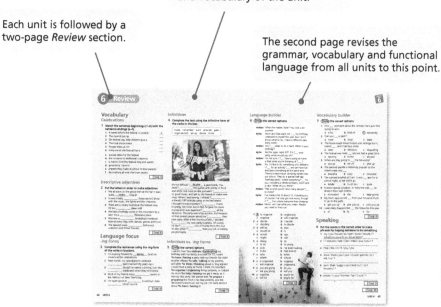

Focus on pronunciation sections provide more extensive practice of pronunciation features such as word and sentence stress and intonation.

The *Speaking extra* pages practise the *Useful Language* from the Speaking pages in the Student's Book.

There is plenty of listening practice to contextualise the language.

The *Language focus extra* pages provide even more practice of the grammar in the Student's Book.

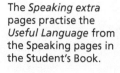

Whenever students are asked to listen, they are given an opportunity to listen for gist first.

Teacher's Book

The unit aims and unit contents include all the video, common learner errors and also the relevant material at the back of the book, such as pronunciation and CLIL.

Each lesson has objectives making it easier for the teacher and the learner to understand and attain the goals.

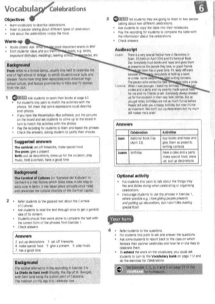

Each lesson starts with an optional warm-up activity to prepare the students for the lesson in a dynamic way.

Each unit contains a detailed list of the CEFR goals covered within it.

Each reading text is supplemented with contextual information on the topic.

Throughout the notes, there are ideas for games to practise the target language.

There are suggestions for dealing with stronger or weaker students throughout the notes.

The first Discovery™ videos have short lesson notes here. If you want to explore the video in more depth, there are thorough lesson notes at the back of the book.

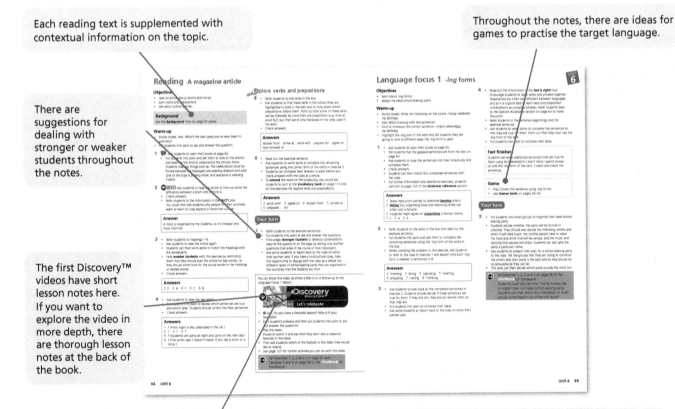

Video clips on these pages can either be done as a lead-in to the *Language focus 1* lesson, or as a follow-up to it.

Language note boxes alert teachers to typical mistakes students make with the target language.

Audio scripts can be found together at the back of the book.

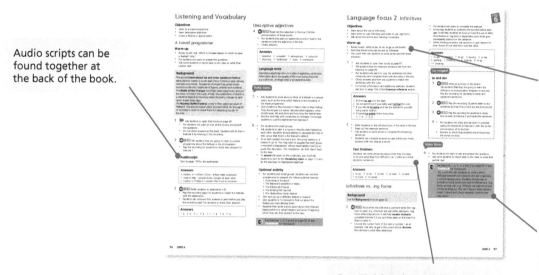

Teaching notes include 'off the page' activities with Student's Books closed.

Homework suggestions point teachers to the relevant workbook pages, but also offer creative, learner-centred alternative ideas.

Fast Finishers boxes help with class management.

The *Discover Culture* video lesson contains step-by-step lesson notes, as well as the video script. Video self-study activities for students are available on the Cambridge Learning Management System (CLMS), accessible via the Workbook.

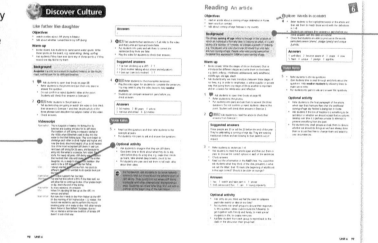

Each reading text is supplemented with contextual information on the topic.

Video scripts are embedded within the teacher's notes.

Optional activity boxes provide a variety of ideas for motivating activities.

Where the teacher needs to prepare before the class, this is clearly highlighted at the start of the lesson notes.

Answer keys are embedded within the notes, in the appropriate place.

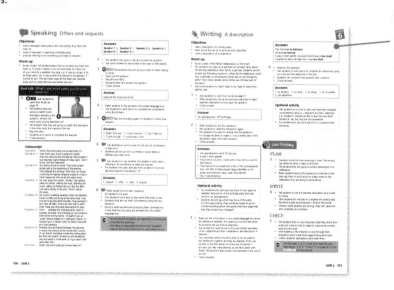

Presentation Plus digital classroom software

Engage students with lively multimedia content including easy access to all the videos with subtitles.

A link to the Cambridge Learner Dictionary

Fully interactive Workbook

Fully interactive Student's Book

Check students' answers with the answer key.

Extra teacher's resources such as the Teacher's Book, tests and photocopiable activities

The zoom feature allows you to zoom anywhere on the page.

Listen to the audio with the option to show the script.

Access this content via the *Presentation Plus* DVD-ROM, available separately.

Each page in each unit features interactive activities.

Presentation Plus gives you easy access to digital versions of all the teaching resources you need in one place.

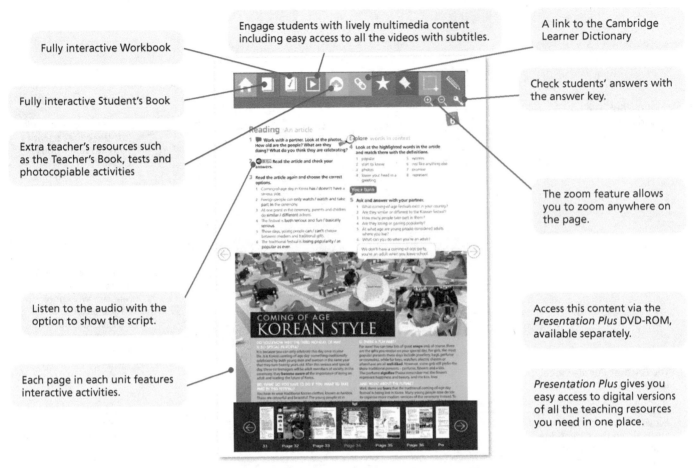

Online Workbook with Online Practice on the Cambridge Learning Management system

Click on the Resources tab to open the Online Practice.

The Cambridge Learning Management system gives students extra language practice with even more games and activities.

Click on the Content tab to open the Online Workbook.

You and your students can see how much of each unit, section or exercise has been attempted.

The Workbook gives free access to the *Resources* area, where students will find the Workbook audio and Wordlists.

The teacher view also has access to a full online teacher training programme.

In the gradebook, students and teachers can see scores by unit or section for individual students or the whole class.

The teacher decides when to unlock content.

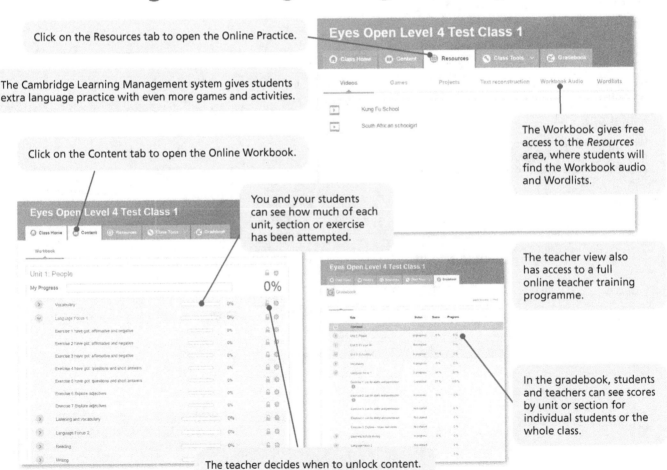

Using video in *Eyes Open*

Using video in the classroom can often appear to be something of a challenge, especially if the necessary equipment isn't always available. But teachers who use video report increased levels of motivation and enthusiasm in students.

Eyes Open offers four video clips per unit, a total of 32 sequences in the course. These high-quality clips have been produced in collaboration with Discovery Education™. The Discovery Education™ footage has been edited by Cambridge University Press to meet the needs of the secondary classroom and the audio has been specially written to fit the syllabus and level of the students.

The clips maintain the appeal and exciting content of all Discovery Education™ videos, featuring a wide variety of countries from around the world (both English and non-English speaking). The themes have been carefully selected to appeal to learners in the target age range. They often focus on aspects of teenagers' lives around the world and inspire learners to continue to explore the topics in the videos outside the classroom.

The videos can be used as much or as little as the teacher chooses. In the Teacher's Book, each video is accompanied by a number of suggested exercises which can be completed in a short time within the course of a normal class. The Student's DVD-ROM, which accompanies the Student's Book, contains all 32 videos from the course as well as interactive exercises which students can complete while watching the videos. Extra ideas for building on the content and themes of the videos are provided in the Teacher's Book. If the teacher prefers to make a full lesson out of the video, he/she can print out the corresponding worksheets from the *Presentation Plus* software.

Video in the classroom

Why video?

Video is becoming the primary means of information presentation in digital global media. Recent statistics suggest that 90% of internet traffic is video-based. Because of this, teaching a language through text and image alone may not completely reflect how many of today's teenagers communicate and receive and transmit information. Due to the increasing prevalence of video in all walks of life, being visually literate and knowing how to process visual data is an increasingly necessary skill in today's digital world. So why not use video in the language classroom?

How to exploit video

Video can be exploited in a variety of ways in the language classroom. Primarily, teachers may use video for listening skills practice. Video is an ideal tool for practising listening comprehension. The obvious advantage it has over audio alone is the visual support it can offer the viewer. Students are sometimes able to see the speaker's mouth, facial expressions and gestures, as well as being able to see the context clearly and any visual clues which may aid comprehension. All of the essential micro-skills such as listening for specific information, predicting and hypothesising can be taught very effectively through this medium.

Video can also act as visual stimulus. Here the moving image acts as a way to engage interest and is a catalyst for follow-up classroom tasks, such as summarising the video content or post-viewing discussions. Teachers can also make use of the visual image alone to practise prediction or encourage students to invent their own soundtrack based on what they see rather than what they hear.

Finally, video can be a great source of information and provides learners with the content for subsequent tasks such as project work. The factual nature of Discovery Education™ provides a very useful tool when teaching CLIL (Content and Language Integrated Learning), in which students learn academic subjects in English.

For more detailed information about use of videos in *Eyes Open* and extra worksheets, see pages 122–137.

Videos in *Eyes Open*

Our approach to integrating video into Cambridge's new secondary course, *Eyes Open*, was to adapt authentic material from Discovery Education™. The content and subject matter of these videos is ideal for the secondary school classroom. Learners of this age are curious about the world and keen to learn about different cultures, natural history and people of their own age around the globe. Many teenagers also watch similar documentary-style programmes outside the classroom. The videos in *Eyes Open* are short and fast-paced, with plenty to engage the teenage viewer without overloading them with information.

The voiceovers in the videos are delivered in a clear, concise manner with language specially graded to match the syllabus and to reflect what students have learned up to each point on the course. By providing subtitles in a simplified storyboard format, we have added an extra aid to student comprehension which teachers can make use of should the need arise.

There are four videos in each unit of *Eyes Open*. Video sections can be found on the *Language focus 1* page, the *Discover Culture* page, the *Speaking* page and the *CLIL* page at the back of the book. Discovery Education™ video supplements and extends the unit themes throughout the course. With a strong cultural focus and a variety of topics from countries around the world, these videos act as a way to encourage intercultural awareness and lead students to seek out similarities and differences between their own culture and other cultures around the world.

The videos which accompany the *CLIL* pages at the back of the book are an ideal complement to the content being taught in class. Subjects such as Science, Maths and History are brought to life in informative and highly educational videos which are a natural progression from the lesson on the page.

Of the four videos, the only one not to feature documentary material is on the *Speaking* page. These *Real Talk* videos include interviews with British, American and Australian teens in which the young people talk to camera on a variety of subjects both relevant to the topic on the page and to teenagers' own lives. These voices are fresh and act as sympathetic role models for the learners.

The future of video in class

Who knows where we will end up with video? New video genres are being born all the time. Software offering the latest innovations in interactive video work is constantly being developed, and, before long, it will be possible to show a video in class that your students will be able to change as they watch.

We are living in an age in which digital video reigns supreme. For this reason, try to make video a central part of your lessons, not just an added extra. Hopefully, courses with integrated video content such as *Eyes Open* will make it easier for teachers to do this. It's hoped that working with video in this way will bring the world of the classroom a little closer to the world our learners are experiencing outside the classroom walls. That must surely be motivating.

The use of image in *Eyes Open*

Using images in the language classroom is something we take for granted. However, although our classroom materials are full of images, most of these are used as a support with written or spoken texts. As text provides the main focus of our attention in class, the images used alongside often perform a secondary role or are simply decorative.

The information of the digital age in which we live is highly visual. These days, people often communicate through images and video, or through a combination of image and text. We therefore believe it appropriate to rethink the role of images in learning materials and place more emphasis on 'the visual'. This brief introduction outlines the different roles that images can have in our teaching practice and what we have done in *Eyes Open* to make the image more central to the course and to more fully exploit image.

High-impact images

In *Eyes Open*, we provide high-impact photos on the opening page of each unit. These images have multiple functions. Firstly, they provide an engaging link with the unit content, stimulating the students to take an interest in the topic. An image is a more efficient and impactful way of conveying a message. In this sense, a picture can really be worth 'a thousand words'. Secondly, the *Be Curious* section beside the image poses specific questions related directly to the image. Thirdly, the image often acts as a cultural artefact which is open to multiple readings. In the *Be Curious* section, students are often encouraged to hypothesise about the image in question. For example, looking at the photo of a busy street market, they might be asked, 'Where do you think it is?' Students should feel confident here that they can provide their own answers, using their imagination as much as possible providing they can justify their opinions.

The images in both these opening pages and in others have been selected because they offer an original angle on a well-known topic, or show a different perspective.

Intercultural awareness and critical thinking

The images have also been carefully selected to encourage intercultural awareness and critical thinking. For example, in Level 4 Unit 6 (Celebrate in style), the image shows national celebrations from Brazil and asks students to consider where the figure is and what the celebration is about. If you are not in Brazil, you can encourage students to compare the celebrations with their own experiences and learn about cultural similarities and differences between the origins and traditions. Similarly, in Unit 8 the image does not provide us with all of the information we need to understand the situation and what has happened previously. Students could be encouraged to hypothesise using the evidence which they have before them. The important concern again here is that students can provide their own answers rather than simply second-guess a 'correct' answer from the answer key.

This may be something new and even daunting but, if done in stages, students will soon get the hang of analysing images in this way and thinking more deeply about them. Notice that in the *Be Curious* section, the first question is sometimes, 'What can you see in the photo?' So, before analysing, students merely *describe*. Such scaffolding supports a gradual increase in cognitive load and challenge. Students are not expected to hypothesise immediately, but reflect on the image once they have described it and visualised it.

Teaching tips for exploiting images in class

If your class has problems analysing the images, consider three different ways of responding to them: the *affective* response – how does the image make you feel?, the *compositional* response – how is the image framed? (i.e. what is in the foreground/background, where the focus is, etc.), and the *critical* response – what message does the image communicate; what conclusions can we draw from it? This can be a useful framework for discussing any image.

Moving on: selecting your own images and student input

Taking this further, you could select your own images for use in class to supplement those found in the course. Some criteria for selecting images could be: *impact* (will the images be able to stimulate or engage the learner on an imaginative level?), *opportunity for personalisation* (how can the students make these images their own?) and *openness to multiple interpretation* (how many different readings can be drawn from a certain image?).

There are a number of great websites and image-sharing platforms where you can access high-quality and high-impact copyright-free images to be used in class. These include:

http://unsplash.com

http://littlevisuals.co

http://www.dotspin.com

http://www.lifeofpix.com

You can also then allow students to take a more active role by inviting them to bring their own images to class. Thus, images provide an even more central focus, functioning both as objects for analysis in their own right and as a clear way for students to provide their own input. This can be easily achieved digitally. Why not set up an Instagram page with your class, or a blog, or even a class website? This will allow students to upload their own images and interact with them by sending posts or messages describing or commenting on the images. In this way, they get extra practice at writing and even speaking. This interaction can then inform the face-to-face classroom to create a blended learning environment, as you prompt face-to-face discussion and negotiation of ideas based on what you view online.

Role of culture in *Eyes Open* by Ben Goldstein

It is a truism that language and culture are inseparable and yet this is something that is often overlooked in English language teaching materials which focus exclusively on a linguistic agenda. For this reason, each unit of *Eyes Open* includes a *Discover Culture* spread which clearly emphasises culture. These spreads include a video-based page and an extended reading which are related in topic. The Discovery videos and accompanying texts have been carefully chosen to offer insights into life and realities across the planet. Unlike other textbooks, *Eyes Open* offers a truly global focus, concentrating both on the English-speaking world and also on other countries. Why have we chosen to do this?

English as an international language

Due to globalisation, English is spoken in more places in the world than ever before and the number of proficient non-native speakers of English now outnumbers natives by approximately five to one. For this reason, it is likely that your students will speak English in later life in global contexts with a majority of non-native speakers present. This has obvious repercussions for pronunciation. For example, is it now desirable for learners to sound native-like? But it also has an effect on the cultural input that we present in class. It may be counter-productive to present only examples of native-speaker culture if your learners will rarely find themselves in a purely native-speaker environment.

For this reason, in its *Discover Culture* spread (and throughout the units) *Eyes Open* features cultural input from many different societies. For example, Level 3 Unit 3 features a video focusing on characteristic musical styles from three different countries: Australia (where English is spoken as a first language), India (where it is spoken as a second language) and Mexico (where it is learnt as a foreign language). This is not to say that target culture is ignored. One advantage of this approach, of course, is that the students' own country may appear in these pages thus engaging learners even further and offering an opportunity to use students' real-world knowledge and experience to analyse a text critically.

An intercultural 'glocal' approach

Eyes Open is a course that will be used in many different countries. Therefore the topics chosen are global in reach and appeal. However, they are also sufficiently familiar to students for you to 'localise' them. Put simply, this means that you could seek out local angles on global topics. For example, if the unit discusses a subject such as graffiti (a truly global phenomenon), you could get students to find examples of graffiti from their local context. This is, of course, facilitated by the *Your turn* sections which always attempt to bring out the students' own views on a particular subject and allow them to reflect on their own world. Such an approach is very much in line with the Common European Framework's principles in which intercultural awareness predominates. Such an approach encourages learners to reflect on their own culture and identity and seek out differences and similarities between that and the target culture. As a consequence learners will see that their own culture is plural and diverse, and they may begin to challenge stereotypes and misconceptions about how their own culture is seen by others.

Challenging stereotypes

While featuring topics which are familiar to teachers and students, *Eyes Open* also offers an alternative vision of certain widely-established cultural traditions. Cultural phenomena are truly representative of different countries rather than merely reiterating cultural clichés and stereotypes which may no longer be true.

For example, rather than focus on well-known British sports like rugby or cricket, Level 1 Unit 8 focuses on Scotland's lesser-known Highland Games. Likewise, the course features exciting and teen-relevant material such as the Burning Man music and culture festival in the USA (Level 3 Unit 3), rather than more established traditional music festivals like the Proms in the UK.

How have we implemented our approach to culture?

Discover Culture sections

Video exploitation

As in other parts of *Eyes Open*, the visual aspect is taken very seriously. After a series of warmer questions to activate the learners' schemata, students watch the video for gist and specific comprehension, but there are also questions which focus on visual stimuli. For example, students might be asked to test their memory on the images that they have or have not seen in the clip. Likewise, before watching, students might be asked to imagine which images they think would appear in the clip and then watch and check their answers. Students in the *Your turn* are then asked to find a personal connection with the topic shown in the video and/or give an extended opinion about it. As explained above, the approach embraces all cultures in which English is spoken as first, second or foreign language, from entrepeneurs in Mexico, to Maths lessons in Singapore to winter survival in Alaska. Very often, different countries' cultures are compared within the same video such as one clip which focuses on the distinct animals which live in the world's cities. In this way, students are learning about world culture through English but via the dynamic and motivating medium of Discovery Education™ video.

Reading exploitation

As in the video section of *Discover Culture*, images play a key part in activating students' interest in the topic. Images have been chosen specifically to trigger a response, encouraging students to hypothesise about what they are about to read. Once again, the topics here offer interesting focuses and contrasts on a topic related to the previous video spread. For example, in Level 3 Unit 2 two different schooling traditions are highlighted: The Royal Ballet in London is compared to La Masía, FC Barcelona's football academy for teens, which provides many of the team's best players. This is in line with the approach taken to culture in the series. By exploring world contexts (such as Spain here) where English is spoken as a foreign language, it is hoped that that teachers and students will feel able to localise the material to suit their own context. For example in the case above, the follow-up question after the reading could then be "Is there a football academy that functions in a similar way in your country?" At the same time, connections between target and world culture can be forged. For example, students might be asked if they have ever stopped to reflect on the similarities between training to be a ballet dancer or a footballer.

Ideas for further exploitation

If a *Discover Culture* spread has proved popular with your class, why not get students to produce a mini project on a similar topic? This could either feature a local context similar to the one in the spread or describe a related personal experience. Encourage them to use digital resources to research the project. These projects can be showcased in class by way of student presentations using digital tools for added effect. The Teacher's Book has an *Extension Activity* box at the end of each *Discover Culture* section, with specific ideas for further exploitation of the topics.

Speaking and writing in *Eyes Open*

Speaking and writing use vocabulary and grammar that learners have already internalised, or are in the process of internalising. They both allow the writer or speaker to be creative, but often use formulaic phrases and expressions such as functional language, which can become automated and prepare the listener to expect predictable content. However, although similar in that they are both productive skills, in many ways speaking and writing are very different and need a different pedagogical approach.

Writing

Writing is a skill that students often find difficult, even in their L1. It involves thinking about vocabulary, grammar, spelling and sentence structure, as well as how to organise content, and of course register is important too.

How does *Eyes Open* help students improve their writing skills?

Motivation through real life tasks

It helps a writer to have an idea of who the reader is (as opposed to the teacher!) and what the purpose of the writing is. In real-life tasks this is easier to see.

Genre (type of text) is important here too, so in *Eyes Open* a range of appropriate text types have been selected, using the CEFR for guidance, and the type of text is always indicated for students. Genre tells us what kind of language is used, be it set formulae or functional language, vocabulary, and formal or informal register, all related to the purpose of the text and its expected content. On each writing page the *Useful language* box focuses learners on an integral aspect of that type of test. The *Eyes Open* syllabus has been carefully planned across the four levels to deal with a range of relevant language issues related to the different genres.

The writing page starts with a **model text**. This serves to show students what kind of text they are aiming for. It is also designed to focus attention on how the useful language is used in the text, which allows for a process of noticing and discovery learning. This useful language often includes appropriate functional expressions. Writing in one's own language is a process involving planning, drafting and redrafting, and checking for mistakes. Within this process you have time to think, look things up and so on. The way writing is dealt with in *Eyes Open* encourages learners to follow the same process. The workbook then provides more work on the same genre, with another model text and exercises which recycle and extend the highlighted features from the SB, before suggesting another title for further practice.

TIPS:

- With some genres, get students to predict what they expect to find in the model text.
- As well as focusing on the Useful language, ask students to underline phrases in the model they could use for their own text.
- Brainstorm ideas and do the planning stage in pairs. The drafting can also be done collectively.
- Write the SB text in class and the WB pages individually for homework.
- Get students to use the checklist on each other's work to raise their awareness. Then allow students to write a final draft.
- Using a digital device for writing makes the whole process easier and more like the modern world, and so is more motivating.

Speaking

Speaking is challenging, and can be daunting (it involves thinking and speaking at the same time, and listening and responding to someone else). Teenagers may lack confidence or feel embarrassed when speaking English. *Eyes Open* takes a **step-by-step approach**, where students are provided with sufficient **support** and a structure to enable them first to practise in a controlled way but later to create their own conversations. As with writing, speaking can involve set phrases or functional language used in the context of a particular genre. The more these phrases can be practised and memorised, the easier creating a new conversation will be. This is known as automatisation. To try and mirror speaking outside a classroom, there is no written preparation. Instead, *Eyes Open* starts with a model conversation in a clear, **real-life context**, to motivate students and highlight useful language. Students **listen first** to answer a simple question designed to focus on content rather than language. The focus then shifts to the useful language, which may be complete fixed phrases or functional exponents to begin a sentence. Students use these to complete the conversation and listen again to check. They then read the model conversation in pairs, and often do a follow-up exercise using some of the useful language as well, in order to give them confidence and prepare them for developing their own conversation, either by adapting the model (at lower levels) or by creating their own. In both cases prompts are provided, and students are encouraged to use the phrases from the useful language box in their own conversations.

TIPS:

- Students can read the model conversation several times; after they have done this once or twice, encourage one of them to read and the other to respond from memory. Then they swap, and finally they see if they can both remember the conversation.
- Use the model and audio to concentrate on pronunciation, drilling at natural speed. Students can look for features of speech (eg. words being joined together, or sounds disappearing in connected speech).
- Get students to "act" the model conversations in character. This helps lessen embarrassment, and can be fun.
- Encourage students to do the final task several times with different partners.

Your turn

Throughout the SB there are *Your turn* sections on every page (except the Speaking and Writing sections). These are included to practise writing and speaking – the writing stage often helps to scaffold a subsequent speaking activity – linked with new vocabulary and grammar, or listening and reading. Students are encouraged to actively use new language in a **personalisation activity.** This approach has been shown to help learners activate and relate new language to their own lives, i.e. in a relevant and familiar context.

TIPS:

- In class, students can compare what they have written in the Student's Book or the Workbook for homework. They could then tell the class if they are "similar or different".
- Doing the speaking activities in pairs or small groups makes them feel more confident. After this "rehearsal" they could be asked about what they said in an open class report back stage.
- Turn sentences into questions as the basis of a class "survey" in a milling activity.

Managing teenage classes

Classroom management is one of the main everyday anxieties of teachers of teenage classes. Classroom management involves discipline, but it also involves lesson planning, time management and responsiveness to the needs of teenage pupils.

Tips for the first lessons

The first few lessons with any new group of teenage pupils will set the stage for the rest of the year. New pupils will invariably put us to the test so it is important to be prepared and well-equipped from day one.

It is best not to let pupils sit where they want. If possible, speak to other teachers who know your new pupils and get advice on who should and should not be seated together. Have a seating plan prepared. This will also help learn pupils' names quickly. We rarely feel 100% in control until we know our pupils' names!

Prepare a number of class rules and consequences which apply to your personal expectations and suggest these to the class. Invite pupils to discuss each rule and the possible reasons behind them. Pupils may adapt your suggestions or change the wording. Type out the final 'contract' and ask everyone to sign it and sign it yourself. Pupils may even take it home to show their parents.

The greatest source of real communication in any language classroom is the day-to-day interaction between teacher and pupils. It is essential to work on and develop the language that they will be using for the next few years at school. It is the key to establishing a classroom atmosphere of confidence, security and motivation.

Recommended approaches and *Eyes Open*

Although they would probably never admit it, teenagers want and need structure in the classroom because it gives them a sense of security. If the lesson is not organised, instructions are not clear, the material or tasks too difficult (or too easy!), then discipline problems are sure to arise.

If lesson aims are made clear to pupils, this can help. *Unit aims* are summarised on the first page of each unit in the Student's Book expressed as *I can …* statements. These aims are clear and simple for pupils to understand. For more detailed aims, the Teacher's Book starts each page with *Objectives* for the lesson. Use the accompanying exercises and tasks which have been designed to determine if pupils are able to achieve these objectives.

At the beginning of the lesson you might write a summary of your lesson plan on the board in the form of bullet points. At the end of the lesson draw your pupils' attention back to these points, ask them to reflect on the lesson and tick off each point covered.

Young teens do not have a one-hour attention span so we try to include variety in lesson plans. The *Eyes Open* Student's Book has been developed to help here. For example, each section ends with a communicative *Your turn* section, where students are offered quiet time to plan before they are given the opportunity to speak with a partner or in a small group. The optional activities in the Teacher's Book provide you with additional ideas to have up your sleeve to use when you need to vary the pace of the lesson.

Motivation is key. All teenagers are talented at or interested in something and have varied learning styles, so incorporate your pupils' interests into your lessons, exploit their skills and cater to their different learning styles. The themes, videos and images in *Eyes Open* have been carefully chosen to maintain pupils' interest and motivation throughout the year. These features of the course should especially appeal to visual learners. The *CLIL* section brings other school subjects into the English lesson and includes one of the three Discovery Education™ videos which appear in each unit. The *Discover Culture* section in each unit features an integrated video page and a reading page and aims to raise awareness of and interest in global cultures. The *Speaking* sections offer further communicative practice and include the fourth video sequence, this time featuring teens modelling language.

Mixed ability

Another challenge we face in the teen classroom is the issue of mixed ability. Mixed ability refers to stronger and weaker pupils, but teenagers are different in a variety of other ways too: adolescent pupils have different levels of maturity and motivation; work at different speeds; possess different learning styles; have different attention spans and energy levels; and are interested in different things. The challenge for us as teachers is to prepare lessons which take all these differences into account and to set achievable goals so that at the end of a lesson, every pupil leaves the classroom feeling that they have achieved something.

Practical ideas for teaching mixed-ability classes

Working in groups

In large classes there is not much opportunity for individual pupils to participate orally. Most pages in *Eyes Open* end with a *Your turn* activity which offers pupils the opportunity to talk in pairs and small groups. By working together, pupils can benefit from collaborating with classmates who are more proficient, or who have different world experiences. When working in groups there is always the risk that one or two pupils end up doing all the work. Avoid this by assigning each pupil with an individual task or specific responsibility.

Preparation time

Give pupils time to gather their ideas and let them make notes before a speaking activity. This 'thinking time' will give less proficient pupils the chance to say something that is interesting, relevant and comprehensible. In a similar way, give pupils time to rehearse interviews and role plays before 'going live' in front of the class.

Similarly, let students compare and discuss their answers before feeding back to the class. This provides all students with confidence and allows weaker students the opportunity to take part.

Task repetition

After giving feedback on a speaking activity, get pupils to do it again. By getting a second, or even a third opportunity to do something, pupils become more self-assured and are therefore more likely to succeed. Practice makes perfect! Pupils will be able to use these multiple attempts to develop accuracy and fluency, while stronger students can also be encouraged to build complexity into later attempts.

Teacher's notes

The unit-specific Teacher's notes also offer further differentiated activities for each lesson so that you can tailor your lesson according to the abilities of each of your students.

Fast finishers

Prepare extra tasks for fast finishers to reward them for their effort and/or to challenge them more. Place these tasks in numbered or labelled envelopes to increase their curiosity. These envelopes should not be seen as punishments so their contents should be activities which are interesting, relevant and straightforward enough that they can be done without teacher support. Fast finishers can create self-access materials (wordsearches, crosswords, vocabulary cards, jumbled sentences, quizzes) that could be used by the rest of the class in future lessons. *Eyes Open* also provides a wealth of ready-made fast finisher activities in the Teacher's notes. The Student's Book also includes a *Vocabulary Bank* for fast finisher revision.

Homework

The Workbook has graded vocabulary, language focus, listening and reading exercises: basic (one star), standard (two stars) and higher (three stars). Teachers can direct pupils to the appropriate exercises. These exercises could also be used in class.

What is a *corpus*?

A corpus is a very large collection of natural, real-life language, held in a searchable electronic form.

We use corpora to analyse and research how language is used. Using a corpus we can rapidly and reliably search through millions of words of text, looking for patterns and exploring how we use English in a range of different contexts and situations.

We can use a corpus to look at which words often go together, which words are the most common in English, and which words and phrases learners of English find most difficult. This can inform both *what* we teach to learners, *when* we teach it, and *how* we present it in our materials.

We use information from corpora to improve and enhance our materials for teachers and learners.

The Cambridge English Corpus

The Cambridge English Corpus is a multi-billion word collection of contemporary English.

The Cambridge English Corpus has been put together over a period of 20 years. It's collected from a huge range of sources – books, magazines, lectures, text messages, conversations, emails and lots more!

The Cambridge English Corpus also contains the Cambridge Learner Corpus – the world's largest collection of learner writing. The Cambridge Learner Corpus contains more than 50 million words of exam answers written by students taking Cambridge English exams.

We carefully check each exam script and highlight all errors made by students. We can then use this information to see which words and structures are easy and difficult for learners of English.

The Cambridge Learner Corpus allows us to see how students from particular language backgrounds, achievement levels and age groups perform in their exams. This means that we can work out how best we can support and develop these students further.

Why use a corpus to develop an ELT course?

Using research and information from a corpus in our ELT material allows us to:

* Identify words and phrases that occur most **frequently** – these are words that learners need to know.
* Look at **word patterns** and make sure we teach the most useful phrases and collocates.
* Include language that is **up-to-date** and relevant to students.
* **Focus on certain groups of learners** and see what they find easy or hard.
* Make sure our materials contain **appropriate content** for a particular level or exam.
* Find mistakes which are universal to English language learning, and those which are a result of **first-language interference**.
* Find plenty of **examples** of language used by students and use this to help other students.

At Cambridge, we use the Cambridge English Corpus to inform most of our English Language Teaching materials, making them current, relevant, and tailored to specific learners' needs.

How have we used the Cambridge English Corpus in *Eyes Open*?

In *Eyes Open*, we've used the Cambridge Learner Corpus in order to find out how best we can support students in their learning.

For the grammar and vocabulary points covered in each unit, we've investigated how students perform – what they find easy and what they find difficult. Using this information, we've raised further awareness of the particular areas that learners make errors with; in the form of *Get it right!* boxes in the Student's Book containing tips and *Get it right!* pages in the Workbook containing short exercises. These tips and exercises highlight and test particular areas that previous students have found difficult. For example, you'll find exercises which focus on spelling in order to help learners avoid common errors made by other students at each level.

Using this information, we've developed activities and tasks that provide practice for students in those areas where we've proven that they need the most help. This customised support will allow students to have a better chance at avoiding such errors themselves.

How could you use corpora in your own teaching?

There are lots of corpora that are accessible online – why not try typing 'free online corpora' into your search engine to see what is available? Alternatively, you don't necessarily need to use a corpus in order to use corpus principles in your classroom – corpora involve using real examples of language, so why not type your search word or phrase directly into your search engine to see examples of that word or phrase in use online?

Whichever method you decide to use, there are a number of ways in which you can use corpus-type approaches in your teaching. Here are three examples:

1 Choose two similar words (why not try, for example, *say/tell* or *make/do*) and search for these either in a corpus or in your search engine. Choose sentences with these examples in and paste them into a document. Then, remove these search words from the sentences and ask students to fill in the correct word. As an extension activity, you could also ask them to discuss why each example is *say* and not *tell*, for example.

2 Choose a word (why not try *at* or *in* for example) and paste some examples into a short text. Ask students to describe when you would use each one, by looking at the context the examples are found in (e.g. *in* is used with parts of the day; *in the morning*; *at* is used with a particular time; *at five o'clock*)

3 Choose a word or phrase and paste some examples into a short text. Make changes to the examples to introduce errors and ask students to spot and correct them.

Remember – look out for this symbol to see where corpus research has been used in our other materials!

Using the *Review* sections in *Eyes Open*

In *Eyes Open*, the *Review* sections appear after every two units. They are designed to provide students with the opportunity to test themselves on the vocabulary, language focus and speaking sections which they have studied in those units.

When to use the *Review* sections

It is advisable that you make use of the *Review* sections at the end of every two units. Doing this will not only allow you to keep a check on students' progress, but will also enable you to find out which areas are presenting students with difficulties.

Using the *Review* sections in the classroom

If you choose to do the *Review* sections in class, we suggest that you follow a set procedure so that students know what to expect.

- Tell students the vocabulary or grammar that is to be practised.
- Revise the language needed by putting example sentences on the board.
- Pair **stronger students** with **weaker students**.
- Give each pair two minutes to note down what they know about the particular vocabulary area, grammar point or function, for example grammar rules, spelling changes, how particular vocabulary is used in a sentence, what function certain phrases are used for, etc.
- Elicit ideas from the class. At this point deal with any uncertainty or confusion, but do not go into great detail.
- Read out the example in the exercise and check students understand what they have to do.
- Set a time limit for the completion of the exercise: 3–4 minutes for the shorter exercises and 5–6 minutes for the longer ones.
- Students work alone to complete the exercise.
- Ask students to swap their work with a partner.
- Check answers. Students mark their partner's work and give it a mark. For example, if there are five questions in an exercise, students could record anything from 0 to 5 marks.
- Put students into pairs to act out the conversation in the *Speaking* section.

Keeping track of marks

- Encourage students to keep a note in their notebooks of their overall mark in each *Review* section.
- Challenge them to improve their mark each time.
- If students are dissatisfied with their original mark, encourage them to do the exercises on the *Review* section again at home in a few days' time with the aim of improving their mark.

Alternative ways of using the Review sections

Language gym

- Designate different parts of the classroom 'Vocabulary 1', 'Vocabulary 2' and 'Vocabulary 3'.
- Put students into groups and tell each group to go to one of the designated areas.
- Set each group different exercises to do from the Vocabulary part of the *Review* section. Set 1–2 exercises per group.
- Set a five-minute time limit per exercise.
- Photocopy the answers from the Teacher's Book and give one copy to each group. Name one student in each group 'Answer Master' and explain that it is that student's job to read out the answers to the group once the group has completed the exercises. Alternatively, if you have the *Presentation Plus* software, put the answers on the interactive whiteboard.

- Groups may finish at different times. Keep an eye on the progress each group is making. Go over to groups that finish early and ask them about the exercises they have just done. Did they find them easy or difficult? What marks did they get on the exercises? Is there anything they didn't understand or would like to do more work on?
- Once students have completed the exercises in their area, they move on to the next one.
- You could then do the same thing with the *Language focus* sections.
- Remember that this activity can only be done if exercises in one part of the *Review* section do not refer to exercises in another part.

Review quiz

- Put students into groups.
- Make one student in each group the captain.
- If you have the *Presentation Plus* software, put the *Review* section on the interactive whiteboard.
- Go through each exercise in turn, eliciting answers.
- All answers must go through the captain.
- The first captain to raise his or her hand gets the chance to answer the question.
- Groups receive one point for each correct answer.
- If the answer is incorrect, the next captain to raise his or her hand gets the chance to answer the question and so on.
- The group with the most points at the end wins.

Review football

- Split the class into two teams.
- Appoint **weaker students** as team captains. This means that it is their job to tell you their team's answer to a question.
- Draw a football pitch on the board divided into segments, which could correspond to the number of questions there are in a particular exercise.
- Draw a picture of a football on a piece of paper, cut the ball out, put Blu-Tack on the back of it and attach it to the centre circle on the pitch you have drawn on the board.
- Toss a coin in the air and ask teams to choose 'heads' or 'tails'. The team which guesses correctly gets possession of the ball.
- If that team then answers its first question correctly, it moves forward on the pitch and gets to answer another question. If it answers incorrectly, it loses possession of the ball.
- After an initial game with the whole class, students can play this in small teams, with **weaker students** acting as referees.

Review language throughout the course

- The most successful language students continue to review what they have learnt long past the point at which they might be said to have learnt it. Make the review of language a feature of your lessons.
- At the end of every lesson, set homework.
- At the beginning of the following week, do a classroom activity making use of some or all of the new language introduced the previous week. For example, students could play the *Correct the sentence* game (see *Games Bank*, page 28).
- At the beginning of the next month, do a classroom activity making use of some or all of the new language introduced the previous month. For example, students could write a conversation based on a theme from a recent unit in which they try to use all of the new language they have learnt.
- At the end of each unit, put students into groups and ask them to write their own *Review* section quiz, which they can then share with another group.

CLIL explained

Content and Language Integrated Learning (CLIL) is a matrix where content learning, language fluency and cognitive agility develop together. Students are given the opportunity to acquire both knowledge and language. At the same time, they develop a range of cognitive skills and social competences required inside and outside the classroom.

CLIL is an educational response to the demands and resources of the 21st century. Students are increasingly aiming to use English in a dynamic, fast-paced workplace where they will be expected to analyse and create material in English. CLIL's unique emphasis on cognitive agility in addition to content and language learning introduces students to creative and analytical thinking in a foreign language at a young age.

There are two possible scenarios in a CLIL classroom. CLIL classes can be English language classes in which the topic material used corresponds with content objectives from another subject such as biology or technology. Alternatively, the CLIL class could be a subject class, such as History or Geography, taught in English. Either way, the objectives of the CLIL classroom are much broader that a traditional English class or a traditional subject class. As a consequence of these broad learning objectives, learning styles are vitally important and must be taken into consideration when planning a CLIL class. In order to attain all the learning objectives, a CLIL class is required to be more interactive or practical than a traditional one.

CLIL classes break down the barriers between subjects, generating an experience more representative of the real world. Motivation and confidence improve as students become accustomed to carrying out both creative and analytical work in an English-speaking environment.

Methods and Tips

When planning a CLIL lesson it is vital to keep in mind the principles of CLIL: content learning, language fluency and cognitive agility.

Content Learning

Content learning is foremost in the CLIL classroom. So that language is not a barrier to learning, classes should be both dynamic and visually rich. The graphics and videos used in *Eyes Open* help teachers to achieve this environment. The interactive style of learning promoted in the *CLIL* pages enables students to understand concepts quickly and avoid frustration.

The learning objectives of each CLIL class must be clear.
Each *CLIL* page in the *Eyes Open* series has been specifically designed to meet a particular content learning objective from subjects such as History, Technology and Geography.

Multiple activities should be used to check content comprehension. The unique nature of the CLIL classroom requires multiple activities to check students' comprehension. *Eyes Open CLIL* pages use a wide variety of styles so as not to seem repetitive and to appeal to all levels in the classroom.

Language Fluency

CLIL classes must develop all four skills. It is fundamental that all four basic skills are developed: reading, writing, speaking and listening. A range of engaging activities is provided in the *CLIL* pages of *Eyes Open* so that all these skills can be addressed.

Introduction activities should be used to refresh vocabulary.
Before starting on content material, introduction activities should be used to refresh vocabulary as well as to check content knowledge. Every *CLIL* page in the *Eyes Open* series starts with an introduction activity.

Cognitive Agility

Tasks should reflect mixed learning styles of students. There has to be a flexible approach to learning in any CLIL classroom so that all students are given the opportunity to thrive. *Eyes Open* allows teachers to create this atmosphere by including open activities where the students are asked either to do a creative piece of work or to share their reflections and opinions. Students are not restrained to right or wrong answers but rather are encouraged into critical and creative thinking.

Student-led learning. Students should be encouraged to support each other's learning through teamwork and feedback activities, with teachers, at times, taking a backseat. Teachers should encourage students to use and share their technological skills and global knowledge to enrich the class. This allows students to gain confidence in language fluency and content presentation. Students also learn to adapt their language and content knowledge to a variety of situations. Teachers can use the wide range of teamwork tasks provided in *Eyes Open CLIL* pages to create an inspiring classroom and to encourage student-led learning.

Challenging activities and material which invite students to think and discover for themselves. Students should be given plenty of opportunities to contemplate the content material. The *CLIL* videos and *Your turn* activities provided in the *Eyes Open* series challenge students to make the cognitive leap into dynamic learning by encouraging them to view the content theory in real-life scenarios.

Eyes Open CLIL pages

In this unique series of English text books, each *CLIL* page has been specially designed to meet a specific learning objective from a content subject. Teachers will find it both straightforward and enjoyable to teach content material included in the *CLIL* pages thanks to the well-planned exercises and attractive presentation.

The *Eyes Open CLIL* pages use a wide range of procedurally rich activities to enhance learning, with an emphasis on promoting critical and creative thinking. Developed to stimulate learning in a way which is attractive to all students in the classroom, every student in the class should be able to find something appealing in the *CLIL* pages, be it the *CLIL* video, the *Your turn* activity, a curious fact or the introduction activity.

Eyes Open prides itself on its use of authentic video material which teachers can use to extend content learning and to make a meaningful connection with the world outside the classroom. Teachers can use these videos to encourage students to draw on their knowledge of the world around them and share it in the classroom. This shared extended learning can be as simple as teachers encouraging students to bring in newspaper cuttings or as demanding as group projects on topics related to the *CLIL* page.

The *Eyes Open CLIL* pages provide a competence-based education; suited to the 21st century and in line with the learning patterns of the internet generation and the global citizen. English taught through integrated material which stimulates critical thinking pushes each individual student to participate in a meaningful manner in classroom activities. The content material in *Eyes Open* can be used to stimulate each student's curiosity and allow students to exploit their individual interests in order to reach their potential as critical and creative English speakers. Teachers can use the model developed in the *Eyes Open CLIL* pages as a platform for further learning, thus ensuring that students remain engaged in their own learning both inside the classroom and out.

Introduction to project work in *Eyes Open*

Project work can provide several advantages for learners by helping them to gain valuable skills which can benefit them in all areas of the curriculum, not just in English language learning. The following are just some of the many advantages project work can provide. It can:

- be highly motivating, as students can harness their own curiosity about a particular topic, giving them greater ownership of what they're learning and how it can be presented.
- encourage students to work independently, to research information, plan work, organise and present it.
- provide a contrast to standard lessons and give students the opportunity to have fun with English.
- build team-working skills by encouraging discussion and collaboration with peers in order to achieve a successful outcome.
- reinforce and consolidate new language that has been presented in class.
- help struggling students improve their language skills by collaborating closely with stronger peers.
- encourage stronger students to develop their skills further, by giving them the freedom to experiment with language.
- build speaking and writing confidence and fluency, for example via writing and conducting surveys and presenting written work in easy-to-read formats.
- improve presentation skills, both spoken and written.

Projects in the Student's Book

Eyes Open Student's Book contains three projects, which can be used at any point in the school year. The topics are based on selected units from the Student's Book. The project pages are designed to be used in class, but in a simple and easy to follow format to allow students to work as independently as possible.

Each project page is divided into three sections: *Look* provides a visual stimulus of some kind which serves as a model for students to help them create their own work; the *Prepare* section contains step-by-step instructions for students working in pairs or groups; and the final *Present* section tells students how to display their information. See pages 123–125 of the Student's Book for each project, and pages 146–148 of the Teacher's Book for detailed teaching notes on them.

Projects on the Cambridge Learning Management System

In addition to the Student's Book projects, *Eyes Open* includes a number of ideas for projects utilising technology. These are available via the Cambridge Learner Management System (CLMS) in the resources section. The CLMS can be accessed via a link from the *Presentation Plus* software.

The digital projects enable students not only to engage in language practice, but to use and develop their digital skills and digital literacy through researching a topic and presenting their work in a digital format. Options include picture collages, audio slideshows and videos. For the teacher, there is a connection between these projects and the Secondary Digital Teacher Training Course, which is designed to introduce teachers to various type of digital project. Students interested in using technology will be particularly motivated by producing work using digital devices and applications.

Guidance on using projects in *Eyes Open*

The success of project work can greatly depend on how carefully a project is set up, and how motivated your students are to do projects. If your time is limited, you might decide you only have time for one or two projects, so you'll need to assess each one to decide which you think would benefit your students the most. Consider your students' particular interests and strengths, in addition to which topics are areas of language they need most practice in. Depending on how much time you have available, you might want to spend two lessons working on a project, or just one, with students doing most of the preparation and writing for homework. Once you've selected a project you're going to do, you'll need to prepare your students carefully.

Motivating students to do a project

It's important to get students interested in the topic before launching into the project work itself as motivated students are, of course, much more likely to produce good work and enjoy it. Before asking students to turn to a particular project in the Student's Book, you could show them an authentic example of a presentation (for *Project 1*), an advertisement (for *Project 2*) or a comic strip (for *Project 3*). Then explain that you'd like them to produce something similar (if you anticipate difficulties sourcing examples in English, use L1 examples). You could ask them if they think the format is the best way to present the information that's there, and ask them if they can think of any other ways the information could be shown (for example, perhaps a poster for *Project 3* or a TV report for *Project 1*). You could also brainstorm any other ways that information is often presented (for example, PowerPoint presentations, short video clips, etc). Encourage them to think broadly at this stage, as they may be inspired by their own ideas. The students could choose whether to produce work in a digital or paper-based format.

Preparing for a project

Once students understand the goal they need to achieve, you can then turn to the project page in the Student's Book. Ask them to critically assess the way the material is presented. For example, in *Project 2* do they think the advertisement is visually appealing? Can they think of an alternative way of presenting similar information? Encouraging students to be creative and think beyond what's on the page is important, as it will help them take ownership of the task. You'll then need to ask students what stages will be needed to produce their end result, and what equipment may be needed. Write these up so the whole class can see as you elicit the details from them. You'll also need to set a clear time limit for each stage, depending on how much time you've allocated for the whole task.

Once students have understood the goal and the individual steps needed to achieve it, you can put them into small groups. Groups of three or perhaps four students are ideal, depending on the nature of the project. Any more than this and it's more likely that quiet or weaker students will be left out and dominated by more confident members of the group. You might want to mix weaker students with stronger students to allow the weaker ones to learn from the stronger, or you might prefer to group according to ability, with weaker students grouped together.

Managing the project work in class

Depending on the abilities of the groups, you might want to encourage students to consider alternative sub-topic areas to those given in addition to alternative ways to present the information if they prefer. For example, in *Project 1* students may think of additional or replacement sub-topics to include in their poster. For *Project 2*, students might want to use questions and answers or a personal recommendation. For a project that requires research beyond the classroom, ask students what sources they're going to use to gather the information they need. If necessary, provide guidance by suggesting some yourself in the form of useful websites or books, for example. You may need to provide them with the facilities they'll need to access them; for example if they don't have a computer at home they'll require access to one at school, or another alternative. They can then note these down in their groups, in addition to the specific information they need to find out and, if they have the facilities, start the research in class together. If they have to do the research outside class, they'll need to decide who is going to research which pieces of information. You'll also need to ask them to consider what visual material they'll want to include in their presentation, and where they will source it.

The teacher's role as facilitator

Whilst students are working on the stages of the project, you'll need to take the role of facilitator, moving round the groups and encouraging students to work things out for themselves by asking questions. More confident individuals are likely to take on the role of leader within each group, and you might have to encourage quieter students to contribute more by asking them questions and giving them specific tasks. When required, help students with the necessary language, but try to encourage as much autonomy as possible at this stage. Monitor the time, and periodically remind students how much time they have left. Students are likely to lapse into L1. This is probably unavoidable at lower levels, but it's also a good opportunity to encourage them to use English when they should be familiar with the language they need, or could provide valuable opportunities for extending their language. By asking 'How can you say that in English?' and encouraging them to note down useful language you give them, they can gradually build up their fluency.

The presentation stage

Once the preparation stage is complete and students are happy with the information they have gathered, they'll need to present it in a format that is attractive and easy to understand. At this stage you might want to take on more of a supporting role. Ask them to assign responsibilities within their groups. Who is going to write up the information? Can it be shared within the group? What is the best way to organise the information? They'll need to be provided with any necessary equipment, and given a clear time limit if the project is to be done in class. If this is to be done for homework, establish what equipment they have at home, and what may need to be given to them to take home. Once students have finished their presentations, check it and elicit or make any corrections necessary to improve their work. It's important to strike a balance so as not to discourage students and potentially demotivate them. If you have time, and if motivation is unlikely to be an issue in your class, you might want them to produce a second, or even a third draft incorporating any corrections or suggestions you might have. Once you and your students are satisfied with the outcome, they can either present the project themselves in groups, perhaps by taking turns to present different pieces of information, and/or by displaying the projects. How they are displayed will obviously depend on the facilities you have, and the type of project. If you have classroom space, you might wish to display posters on the wall. If students have created work in a digital format, this material could be uploaded to the CLMS.

Games Bank

Board race and wipeout

(10 minutes)

- Draw a vertical line down the middle of the board.
- Divide the class into two teams. Tell them to form two lines so the two students who are first in line face the board.
- Give each student at the front of the line a different colour board pen.
- Choose a category, e.g. jobs, and tell them they have two minutes to write as many words as possible from this category on the board. The students at the front of the line write the first word, then pass the pen to the student behind them and join the back of the queue, repeating the process until the two minutes are up.
- Each team wins a point for each correctly spelt word that they wrote on the board.
- Tell students to sit down and, while they do this, wipe your board rubber over the board randomly so that most letters of all of the words are erased but some remain. The first team to remember and write down all of the words wins a point for each word.

Correct the sentence

(5–10 minutes)

- Put students into teams of four or five.
- Write a sentence on the board, e.g. *We mustn't send text messages in class.*
- Students confer in their teams and quickly decide if the sentence is correct or incorrect. The sentence may be incorrect in terms of its content or its grammar.
- If the sentence is incorrect, students must come up with the correct sentence.
- The first team to tell you the right answer wins a point.
- Repeat with further sentences.
- The team with the most points at the end of the game wins.

Could you spell that, please?

(5 minutes)

- Put students into pairs (A and B).
- Student B closes his/her book.
- Student A reads out a word from a particular vocabulary list, then asks *Could you spell that, please?* Student B tries to spell the word.
- Students swap roles and the game continues until all the words have been covered.
- Students win a point for correctly spelt words.
- The student who spells the most words correctly is the winner.

Expanding sentences

(5–10 minutes)

- Divide students into two or more teams.
- Write the beginning of a sentence on the board, e.g. *If…*
- Tell the teams that they have to add one or more words to what you have written on the board.
- One member of each team comes to the board in turn to add words to the sentence, e.g.
  If…
  If we…
  If we go…
  If we go to…
  If we go to Mars…
- Teams win a point if the words they add are correct.

Guess the question

(5 minutes)

- Put students into groups of four or five.
- Read out answers to questions, e.g. *I was eating a cheese sandwich.*
- Ask students to guess what the question is, e.g. *What were you eating?*
- Teams win a point for a correct question and the team with the most points at the end of the game wins.

Guess the story

(15 minutes)

- Divide the class into groups of two or three.
- Give each group a list of five words that they have studied. These should be different for each group. The students shouldn't tell anyone else their words.
- You could give more words if you feel that five is not enough. Eight words would be a good upper limit.
- Each group must invent a story which incorporates all of these five words, but tell them they must include them in their story naturally so they don't stand out as being obvious.
- Put two groups together to tell each other their stories. Afterwards, they guess which words the other group had been given. The group with the least correct guesses about their words wins.

Hangman

(5 minutes)

- Choose one student to come to the front of the class and draw dashes on the board to represent the letters of a word.
- The other students call out letters to try to guess the word.
- For every incorrect guess, the student draws a part of the hanged man on the board.
- The student who guesses the correct word comes to the board and chooses the next word.
- Students can also play this game in pairs or small groups.

Head dictation

(5 minutes)

- Give each student a blank piece of paper and a pen.
- Tell the students that you're going to give them three topics they have covered over the last few weeks / the course, and they'll need to draw pictures of words within those categories. You will tell them where on the paper to draw them and how many things.
- Now tell students to each put the piece of paper on their heads. Tell students not to look at their piece of paper or tell anyone what they have drawn until you say they can.
- Whilst they are holding the paper on their heads, read out instructions of what the students should draw, e.g. *On the left of your piece of paper draw one type of shop, in the middle of your piece of paper draw two household appliances, on the right of your piece of paper draw three parts of the body.*
- Now tell students to swap their piece of paper with their partner's. They ask questions to try and find out what their partner has drawn, e.g. Student A: *Is it a knee?* Student B: *No, it isn't. Try again!*

Pelmanism

(5 minutes)

- Before you do this activity you will need to do some preparation.
- On a piece of paper, draw a table with ten numbered spaces in it. Write pairs of associated words in the ten spaces (e.g. *big/ enormous, go/went, do/done*.)
- Draw your table on the board, but leave the spaces empty.
- Students choose number pairs in order to try to reveal the associated words. Write the two words which correspond to those numbers on the board.
- If students have chosen a pair, they say *Match!* If not, rub off the words they have revealed.
- Students work as a class to reveal all the matches.

Pictionary

(5–10 minutes)

- Divide students into two teams.
- A member of each group comes to the front of the class in turn. Draw a line down the middle of the board.
- Write a word or a phrase on a piece of paper and show it to the two students at the board, but not the others.
- The two students then draw a picture of the word or phrase on their side of the board. The rest of the class tries to guess what the word or phrase is.
- Teams win a point for a correct answer and the team with the most points at the end of the game wins.
- Students can also play this game in pairs.

Stop the bus

(10 minutes)

- Divide the class into teams of three or four.
- Draw a table on the board with four columns. Write a category in each column, e.g. *adjectives, countries, things in the home, sports and activities,* etc.
- Choose a letter of the alphabet and tell students to write down one word beginning with the chosen letter for each category. Do an example together first.
- The first team to write one word for each of the categories shouts *Stop the Bus!*
- Write their answers on the board and award a point if all the answers are correct.
- If it's taking a long time to think of a word for each of the categories because it's too difficult with one of the letters, reduce the number of categories for that round. Give the point to the team who have different words from the other teams as this will encourage them to think of more difficult words.

The ball game

(5 minutes)

- Play this game with the whole class.
- Students take it in turns to hold a ball. While holding the ball they say a word, e.g. *go.*
- They then throw the ball to another student who has to use that word in a sentence or with a phrase, e.g. *go sailing.*
- If this student makes a correct sentence, he or she then chooses the next word and throws the ball to a new student. If not, he or she drops out and the ball passes to his or her neighbour.
- The last students left is the winner.

The chain game

(5–10 minutes)

- Start the chain by saying a sentence, e.g. *I've done my History homework, but I still haven't studied for my Maths test.*
- Students then continue the chain in groups, taking the last noun or the last verb from the previous sentence as their starting point, e.g. *I still haven't studied for my Maths, but I've already studied for my English test.*
- On it goes until you bring the game to an end. (Students should, ideally, have a chance to make three or four sentences each.)
- At the end students make notes on what they can remember about what was said by different students in the chain, e.g. *Carlo still hasn't studied for his Maths test.*

The memory game

(5 minutes)

- Put students into groups of four or five.
- One student in the group begins by making a sentence using a new item of vocabulary and/or grammar structure, e.g. *I must send my grandmother a birthday card.* or *I should do my homework.*
- The next student repeats what the first student says and adds a sentence of his or her own.
- The game continues in this way, with each student in the group repeating what the others have said before adding to it.
- If a student cannot recall everything that has been said before, he or she drops out.
- The last student left is the winner.

The mime game

(5 minutes)

- Put students into pairs.
- Students take it in turns to mime words, phrases or sentences, e.g. *dinner, have dinner, you're having dinner,* for their partner to guess.
- Students win a point if they guess the correct word, phrase or sentence.
- The student who guesses the most words, phrases or sentences is the winner.

The thirty-seconds game

(5 minutes)

- Put students into pairs.
- Students have 30 seconds to speak on a theme of their choice using a particular grammatical structure (e.g. *present continuous, present simple, be going to, the present simple passive*) as often as they can.
- Students win one point for each correct sentence using that structure, but get stopped and have a point taken away for each incorrect sentence.

Revision and recycling

Teachers can control what is taught in class but we cannot control what is actually learned by our pupils. Teachers provide pupils with a certain amount of input during a lesson, but that input does not necessarily transform itself into output. According to experts, unless we review or re-read what we have studied in a lesson, we forget 50–80% of it within 24 hours! (Reference: *Curve of forgetting*, University of Waterloo https://uwaterloo.ca/counselling-services/curve-forgetting). This high rate of forgetting clearly has implications for language teaching. In order to ensure that what we teach will be permanently retained in our pupils' long-term memory, language needs to be reviewed as soon as possible in subsequent lessons and recycled on a regular basis. Unless language is taught in a memorable way and then seen and understood on a number of occasions, this language will fade from our pupils' memory and disappear. Therefore, teachers need to allocate class time to revision and to create regular opportunities for recycling previously taught language and vocabulary. Frequent recycling is essential for effective language learning.

For each unit in *Eyes Open* there is a *Vocabulary Bank* at the back of the Student's Book which can be used to jog pupils' memories. In addition, pupils can go over both the vocabulary and language covered in class in the *Reviews* which can be found after every two units. The Workbook also provides pupils with plentiful opportunities for revision: every unit ends with a *Review* and, at the back of the Workbook, there is a *Language focus extra* for every unit. Online, on the Cambridge Learning Management System (CLMS), students can also revise vocabulary and grammar through playing arcade-style games at the end of each unit. Finally, the presentation software disc (*Presentation Plus*) includes video worksheets for teachers to use, and these include activities to practise grammar points from the unit.

A good start to the English lesson can set the tone for the rest of the lesson. A warmer is an activity designed to get the lesson rolling and to awaken pupils' brains, to prepare their ears, eyes and mouths for English! Warmers should be short, interactive, competitive and fun. They should get pupils thinking and speaking in English. They are an effective way of revising and recycling previously taught language; motivating pupils and making them feel positive about the lesson from the start. Most warmers can be used as fillers too at the end of a lesson. Pupils review what has been covered in the lesson and leave the class in a positive frame of mind and with a sense of achievement.

Vocabulary warmers

Six things

Divide the class into small groups. Prepare one sheet of paper for each group. Each sheet of paper should have different headings beginning with *Six things …* Possible headings could be *Six things … that are yellow / that are round / that you find in the bathroom / that are battery-operated*, etc. Pupils have one minute to write down their six ideas in secret. Once finished, each group reads out their heading and the rest of the class have a time limit in which to guess the six things on their list.

Last man standing

Give each pupil a slip of paper. Give the class a lexical set (for example, ball sports, wild animals, vegetables, etc) and each pupil secretly writes down a word belonging to that lexical set on the slip of paper. Once finished, pupils fold their slips of paper, put them away in their pocket or under their books and stand up. When the whole class is standing, the teacher makes the first guess and writes it on the board for reference. Any pupil who wrote that word is eliminated and sits down. Eliminated pupils take turns to guess the words of those standing. Write each guess on the board so that pupils do not repeat words. The winner is the last person left standing because no-one has been able to guess his/her word.

Word swap

Give each pupil a slip of paper on which they must write down a word or phrase that they have learned in class. They must remember what it means! Once finished, pupils stand up and move around the classroom while music is played. When the music stops, pupils quickly get into twos with the person nearest to them. Give the pupils enough time to explain or define their words to one another. When the music starts again, they must swap slips of paper and move around the classroom again. The same process is repeated, but this time each pupil has another word/phrase to explain to a new partner. Repeat several times.

Stories from the bag

Vocabulary bags (or boxes) are a simple way of keeping a written record of vocabulary studied in class, and they provide an immediate selection of words/phrases for revision activities. For this writing activity, invite 10–15 pupils to take a word from the bag. Write these words on the board in the order that they are picked from the bag. When you have the complete list, pupils work in pairs or small groups to invent a story which must include all the words, and they must appear in the story in the same order as they appear on the board. The first word on the list should appear near the start of the story and the last word on the list should appear near the end of the story. Set a time limit of ten minutes. Groups read out their stories and vote for the best one.

Grammar warmers

Disappearing text

This activity can be used whenever you have a short text on the board. Pupils take turns to read out part of the text aloud. Each time someone finishes reading the text, rub out or delete three or four words. You can draw a line in its place or you can leave the first letter of the missing words. Pupils continue taking turns to read out the complete text remembering to include all the missing words. Challenge pupils to see how much of the text they can remember when most of it has disappeared. Pupils work in pairs and reconstruct the original text, thinking carefully about how each sentence is formed grammatically. This can be done either orally or in writing.

Assessment in *Eyes Open*

Introduction to the tests

A wide range of tests is available on our *Presentation Plus* software in the Cambridge Test Centre. There are *Diagnostic*, *Unit*, *Mid-* and *End-year Progress* tests, as well as *Speaking* tests for every unit, which are all available to download as editable PDFs, with the answer keys and audio. The tests author is an expert test writer and has ensured that the tests are valid, in that they:

- measure what they are meant to measure, in this case, students' understanding of the items in the *Eyes Open* syllabus,
- have been written to match the learning objectives of each level of *Eyes Open*,
- are aligned to the CEFR.

Diagnostic test

The *Diagnostic* test is designed for use at the beginning of the course and, like the Starter unit in the Student's book, revises the core grammar and vocabulary which most students will have studied previously. You might want to use this test to assess which parts of the Starter unit need special remedial work with your class, before starting Unit 1.

Unit tests

Each *Unit* test is divided into a number of sections to reflect the contents of the corresponding unit: *Language focus* (grammar), *Vocabulary*, *Useful language* (expressions from the *Speaking* page), *Listening*, *Reading* and *Writing*. There is also an accompanying *Speaking Test* for each unit. This is independent of the main *Unit* test so that you can decide when or if you want to use it, depending on your classroom context.

Mid- and End-year Progress tests

The *Mid-year* and *End-year Progress* tests have been developed for use at the mid and end points of the course (after Units 4 and 8), in order to assess students' grasp of the language covered in the previous units of the corresponding level of *Eyes Open*.

Cambridge Exams

If you are preparing your students for **Key (for Schools),** or **Preliminary (for Schools)**, then you will find that many of the *Unit* tests, the *Speaking* tests, and all of the *Mid-* and *End-year Progress* tests include question types which reflect those found in those exams.

Adapting the tests

All of the above tests are provided as editable PDF documents to make it easy for you to make changes at question level, add or cut whole exercises, or move questions from one test to another if you have covered the syllabus in a different order. The Answer Key will also need to be updated of course. Please note that you'll need Adobe Acrobat Pro in order to make changes to the PDFs.

Mixed Abilities

Both the *Unit* tests and *Mid-* and *End-year Progress* tests are available at two levels: *Standard* and *Extra*. This allows you to challenge and extend the learning of those students who need it, whilst still providing a degree of achievability for those students who require more support. However, the same audio is used in both versions of the test, but with a different set of questions for each version, to help make classroom management easier.

Preparing your students for tests

One of the principal reasons for testing our students is to promote revision and deeper learning before the test. Each level of *Eyes Open* offers a wide range of material which can be used with students to prepare for tests. The Student's book contains a two-page *Review* section after every two units, and a *Vocabulary Bank* at the back of the book, containing activities which cover the full lexical syllabus of each. The Workbook also contains a three-page *Review* section at the end of each unit, together with *Get it right!* pages which focus on common learner errors, based on real examples of learner errors from the Cambridge Learner Corpus (for more information please see page 23). There is also extra grammar practice in the *Language focus extra* section at the back of the Workbook. Finally, online on the Cambridge Learning Management System, there is a variety of self-study vocabulary and grammar games, further writing practice and additional grammar-based interactive video activities.

Using the results

The score of each test, including the corresponding *Speaking* test, totals 100 marks. This will make it easy to store results, translate then into whichever grading system is used in your context, and to communicate them both within the school and to parents. Such summative assessment is sometimes referred to as Assessment of Learning.

The results will help you to assess where individuals are struggling and where the whole class needs further practice and this, in turn, should help inform your teaching for the coming lessons.

Online Workbook

The Online Workbook offers similar opportunities for formative assessment (Assessment for Learning). Because most work in the Online Workbook is marked automatically, this frees up time for you to focus on your students' learning. The gradebook in the Cambridge Learning Management System (CLMS) will allow you to see quickly and clearly where individuals need extra personalised support and guidance on a particular area of grammar, or in a skill, such as listening. You can also see where a large part of the group is finding a learning objective challenging.

The CEFR

The Common European Framework of Reference for Languages (abbreviated to CEFR, or CEF) is a description of language ability. It is divided into six main levels, ranging from A1 (beginner) to C2 (advanced). It is 'language neutral' and describes what learners can do in terms of the different language **skills** like speaking or reading, as well as looking at language **competencies** like the learners' vocabulary range, and **communication strategies** – how learners use their resources to communicate.

It was envisaged as something which could provide a common language for describing objectives, methods and assessment in language teaching. Put simply, if a learner says 'I am B1 in French' or 'I have passed a C1 exam in English', people like employers or teachers should have a good chance of understanding what this means. The different educational systems and qualifications in different countries might otherwise make this more difficult. As the CEFR authors write, "*the Framework will enhance the transparency of courses, syllabuses and qualifications". (Council of Europe, 2001: 1)*

The levels are described through illustrative descriptors, and you will find the descriptors for each level of *Eyes Open* on the next page. Part 1 of this guide describes the general degree of proficiency achieved at this level as an overview, while Parts 2 and 3 show how the CEFR descriptors relate to each unit of *Eyes Open* Student's Books. Part 2 is organised by skill. Part 3 is organised by unit and appears at the beginning of each unit as a table showing a breakdown of how each of the lessons relates to the CEFR goals.

English Profile and the CEFR

Since the CEFR is language neutral, each language needs a 'profile' project which will detail what learners can do in each specific language. English Profile is the official English language profiling project, registered with the Council of Europe. It aims to provide descriptions of the grammar, vocabulary, etc. required at each level of the CEFR by learners of English that will give the ELT 'community' a clear benchmark for learner progress.

The authors of the CEFR emphasise that: "We have NOT set out to tell practitioners what to do or how to do it. We are raising questions not answering them. It is not the function of the CEF to lay down the objectives that users should pursue or the methods they should employ." (Council of Europe, 2001: xi) English Profile follows this philosophy, and aims to **describe** what learners can do at each level. EP researchers are looking at a wide range of course books and teacher resources to see what learners are being taught, but crucially they are also using the Cambridge Learner Corpus (CLC), a multi-billion word expert speaker corpus of spoken and written current English, covering British, American and other varieties. This allows researchers to analyse what learners are actually doing with the English language as they progress through the levels and use their findings to produce resources like the English Vocabulary Profile.

The English Vocabulary Profile

The English Vocabulary Profile offers reliable information about which words (and importantly, which meanings of those words), phrases and idioms are known and used by English language learners at each level of the CEFR. It is a free online resource available through the English Profile website, (www.englishprofile.org), invaluable for anyone involved in syllabus design as well as materials writers, test developers, teachers and teacher trainers. The authors of *Eyes Open* have made extensive use of it to check the level of tasks and 'input texts', for example listening or reading texts, and also to provide a starting point for vocabulary exercises.

The Common European Framework of Reference for Languages (CEFR)

The Global Scale descriptors for CEFR levels [Council of Europe 2001:24]

C2	Can understand with ease virtually everything heard or read. Can summarise information from different spoken and written sources, reconstructing arguments and accounts in a coherent presentation. Can express him/herself spontaneously, very fluently and precisely, differentiating finer shades of meaning even in more complex situations.
C1	Can understand a wide range of demanding, longer texts, and recognise implicit meaning. Can express him/herself fluently and spontaneously without much obvious searching for expressions. Can use language flexibly and effectively for social, academic and professional purposes. Can produce clear, well-structured, detailed text on complex subjects, showing controlled use of organisational patterns, connectors and cohesive devices.
B2	Can understand the main ideas of complex text on both concrete and abstract topics, including technical discussions in his/her field of specialisation. Can interact with a degree of fluency and spontaneity that makes regular interaction with native speakers quite possible without strain for either party. Can produce clear, detailed text on a wide range of subjects and explain a viewpoint on a topical issue giving the advantages and disadvantages of various options.
B1	Can understand the main points of clear standard input on familiar matters regularly encountered in work, school, leisure, etc. Can deal with most situations likely to arise whilst travelling in an area where the language is spoken. Can produce simple connected text on topics, which are familiar, or of personal interest. Can describe experiences and events, dreams, hopes & ambitions and briefly give reasons and explanations for opinions and plans.
A2	Can understand sentences and frequently used expressions related to areas of most immediate relevance (e.g. very basic personal and family information, shopping, local geography, employment). Can communicate in simple and routine tasks requiring a simple and direct exchange of information on familiar and routine matters. Can describe in simple terms aspects of his/her background, immediate environment and matters in areas of immediate need.
A1	Can understand and use familiar everyday expressions and very basic phrases aimed at the satisfaction of needs of a concrete type. Can introduce him/herself and others and can ask and answer questions about personal details such as where he/she lives, people he/she knows and things he/she has. Can interact in a simple way provided the other person talks slowly and clearly and is prepared to help.

PART 1

The level of *Eyes Open 4* covers level B1+ of the CEFR. The table below describes the general degree of skill achieved by learners at this level.

Skill	Learners will be able to:
Listening	understand extended speech and follow lines of argument on familiar matters regularly encountered in work, school, leisure, etc; understand the main point of many radio or TV programmes on current affairs or topics of personal or professional interest.
Reading	read articles and reports concerned with contemporary problems in which the writers adopt particular stances or viewpoints; understand the description of events, feelings and wishes in personal letters.
Speaking	deal with most situations likely to arise whilst travelling in an area where the language is spoken; enter unprepared into conversation, including explaining a viewpoint, on topics that are familiar, of personal interest or pertinent to everyday life (e.g. family, hobbies, work, travel and current events); give reasons and explanations for opinions and plans; narrate a story or relate the plot of a book or film and describe their reactions.
Writing	write personal letters describing experiences and impressions; write a short essay or report, passing on information or explaining a viewpoint on topics which are familiar or of personal interest.
Communicative language competence	give clear descriptions and express viewpoints on most topics without much searching for words; show a relatively high degree of grammatical control; keep going comprehensibly when speaking, though pausing for grammatical and lexical planning and repair, especially in longer stretches of free production; perform and respond to a wide range of language functions; use awareness of the salient politeness conventions to act appropriately; speak clearly and intelligibly even if a foreign accent is evident and occasional mispronunciations occur.
Communication strategies	initiate, maintain and close simple conversations, and intervene in a discussion on a familiar topic, using a suitable phrase to get the floor; identify unfamiliar words from the context, extrapolate the meaning of occasional unknown words, and deduce sentence meaning if the topic discussed is familiar; ask someone to clarify or elaborate what they just said; exploit a basic repertoire of language and strategies to help keep a conversation going, including summarising the point reached in a discussion to help focus the talk, and inviting others into the discussion.

PART 2

How the goals of the CEFR are realised in *Eyes Open 4*.

LISTENING

OVERALL LISTENING COMPREHENSION
Can identify both general messages and specific details.
Can follow extended speech, short narratives and complex lines of argument provided the topic is reasonably familiar, and the direction of the talk is sign-posted by explicit markers

Starter	Unit 1	Unit 2	Unit 3	Unit 4	Unit 5	Unit 6	Unit 7	Unit 8
1-3 p4	3 p9	3 p19	4 p31	3 p41	3–4 p53	3 p63	3 p75	1–2 p92
2–3 p5	1–2 p16	1–2 p26		1–2 p48		1–2 p70	1–2 p82	
3–4 6								
2–3 p7								

UNDERSTANDING INTERACTION
Can generally follow the main points of extended discussion and animated conversation around them.

Starter	Unit 1	Unit 2	Unit 3	Unit 4	Unit 5	Unit 6	Unit 7	Unit 8
6–7 p5	1–4 p12	3–5 p26	1–6 p38	3–6 p48	1–6 p60	3–6 p70	3–6 p82	
	3–5 p16							

LISTENING TO MEDIA & RECORDINGS

Can understand the most of various types of TV and radio programmes, including news bulletins and interviews, documentaries, live interviews and talk shows.

Starter	Unit 1	Unit 2	Unit 3	Unit 4	Unit 5	Unit 6	Unit 7	Unit 8
	1–8 p14	1–4 p22	1–5 p34	3–5 p44	1–4 p56	1–3 p66	1–4 p78	4 p85
		1–6 p24	1–6 p36	1–7 p46	1–5 p58	1–5 p68	1–4 p80	4–7 p88
								1–7 p90
								3–6 p92

READING

READING CORRESPONDENCE

Can understand the description of events, feelings and wishes in personal letters well enough to correspond regularly with a pen friend.

Starter	Unit 1	Unit 2	Unit 3	Unit 4	Unit 5	Unit 6	Unit 7	Unit 8
		1–4 p27						

READING FOR INFORMATION & ARGUMENT

Can identify the main conclusions in clearly signalled argumentative texts.
Can recognise the line of argument in the treatment of the issue presented, though not necessarily in detail.
Can recognise significant points and obtain information, ideas and opinions from straightforward articles on familiar subjects.

Starter	Unit 1	Unit 2	Unit 3	Unit 4	Unit 5	Unit 6	Unit 7	Unit 8
	1–5 p10	1–3 p20	1–6 p32	1–4 p42	1–5 p54	1–4 p64	1–3 p76	1–3 p86
	1–3 p15	3 p22	3 p34	1–3 p47	1–4 p59	1–4 69	1–3 p81	1–3 p91
	1–5 p17	1–6 p25	1–4 p37	1–4 p49	1–4 p61	1–4 p71		1–4 p93

SPEAKING

OVERALL SPOKEN INTERACTION

CONVERSATION

Can convey degrees of emotion and highlight the personal significance of events and experiences.
Can express and respond to feelings such as surprise, happiness, sadness, interest and indifference.

Starter	Unit 1	Unit 2	Unit 3	Unit 4	Unit 5	Unit 6	Unit 7	Unit 8
	7 p16	6–7 p20				5 p68		
		1–8 p26						

INFORMAL DISCUSSION (WITH FRIENDS)

Can express thoughts on more abstract, cultural topics such as films, books, music, etc.
Can give or seek personal opinions and give brief comments on the views of others.
Can express belief, opinion, agreement and disagreement politely.
Can make their opinions understood when discussing problems or practical questions of where to go, what to do, who or which to choose, how to organise an event (e.g. an outing), etc.

Starter	Unit 1	Unit 2	Unit 3	Unit 4	Unit 5	Unit 6	Unit 7	Unit 8
	4 p12	4 p22	6 p32	7 p47	4–5 p55	5–6 p66	4–5 p75	5–6 p85
			6 p34		6 p58	4 p67	6 p76	5–6 p86
			6–7 p35				5–6 p81	8 p88
			5–6 p37					7 p90
			1–8 p38					6 p91

GOAL ORIENTED CO-OPERATION

Can explain why something is a problem, discuss what to do next and compare and contrast alternatives, giving brief reasons and explanations.

Starter	Unit 1	Unit 2	Unit 3	Unit 4	Unit 5	Unit 6	Unit 7	Unit 8
						4 p70		
						7–8 p70		

INFORMATION EXCHANGE
Can exchange, check and confirm information.
Can describe how to do something, giving detailed instructions.
Can summarise a short story, article, talk, discussion interview, or documentary and answer questions of detail.
Can ask for and follow detailed directions.

Starter	Unit 1	Unit 2	Unit 3	Unit 4	Unit 5	Unit 6	Unit 7	Unit 8
6 p4	5 p9	6–7 p20	5–6 p31	4–5 p41	6 p56	4 p63	5–6 p80	7–8 p89
8 p5	5 p10	5–6 p21	6–7 p33	5 p42	2 p58	7 p64	8 p82	7–8 p92
6 p6	5 p11	7 p23		6 p44	5 p59	5 p69		
6 p7	6 p13	5–6 p25		8 p46	6–7 p60			
	8 p14			6–7 p48				
	6 p15							

OVERALL SPOKEN PRODUCTION

SUSTAINED MONOLOGUE: Describing Experience
Can give detailed accounts/descriptions of
* experiences, describing feelings and reactions.
* events (real or imagined), dreams, hopes and ambitions.
Can relate the plot of a book or film and describe their reactions.
Can narrate a story.

Starter	Unit 1	Unit 2	Unit 3	Unit 4	Unit 5	Unit 6	Unit 7	Unit 8
	3 p13							

WRITING

OVERALL WRITTEN PRODUCTION
Can write straightforward connected texts on a range of familiar subjects within their field of interest, by linking a series of shorter discrete elements into a linear sequence.

Starter	Unit 1	Unit 2	Unit 3	Unit 4	Unit 5	Unit 6	Unit 7	Unit 8
6 p11				5 p53				

CORRESPONDENCE
Can write letters or emails asking for or giving simple information, giving news, expressing thoughts or conveying degrees of emotion, and highlighting the personal significance of events and experiences.

Starter	Unit 1	Unit 2	Unit 3	Unit 4	Unit 5	Unit 6	Unit 7	Unit 8
		5–7 p27						

CREATIVE WRITING
Can write a description of an event, a recent trip (real or imagined).
Can write accounts of experiences, describing feelings and reactions in some detail.
Can narrate a story.
Can write a review of a film, book or play.

Starter	Unit 1	Unit 2	Unit 3	Unit 4	Unit 5	Unit 6	Unit 7	Unit 8
					5–7 p61	5–7 p71	5–6 p78	5–7 p83

COHERENCE
Can use a variety of linking words and cohesive devices efficiently.

Starter	Unit 1	Unit 2	Unit 3	Unit 4	Unit 5	Unit 6	Unit 7	Unit 8
	3–5 p17		2–4 p39					

REPORTS AND ESSAYS
Can write short, simple essays on topics of interest.
Can summarise, report and give their opinion about accumulated factual information.
Can write very brief reports to a standard conventionalised format, which pass on routine factual information and state reasons for actions.

Starter	Unit 1	Unit 2	Unit 3	Unit 4	Unit 5	Unit 6	Unit 7	Unit 8
	6–8 p17		5–7 p39	5–7 p49				5–7 p93

COMMUNICATIVE LANGUAGE COMPETENCE

VOCABULARY RANGE
Have sufficient vocabulary to express themselves with some circumlocutions on most topics pertinent to their everyday life such as family, hobbies and interests, work, travel, and current events. Can vary formulation to avoid frequent repetition.

Starter	Unit 1	Unit 2	Unit 3	Unit 4	Unit 5	Unit 6	Unit 7	Unit 8
1 p5	1–5 p9	1–5 p19	1–9 p31	1–5 p41	1–5 p53	5–6 p64	1–5 p75	1–4 p85
1 p6	4 p10	4–5 p20	4–5 p32	4 p42	4–6 p56	4 p66	4–5 p76	4 p86
1 p7	5–7 p12	5–7 p22	4–5 p34	1–2 p44	1–4 p63	4 p69	4 p78	1–3 p88
5 p7	4–5 p15	4 p25	4 p37				4 p81	4 p91
							3–4 p83	3–4 p93

GRAMMATICAL ACCURACY
Shows a relatively high degree of grammatical control. Does not make mistakes which lead to misunderstanding, and can make some corrections in retrospect.

Starter	Unit 1	Unit 2	Unit 3	Unit 4	Unit 5	Unit 6	Unit 7	Unit 8
1–6 p4	1–6 p11	1–6 p21	1–5 p33	1–4 p43	1–5 p55	1–5 p65	1–5 p77	1–6 p87
2–8 p5	1–6 p13	1–7 p23	1–5 p35	1–7 p45	1–5 p57	1–3 p67	1–5 p79	7 p88
2 p6				4–7 p47				1–6 p89
5 p6								5 p91
2–6 p7								

PHONOLOGICAL CONTROL
Pronunciation is clearly intelligible even if a foreign accent is sometimes evident and occasional mispronunciations occur.

Starter	Unit 1	Unit 2	Unit 3	Unit 4	Unit 5	Unit 6	Unit 7	Unit 8
	1 p9	1 p19	2 p31	1 p41	1 p53	1 p63	1 p75	1 p85
	4 p13	5 p22	5 p35	4 p45	4 p56	3 p67	3 p77	1 p88
	6 p16	6 p23	6 p38	6 p48	3 p57	6 p70	6–7 p82	6 p89
		6 p26			6 p60			6 p92

SOCIOLINGUISTIC APPROPRIATENESS
Are aware of the salient politeness conventions and act appropriately.
Can sustain relationships with native speakers without unintentionally amusing or irritating them.

Starter	Unit 1	Unit 2	Unit 3	Unit 4	Unit 5	Unit 6	Unit 7	Unit 8
		4 p26						

COMMUNICATION STRATEGIES

IDENTIFYING CUES AND INFERRING
Can identify unfamiliar words from the context and deduce sentence meaning provided the topic is familiar.

Starter	Unit 1	Unit 2	Unit 3	Unit 4	Unit 5	Unit 6	Unit 7	Unit 8
	4 p10	4 p25	4 p37	4 p42	4 p54	4 p66	4 p81	4 p86
				3 p49	4 p59	4 p69		4 p91

TAKING THE FLOOR (TURNTAKING), COOPERATING, ASKING FOR CLARIFICATION, COMPENSATING, MONITORING & REPAIR
Can intervene in a discussion on a familiar topic, using a suitable phrase to get the floor.
Can ask someone to clarify or elaborate what they have just said.
Can ask follow up questions to check that they have understood what a speaker intended to say, and get clarification of ambiguous points.

Starter	Unit 1	Unit 2	Unit 3	Unit 4	Unit 5	Unit 6	Unit 7	Unit 8
			4 p38				4 p82	4–8 p92

Unit contents

Vocabulary *-ed* and *-ing* adjectives, phrasal verbs, energy issues, *make* and *do*, art around us, performing, adventure sports and activities, survival essentials

Language focus Past simple vs. past continuous, question words, present perfect and past simple, present perfect with *still*, *yet*, *already* and *just*, word order in questions, subject/object questions, present perfect with *ever*, *never*, *for* and *since*, present perfect questions

CEFR

SKILL AREA	GOAL	EXERCISE
Listening	OVERALL LISTENING COMPREHENSION	1–3 p4 2–3 p5 3–4 p6 2–3 p7
	UNDERSTANDING INTERACTION	6–7 p5
Speaking	INFORMATION EXCHANGE	6 p4 8 p5 6 p6 6 p7
Writing	OVERALL WRITTEN PRODUCTION	6 p11
Communicative language competence	VOCABULARY RANGE	1 p5 1 p6 1 p7 5 p7
	GRAMMATICAL ACCURACY	1–6 p4 2–8 p5 2 p6 5 p6 2–6 p7

Summer holidays

Objectives

- revise the past simple and the past continuous, question words, *-ed* and *-ing* adjectives and phrasal verbs.

Past simple vs. past continuous

1 💬 Books closed. Ask students if they have ever had a bad experience on holiday, e.g. building work going on in their hotel, being given the wrong room, bad food in a restaurant. Discuss it with the class as a whole.

- Ask students to open their books at page 4.
- Put students into pairs to describe the picture and answer the question.
- Elicit answers to the question, but do not confirm or reject them at this stage. Students will check their ideas in Exercise 2.

2 🔊 **1.01** Play the recording for students to check their answer to Exercise 1.

Suggested answer

They were on a cruise holiday. They were swimming, but they saw some sharks in the water and they swam to the island.

3 🔊 **1.01** Write *past simple* and *past continuous* on the board.

- Elicit everything students know about these forms.
- Put students into pairs to complete the text using the verbs in brackets in the correct form.
- For further information, ask students to turn to page 98 of the **Grammar reference** section.
- Play the recording again for students to listen and check their answers.

Answers

2 was sailing **3** stopped **4** jumped **5** were swimming
6 pushed **7** saw **8** swam **9** began **10** shouted
11 were relaxing

Optional activity

- Put students into small groups.
- Ask students to write a short story about a disastrous holiday (*disastrous* is commonly used to exaggerate the fact that something was *unsuccessful*) using the past simple and past continuous.
- Help weaker students by giving them a particular scenario, e.g. a delayed flight.
- Ask one member of each group to read their group's story out to the class.

Question words

4 • Books closed. Elicit the question words, e.g. *why*, *where*, *how*, *which*, etc., and write them on the board. Ask students to make some simple questions with the question words.

- Ask students to open their books at page 4 and complete the questions Pete and Maria were asked with the words in the box.

Answers

2 What **3** Who **4** Which **5** Where **6** When
7 Why

-ed and -ing adjectives, phrasal verbs

5 🔊 **1.02** Books closed. Write the following on the board:
I went to the cinema last night to see a sci-fi film. It was really <u>boring</u>. I was so <u>bored</u> that I left after half an hour.

- Highlight the *-ed* and *-ing* adjectives in the sentences and ask students to explain the difference between these types of words: *-ed* adjectives are used to describe personal feelings, e.g. *I'm so tired*; *-ing* adjectives are used to describe situations and people's characters, e.g. *Janna's very interesting. The holiday was exciting.*
- Write *phrasal verbs* on the board, elicit some common examples, e.g. *get up* or *go out*. Then ask students to explain what phrasal verbs are, i.e. verbs which take prepositions or adverbs.
- Ask students to open their books at page 4.
- Students work in pairs to choose the correct words in each case to complete the answers to the questions in Exercise 4.
- Play the recording for students to check their answers.

Answers

2 setting off **3** worrying **4** terrified **5** come back
6 look round **7** interesting **8** bored **9** found out
10 excited

Optional activity

- Put students into pairs to write definitions for the phrasal verbs used in Exercise 4.
- The phrasal verbs are:
  come back – to return, e.g. *We came back home very late*;
  find out – to discover something, e.g. *I found out that our teacher was from Glasgow*;
  look round – inspect and investigate an area, e.g. *We looked round Prague's Old Town for a few hours*;
  pick up – to learn, e.g. *I picked up a lot of French words on holiday.*;
  set off – to begin a journey, e.g. *We set off for Paris at 7.*
- Ask one student from each pair to read out one of their definitions.

Your turn

6 • Read out the example questions and answer.

- Give students some time to think of a holiday that they would like to talk about.
- Put students into pairs to ask and answer questions about a holiday using the words in the boxes.
- Encourage students to say as much as they can.

 Set Exercises 1, 2 and 3 on page 3 of the **Workbook** for homework.

Home life

Objectives

* revise verbs related to energy, the present simple and the past simple, *make* and *do*, and the present perfect with *still*, *yet*, *already* and *just*.

Energy issues

1 • Books closed. Ask students if they can name any verbs related to energy. Write the verbs on the board. You might expect them to come up with *save* or *waste*.
  * Ask students to open their books at page 5.
  * Refer them to the matching exercise and then ask them to complete it. **Weaker students** can use their smartphones to look up definitions of the words.
  * Check answers.

Fast finishers

Students can think of further ways we might save energy at home, e.g. use energy-saving light bulbs, don't have a bath every day.

> **Answers**
> 2 c 3 d 4 a 5 f 6 b

Present perfect and past simple

2 🔊 **1.03** Tell students they are going to listen to a girl talking about energy use.
  * Play the recording for students to answer the question.
  * Check answers.

> **Answer**
> her family

3 🔊 **1.03** Write *present perfect* and *past simple* on the board.
  * Elicit everything students know about these forms.
  * Put students into pairs to complete the text using the verbs in brackets in the correct form.
  * For further information, ask students to turn to page 98 of the **Grammar reference** section.
  * Play the recording again for students to listen and check their answers.

> **Answers**
> 2 spent 3 've saved 4 had 5 didn't waste
> 6 've stopped 7 left 8 switched 9 has bought

Your turn

4 • Refer students to the sentence beginnings and the example.
  * Ask them to complete the sentences with information about how they use energy at home.
  * Students can compare their sentences in pairs.
  * Ask some students to tell the class about their partner.

make and *do*

5 • Refer students to the photo. Ask them to describe it.
  * Write *make* and *do* on the board.
  * Elicit some examples, e.g. *do your homework*, *do an exercise*, *make a mistake*, *make a phone call*.
  * Ask students to open their books at page 5 and complete the sentences with *make* or *do*.
  * Check answers.
  * To **extend** the work on this, you could put students into small groups and ask them to think of other ways to keep parents happy (using phrases with *make* or *do*), e.g. make them breakfast on Sundays or do the dishes.

> **Answers**
> 2 make 3 do 4 Make 5 Make 6 make 7 make
> 8 do

Language note

Generally speaking, *do* is used with duties, leisure activities and jobs (e.g. *do the dishes*), whereas *make* is used when we talk about performing or building something (e.g. *make a bookshelf*). However, there are many contradictions to the general distinction referred to above, e.g. *make the bed*.

Present perfect with *still*, *yet*, *already* and *just*

6 🔊 **1.04** Play the recording of a conversation between Tina and her mother for students to answer the two questions.
  * Students can compare their answers in pairs before you check answers with the whole class.

> **Answers**
> Tina is doing her homework. Her mum has made a cake.

7 🔊 **1.04** Write *still*, *yet*, *already* and *just* on the board. Elicit example sentences with each of the adverbs. Encourage students to note both the position of the words in the sentence as well as their meaning.
  * For further information, ask students to turn to page 98 of the **Grammar reference** section.
  * Put students into pairs to complete the conversation by choosing the correct word in each case.
  * Play the recording for students to check their answers.
  * Students can act out the completed conversation twice, taking a different part each time.

> **Answers**
> 2 yet 3 just 4 still 5 just 6 already

Your turn

8 • Read out the example questions and answers.
  * Put students into pairs to ask and answer similar questions.
  * Give students further practice of present perfect questions by giving them the opportunity to ask you questions about what you have done today.

> Set Exercises 4, 5, 6, 7 and 8 on page 4 and Exercise 9 on page 5 of the Workbook for homework.

Arts and entertainment

Objectives

- revise vocabulary relating to art, word order in questions, vocabulary relating to performing and subject/object questions.

Art around us

1
- Books closed. Put students into groups to brainstorm vocabulary associated with the arts and entertainment. Make this activity competitive by telling students that the team which comes up with the most correct words wins.
- Ask students to open their books at page 5.
- Students work in pairs to match the words in the box with the pictures.
- Check answers.

Answers

a orchestra b mural c exhibition d sculpture
e portrait f gallery g juggler h microphone

Game

- Play *Could you spell that, please?* using the arts and entertainment vocabulary.
- See **Games Bank** on pages 28–29 .

Word order in questions

2
- Ask: *What is the order of words in a question in English?*
- Elicit the basic structure of a question in English and put it on the board: *question word + auxiliary verb + subject + verb.*
- Order the words in item 1 to make a question as an example. Put this on the board and encourage **weaker students** to use it as a model to follow when completing the exercise.
- For further information, ask students to turn to page 98 of the **Grammar reference** section.
- Put students into pairs to order the words in the remaining items to make questions.
- Check answers.

Answers

2 How did you all meet?
3 Who writes all the songs you play?
4 When was your first concert?
5 What other instruments can you play?
6 What do you do in your free time?
7 What other music do you like?
8 Where are you going after you finish here?

Performing

3 🔊 **1.05** Tell students they are going to listen to an interview with a band. The interview will feature the questions from Exercise 2.
- Play the recording for students to answer the question. Read out the example sentence.
- Check answer.

Audioscript

Turn to page 178 for audio script.

Answer

They met at an arts festival.

4 🔊 **1.05** Refer students to the incomplete notes about the band from the interview.
  Before you play the recording, check students' understanding of the following vocabulary:
  busker /ˈbʌsk ər/: someone who performs in a public place such as a street corner or a square;
  concert hall: a venue which is used primarily for the performance of classical music.
- Play the recording again for students to complete the notes.
- Check answers.

Answers

2 buskers 3 guitar 4 guitar 5 graffiti 6 concert hall
7 on stage

Subject/object questions

5
- Books closed. Check students understand the difference between a subject and an object in a sentence. Do this by writing a simple sentence on the board, e.g. <u>The dog</u> chased <u>the cat</u>. Underline the words *the dog* and *the cat*, then ask students to indicate that *the dog* is the subject and *the cat* is the object.
- Elicit the idea that the subject in a sentence refers to a noun or phrase which comes before the verb, and which performs the action described by the verb, whereas the object is a noun or phrase which comes after the verb in English and which is affected by it.
- Ask students to open their books at page 6.
- Read out the example and then ask students to turn to the **Grammar reference** section on page 98. Students should use the information there to help them complete the exercise.
- Students can work in pairs to do this task.
- Check answers.

Answers

2 do you have for breakfast 3 taught you to play
4 gives you ideas for songs 5 do you listen to
6 did you do last night

Game

- Play *Correct the sentence* using subject/object questions.
- See **Games Bank** on pages 28–29.

Your turn

6
- Divide students into pairs (A and B).
- Tell Students A that they are in a band. They need to give their band a name as well as think of a history for it. Tell Students B that they are music journalists and that they should think of questions to ask. You may want to put students into groups, i.e. all band members in one, all music journalists in another, to do this stage of the activity.
- Put students into A and B pairs to act out their interviews.

 Set Exercises 9, 10, 11, 12 and 13 on page 5 of the **Workbook** for homework.

Exciting lives

Objectives

* revise the names for adventure sports and activities, present perfect with *ever, never, for* and *since*, present perfect questions and objects needed to help survive in difficult environmental conditions.

Adventure sports and activities

1 • Books closed. On the board draw a basic picture of someone rock climbing. Elicit the activity and then ask students what type of activity it is: *adventure sport*.
* Ask students to open their books at page 7.
* Read out the example.
* Ask students to work alone to order the letters in brackets to make adventure sports and activities.
* Check answers.

Answers
2 skiing   **3** sailing   **4** climbing   **5** safari   **6** theme park
7 summer camp   **8** school exchange

Present perfect with *ever*, *never*, *for* and *since*

2 🔊 **1.06** Tell students they are going to listen to Sam talk about travelling.
* Play the recording for students to listen and answer the question.
* Check answer.

Answer
When he was a small child.

3 🔊 **1.06** Write *ever, never, for* and *since* on the board.
* Elicit example sentences using each of the words and the present perfect.
* For further information, ask students to turn to page 98 of the **Grammar reference** section.
* Put students into pairs to complete Sam's blog post by choosing the correct word in each case.
* Play the recording again for students to check their answers.

Answers
2 never   **3** for   **4** never   **5** for   **6** ever

Optional activity
* Refer students to the use of *for* and *since* in Sam's blog post.
* Elicit how these words are used with the present perfect: *for* is used with periods of time and *since* with moments in time, e.g. *I've lived in Amsterdam for ten years. My grandparents have lived in their house since 1995.*
* Ask students to write sentences about their lives using *for* and *since* and the present perfect. You could ask students to write their sentences on some of the topics from the Starter Unit.
* Put students into pairs to compare their sentences.

Present perfect questions

4 • Read out the example question.
* Put students into pairs and ask them to complete the remaining questions using the present perfect.
* Check answers.

Answers
2 have you lived   **3** have you finished packing yet
4 have you had   **5** Have you ever been
6 Have you visited Hawaii yet

Optional activity
* Put students into pairs (A and B).
* Students ask each other questions about where they have and haven't been, e.g. Student A asks Student B *Have you ever been to Australia?* Student B either answers *Yes, I have* or *No, I haven't.*
* If Student B answers *Yes, I have*, Student A then asks further questions in the past simple, e.g. *When did you go? Who did you go with? Where did you stay? How long did you go? What did you think of it?*

Survival essentials

5 • Remind students that the verb *survive* means *to remain alive despite difficulty*, e.g. *They survived the tsunami.* Point out that *survival* is the noun form of the word.
* Put students into pairs. Ask them to match the words to make compound nouns, each of which is an object essential to survival in difficult environments.
* Check answers.

Answers
2 a   **3** b   **4** d   **5** f   **6** e

Optional activity
* Put students into pairs.
* Students take it in turns to define the objects in Exercise 5 for their partner to guess the word, e.g. *This is something you need to protect yourself in hot weather.*

 Your turn

6 • Ask students to imagine that they are adventure travellers. Give students time to think about the kind of life they have. They should think about where they have been, how they have travelled to places, any difficult experiences they have had, etc.
* Read out the example questions and answer.
* Put students into pairs to take it in turns to interview one another.
* Ask some students to report back to the class on their partner.

🔄 Set Exercises 14, 15, 16 and 17 on page 6 of the **Workbook** for homework.

Unit aims

I can ...

* talk about the kind of clothes I like to wear.
* understand short online texts about fashions and an article about style icons.
* talk about past habits and experiences.
* understand a radio interview with an actor.
* buy clothes in a shop.
* write a short biography of a famous person.

Unit contents

Vocabulary	Clothes
	Words in context
	Adjectives and dependent prepositions
	Compound nouns
Reading	Short online texts
	● Milan fashion week
	A magazine article
Language focus	*used to* and *would*
	Past perfect
Listening	An interview
Discover culture	● Inside the guitar
Speaking	Buying clothes
	● Real Talk: What music and fashion were your parents into when they were growing up?
Pronunciation	Sentence stress in past perfect
Writing	A biography
	Sequencers and connectors
CLIL	Social Science: The history of jeans
	● Trendsetters

Background

Cosplay is a portmanteau word formed from a blend of the words *costume* and *play*. It refers to the art of practice of dressing up as characters from films, books, TV shows or video games, and in particular to characters science fiction as well as from the Japanese comic-book genres of animé and manga. It has become a significant pop-cultural phenomenon over the last 20 years.

Be curious

* Books closed. Write *fashion* on the board. Elicit the meaning of the noun, which refers to styles of clothing, hair, decoration, language, music, film and behaviour that are popular at a given moment in time.
* Ask students to open their books at page 8.
* Ask them to describe the photo and then ask them to close their books and say what they remember about it.
* Give students a couple of minutes to answer the three questions.
* Students can then compare answers in pairs before you check answers with the class.
* Tell students that the themes of Unit 1 are trends, fashion and clothes.

Suggested answers

* In the photo, there is a girl with pink hair. She's wearing strange clothes: a kind of red and white uniform. She looks like a character from a Japanese comic book.
* She's outside on the street. Maybe she is playing the part of a character in a film or comic.
* In my free time, I like to play computer games with my friends. There are some good games that we can play together online. I also often go to the cinema with them.
* My parents prefer to watch films at home. And my sisters are younger than me, so they can't go out on their own.

CEFR

SKILL AREA	GOAL	EXERCISE
Listening	OVERALL LISTENING COMPREHENSION	3 p9 1–2 p16
	UNDERSTANDING INTERACTION	1–4 p12 3–5 p16
	LISTENING TO MEDIA AND RECORDINGS	1–8 p14
Reading	READING FOR INFORMATION & ARGUMENT	1–5 p10 1–3 p15 1–5 p17
Speaking	CONVERSATION	7 p16
	INFORMAL DISCUSSION (WITH FRIENDS)	4 p12
	INFORMATION EXCHANGE	5 p9 5 p10 5 p11 6 p13 8 p14 6 p15
	SUSTAINED MONOLOGUE: Describing Experience	3 p13
Writing	COHERENCE	3–5 p17
	REPORTS AND ESSAYS	6–8 p17
Communicative language competence	VOCABULARY RANGE	1–5 p9 4 p10 5–7 p12 4–5 p15
	GRAMMATICAL ACCURACY	1–6 p11 1–6 p13
	PHONOLOGICAL CONTROL	1 p9 4 p13 6 p16
Communication strategies	IDENTIFYING CUES AND INFERRING	4 p10

Vocabulary Clothes

Objectives
* learn vocabulary for different types of clothing.
* describe the clothes I like wearing.

Warm-up
* Books closed. Write *clothes* /kləʊ(ð)z/, *pattern* /ˈpat(ə)n/ and *material* /məˈtɪərɪəl/ on the board. Drill the pronunciation of the three words.
* Draw three T-shirts on the board: one with vertical stripes, one with horizontal stripes and one with dots. Explain that each T-shirt has a different *pattern*.
* Explain *material* by referring to the material that one item of clothing you are wearing is made from. For example, you may be wearing trousers made from cotton.

1 **1.07** Ask students to open their books at page 9.
* Put students into pairs to match the words with the clothes in the pictures.
* If you have the *Presentation Plus* software, put the pictures on the board and ask students to come up to the board in turn to match the words with the photos.
* Play the recording for students to listen, check their answers and repeat the phrases.

> ### Answers
> **a** silk scarf   **b** flowery dress   **c** baggy jumper
> **d** flat shoes   **e** fitted coat   **f** cool T-shirt   **g** tight jeans
> **h** stripy shirt   **i** leather jacket   **j** denim skirt

2 • Refer students to the phrases in the box in Exercise 1. Focus on the words for materials: *leather*, *silk* and *denim*.
* Ask students to use their smartphones to find out both the meaning of these words and the translations into their own language. Students could also look up at the meaning as well as a translation of the word *fitted*.
* Ask students to work alone to find words in Exercise 1 to describe what it listed in a–d.
* Check answers.

> ### Answers
> **a** leather; silk, denim   **b** stripy; flowery
> **c** flat; tight; baggy; fitted   **d** cool

3 **1.08** Tell students they are going to listen to three people talking about the clothes they are wearing.
* Play the recording for students to identify the people on the recording in the pictures in Exercise 1.
* Students can compare answers before you check answers with the whole class.

Audioscript
1 My dad bought this dress for me. I really love the colours and it's the perfect length for me – just above the knee. I also really like the way the top part is fitted, but not really tight.
2 I love making things. I painted this T-shirt. Do you like the design? I love wearing it with jeans. My sister sells them on her stall at the market. I paint designs on denim skirts too, and leather jackets.
3 I feel really comfortable in casual clothes. This is my favourite jumper. I got it for my birthday. I wear it all the time! It's so warm and comfortable. My mum always complains. She says it's too baggy and asks me why can't I wear a shirt or a nice jacket. She doesn't understand!

> ### Answers
> Speaker 1 girl with dress   Speaker 2 girl with green coat
> Speaker 3 girl with yellow trousers

> ### Game
> * Play *Pictionary* using the clothes vocabulary.
> * See **Games Bank** on pages 28–29.

Your turn

4 • Ask students to write down phrases to describe the clothes they like wearing. In some cases, this will mean that they change the phrases in the box in Exercise 1, e.g. they might like wearing *woollen* rather than *silk* scarves.

5 • Ask a student to read out the questions and then refer students to the example answers in the speech bubbles.
* Put students into pairs to ask and answer the questions.
* To **extend** the work on the vocabulary, you could ask students to turn to the **Vocabulary bank** on page 107 and do the exercises for *Clothes*.

> ### Optional activity
> * Ask students to write a short description of one of their favourite items of clothing. Students should include the following information: when and where they bought it (or who gave it to them), how frequently they wear the item and why it means so much to them.
> * Put students into pairs to talk about the items of clothing they wrote descriptions of.
> * Ask some students to report back to the class on their partner.

> Set Exercises 1, 2, 3, 4 and 5 on page 7 of the **Workbook** for homework.
> Students could also complete the following exercises on patterns and materials: http:// learnenglishteens.britishcouncil.org/grammar-vocabulary/vocabulary-exercises/patterns-and-materials

Reading Short online texts

Objectives
- read an article about teenage fashion from the past.
- learn words in context.
- talk about fashions in my country.

Background

Teddy boys based their style on the fashion of the Edwardian era, the name given to the period between 1901 and 1910 when King Edward VII was on the British throne. *Teddy* is an affectionate form of *Edward*.

The **Punk** movement is associated with a loud, aggressive form of rock known as *punk rock*, which developed in the 1970s in New York and later spread to the UK.

The noun **Hippy** (also spelt *hippie*) was coined from the adjective *hip*, meaning *fashionable* or *aware of the latest style and developments*. Hippies are associated with the counter-culture, a movement of the late 1960s which rejected conventional values, and which chose, instead, to champion freedom, love and individuality.

New Romantic describes both a type of synthesised 1980s pop music and a particular look involving make-up and flamboyant style. The wearing of frilly shirts by men was reminiscent of the Romantic era of the 19th-century, which had a huge influence on European culture.

Warm-up

- Books closed. Ask students if they know of any words (in English or their L1) to describe people who follow a particular fashion in clothes, music, language, behaviour, etc. Students may think of words such as *emo*, *hipster* or *geek*.
- Find out if any students identify with a particular fashion.

1
- Ask students to open their books at page 10.
- Give students a minute or so to study the photos, decide the order the fashions shown in them come in, and to read the introduction to the quiz and answer the questions.

2 🔊 **1.09** Ask students to read the text to check their answers to Exercise 1.
- Refer students to the information in the **FACT!** box. Check students' understanding of the noun *peer* /pɪə/, which refers to a person who has the same age, social position or ability as other people in a group.
- Ask students if they get most of their ideas for clothes and fashion from their friends or from things such as magazines and TV.

Answers
4 – 1 – 3 – 2
1 Hippies 2 New Romantics 3 Punks
4 Teds (teddy boys and girls)

3
- Refer students to the gapped sentences.
- Read out the example.
- Put students into pairs and ask them to complete the sentences with the names of the people who followed the four distinct styles.
- Check answers.

Answers
2 Teds 3 Hippies; New Romantics
4 Hippies, New Romantics 5 Teds; Punks
6 Teds; Punks 7 New Romantics 8 Hippies

Explore words in context

4
- Refer students to the words in the box. Drill the pronunciation of the following words: *quiff* /kwɪf/, *dyed* /dʌɪd/ and *extravagant* /ɪk'stravəg(ə)nt/.
- Put students into pairs to first find the words in the text and then look for examples of the words in the photos. Students can use their smartphones to look up the meanings of the words online.
- Check answers.
- You could **extend** the work on this vocabulary by asking students to say whether they know anyone who uses extravagant make-up or who dresses extravagantly, who has a quiff or dyed hair, etc.

Suggested answers
Picture 1: loose clothes   **Picture 2:** extravagant makeup
Picture 3: dyed hair   **Picture 4:** quiff

Your turn

5
- Ask a student to read out the questions.
- Put students into pairs to ask and answer the questions. Encourage **stronger students** to develop conversations beyond the questions on the page by asking one another questions that arise in the course of their discussion.
- Ask some students to report back to the class on what their partner had to say.

You can show this video as either a lead-in or a follow-up to the Language Focus 1 lesson.

Discovery EDUCATION
1.1 Milan fashion week

- ▶ Ask: *Can you name any top models?*
- Elicit student's answers and then put students into pairs to ask and answer the questions.
- Play the video.
- Students watch it and say what they learnt about Milan and the designer featured.
- Then ask students if they would like to go to Milan fashion week.
- See page 122 for further activities you can do with this video.

Suggested answers
- Milan is in the north of Italy. It's the fashion capital of the world, as an important fashion show takes place there every year.
- Missoni (in the video), Giorgio Armani, Emilio Pucci, Gianni Versace

Language focus 1 *used to* and *would*

Objectives

- learn *used to* and *would*.
- talk about my school when I was nine.

Warm-up

- Books closed. Write the following on the board:
  1 *I played football every Sunday.*
  2 *I used to play football every Sunday.*
  3 *I loved doing sport when I was a boy. I would play football every Sunday.*
- Elicit the fact that the sentences refer to the same habitual action in the past.

1
- Ask students to open their books at page 11.
- Tell students that the gapped sentences are from the text on page 10.
- Ask students to copy the sentences into their notebooks and complete them.
- Check answers.
- Ask students to translate *used to* and *would* into their own languages.
- For further information and additional exercises, students can turn to page 99 of the **Grammar reference** section.

Answers

	used to
+	Both boys and girls **used** to wear extravagant make-up.
–	They **didn't use** to spend a lot of money on clothes.
?	What **did** the different groups **use** to call themselves? **Did** you **use to be** a hippy? Yes, I **did**. No, I **didn't**.
	would
+	They **would** put a lot of gel in it. They **would** paint flowers on their hands and faces.
?	**Would** he **break** the rules? Yes, he **would**. No, he **wouldn't**.

- We use *used to* and *would* to talk about **past habits**.
- We only use ***would*** with actions. We used ***used to*** with actions, states and feelings.

2
- Refer students to the gapped text.
- Complete the first gap with the class.
- Ask students to work alone to complete the text with the correct form of *used to*.
- Check answers.

Answers

1 used to be   2 used to go   3 used to like
4 used to dress   5 used to have   6 didn't use to go out
7 used to love

3 Help students with this exercise by guiding them to the correct answer for item 1: *would* cannot be used to complete the gap as it is not used with state verbs such as *be*. That means we can say *He used to be a New Romantic*, but not *He would be a New Romantic.*
- Ask students to look back at the gaps in Exercise 2 to decide where *would* can be used.
- Check answers.

Answers

When my dad was a student he **used to** be a New Romantic. He and his friends **would go** to concerts together all the time. They **used to like** wearing really extravagant clothes. They **would dress** as pirates and paint their faces. He **used to have** long, blond hair, but then he started working in a bank in the city and he **didn't use to go out** so much. He forgot about all the thing he **used to love** doing with his friends. Now he looks completely different!

4
- Read out the information in the **Get it right!** Box.
- Point out that *use to* rather than *used to* is also used in negative sentences, e.g. we say *I didn't use to like Maths* not *I didn't used to like Maths*.
- Read out the example.
- Put students into pairs to complete the exercise.
- Check answers.

Answers

2 Did you use to do any sports?
3 Did you use to wear a uniform?
4 Did your teachers use to give you a lot of homework?
5 Who did you use to play with in the playground?

Your turn

5
- Put students into pairs to ask and answer the questions from Exercise 4.
- Ask some students to tell the class about their partner's past habits.

6
- Read out the example sentence.
- Give students a few minutes to write four or five sentences about the difference between their life now and when they were nine.
- Monitor while students write their sentences. Help as necessary.
- Students can compare the sentences they wrote with a partner.

➡ Set Exercises 1, 2, 3, 4 and 5 on page 8 of the Workbook for homework.

Listening and Vocabulary

Objectives

- listen to a radio interview with an actor.
- learn adjectives and dependent prepositions.
- write sentences about my partner using adjectives and dependent prepositions.

An interview

Background

Back to the Future was the most successful film of 1985, which turned its lead, Michael J. Fox, into a global star.

Warm-up

- Books closed. Read out a list of some American films of the 1980s that were popular with young people, e.g. *Ghostbusters*, *Gremlins*, *ET*, *Karate Kid*, *A Nightmare on Elm Street*.
- Find out if any students have heard of or seen any of these films.
- Alternatively, you could simply put students into pairs and ask them to tell one another about the best film that they have seen recently. If you choose to do this alternative warm-up, make sure that you ask some students to report back to the class on what their partner said.

1   💬 Ask students to open their books at page 12.
- Put students into pairs to answer the questions.
- Do not check answers at this point. Students will do that in Exercise 2 by listening to the recording.

2   🔊 1.11 Tell students they are going to listen to an interview with an actor taking part in a stage version of *Back to the Future*.
- Play the recording for students to check their answers to Exercise 1.

Audioscript

Turn to page 178 for audio script.

Suggested answers

1 *Back to the Future* is a classic film. It came out in 1985.
2 In the film, Marty McFly, travels back in time. The photos show people now and in the past.
3 The technology has changed: people didn't have Internet and their computers were much bigger.

3   🔊 1.11 Play the recording again for students to listen and choose the correct answers.
- Students can compare their answers in pairs before you check answers with the whole class.

Answers

1 1985   2 1980s to the 1950s   3 1980s   4 in the past
5 1980s   6 were   7 weren't   8 hasn't

Your turn

4   • Read out the questions.
- Put students into pairs to ask and answer them.
- Ask some students to tell the class about their partner.

Optional activity

- Give students time to think of which period of history they would go back to if they had a time machine.
- Put students into pairs and ask them to tell each other which period of history they have chosen and why, e.g. *I would go back to the Middle Ages.*
- Ask some students to report back to the class on what their partner said.

Adjectives and dependent prepositions

5   🔊 1.12 Tell students that some adjectives are used with particular prepositions, e.g. *She's good at playing chess.*
- Put students into pairs and ask them to complete the sentences by choosing the correct preposition in each case.
- Play the recording for students to check their answers.

Answers

2 by   3 in   4 on   5 by   6 with   7 of   8 of

Optional activity

- Put students into pairs (A and B).
- Students take it in turns to test each other on adjectives and dependent prepositions.
- Student A closes their book. Student B says one of the adjectives from Exercise 5. Student A says what preposition is used with that adjective.
- Students swap roles and continue in this way until all the adjectives in Exercise 5 have been used.

Your turn

6   • Read out the example sentence.
- Put students into pairs and give students time to write five sentences describing their partner using the adjectives and prepositions from Exercise 5.

7   • Refer student to the example conversation.
- Put students into pairs to ask and answer questions based on the sentences they wrote in Exercise 6.
- If none of the sentences that students wrote are true for their partner, they should ask their partner to use the adjectives and dependent prepositions to say a few things about him or herself that are true.
- Ask some students to report back to the class on what their partner said.
- To **extend** the work on the vocabulary, you could ask students to turn to the **Vocabulary Bank** on page 107 and do the exercises for *Adjectives and dependent prepositions.*

↪ Set Exercises 1, 2, 3 and 4 on page 9 of the **Workbook** for homework.
For homework, you could also ask students to watch *Back to the Future*. They can then say what they think about the film with a partner in the next lesson.

Language focus 2 Past perfect

Objectives

*   learn the past perfect.
*   talk about the first time I did or saw something special.

Warm-up

*   Books closed. Write the following sentences on the board:
    1 *Cristiano Ronaldo joined Real Madrid in 2009.*
    2 *He had wanted to play for the Spanish club for years.*
*   Focus on the underlined verbs in each sentence. Elicit the fact that the first sentence is in the past simple. Explain that the second sentence is in the past perfect and that this is a different way of talking about events in the past.
*   Highlight the form of the past perfect: *had* + past participle.

1
*   Ask students to open their books at page 13.
*   Tell students that the example sentences are from the listening on page 12.
*   Ask students to copy the sentences into their notebooks and complete them using the words in the box. Then, ask them to answer the questions.
*   Check answers.
*   For further information and additional exercises, students can turn to page 99 of the **Grammar reference** section.

Answers

+	I **had** always **wanted** to be in a big show.
–	I **hadn't** really **thought** about it before.
?	**Had** you **seen** it before you started on the production? Yes, I **had seen** it twice. No, I **hadn't** seen it.

1 a   2 a

Language note

The past perfect and the present perfect connect different points in time. The present perfect relates the past to the present moment, whereas the past perfect joins two past events. Compare the following:
1 *She's lived in that flat for years. She enjoys living there.*
2 *She'd lived in that flat for years. She enjoyed living there.*

2
*   Read out the example. Check students' understanding of why the past simple is used in the first item. Explain that only one past action is referred to; there is no other context.
*   Put students into pairs and ask them to complete the remaining sentences with the correct form of the verbs.
*   Check answers.

Answers

1 hadn't heard   2 had gone; didn't see
3 hadn't been; was   4 arrived; had started

3 Ask students to describe the pictures briefly.
*   Put students into pairs and ask them to tell the story the pictures show using the verbs in the box.

4 🔊 **1.13** Complete the first gap with the class as an example.
*   Ask students to work alone to complete the remaining gaps in the text with the verbs in the box in Exercise 3.
*   Students can compare answers in pairs.
*   Play the recording for students to check their answers.

Answers

1 was   2 had wanted   3 saw   4 asked   5 said
6 hadn't let   7 got on   8 arrived
9 had put up their tents   10 waited   11 had
12 sold out

Say it right!

Sentence stress in past perfect

1 🔊 **1.14** Remind students that certain words in a sentence are given particular stress if they carry a meaning the speaker wishes to convey and that the same sentence can be given different meanings according to which words are stressed.
*   Play the recording for students to listen to and repeat the sentences.

2 🔊 **1.15** Play the recording for students to mark the main stress in the sentences.

3 🔊 **1.15** Play the recording for students to check their answers to Exercise 2 and repeat the sentences.

Answers

1 The **show** had **sold out** really **quickly**.
2 We'd **wanted** to **go** to that **restaurant** for **ages**.
3 **What**? He hadn't **seen** that **film**? **Ever**?
4 **Lots** of other **people** had **arrived** before us.
5 I hadn't **expected** to **see** him there. What a **surprise**!

4 Put students into pairs to practise saying the sentences in Exercise 2.

Optional activity

*   Students can use their smartphones to record each other saying the sentences in Exercise 2.
*   Students can then listen back to check whether they are used sentence stress correctly in each case.

Your turn

5
*   Read out the example note about the first time someone did something or saw something special.
*   Give students a few minutes to write notes about their own experiences.
*   You could encourage **weaker students** to write full sentences as these will help them with the next activity.

6
*   Put students into pairs to talk about the experiences they made notes on in Exercise 5. Students can use questions 1–6 and any other they can think of.
*   Ask some students to report back to the class on their partner.

➡ Set Exercises 1, 2, 3, 4 and 5 on page 10 of the **Workbook** for homework.

Discover Culture

Inside the guitar

Objectives

- watch a video about how guitars are made.
- talk about guitars and other musical instruments.

Warm-up

- Books closed. Write the following names on the board: *Fender*, *Gibson*, *Ibanez*.
- Ask: *Do you know the connection between these names?* (They are all makes of guitar, with Fender and Gibson being most famous in the world of rock.)

1 💬 Ask students to open their books at page 14 and look at the photos of the acoustic and electric guitars.
- Drill the pronunciation of *fret* /**fret**/. Then check students' understanding of:
  body: the central part of the guitar, which is attached to the neck;
  frets: ridges on the fingerboard on the neck of a guitar, which divide it into semitones;
  strings: wires on a guitar, which produce notes by vibration.
- Put students into pairs to ask and answer the questions.
- Check answers.

Suggested answers

Both guitars have the same basic parts (frets, body and strings), but their construction is different. You need electricity to play the electric guitar. The sounds these instruments make are different, too.

2 💬 Put students into pairs to answer the two questions.

3 ▶ **1.2** Refer students to the three options a–c.
- Play the recording.
- Students watch the video and say which of the options best describes the main focus of the video.

Videoscript

What role has the guitar played in popular culture? Well, guitars have been around for a long time. You hear the guitar in all different types of music. Traditional, or *acoustic*, guitars like these here have a deep body. This deep body amplifies the sound. And then there's the electric guitar. Its sound is quite different from the acoustic guitar. Many musicians have a favourite brand of electric guitar. Some love their Fenders. And others prefer Gibsons. We visited the Gibson guitar factory in the US to learn more about these amazing instruments. First, we learned that electric guitars, unlike acoustic guitars, have a solid body. At the factory, they use big machines to make the bodies – lots of them. But they also do a lot of things by hand, like adding the frets. These guitars look just like the original Gibson did in 1952 with the same colours and the same pattern. When we arrived, the factory had just received an order for 500 of these! But one thing is still missing! The sound! They put small magnets, like these, under the strings. When the strings move, they create waves. The magnets change these waves into electricity. The electricity goes through a wire, and we hear sounds! Then, they add the strings, and it's done! So you see, the electric guitar was part of a revolution in music and it still is today.

Answer

c

4 • Refer students to the six questions. Give them a few minutes to answer them.
- This exercise is a test of students' memory and some will do better at it than others.

5 ▶ **1.2** Play the recording again for students to check their answers to Exercise 4.

Answers

1 electric guitar   2 with a group of musicians
3 electric guitars   4 the body   5 frets   6 a concert

6 • Read out the words and phrases on the picture and explain that they are all used in the video to describe how an electric guitar works.
- Put students into pairs to write their own description of how a guitar works using the words and phrases.

7 ▶ **1.2** Play the recording from 02.04 to 02.35 for students to check their answers.

Answers

See the videoscript in Exercise 3 above.

Your turn

8 • Refer students to the questions about guitars and other musical instruments.
- Put students into pairs to ask and answer the questions.

Optional activity

- Students can read this story of the evolution of the electric guitar.
  http://www.sixstringtheories.com/wp-content/uploads/2011/05/eguitar_infographic2.jpg
- Students can then tell a partner which of the guitars pictured they would most like to play.

 For homework, you could give students a list of some of the best guitarists of all time and ask them to watch some videos of them on YouTube, e.g. Django Reinhardt, Paco du Lucia or Jimi Hendrix. At the beginning of the next lesson, students could tell a partner whose playing they most enjoyed.

Reading A magazine article

Objectives
* read a magazine article about objects that symbolise the UK.
* learn compound nouns.
* talk about people or objects that are popular in my country.

Warm up
* Books closed. Write the following on the board: *the Eiffel Tower, the Statue of Liberty, the Coliseum.*
* Ask students which cities these monuments represent. Elicit: *Paris, New York* and *Rome.*
* Elicit examples of other buildings, monuments, objects or people that are in some way representative of particular cities or countries. You may wish to introduce the adjective *iconic* at this point.

Language note
The adjective **iconic** means *relating to an icon. Icon* originally referred to devotional paintings of holy figures which were used in religious ceremonies, but is now mostly used to refer to someone regarded as being representative or symbolic of something and therefore worthy of admiration, e.g. *Marilyn Monroe is one of the icons of Hollywood. Iconic* is now used with the meaning *well-known, popular* or *commercially successful,* and has become a cliché in the worlds of media and marketing. The adjective **retro** refers to fashion or style that borrows a look common at a point in the recent past.

1 Ask students to open their books at page 15.
* Refer students to the photos and then ask the class the questions.
* Elicit answers, but do not confirm or reject them at this stage. Students will check their answers in Exercise 2.

2 🔊 `1.16` Ask students to read the magazine article to check their answers from Exercise 1.

Suggested answers
the Beatles – a band from the 1960s; they're still popular
a telephone and a red telephone box – you can still see some the boxes in the UK
the Mini – a British car; its production stopped in 2000, but there's a new (German) Mini
a black cab – a London taxi; they're still used, but often covered in adverts

Language note
Fab is short for *fabulous* and in some areas of the UK is a commonly used adjective meaning *great* or *fantastic,* e.g. *I thought the film was fab.*

3
* Refer students to sentences a–c.
* Ask students to read the magazine article and then ask them to say which sentence describes what the four icons featured in the article have in common.
* Read out the information in the **FACT!** box. Then ask the class why we romanticise objects, buildings, monuments, etc., from the past and why it is we try to preserve or celebrate them.

Answer
c

Explore compound nouns

4
* Read out the example compound noun.
* Ask students to make further compound nouns by matching the words in A with those in B.
* Students can compare their answers in pairs and then find the compound nouns in the text.
* Check answers.

Answers
style changes   telephone box   street corners
motor industry   taxi fare

Language note
Compound nouns are formed from a noun plus another word, usually a noun, but sometimes adjectives and verbs. They are either written as two words (e.g. *post office*) or as one (e.g. *postman*). In the past compound nouns were commonly hyphenated (e.g. *post-man, post-office*) although they now tend to be written as either one word or two.

5
* Read out the example.
* Put students into pairs to decide which of the words in each group are *not* used with the words in bold to form compound nouns. Encourage students to say each of the compounds while making their decisions. The non-compound nouns should sound unusual in that they will not be words that the students have ever heard.
* Check answers.
* To **extend** the work on the vocabulary, you could ask students to turn to the **Vocabulary Bank** on page 107 and do the exercises for *Explore compound nouns.*

Answers
2 model   3 name   4 house   5 driver   6 call

Your turn

6
* Put students into pairs to ask and answer the questions. Students can search online for examples of people or objects that are icons in their country.
* Ask students to share the images of these icons with each other by emailing them if possible. You can then discuss with the class as a whole which of the icons chosen are most representative of the students' country.

➡ Set Exercises 1, 2, 3, 4 and 5 on page 11 and Exercise 6 on page 10 of the Workbook for homework.

Speaking Buying clothes

Objectives
- watch teenagers talking about the music and fashion their parents liked.
- listen to teenagers talk about buying clothes.
- practise asking and answering questions in a clothes shop.

Warm-up
- Books closed. Write the phrase *to be into something* on the board.
- Explain that it is an informal way of saying you are interested in something, e.g. *I'm really into rock*.

Real talk: What music and fashion were your parents into when they were growing up?

1 ▶ **1.3** Ask students to open their books at page 16.
- Tell students they are going to watch some teenagers answering the following question:
  What music and fashion were your parents into when they were growing up?
- Refer students to the music styles and people in the box as well as the list of sentences.
- Tell students that they are going to match the sentences with the music or people.
- Play the video or the recording.
- Students work alone to complete the exercise.
- Check answers.

Videoscript

Narrator: What music and fashion were your parents into when they were growing up?

Speaker 1: My parents? My dad didn't like anything popular when he was young. He's a classical violinist so he only likes classical music! But Mom was crazy about pop music … I think she still is!

Speaker 2: My parents weren't that into music, but they both liked fashion, especially my mom. She followed the latest trends, like tight jeans, and those dresses with bows everywhere and shoulder pads. Her wardrobe is still full of them but she doesn't wear them anymore.

Speaker 3: I've no idea. They haven't got any pictures from that time. The photo albums disappeared in a move when I was little. When I ask them about it, they never say! I guess they liked disco since they grew up in the 70's, but they don't admit it!

Speaker 4: I'm not sure about my parents, but my grandparents were into the Beatles. My grandma even went to one of their first concerts. She still seems excited when she talks about it.

Speaker 5: My parents were both really into Michael Jackson. It's a little embarrassing … My dad still has a copy of the famous white glove. And my mom can do all of those crazy dance moves. Whenever they play his songs, we just sit back and laugh!

Speaker 6: They were into punk music and everything that went with it – the crazy hair, the weird clothes, the makeup. It's really funny to see pictures of them from that time. They look so serious, but they have dyed hair and leather jackets!

Narrator: What music and fashion were *your* parents into when they were growing up?

Answers
1 classical and pop   2 no music   3 disco   4 the Beatles
5 Michael Jackson   6 punk

2 💬 Put students into pairs to ask and answer the question.
- Ask some students to report back to the class on what their partner said.

3 🔊 **1.17** Tell students they are going to listen to Olivia telling Raquel talking in a clothes shop.
- Read out the question.
- Play the recording.
- Students listen and answer the question.
- Check answer.

Answer
a top

4 - Refer students to the phrases in the *Useful language* box.
- Check students' understanding of the language, particularly the verb *suit*, which, in this context, means *make someone look more attractive*, e.g. *That dress really suits you*.
- Students can work alone to complete the conversation using the phrases in the *Useful language box*.

5 🔊 **1.17** Play the recording for students to check their answers.

Answers
2 they're my size   3 are the changing rooms
4 the top suits me   5 look great   6 fit very well

6 💬 Ask students to work in pairs to act out the conversation in Exercise 4.
- Students can act out the conversation twice, taking a different part each time.

7 💬 Read out the instructions and make sure that students understand what they have to do.
- Put students into pairs (A and B).
- Give students some time to plan what they want to say.
- Students then act out their conversations.
- Monitor while students are practising their conversations. Check that they are using the phrases from the *Useful language box*.

⊙ Ask students to watch this video about Camden Market, famous for its clothes stalls, and complete the accompanying exercises:
http://learnenglishteens.britishcouncil.org/uk-now/video-uk/camden-fashion

✏️ Writing A biography

Objectives
- read a biography of the pop group ABBA.
- learn about the use of sequencers and connectors.
- write a biography of an artist or band from the past.

Warm-up
- Books closed. Ask students if they know of any English-language bands or artists that were successful in the 1970s.
- If students cannot name any, introduce them to some examples e.g. *Queen, Led Zeppelin, Pink Floyd, David Bowie, Stevie Wonder.*

1
- Ask students to open their books at page 17.
- Refer students to the photo and ask them the questions.
- Students then read the biography to check their answers.

Answers
They're a group called ABBA. They were popular in the 1970s.

2
- Refer students to the fact file.
- Put students into pairs and ask them to read the text again and complete the facts about ABBA.
- Check answers.

Suggested answers
1 ABBA 2 Sweden 3 1972 / 1982
4 at the Eurovision Song Contest in 1974
5 *Waterloo, Dancing Queen, SOS* 6 pop and disco
7 glam-rock 8 380 million 9 They were two couples.
10 They released two albums in Spanish. Their music has become popular again recently.

3
- Ask students to identify the paragraphs in which the information in the Exercise 2 appears in the biography of ABBA.
- Students can compare their answers in pairs before you check answers with the class.

Suggested answers
Paragraph 1: facts 1, 2, 3, 9, 10
Paragraph 2: facts 4, 5, 6, 7, 10
Paragraph 3: facts 8, 10

4
- Read out the information about sequencers and connectors in the *Useful language box.*
- Explain that words and phrases such as *although* and *as a result* are used to make a piece of writing coherent. Drill the pronunciation of *although* /ɔːlˈðəʊ/.
- Ask students to work alone to find three further examples of such words and phrases in the biography in Exercise 1.
- Check answers. You could then elicit further example sentences using these words and phrases as a means of checking students' understanding. If you do this, write the example sentences on the board and ask students to copy them into their notebooks.

Suggested answers
Later on both couples got married.
Over the next eight years they became one of the most famous pop groups ever.
During that time they played pop and disco, and were famous for their glam-rock stage costumes.
In the last few years their music has become popular again with the musical (and film) *Mamma Mia.*

5
- Put students into pairs and ask them to complete the sentences about ABBA using the words and phrases in the box.
- Check answers.

Answers
1 Although 2 as a result 3 After 4 Over the next
5 the last few years

Optional activity
- If students do not know ABBA's music, you could introduce them to some of the band's songs on YouTube. They could listen to the songs referred to in the biography or the band's performance of Waterloo at the Eurovision Song Contest in 1974.
- You would probably be advised to do this as a whole class activity. Otherwise the class may become a cacophony of competing songs.

✏️ Get Writing

PLAN
6
- Students should do their planning in class. The writing can either be done in class or at home.
- Tell students they are going to write a biography of a band or artist from the past.
- You may want to brainstorm some bands or artists with the class as a whole to give the class some ideas.
- Refer students back to the headings in Exercise 2 and then ask them to work alone to make notes. If you choose to do the writing in class, encourage students to use their smartphones to look up information online.

WRITE
7
- Tell students to use the biography of ABBA as a model to follow.
- Give students ten minutes to complete the writing task. Students should write between 140 and 160 words.
- Monitor while students are writing. Help with grammar and vocabulary as necessary.

CHECK
8
- Tell students that it is very important that they check their writing in order to look for ways to improve its content, style and structure.
- Give students a few minutes to look through their biographies and check them against the points here.
- Collect students' texts and mark them.

 Set Exercises 1, 2, 3 and 4 on page 12 and Exercises 5, 6, 7, 8, 9, 10 and 11 on page 13 of the **Workbook** for homework.

2 A helping hand

Unit aims

I can ...
- talk about a person's qualities.
- understand a magazine article and a blog about people and their lives.
- talk about things I've done and things happening in my life.
- understand a news report about an educational project.
- show concern.
- write a personal email.

Unit contents

Vocabulary	Personal qualities
	Word building
	Phrasal verbs (learning and socialising)
	Words in context
Reading	A magazine article
	● Born to dive
	A blog post
Language focus	Reflexive pronouns and *each other*
	Present perfect simple
	Present perfect continuous
	Present perfect simple vs. present perfect continuous
Listening	A news report
Discover culture	● A very Indian wedding
Speaking	Showing concern
	● Real talk: Have you helped a friend through a difficult situation?
Pronunciation	Stress and intonation in questions with *How long?*
Writing	A personal email
	Expressing how we feel
CLIL	Technology: The changing classroom
	● The house of the future

Be curious

- Books closed. Write the common phrase *to give someone a helping hand* on the board. (It can also be *to lend someone a helping hand*). Elicit the idea that the phrase refers to one person helping another to do a particular task, e.g. *I was struggling with my Physics homework, but my brother gave me a helping hand*.
- Ask students to open their books at page 18 and describe the photograph.
- Give students a couple of minutes to answer the three questions.
- Students can then compare answers in pairs before you check answers with the class.
- Tell students that the theme of Unit 2 is helping others.

Suggested answers

- In the photo, there are two pandas outside by the branches of a tree.
- One of the pandas is helping the other to climb up the tree, maybe because it isn't tall enough to climb by itself.
- Other animals help each other in the wild. For example, there are birds that eat the insects off the backs of large mammals. Animals that live in groups, for example, monkeys, make warning noises when they see a predator.

CEFR

SKILL AREA	GOAL	EXERCISE
Listening	OVERALL LISTENING COMPREHENSION	3 p19 1–2 p26
	UNDERSTANDING INTERACTION	3–5 p26
	LISTENING TO MEDIA AND RECORDINGS	1–4 p22 1–6 p24
Reading	READING CORRESPONDENCE	1–4 p27
	READING FOR INFORMATION & ARGUMENT	1–3 p20 3 p22 1–6 p25
Speaking	CONVERSATION	6–7 p20 1–8 p26
	INFORMAL DISCUSSION (WITH FRIENDS)	4 p22
	INFORMATION EXCHANGE	6–7 p20 5–6 p21 7 p23 5–6 p25
Writing	CORRESPONDENCE	5–7 p27
Communicative language competence	VOCABULARY RANGE	1–5 p19 4–5 p20 5–7 p22 4 p25
	GRAMMATICAL ACCURACY	1–6 p21 1–7 p23
	PHONOLOGICAL CONTROL	1 p19 5 p22 6 p23 6 p26
	SOCIOLINGUISTIC APPROPRIATENESS	4 p26
Communication strategies	IDENTIFYING CUES AND INFERRING	4 p25

Vocabulary Personal qualities

Objectives

* learn words for personal qualities.
* listen to descriptions of people who help or teach others.
* describe someone I know who helps me.

Warm-up

* Books closed. Write *personal qualities* on the board.
  Check students' understanding of the word *qualities* (a *quality* is a characteristic someone possesses).
* Write an example on the board, e.g. *Jane should captain the team because she's got good leadership qualities. She's calm and confident.* Focus on the words describing Jane's qualities (*calmness and confidence*).
* Explain that the word *qualities* tends to be used positively.
* Brainstorm examples of positive character adjectives and put them on the board, e.g. *patient, generous, friendly.*

1 🔊 **1.18** Ask students to open their books at page 19.
* Put students into pairs to match the sentences with the photos.
* If you have the *Presentation Plus* software, put the pictures on the board and ask students to come up to the board in turn to match the words with the photos.
* Play the recording for students to listen, check their answers and repeat the phrases.

Fast finishers

Fast finishers may describe the photos.

Answers

1 c 2 e 3 a 4 d 5 b

Language note

Rather than say *I am interested in something*, some people say they are **passionate about** it. This form of exaggeration is common in advertising where, for example, a shoe retailer may advertise its products saying: *We're passionate about comfortable footwear.*

2
* Ask students to work alone to match the sentences with the adjectives in Exercise 1.
* Students can compare answers in pairs before you check answers with the class.

Answers

1 shy   2 passionate about   3 strict   4 determined
5 hard-working   6 impatient

3 🔊 **1.19** Tell students they are going to listen to three people talking about a person who helps or teaches them.
* Play the recording for students to note down the adjectives that are used to describe each of the people referred to.
* Students can compare answers before you check answers with the whole class.

Audioscript

1 Krista is my art teacher, I've been in her classes for three months now and she's such a good teacher. She's never impatient, she never gets angry. She's a very talented artist too. Her paintings are so beautiful and she's really passionate about art. It's her life!

2 Steff's a great guy. He's easy-going and sociable. He never gets stressed and he's always good fun to be with. But when something is important to him he can be very determined!

3 Toni can be really shy when he's with people he doesn't know, but when he's in the theatre, he's a completely different person. He's hardworking and he's very strict, he makes us practise for hours – we can't stop until it's perfect!

Answers

1 talented, passionate about
2 easy-going, sociable, determined
3 shy, hard-working, strict

Game

* Play *Could you spell that, please?* using the adjectives for personal qualities.
* See **Games Bank** on pages 28–29.

Your turn

4
* Read out the example.
* Ask students to think of someone they know well and who helps them in some way. This could be a family member who helps them with homework, a teacher who helps them understand difficult areas of a particular subject, or a friend who has taught them how to do something, e.g. write computer code.
* Monitor while students write their sentences. Help as necessary.

5
* Read out the example and then focus on the word *both*. Check students understand its meaning (*both* is a word used to emphasise the fact that we are referring to two people or things) and show how it is used before the *main* verb or after the verb *to be*, e.g. *We both like films. We are both sociable.*
* Give students a few minutes to work in pair and discuss their descriptions from Exercise 4.
* To **extend** the work on the vocabulary, you could ask students to turn to the **Vocabulary Bank** on page 108 and do the exercises for *Personal qualities*.

Optional activity

* Ask students to choose two of the character adjectives in Exercise 1 that apply to them.
* Put students into pairs to tell their partner the adjectives they chose, e.g. *I think I am impatient and strict. What about you?*

 Set Exercises 1, 2, 3, 4 and 5 on page 17 of the Workbook for homework.

Reading A magazine article

Objectives
- read an article about a climber.
- learn how to build words.
- talk about my best qualities and qualities I would like to have.

Warm-up
- Books closed. Write the following on the board: *How do you become good at something?* This 'something' could refer to anything from doing a sport to playing a musical instrument or learning a language.
- Elicit answers from the class, e.g. *by practising a lot* or *by hard work.*

1
- Ask students to open their books at page 20.
- Ask students to look at the headline and the photo. They should then choose three adjectives to describe Brooke.
- Students can compare the adjectives they choose with a partner.

> ### Answers
> Brooke: determined, hard-working
> Mum: strict, passionate

2 🔊 **1.20** Write the phrase *to push yourself* on the board. Elicit or introduce the meaning of the phrase (to use determination, hard work, effort and commitment to achieve something), e.g. *Mia has a real talent for Maths, but she needs to push herself to achieve everything she is capable of achieving.*
- Ask students to read the text to check their answers to Exercise 1.
- Refer students to the information in the **FACT!** box. Ask students if they have ever been rock climbing or if they would ever consider trying it.

> ### Answers
> She loves climbing because when she's on a high rock she feels happy.

3
- Put students into pairs and ask them to complete the exercise by scanning the magazine article for key words which should lead them to the information they are looking for.
- Check answers.

> ### Answers
> **1** She has really strong fingers and the incredible flexibility of a child.   **2** Both her parents are past climbing champions.   **3** They really respect and trust each other.
> **4** She runs a club for young climbers.   **5** She passes her passion on to her students.   **6** She feels happy.

🔍 Explore word building

4
- Write the word *happy* on the board. Elicit that it's an adjective. Ask students if they can turn it into a noun (*happiness*).
- Refer students to the words in the table and explain that they are going to look at how one word can be built from another.
- Put students into pairs and ask them to copy and complete the table by finding the words in the article.
- Check answers.

> ### Answers
> **2** passion **3** determined **4** challenge **5** success
> **6** happy

5
- Brainstorm examples of world-class sportspeople, e.g. Cristiano Ronaldo, (football), Serena Williams (tennis), Floyd Mayweather (boxing), Lewis Hamilton (motor racing) or Jessica Ennis-Hill (athletics).
- Read out the example sentence.
- Ask students to work alone to write three sentences of their own about what it takes to be a world-class sportsperson.
- Students can compare their ideas in pairs before you ask some students to read their sentences out to the class.
- To **extend** the work on the vocabulary, you could ask students to turn to the **Vocabulary bank** on page 108 and do the exercises for *Explore word building*.

Your turn

6
- Ask a student to read out the two questions.
- Give students time to make notes in response to the questions.

7
- Refer students to the example and then put them into pairs to ask and answer the questions from Exercise 6.
- Encourage **stronger students** to develop conversations beyond the questions on the page by asking one another questions that arise in the course of their discussion.
- Ask some students to report back to the class on what their partner said.

You can show this video as either a lead-in or a follow-up to the Language Focus 1 lesson.

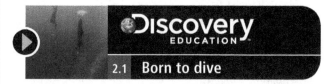

- ▶ Ask: *Have you ever been diving?*
- Elicit student's answers and then put students into pairs to ask and answer the questions.
- Play the video.
- Students watch it and say what they learnt about free diving.
- Then ask students if they would like to try the type of diving featured in the video
- See page 123 for further activities you can do with this video.

> ### Suggested answers
> - Free diving means diving without any breathing equipment.
> - This sport can be dangerous. You need to train for a long time.
> - You have to be passionate about it and hard-working.

 Set Exercises 1, 2, 3, 4 and 5 on page 21 and Exercise 7 on page 18 of the **Workbook** for homework.
You could ask students to watch some videos of Brooke Raboutou climbing. Several can be found online.

Language focus 1 Reflexive pronouns and *each other*

Objectives

* learn reflexive pronouns and *each other*.
* talk about the last time I did something.

Warm-up

* Books closed. Mime knocking your fingers on the table. Wince as if you are in pain, then ask the following question: *What did I do?*
* Say: *I hurt myself*. Write this sentence on the board.
* Underline *I* and *myself*. Tell students that *myself* is an example of a reflexive pronoun and that they are going to look at how such words are used in a sentence.

1
* Ask students to open their books at page 21.
* Tell students that the gapped sentences are from the text on page 20.
* Ask students to copy the sentences into their notebooks and complete them.
* Check answers.
* You may want to explain that verbs like *feel*, *relax* or *concentrate* are not used reflexively in English, e.g. *She felt sorry for him* not ~~She felt herself sorry for him~~.

Answers

1 each other   2 herself   3 yourself

2
* Refer students to the gapped table.
* Put students into pairs and ask them to copy and complete the table with the reflexive pronouns from Exercise 1.
* Check answers.
* Students can then answer the three questions.
* Check answers.
* For further information and additional exercises, students can turn to page 100 of the **Grammar reference** section.

Answers

subject pronoun	object pronoun	reflexive pronoun
I	me	myself
you	you	[1]**yourself**/yourselves
he	him	himself
she	her	[2]**herself**
it	it	itself
we	us	ourselves
they	them	themselves

1 Brooke trusts her mother. Her mother trusts Brooke.
2 Brooke   3 the athlete himself/herself

Language note

Verbs referring to everyday activities (e.g. *get up, dress*) are only used reflexively in English when we want to express surprise that someone has done an action on their own, e.g. *Although he was seriously injured, Joe is still able to wash and dress himself.*

3
* Read out the example.
* Put students into pairs to complete the matching exercise.
* Check answers.

Answers

2 g 3 a 4 h 5 d 6 b 7 f 8 e

4 **1.21** Read out the information in the **Get it right!** box.
* Read out the example in Exercise 4.
* Ask students to work in pairs to complete the exercise.
* Encourage **weaker students** to ask themselves a question about each of the sentences, e.g. *Who is busy preparing for the world championship? Who hadn't seen someone for ages?* This will make it easier for students to decide if they need to use a reflexive pronoun or *each other* in each of the gaps in the sentences.
* Check answers with the class.

Answers

1 himself   2 yourself; myself   3 yourselves; each other
4 each other; herself

Your turn

5
* Refer students to the four items in the list.
* Give students to think of the last time they did the things in the list.
* Monitor while students make their notes. Help as necessary.

6
* Read out the example sentence.
* Put students into pairs to discuss their ideas from Exercise 5.
* Ask some students to report back to the class on what their partner said.

Set Exercises 1, 2, 3, 4, 5 and 6 on page 18 of the **Workbook** for homework.

Listening and Vocabulary

Objectives

* listen to a news report about a community learning project.
* learn phrasal verbs for learning and socialising.
* practise using the phrasal verbs by talking about people I know.

A news report

Warm-up

* Books closed. Write *community* on the board.
* Elicit a definition of the word (it refers to people living in a specific area who have something in common, e.g. *the Swedish community in London*).
* Ask: *How can people help each other in the community?*
* Elicit ideas. Encourage students to think of how old people can help young people and vice versa.

1 💬 Ask students to open their books at page 22.
* Put students into pairs to look at the photo and answer the questions.
* Do not check answers at this point. Students will do that in Exercise 2 by listening to the recording.

2 🔊 **1.22** Tell students they are going to listen to a news report.
* Play the recording for students to check their answers to Exercise 1.

Audioscript

Turn to page 178 for audioscript.

> #### Suggested answers
> 1 An older person from the community and a student from a secondary school in Nottingham.
> 2 The student is teaching the older person how to use a computer.
> 3 The student is helping the older person. The older person is helping the student learn how to teach.

3 🔊 **1.22** Refer students to the article about the community project featured in the news report.
* Tell students that there are mistakes in the article. The first one can be seen in the example.
* Ask students to read the article. Then play the recording for students to find five mistakes in it.
* Check answers.

> #### Suggested answers
> A great new project started at a Nottingham **primary secondary** school at the beginning of ~~October~~ **September**. Once a ~~month~~ **week**, older people from the community come to the school to learn how to use the Internet and their mobile phones. ~~The same~~ **More and more** people come every time. So far they've all learned to share photos on their phones and set up a Facebook page. The students are great teachers, ~~but and sometimes~~ they're ~~a little impatient~~ always patient! '~~Sometimes their explanations are too difficult~~ **Their explanations are always simple**!' said one of the older participants. The teenagers are really enjoying the chance to help people in their community.

Your turn

4 * Read out the questions.
* Put students into pairs to ask and answer them.
* Ask some students to report their ideas to the class.
* To **extend** this activity, ask students for their views on the best way to teach someone about digital technology.

Phrasal verbs (learning and socialising)

5 🔊 **1.23** Focus on the words in bold. Explain that they are all phrasal verbs relating either to learning something or socialising.
* Match the first phrasal verb with its definition as an example.
* Ask students to work alone to complete the matching exercise.
* Play the recording for students to check their answers.
* Encourage students to make digital dictionaries of the phrasal verbs they learn. They could include the following information: a definition of the phrasal verb, an example sentence containing the phrasal verb, a translation of the phrasal verb into the students' language.

> #### Fast finishers
> Students can write gapped sentences using two or three of the phrasal verbs. Collect and check these, and then put the sentences on the board for the class to complete.

> #### Answers
> 1 h 2 g 3 d 4 f 5 c 6 b 7 e 8 a

Your turn

6 * Refer students to the information in the list.
* Help **weaker students** by telling them about *somebody* you look up to, get on well or can count on as well *something* that you have given up, set up, passed on or signed up for.
* Ask students to work alone to make notes on two people and two things from the list.

7 💬 Refer student to the example.
* Put students into pairs to discuss the ideas they made notes on in Exercise 6.
* Ask some students to tell the class about their partner.
* To **extend** the work on the vocabulary, you could ask students to turn to the **Vocabulary Bank** on page 108 and do the exercises for *Phrasal verbs (learning and socialising)*.

 Set Exercises 1, 2, 3 and 4 on page 19 of the Workbook for homework.
Students can also find out about community educational projects in their area. They can share what they find out with a partner in the next lesson and say which projects they would like to get involved in.

Language focus 2 Present perfect simple

Objectives

- revise the present perfect.
- learn the present perfect continuous.
- talk about something I have been learning to do recently.

Warm-up

- Books closed. Elicit the form of the present perfect: *has/have* + past participle.
- Elicit the fact that it is used to describe experiences in the past and actions that started in the past and continue to the present.

1
- Ask students to open their books at page 23.
- Tell students that the example sentences are from the listening on page 22.
- Put students into pairs to answer the questions.
- Check answers.
- For further information and additional exercises, students can turn to page 100 of the **Grammar reference** section.

> ### Answers
> **1** no **2** a series of actions **3** yes

2
- Elicit the full question for the first item as an example.
- Check answers.

> ### Answers
> **1** How many times have you logged on to the Internet today?
> **2** How many text messages have you sent on your phone since this morning?
> **3** How many birthday parties have you been to in the last month?
> **4** How many text messages have you received today?
> **5** How many English classes have you had this week?

3 💬 Put students into pairs and ask them to ask and answer the questions from Exercise 2.

Present perfect continuous

4
- Ask students to look at the table in Exercise 4.
- Tell them that the sentences are from the listening on page 22.
- Ask students to copy the sentences into their notebooks. Play the listening again for students to fill the gaps.
- Check answers.
- For further information and additional exercises, students can turn to page 100 of the **Grammar reference** section.

> ### Answers
>
> | + | You[1]**'ve been coming** to classes for three weeks. We[2]**'ve been meeting** once a week here in the school. |
> |---|---|
> | ? | **Have** you **been checking** your Facebook page every day? Yes, I **have**. No, I **haven't**. |
>
> The examples above, …
> **1** refer to a time period that **hasn't** finished.
> **2** talk about **a series of actions**.
> **3** **say** how long or how regularly an action has been happening.
> **4** refers to actions we **expect** to continue in the future.

5
- Put students into pairs to order the sentences.
- With **weaker students**, you could do this as a whole-class activity.

> ### Answers
> c – e – d – b – a
> There are six examples of the present perfect continuous.

Present perfect simple vs. present perfect continuous

6
- Ask students to write sentences in the present perfect simple or continuous based on the prompts.
- Check answers. Note the alternative answers for item 6.

> ### Answers
> **1** I've been studying English for five years.
> **2** I've had two mobile phones since I was 12.
> **3** She's been studying every evening for the exam next week.
> **4** He's had three different teachers this year.
> **5** We've taken four exams in the last month.
> **6** I've read a lot since September. (I have read an unspecified number of books and I am not reading any more now.) I've been reading a lot since September. (I have read an unspecified number of books and I am continuing to read.)

> ### Say it right!
>
> #### Stress and intonation in questions with *How long?*
>
> **1** 🔊 **1.24** Play the recording for students to listen to the questions and repeat them.
>
> **2** 🔊 **1.25** Play the recording for students to mark the main stresses in each of the questions.
>
> **3** 🔊 **1.25** Play the recording for students to check their answers to Exercise 2 and repeat the sentences.
>
> > ### Answers
> > **1** How **long** have you been **rea**ding that **book**?
> > **2** How **long** has she been **li**ving in this **street**?
> > **3** How **long** has he been **wor**king in that **shop**?
> > **4** How **long** has it been **rai**ning?
> > **5** How **long** have they been **lear**ning **French**?
>
> **4** Put students into pairs and ask them to practise saying the questions in Exercise 2 with the correct stress and intonation.

Your turn

7
- Give students a few minutes to write notes about something they have been learning to do recently.
- Put students into small groups to talk about the experience they made notes on.

> Set Exercises 1, 2, 3, 4, 5 and 6 on page 20 of the **Workbook** for homework.

Discover Culture

A very Indian wedding

Objectives

* watch a video about an Indian wedding.
* talk about a traditional ceremony in my country.

Warm-up

* Books closed. Write *bride* /braɪd/ and *groom* /gruːm/ on the board.
* Drill the pronunciation of the words and then ask students if they know what the words refer to (Answer: a *bride* is a woman on her wedding day; a *groom* is a man on his wedding day).

1 💬 Ask students to open their books at page 24.
* Refer students to the photos and the words in the box.
* Put students into pairs to describe a wedding they have been to and say whether it was similar to the weddings in the photos. If two students in a pair have not been to a wedding, they could describe weddings they have seen in films or TV dramas.

2 ▶ **2.2** Play the video for students to note down the people and things in the box in Exercise 1 appear.
* Check answers.

Videoscript

Narrator: In India, weddings are a family affair. Everyone takes part. They are also full of traditions and some traditions are thousands of years old. This is the bride – the future wife. The night before the wedding, the women in her family draw on her hands with henna, a natural dye. People say dark henna is a good sign. It means friendship between the bride and her husband's mother. The women have done a good job. The henna looks dark, and her future mother-in-law loves it! When they've finished the henna drawing, the bride's family and friends dance for her. It is the morning of the wedding and the workers are busy in the garden. They have been preparing for the big day since the early morning. More than fifty people have been working on the flowers! It is time for the future husband, the groom, to go to the wedding. He rides a white horse, another tradition. The bride is ready and waiting for her groom to come.
Bride: Wherever I go, I'll always be an Indian bride.
Narrator: And the wedding begins. It is a tradition to tie the bride and groom's hands together with a red ribbon. The bride gives the groom a handful of rice as a sign of her love. The third tradition involves walking around the fire to show that they will walk together today and for the rest of their lives. Finally, the groom gently colours the bride's hair with red paste. They believe that the colour red will bring them good luck. They are now husband and wife.

Answers

the clothes, the music, the couple, the decorations, the ceremony, the guests, the other members of the family

3 ▶ **2.2** Ask students to work alone to decide whether the six sentences are true or false.
* Students can compare answers in pairs before you play the video again for students to check their answers.

Fast finishers

Fast finishers may try to correct the false sentences.

Answers

1 F   2 T   3 F   4 F   5 T   6 F

4 💬 Put students into pairs to answer the five questions.
* This exercise is a test of students' memory and some will do better at it than others. Help guide those students who struggle with this to the correct answers.

5 ▶ **2.2** Play the recording again for students to check their answers to Exercise 4.

Suggested answers

1 It's a good sign. It means friendship between the bride and her husband's mother.
2 They set up the decorations, e.g. the flowers.
3 The groom arrives on a white horse.
4 It's a sign of her love.
5 To show that they will walk together today and for the rest of their lives.

Your turn

6 • Put students into pairs and ask them to think of a traditional ceremony in their country to describe. They can look online for information about it using their smartphones.
* Ask students to answer the three questions.
* Ask some students to report back to the class on the ceremony they choose to describe. Encourage other members of the class to add to the description that is given.

 Ask students to do this listening exercise on celebrations and complete the accompanying exercises:
http://learnenglishteens.britishcouncil.org/skills/listening-skills-practice/celebrations

Reading A blog post

Objectives
* read a blog post about a traditional Chinese wedding.
* learn words in context.
* talk about celebrations.

Warm up
* Books closed. Put students into small groups and give them one minute to note down as many words as they can connected to weddings.
* Make this competitive by telling students that the group to come up with the most correct words wins.

Suggested answers
bride, groom, guests, ceremony, ring, decorations, gifts, family, get married, marriage

1 Ask students to open their books at page 25.
* Refer students to the photos of a traditional Chinese wedding.
* Put students into pairs and ask them to describe what they think is happening in each of the photos.

2 🔊 **1.26** Ask students to read the blog post and then ask them to say which of the photos best fits the story in the blog and who it is that is telling the story. to check their answers from Exercise 1.

Suggested answers
The top photo best fits the story. (The text is about a cross-culture wedding. The bride in the bottom photo seems to be Chinese, so the best photo must be the top one.)
The bride's sister is telling the story.

3 • Refer students to the information numbered 1–6.
* Ask students to read the blog post again and then put them in pairs to note down which paragraphs the information can be found in.
* Check answers.
* Read out the information in the **FACT!** box. Then ask the class for a list of reasons why people get married, e.g. love, financial stability, pressure from family, expectation of society.

Answers
2 Paragraph 4   **3** Paragraph 3   **4** Paragraph 5
5 Paragraph 3   **6** Paragraph 4

plore words in context

4 • Ask students why learning vocabulary in context is useful. Elicit the idea that words in a language exist and take on meaning by their relation to one another. Seeing a word in a particular context not only allows us to make some sense of its meanings but also, if the context is memorable enough, remember it.
* Put students into pairs to match the highlighted words in the text with definitions 1–5.
* You may want to help **weaker students** with this exercise by completing the first one as an example to give them a better idea of what is to be done.
* Check answers.

Answers
1 a bonus   **2** gifts   **3** take a break   **4** sunrise   **5** in turn

Optional activity
* You could test students on their understanding of the vocabulary from Exercise 4 by asking them to write sentences using those words and phrases.
* Put students into pairs to write their sentences.
* Monitor while students do this task. Help as necessary.
* Ask some students to read their sentences out to the class. To make this more interesting, students can omit the word or phrase from Exercise 4 that they have used, e.g. A student would read *I love getting ... on my birthday*. The rest of the class then guesses what the missing word or phrase is.

Your turn

5 • Check students' understanding of the word *formal* in the context of a party or celebration. This refers to an official occasion, one characterised by a specific dress code and etiquette.
* Give students time to read through and think about the questions.
* Ask students to work alone to make notes in response to the questions. Monitor and help as necessary.

6 • Put students into pairs and ask them to ask and answer the questions in Exercise 5. Students should also ask and answer the two questions in Exercise 6.
* Ask some students to report back to the class on what their partner said.

> For homework, you could ask students to write a description of their perfect wedding. Their descriptions should include the following information: where the wedding would take place, how many guests would be invited, the clothes that people would wear, the food that would be served, the music that guests would dance to, how long it would last. Make sure that students understand that they should use *would* in their descriptions rather than *will* as they are describing a hypothetical situation, e.g. *My wedding would take place on a Saturday morning in July.* Collect and check students' descriptions in the next lesson.

Speaking Showing concern

Objectives

- watch teenagers taking about helping friends through difficult situations.
- listen to someone showing concern for a friend.
- practise showing concern.

Warm-up

- Books closed. Introduce the idea of *concern* /kən'sɜːn/. Drill the pronunciation.
- On the board, write: *My friend has lost his job. I'm really concerned about him.*

Real talk: How have you helped a friend through a difficult situation?

1. ▶ **2.3** Ask students to open their books at page 26.

   - Explain that they are going to watch some teenagers answering the question: *How have you helped a friend through a difficult situation?*
   - Tell students that they are going to match the words and phrases in the box with each of the teenagers in the video.
   - Play the video.
   - Students work alone to complete the exercise.
   - Check answers.

Videoscript

Narrator: How have you helped a friend through a difficult situation?

Speaker 1: Well, a friend of mine didn't make the basketball team this past season. The coach just didn't like him, I guess. But I think he's a terrific player, and I've told him that a lot. That seems to help a little.

Speaker 2: I've helped my best friend, Kate, through a lot of things, but most recently when her cat died. That was horrible. The cat was 16 years old, so it wasn't a surprise, but Kate was really sad about it.

Speaker 3: I can't say I've helped anyone through a difficult situation. I've helped friends get into them, though!

Speaker 4: I'm a good listener, so my friends always come to me with their problems. I've helped a lot of people through difficult situations – sometimes just talking helps.

Speaker 5: My friend's dad lost his job recently. That was hard because it was a surprise for the whole family. My friend wants to be strong for his dad, but he's also really worried. I've talked to him a lot on the phone and that helps. But sometimes he just wants to sit and watch a football game and I understand.

Speaker 6: Well, my friend Jenny has had a very hard year. She hasn't done well in two of her main subjects and exams are coming up soon. She's worked really hard but there's so much to learn. I've made some study notes for her so she doesn't have to read everything. I hope that makes it a little easier.

Narrator: How have *you* helped a friend through a difficult situation?

Answers

1 said nice things   2 doesn't say   3 has never had to help
4 listened   5 talked   6 made notes

---

2. Put students into pairs to ask and answer the question. Tell students they are free to give as much or as little information as they like regarding a friend's difficult situation.
   - Ask some students to report back to the class on their partner.

3. 🔊 **1.27** Tell students they are going to listen to Joe talking to his friend about a problem.
   - Read out the question.
   - Play the recording.
   - Students listen and answer the question.
   - Check answer.

Answer

He's had another argument with his brother.

---

4. - Refer students to the phrases in the *Useful language* box.
   - Check students' understanding of the language, particularly the adjective *poor*, which, in this context means that someone is deserving of sympathy.
   - Students work alone to complete the conversation using the phrases.

5. 🔊 **1.27** Play the recording again for students to check their answers.

Answers

2 poor   3 calm down   4 to worry   5 what you mean
6 will be fine   7 I make you feel better

---

6. 💬 Ask students to work in pairs to act out the conversation in Exercise 4.
   - Students can act out the conversation twice, taking a different part each time.

7. 💬 Put students into pairs to take it in turns to say and respond to sentences 1–6.

8. 💬 Give students time to read each of the situations.
   - Put students into pairs and give them some time to plan what they want to say.
   - Students act out their conversations using the two situations.
   - Monitor while students are practising their conversations. Check that they are using the phrases from the *Useful language* box.

➡ For homework, students can use their smartphones to record some friends answering the question: *How have you helped a friend through a difficult situation?* Students can play their video to a partner in the next lesson.

Writing **A personal email**

Objectives

- read a personal email.
- learn about the use of *feel* and *find* to describe feelings.
- write an email to a friend explaining a problem.

Warm-up

- Books closed. Brainstorming different ways of communicating with friends and family members using technology, e.g. text messages, tweets, Facebook posts, phone calls, Skype calls, message boards.
- Ask students if they think that one means of communication is more suited to a particular type of message than another, e.g. *Are emails better for longer messages? Is Facebook the best for news?*

1
- Ask students to open their books at page 27.
- Refer students to the photo and then ask them to read the email and answer the question.
- Check answer.

> ### Answer
> about her new school

2
- Refer students to the five questions.
- Ask students to read the email again.
- Put students into pairs to answer the questions.
- Check answers.

> ### Suggested answers
> **1** She found some subjects confusing because the work at her new school is harder.
> **2** She felt really lost.
> **3** Her grandfather advised her to talk to her teachers. They've been helping her a lot.
> **4** She is shy and so she found it difficult to make friends.
> **5** Her grandfather advised her to smile and ask questions. She's made some friends since then.

> ### Optional activity
> - Put students into small groups.
> - Ask students to think of advice to offer someone who is struggling to settle in at a new school.
> - Ask one student from each group to report back to the class.

3
- Read out the information about *feel* and *find* in the *Useful language* box.
- Ask students to work alone to find two further examples of feel and find in the email in Exercise 1.
- Check answers.

> ### Answers
> I **found** it difficult to join in.
> I**'m feeling** really happy now!

> ### Language note
> *Feel* is used to refer directly to an emotional state, e.g. *I feel tired*. *Find* is used to express the fact that we have discovered through experience that something is the case, e.g. *I find doing homework tiring*. *Find* is used with the gerund, which means that we say *I find meeting people fun* rather than ~~I find meet people fun.~~

4
- Read out the example.
- Ask students to work alone to write sentences with *find* or *feel* using the prompts in 1–6. Monitor and help as necessary.
- Students can compare their sentences with a partner.
- Ask some students to report back to the class on what their partner wrote.

 ## Get Writing

PLAN

5
- Students should do their planning in class. The writing can either be done in class or at home.
- Tell students they are going to write an email to a friend explaining a problem.
- Refer students to the two ideas that they can use in their writing. Point out that the adjective *silly* means *trivial* in this context, e.g. *It would be silly to argue with a friend over who has the most interesting website*.
- Tell students that they can use their own ideas if they prefer. If students seem keen to do this, you may want to brainstorm some ideas of things that friends have arguments about and put these ideas on the board.
- Refer students back to the questions in Exercise 2 and then ask them to work alone to make notes.

WRITE

6
- Tell students to use the example email as a model to follow.
- Give students ten minutes to complete the writing task. Students should write between 140 and 160 words.
- Monitor while students are writing. Help with grammar and vocabulary as necessary.

> ### Optional activity
> - Create a class problems blog using https://wordpress.com/.
> - Students could post messages about problems on the blog you create. Advice could then be offered in the form of comments, and an online discussion could take place.

CHECK

7
- Tell students that it is very important that they check their writing in order to look for ways to improve its content, style and structure.
- Give students a few minutes to look through their emails and check them against the points here.
- Collect students' emails and mark them.

> Set Exercises 1, 2, 3, 4 and 5 on page 22 and Exercises 6, 7, 8, 9, 10 and 11 on page 23 of the **Workbook** for homework.

Unit aims

I can ...

* talk about careers and training.
* understand a personal profile and a newspaper article about special young people.
* talk about future plans and make predictions about the future.
* understand a discussion on a radio news programme.
* use phrases to discuss options and make decisions.
* write an opinion essay.

Unit contents

Vocabulary	Training and qualifications
	Expressions with *take*
	Achievements
	Words in context
Reading	A profile
	❶ Insectmobile
	A newspaper article
Language focus	*be going to* and present tenses for the future
	Predictions with *be going to, will* and *may/might*
	Future continuous
Listening	A discussion
Discover culture	❶ The young and the brave
Speaking	Making decisions
	❶ Real talk: Are you saving up for something special? What?
Pronunciation	Contracted forms in the future continuous
Writing	An opinion essay Linking phrases
CLIL	Natural Science: The Archimedes' Principle
	❶ A cool experiment

Background

James Rodríguez (born in 1991) is a Colombian football player who moved to Real Madrid in 2014 after an impressive display for his national team at the World Cup in Brazil. He had previously spent three seasons at Porto and one at Monaco. He plays as an attacking midfielder.

Be curious

* Books closed. Write the following verb on the board: *achieve* /ə'tʃiːv/. Drill its pronunciation and check that students understand that it means *to succeed in doing something through hard work, effort and skill,* e.g. *James Rodriguez has already achieved a lot in football.*
* Elicit or introduce the associated nouns: *achievement* /ə'tʃiːvm(ə)nt/ and *achiever* /ə'tʃiːvə/. Drill the pronunciation of these words.
* Ask students to open their books at page 30.
* Ask student to describe the photo and then give them a couple of minutes to answer the three questions.
* Students can then compare answers in pairs.
* Ask some students to tell the class about what their partner said in response to the three questions.
* Tell students that the themes of Unit 3 are people achieving things at a young age.

Suggested answers

* I can see a footballer. It looks like he is with his team mates at an important moment in a match.
* I think he is feeling nervous and excited. He looks as though he is concentrating very hard.
* He looks quite young – maybe in his mid-twenties.
* In my country there is a famous gymnast who started to win international competitions when she was a teenager.

CEFR

SKILL AREA	GOAL	EXERCISE
Listening	OVERALL LISTENING COMPREHENSION	4 p31
	UNDERSTANDING INTERACTION	1–6 p38
	LISTENING TO MEDIA AND RECORDINGS	1–5 p34 1–6 p36
Reading	READING FOR INFORMATION & ARGUMENT	1–6 p32 3 p34 1–4 p37
Speaking	INFORMAL DISCUSSION (WITH FRIENDS)	6 p32 6 p34 6–7 p35 5–6 p37 1–8 p38
	INFORMATION EXCHANGE	5–6 p31 6–7 p33
Writing	COHERENCE	2–4 p39
	REPORTS AND ESSAYS	5–7 p39
Communicative language competence	VOCABULARY RANGE	1–9 p31 4–5 p32 4–5 p34 4 p37
	GRAMMATICAL ACCURACY	1–5 p33 1–5 p35
	PHONOLOGICAL CONTROL	2 p31 5 p35 6 p38
Communication strategies	IDENTIFYING CUES AND INFERRING	4 p37
	TAKING THE FLOOR (TURNTAKING), COOPERATING, ASKING FOR CLARIFICATION, COMPENSATING, MONITORING & REPAIR	4 p38

Vocabulary Training and qualifications

Objectives
- learn vocabulary for training and qualifications.
- listen to people talking about plans for when they leave school.
- talk about what I would like to do after I leave school.

Warm-up
- Books closed. Write *training* /ˈtreɪnɪŋ/ and *qualifications* /ˌkwɒlɪfɪˈkeɪʃ(ə)ns/ on the board. Drill the pronunciation. Check students understand the meaning of the words.

Language note
Training refers to acquiring skills needed for a job. A *qualification* refers to the passing of an official exam which means you can practise in a particular field.

1 Ask students to open their books at page 31.
- Refer students to the photos.
- Put students into pairs to decide how each of the photos relates to the themes of training and qualifications. You may ask **stronger students** to describe the photos.
- Check answers.

Suggested answers
They show different ways of learning and teaching, e.g. learning by doing or listening to the teacher, learning in a big class or on your own.

2 🔊 **1.29** Read out the examples.
- Put students into pairs to match more words from the two boxes to make common phrases.
- Play the recording for students to check their answers.

Answers
1 university degree, university course, university fees, university exam
2 work experience
3 application form
4 part-time course
5 entrance fees, entrance exam
6 training course
7 career path

Game
- Play *Hangman* using the vocabulary for training and qualifications.
- See **Games bank** on pages 28–29.

3
- Ask students to work alone to match the expressions from Exercise 2 with the items a–c.
- Students may disagree on the answers, so ask students to give reasons for their choices. Encourage **stronger students** to offer greater detail when you ask them for answers.

Suggested answers
a university degree, university exam, university course, university fees, entrance exam
b work experience, training course
c application form, part-time course, entrance fees, career path

Optional activity
- Put students into pairs to define the phrases from Exercise 2 by texting each other definitions and answers using a free service such as *WhatsApp*.

4 🔊 **1.29** Read out the information in the **Get it right!** box. Point out that we refer to a job but that we cannot say *a work*. Using *a* with *work* is a common error that English language learners make.
- Tell students they are going to listen to two people talking about their plans for when they leave school.
- Read out the two questions.
- Play the recording for students to listen and answer the questions. Encourage **stronger students** to note down as much as they can about what each speaker says.
- Check answers.

Audioscript
Teenage girl: I want to be a vet, which means I have to go to university and study for a degree in veterinary sciences. I need to sit an entrance exam first. It's really difficult! This summer I'm going to get some work experience with my aunt. She works at the local zoo. It's really interesting work.

Teenage boy: I don't want to go to university. I want to do a training course and start working as soon as possible! I'd like to work with my hands. Maybe I could do a part-time course in car mechanics or something similar. The course is quite expensive, but my uncle's offered me a part-time job in his café, so I could work during the day to make some money to pay the fees and study in the evenings.

Answers
Speaker 1
1 vet   2 university, degree, entrance exam, work experience
Speaker 2
1 car mechanic or something similar
2 university, training course, part-time course, fees

Your turn

5
- Read out the information. Check students understand what they have to do.
- Give students time to make notes on two people they know.

6
- Put students into pairs to discuss the people they made notes on in Exercise 5.
- To **extend** the work on the vocabulary, you could ask students to turn to the **Vocabulary bank** on page 109 and do the exercises for *Training and qualifications*.

 Set Exercises 1, 2, 3 and 4 on page 27 of the **Workbook** for homework.
You may ask students to research training courses or degrees in the UK or US that they might be interested in doing in the future. Students can compare their ideas with a partner in the next lesson.

Reading A profile

Objectives

- read an article about a teenager who has built her own sports car.
- learn expressions with *take*.
- talk about my ideal career.

Background

Chevrolet, known, informally, as *Chevy*, is one of the most well-known US brands of automobile.

Warm-up

- Books closed. Ask students how we become good at something. Elicit ideas, e.g. *by working hard*.
- Put students into pairs and ask them to talk about what they think they are best at or what they would most like to become very good at doing, e.g. *I'd love to be able to paint really well*.

1
- Ask students to open their books at page 32.
- Put students into pairs to look at the photo and say what the girl in the picture is doing and how she might be different from other teens.
- Check ideas with the class. Do not confirm or reject any ideas that students come up with at this stage.

2 🔊 **1.30** Ask students to read the text about Claudette to check their answers to Exercise 1.
- Refer students to the information in the **FACT!** box. Draw students attention to the pronunciation of *Arkansas* /ˈɑːkənsɔː/ and *Iowa* /ˈʌɪəwə/. Ask students at what age people can learn to drive in their country. Then find out if the consensus in the class is that the age should be raised or lowered, or if it is fine as it is.

Answers

She's restoring a car.
She's getting a sports car for her next birthday, but she's building it herself.

3
- Refer students to sentences 1–6. Drill the pronunciation of *engineering* /ɛndʒɪˈnɪərɪŋ/.
- Help **weaker students** by doing the first one as an example.
- Students can work alone to complete the true/false exercise. Make sure students correct the false sentences.
- Check answers.

Answers

1 F (She decided to restore a car when she was 12.)
2 F (She used the money she made working as a dog walker.)
3 F (She's going to drive it to school.) **4** T **5** T **6** T

Optional activity

- Put students into pairs and ask them to take a look at the Chevrolet website and choose their favourite car: http://www.chevrolet.co.uk/.
- Ask some students to tell the class which model they choose and why.

Explore expressions with *take*

4
- Books closed. Write the following sentences on the board and ask students to explain the different meaning of the phrasal verb in each case: *I took off my jumper* and *The plane took off on time*. Elicit the two meanings of *take off*: *remove clothes* and *begin flight*.
- Put students into pairs to match the expressions in the box with the synonyms 1–5.
- Check answers.

Answers

1 take exams 2 take place 3 take up 4 take advice
5 take time

5
- Read out the example sentence.
- Put students into pairs and ask them to complete the remaining sentences with the expressions with *take* from Exercise 4 in the correct form.
- Check answers.
- To **extend** the work on the vocabulary, you could ask students to turn to the **Vocabulary bank** on page 109 and do the exercises for *Explore expressions with take*.

Answers

2 take time 3 take up 4 takes place 5 take exams

Your turn

6
- Read out the example sentence.
- Give students time to think about Claudette's career choice and what their own ideal job would be. Doing this will help **weaker students** who might otherwise struggle at being asked to give spontaneous responses.
- Put students into pairs to ask and answer the questions.
- Ask some students to report back to the class on what their partner said.

You can show this video as either a lead-in or a follow-up to the Language Focus 1 lesson.

- ▶ Ask: *How many insects can you name in English?*
- Elicit student's answers. You might expect them to come up with the following: *bees, flies, ants*.
- Refer students to the questions and then play the video.
- Students watch it and say what they learnt about the insectmobile.
- Ask students if they think a vehicle like the one shown in the video could ever be made to work.
- See page 124 for further activities you can do with this video.

 Set Exercises 1, 2, 3, 4 and 5 on page 31 and Exercise 5 on page 28 of the Workbook for homework.

Language focus 1
be going to and present tenses for the future

Objectives

- learn *be going to* and the present tenses for the future.
- talk about my future plans.

Warm-up

- Books closed. Write the following on the board.
  I'm meeting …
  I'm going to meet …
  I'll meet …
- Ask students to complete the sentences with their own ideas. Students can then compare their sentences in pairs. Monitor while students do this.

1
- Ask students to open their books at page 33.
- Tell students that the gapped sentences are from the text on page 32.
- Ask students to copy the sentences into their notebooks and complete them.
- Check answers.
- Ask students to say which tenses are used to talk about future plans and intentions, arrangements at a specific time in the future and scheduled future events in their language.
- For further information and additional exercises, students can turn to page 101 of the **Grammar reference** section.

> ### Answers
> - I**'m going to start** driving lessons as soon as I can.
> - She[1]**'s going to drive** that dream car to school.
> - I**'m starting** my holidays next week.
> - She[2]**'s getting** a sports car for her next birthday.
> - The degree course **lasts** for three years.
> - My course [3]**starts** next week.
> - We use [4]***be going to*** for future plans and intentions.
> - We use [5]**present continuous** for arrangements at a specific time in the future.
> - We use [6]**present simple** for scheduled future events.

2
- Read out the example.
- Put students into pairs and ask them to complete the matching exercise.
- Check answers.

> ### Answers
> 2 e   3 b   4 f   5 a   6 c

Optional activity

- Ask students to write down five plans or intentions, e.g. *I'm meeting my sister at the cinema after school.* Two of the plans should be false.
- Put students into pairs to read their sentences out. Students then try to guess which of the sentences are true and which false.

3
- Ask students to read through the text once to get a general idea of its content. You could ask students a couple of questions to check students' comprehension, e.g. *What has Aaron Lucas always dreamed of being?* (A train driver) *Why is today an important day for him?* (It's his first day at work).
- Put students into pairs and ask them to choose the correct form of the verbs in the text.
- While checking answers with the class, ask students to give a reason for the choices they made, e.g. in item 1 *leaves* is correct because the present simple is used for train schedules.

> ### Answers
> 1 leaves   2 arrives   3 's going to drive   4 isn't travelling
> 5 are taking   6 's going to work

4
- Refer students to the words and phrases in the box.
- Complete the first sentence with the class as an example. Tell students that *hooray* /hʊˈreɪ/ is another word for *hurrah* /hʊˈrɑː/, words used as exclamatory expressions of approval or joy.
- Put students into pairs to complete the exercise.
- Check answers.

> ### Answers
> 1 start   2 finishes   3 'm not going to study
> 4 'm seeing   5 'm not meeting   6 'm going to learn

5
- Read out the completed sentences in Exercise 4 in turn and ask students to say which of them concern plans for the future.
- Students then note down which of the plans are true for them and change the ones that aren't.

Game

- Play *Expanding sentences* to practise *be going to* and the present tenses for the future.
- See **Games bank** on pages 28–29.

Your turn

6 Ask students to make some notes on five plans they have for the coming week.

7 Put students into pairs to tell one another about their plans.

> Set Exercises 1, 2, 3 and 4 on page 28 of the **Workbook** for homework.

Listening and Vocabulary

Objectives
- listen to a discussion about a fashion item.
- learn vocabulary to describe achievements.
- rank different achievements in order of importance.

A discussion

Warm-up
- Books closed. Write the following on the board: *The iPhone is a must-have object*. Check students understand that this word refers to something considered highly desirable or essential to possess.
- Elicit ideas from the class about why some items become seen as 'must-have' and which items, e.g. clothes or devices, currently fit into that category.

1 💬 Ask students to open their books at page 34.
- Put students into pairs to look at the photo and answer the three questions.
- Do not check answers at this point. Students will do that in Exercise 2 by listening to the recording.

2 🔊 **1.31** Tell students they are going to listen to a discussion about the flip-flops shown in the photo.
- Play the recording for students to check their answers to Exercise 1.

Audioscript
Turn to page 178 for the audioscript.

> **Suggested answers**
> 1 a collections of flip-flops
> 2 She's a millionaire because she set up a flip-flop business.
> 3 They're FishFlops®, i.e. flip-flops with fish on them.

3 🔊 **1.31** Refer students to the profile of Madison. Point out the mistake in it.
- Play the recording again for students to listen and identify five further mistakes.
- Check answers.
- You could then ask students whether they would be interested in buying a pair of Madison's FishFlops®.

> **Answers**
> FishFlops® are an amazing new fashion. Teenager Maddie Robinson had the idea for FishFlops® at the age of ~~13~~ 8 and started her business ~~immediately~~ **when she was 13**. She developed the whole project herself and sold ~~70,000~~ 60,000 pairs in her first year. The FishFlops® sold for ~~£25~~ $25 a pair. This is how she became a millionaire. But she's not greedy, she also helps charities. For example, she gave away ~~15,000~~ **10,000** pairs of FishFlops® to people in need. She also does other voluntary work to support the community. Sometimes, she ~~signs them~~ **gets celebrities to sign them** and donates them as well.

Achievements

4 **1.32** Tell students that is a good idea to learn expressions related to a particular theme as it broadens the range of things that they can say about a subject. Explain to students that they are going to look at some expressions to describe achievements, all of which are taken from the recording.
- Read out the first sentence and ask students to say whether the expression in bold is related to money, fame, work or helping others. Help **weaker students** by explaining that there are two expressions in each category.
- Drill the pronunciation of *voluntary* /ˈvɒlənt(ə)ri/.
- Put students into pairs to complete the exercise.
- Play the recording for students to check their answers

> **Answers**
> a) money: made a fortune, become a millionaire
> b) fame: winning awards, break records
> c) work: started a business, developed the project
> d) helping others: does voluntary work, support the community

5
- Read out the example sentence.
- Ask students to work alone to complete the remaining sentences with the correct form of the expressions in Exercise 4.
- Students can compare their answers in pairs before you check answers with the class as a whole.

> **Answers**
> 2 support the community   3 start a business
> 4 made a fortune   5 won an award
> 6 develop the project

Your turn

6
- Give students time to order the achievements in Exercise 4 in terms of their importance. Point out that there is no right answer, but that you are giving students an opportunity to express their own opinion. Tell them to consider *make a fortune* and *become a millionaire* as one achievement.
- Put students into pairs to compare their ideas.
- To **extend** the work on the vocabulary, you could ask students to turn to the **Vocabulary bank** on page 109 and do the exercises for *Achievements*.

> 🔁 Set Exercises 1, 2, 3 and 4 on page 29 of the **Workbook** for homework.
> You could also ask students to find out about young entrepreneurs from their country. Students should make notes on what these people have done and what their plans are. Students can share what they find out with a partner in the next lesson.

Language focus 2
Predictions with *be going to, will* and *may/might*

Objectives

- learn to use *be going to, will* and *may/might* for predictions.
- learn the future continuous.
- make predictions.

Warm-up

- Books closed. Check students' understanding of *predict* (*to say that something will happen*) and *prediction* (*a thing predicted*).

1
- Ask students to open their books at page 35.
- Tell students that the example sentences are from the listening on page 34.
- Ask students to copy the sentences into their notebooks.
- Put students into pairs to complete the sentences and rules.
- For further information and additional exercises, students can turn to page 101 of the **Grammar reference** section.

> #### Answers
> 1 It's on the front page of all the local papers, it**'s going to be** today's top story.
> 2 She **might become** the richest teenager in the States, I don't know.
> 3 Yes, she should, I'm sure she**'ll win**!
> 4 Meanwhile, her FishFlops® **will be** the latest fashion.
> 1 c 2 b 3 a

2
- Ask students to use the verbs in the box to write sentences about what is going to happen.

> #### Suggested answers
> 1 … fall over. 2 They're going to slip.
> 3 It's going to rain. 4 He's going to score.

3
- Put students into pairs to choose the correct form of the verbs.

> #### Answers
> 1 'll make 2 's going to win; might win
> 3 's going to faint 4 's going to be; may change 5 will

Future continuous

4
- Tell students the example sentences are from the listening on page 34.
- Ask students to copy the sentences into their notebooks.
- Play the recording for them to complete the sentences.
- For further information and additional exercises, students can turn to page 101 of the **Grammar reference** section.

> #### Answers
>
> | + | Everybody [1]**will be wearing** them on the beach this summer. She[2]**'ll be winning** awards for her business idea. |
> |---|---|
> | – | He **won't be doing** much voluntary work this year, he's too busy. |
> | ? | So, **will** you **be buying** a pair of FishFlops®, Glenda? Yes, I **will**. No, I **won't**. |
>
> 1 We use the future continuous to **make predictions about the future**.
> 2 We **don't use** the future continuous with state verbs.

5 🔊 **1.33** Complete the first sentence as an example, then ask students to work in pairs to complete the remaining sentences by ordering the underlined words in each case.
- Play the recording for students to check their answers.

> #### Answers
> 1 we will be doing 2 we will be speaking
> 3 we won't be alone 4 we won't be learning
> 5 everybody will know it 6 we won't have
> 7 we will be driving 8 we will be living longer
> 9 doctors will be discovering 10 life won't be better

Say it right!

Contracted forms in the future continuous

1 🔊 **1.34** Ask students to open their books at page 96.
- Play the recording for students to listen to and repeat the sentences.

2 🔊 **1.35** Play the recording for students to identify the contracted forms in the sentences.
- Students compare their answers in pairs.

3 🔊 **1.35** Play the recording for students to check their answers to Exercise 2 and repeat the sentences.

> #### Answers
> 1 I**'ll** still be studying in 10 years' time.
> 2 She**'ll** be making a lot of money by the time she's 21.
> 3 There**'ll** be people living on the moon in 100 years' time.
> 4 Very soon, we**'ll** be talking to our computers and we **won't** be using keyboards.
> 5 He **won't** be doing voluntary work because he **won't** have time.
> 6 You **won't** be learning English anymore, you**'ll** be learning Chinese.

4 Put students into pairs and ask them to practise saying the sentences in Exercise 2.

Your turn

6
- Refer students to the predictions in Exercise 5.
- Put students into pairs to say whether the predictions are positive or negative and which they agree with.

7
- Refer students to the example sentence.
- Put students into pairs to compare their ideas.

> ➡ Set Exercises 1, 2, 3, 4, 5 and 6 on page 30 of the Workbook for homework.

Discover Culture

The young and the brave

Objectives
- watch a video about a festival in Mongolia.
- talk about people I know who have competed in races.

Background
The word **Naadam** is Mongolian for *game*. The two-day Naadam festival is very important in Mongolia and features three main events: wrestling, horse racing and archery.

Warm-up
- Books closed. Ask students if they have ever been horse riding or if horses are common animals in their countries.

1 💬 Ask students to open their books at page 36 and look at the photos.
- If you have the *Presentation Plus* software, put the photos up on the interactive whiteboard.
- Put students into pairs to ask and answer the questions.
- Do not check answers. Students will find out about the horse race pictured at the bottom of the page by watching the video.
- You could tell students that the top photo was taken in Britain.

2 ▶ **3.2** Refer students to the descriptions of images seen in the video.
- Tell student they are going to watch the video without sound and order these descriptions.
- Play the video without sound.
- Students can compare their answers in pairs before you check answers with the class as a whole.

Videoscript
China is an enormous country, with many different regions and many different cultures. Inner Mongolia, in the north of China, is an expansive region, with thousands of kilometres of grasslands and high mountains. These lands have inspired a number of traditions over the years like the Naadam Festival. There are all kinds of games at this festival; games of great skill and courage and horse races! The Mongols are famous for their abilities on horseback. The games they play today are the same games they played eight centuries ago. These children learn how to ride when they're just three years old! Today, they're taking part in a special race with their horses. They're young – from 5 to15 years old – and incredibly determined. They've been training for months for this race. More riders are arriving now. The race is about to start. And they're off! In other parts of the world, horse races are usually short; less than two kilometres. But these children will race for 30 kilometres and they'll ride the horses without saddles. They'll need incredible strength and balance to stay on their horses. When their horses get tired, the children sing to them. Who is the winner of this year's race going to be? We don't know yet, but it is the children's strength and courage that make them all winners.

Answers
e – c – a – b – d

3 ▶ **3.2** Refer students to sentence 1–6.
- Play the video again for students to decide whether the phrases refer to conventional horse races or the Naadam festival horse race.
- Point out, if necessary, that *conventional* means *ordinary* in this context.
- Students can compare their answers in pairs before you check answers with the class as a whole.

Answers
Conventional horse races: 1, 3 and 5
Naadam festival horse race: 2, 4 and 6

4 ▶ **3.2** Read out the three words in the box. Drill the pronunciation: *courage* /ˈkʌrɪdʒ/, *balance* /ˈbal(ə)ns/ and *strength* /strɛŋθ/.
- Ask students to work alone to complete the text with the three words, one of which is used twice.
- Check answers.

Answers
1 strength   2 balance   3 strength   4 courage

Your turn

5
- Put students into pairs to ask and answer the questions.
- Ask some students to report back to the class.
- To **extend** this task, ask students to find out more about the Naadam festival by doing some research online using their smartphones.

6
- Tell students briefly about a race that you have competed in. It doesn't matter if the only time you have done this was in the 100 metres one day at school. Tell students how you did in the race.
- Put students into pairs and ask them to answer the questions.
- Ask some students to report back to the class on what their partner had to say about races, skills and qualities.

 For homework, ask students to find out more about the culture of Mongolia by doing some research online. Students can share what they find out with a partner at the beginning of the next lesson.

Reading A newspaper article

Objectives
- read a newspaper article about Australians who have done special things.
- learn words in context.
- talk about people in my country who have achieved a lot.

Background
Australia Day is celebrated on January 26th. It commemorates the founding in 1788 of the colony of New South Wales.
The **Aborgines** are the original inhabitants of Australia whose culture was undermined by the arrival of European colonisers.

Warm up
- Books closed. Write *prizes* and *awards* on the board. Drill the pronunciation of the words: *prizes* /ˈprʌɪzɪz/ and *awards* /əˈwɔːdz/.
- Check students understand that a prize or an award is something given as a reward to someone who has won a competition or in recognition of a particular achievement, e.g. A Nobel prize is the most prestigious award in science and literature.
- Ask students if they have ever won a prize. If any students have, ask them to tell the class something about it, e.g. what they won it for or what the prize itself was.

1 Ask students to open their books at page 37.
- Put students in pairs to look at the photos and answer the questions.
- Elicit answers, but do not confirm or reject them at this stage. Students will check their answers in Exercise 2.

2 🔊 **1.36** Before students read the article check their understanding of *rural* /ˈrʊər(ə)l/, which means *relating to the countryside not towns*.
- Ask students to read the article to check their answers to Exercise 1.

Suggested answers
1 They have won the Young Australian of the Year Award.
2 Akram Azimi has worked with Aboriginal communities in Western Australia. Ian Thorpe has won medals at the Sydney Olympics. Trisha Broadbridge survived the 2004 tsunami and has set up a charity which helped to build the Broadbridge Education Centre on Thailand's Phi Phi island.
3 Ian Thorpe is a famous swimmer.

3
- Refer students to questions 1–6.
- Ask students to read the magazine article. Then put them into pairs to answer the questions.
- Read out the information in the **FACT!** box. Check students' understanding of *cerebral palsy* /ˈsɛrɪbr(ə)l ˈpɔːlzi/. This condition is a form of paralysis.

Answers
1 Because there are a lot of recommendations.
2 32
3 Because he arrived in Australia as a refugee from Afghanistan when he was 13, so English is not his first language.
4 He became the youngest male ever to represent Australia.
5 Trisha Broadbridge
6 Because it's on the eve of Australia Day.

Explore words in context

4
- Remind students of the importance of learning words by working out their meaning from their context. Learning words in this way encourages students to see how words acquire their meaning from other words.
- Refer students to the highlighted words in the article.
- Ask students to work alone to complete the exercise.
- Check answers.

Fast finishers
Students can write gapped sentences using the words from Exercise 4. You can then put these sentences on the board and ask the class to complete them.

Answers
1 shortlist 2 virtually 3 remote 4 refugee 5 fellow

Your turn

5
- Give students time to think of someone in their country who has achieved something and who is worthy of being rewarded with a prize.
- If students struggle to think of anyone, put some names on the board. Students could then choose one of these people to make notes on.
- Encourage students to use their smartphones to look online for information.

6
- Before students do this exercise, ask them to consider what makes one achievement *bigger* than another, e.g. the age at which the person achieved something, or the relative difficulty of the achievement.
- Put students into pairs to discuss the ideas they made notes on in Exercise 5.

Optional activity
- Ask students to work in small groups to invent a new award. This should recognise achievement in a new area.
- Students should think of a name for their award as well as come up with an explanation for why the award is necessary.
- Ask one student from each group to report back to the class.

🔄 For homework, you could ask students to research the different types of award that are presented in their country each year. These could be sporting, cultural, educational or business awards for either adults or teenagers.

Speaking Making decisions

Objectives

- watch teenagers talking about what they are saving up for.
- listen to teenagers talking about giving money to charity.
- practise giving and asking for opinions, making suggestions and making decisions.

Background

Oxfam is an international aid charity set up in 1942.
UNICEF is an agency of the United Nations set up in 1946.

Warm-up

- Books closed. Ask students whether they prefer saving or spending money as well as asking them to give a reason for their choice.

Real talk: Are you saving up for something special? What?

1 ▶ **3.3** Ask students to open their books at page 38.

- Tell students they are going to watch some teenagers answering the following question:
Are you saving up for something special? What?
- Refer students to the gapped sentences.
- Tell students that they are going to complete the sentences with what each person is saving up for.
- Play the video.
- Students work alone to complete the sentences.
- Check answers.

Videoscript

Narrator: Are you saving up for something special? What?
Speaker 1: Definitely! I go to concerts all the time, almost every weekend and those cost a lot of money. My favourite band is going to be in town next month and I don't want to miss that. The tickets are extremely expensive, though, so I'm saving as much as I can so I can go.
Speaker 2: Yeah, I am. I just joined a band and the guitar I have right now is in horrible condition. I'm saving up for a new electric guitar so I can play a wider range of songs. I hope to have enough by the summer. We're going to practise every day during vacation.
Speaker 3: Well, yes, but I don't think my parents will like it very much – I want to buy a motorbike. I've seen a second-hand one that I really like but, it's really expensive. I'm doing some work in my neighbour's garden on Saturdays, so I hope to have enough to buy it in six months. Of course, I still need to convince my parents.
Speaker 4: Yes, of course! I'm saving up for college in two years. I also want to travel some before I start, so I'm saving for that too. I'm already looking forward to it!
Speaker 5: Not really, but I do want to go on a trip this summer with my friend's family and I don't think my parents will pay for it. I get money from doing chores around the house, so I'm saving some of that to help pay for it.
Narrator: Are *you* saving up for something special? What?

Answers

1 tickets; favourite band **2** new (electric) **3** motorbike
4 college **5** trip

2 💬 Put students into pairs to ask and answer the question.

3 🔊 **1.37** Tell students they are going to listen to two teenagers discussing giving money to charity.
- Read out the question.
- Play the recording.
- Students listen and answer the question.
- Check answer.

Answer

to have a vote in class

4 • Refer students to the phrases in the *Useful language* box.
- Check students' understanding of the language.
- Students can work alone to complete the conversation using the phrases in the *Useful language* box. **Stronger students** can try to complete the conversation without looking at the phrases in the box.

5 🔊 **1.37** Play the recording for students to check their answers.

Answers

2 thinking of **3** I'd rather **4** What kind of thing
5 a good idea **6** shall we decide **7** the best way is

6 💬 Ask students to work in pairs to act out the conversation in Exercise 4.
- Students can act out the conversation twice, taking a different part each time.

7 • Read out the three questions and elicit answers to them with the class a whole.

Answers

a We need to decide … ; Personally, I'd rather … ; I think the best way is … ; That's a good idea, too.
b I was thinking of …
c How shall we decide, then?; What kind of thing do you suggest?

8 💬 Read out the instructions.
- Put students into pairs and ask them to choose to be either Student A or Student B.
- Give students some time to plan what they want to say.
- Students then act out their conversations.
- Monitor while students are practising their conversations. Check that they are using the phrases from the *Useful language* box.

 For homework, ask students to do some research online to find out about the work of Oxfam and UNICEF. Students share what they find out with a partner in the next lesson.

Writing An opinion essay

Objectives

* read an essay about school leaving age.
* learn about the use of linking phrases.
* write an opinion essay about school.

Warm-up

* Books closed. Ask: *When can students leave school in your country? At what age do most students leave school?*
* Elicit answers to these questions and have a brief discussion on school leaving age.

1
* Ask students to open their books at page 39.
* Read out the question in the rubric and the title of the essay.
* Ask students to describe the photos (one shows two girls excitedly doing something with wires; another a group of students looking bored in a lecture).
* Point out that if the photos reflect the writer's opinion about education in general, we might imagine, that he/she doesn't think a university education will suit everyone and that many young people might be better off learning practical skills.
* Ask students to read the essay to find the answer to the question.
* Challenge **stronger students** by asking them additional questions, e.g. *Why does the writer disagree? What does the writer say about studying?*

> ### Answer
> The writer disagrees.

2
* Ask students to identify the paragraphs in which the information in Exercise 2 appears in the essay.
* Students can compare their answers in pairs before you check answers with the class.

> ### Answers
> **Paragraph 1:** b, c   **Paragraph 2:** a   **Paragraph 3:** e
> **Paragraph 4:** d, c

3
* Read out the information about linking phrases in the *Useful language* box. Explain that such phrases are used to introduce contrasts between ideas and give the writer the opportunity to structure his or her paragraphs.
* Ask students to work alone to find two further examples of such words and phrases in the essay in Exercise 1.
* Check answers.
* You could ask students to translate the linking words and phrases into their own language. You may also want to elicit further example sentences using these words and phrases as a means of checking students' understanding of them.

> ### Answers
> * **to show contrast:**
>   **However**, I believe it might not be the best idea to …
>   … **although** those students who want to go to university …
> * **to show the order of arguments:**
>   **In addition**, there is the problem that some over-16s who don't want to stay on at school …
>   **In conclusion** I'm against it …

> ### Language note
> Although words and phrases such as *however*, *whereas* and *in conclusion* are used in spoken language, they are generally only seen in more formal contexts.

4
* Complete the first sentence as an example.
* Put students into pairs and ask them to complete the remaining sentences using the words and phrases in the box.
* Check answers.

> ### Answers
> 1 however   2 Although   3 whereas
> 4 Firstly; in addition   5 In conclusion

 ## Get Writing

PLAN

5
* Students should do their planning in class. The writing can either be done in class or at home.
* Tell students they are going to write an essay on one of the titles in Exercise 5.
* You could brainstorm arguments for and against the view expressed in each essay title as a way of helping **weaker students**. If you choose to do this, draw a line down the middle of the board, diving it in two. Put the essay titles at the top of the board on either side of the line. You can then put ideas relating to one essay title on one side of the line, and ideas relating to the other essay title on the other side of the line.
* Refer students back to the organisation of paragraphs in Exercise 2 and then ask them to work alone to make notes.

WRITE

6
* Tell students to use the essay in Exercise 1 as a model to follow.
* Give students ten minutes to complete the writing task. Students should write between 140 and 160 words.
* Monitor while students are writing. Help with grammar and vocabulary as necessary.

CHECK

7
* Tell students that it is very important that they check their writing in order to look for ways to improve its content, style and structure.
* Give students a few minutes to look through their essays and check them against the points here.
* Collect students' essays and mark them.

> Set Exercises 1, 2, 3 and 4 on page 32 and Exercises 5, 6, 7, 8, 9, 10 and 11 on page 33 of the **Workbook** for homework.

4 Fabulous food

Unit aims

I can ...

- talk about how to prepare simple dishes.
- understand short online texts and an online article about different foods.
- discuss possible and imaginary situations in the present and future.
- understand a game show where people describe food.
- give instructions on how to make a dish.
- describe a local dish.

Unit contents

Vocabulary	Cooking verbs
	Words in context
	Adjectives describing food
	Prepositional phrases
Reading	Short online texts
	◗ Oil from goats
	An online article
Language focus	First conditional with *if, when* and *unless*
	Second conditional with *could* and *might*
Listening	A game show
Discover culture	◗ Fruits of the sea
Speaking	Giving instructions
	◗ Real talk: What would you make if you had to cook for your family for a day?
Pronunciation	Stress and intonation in second conditional questions
Writing	Describing a local dish
	Cooking and eating
CLIL	Technology: Vertical farming
	◗ You are what you eat

Background

Carl Warner (born in Liverpool in 1963) is an English photographer who creates landscapes using food. He calls his compositions *foodscapes*.

Be curious

- Books closed. Divide the class into pairs. On the board write: *vegetables* and *fruit*. Give students 90 seconds to write down as many names as they can. When the time is over, collect their ideas as a class. Make sure to revise *broccoli* /'brɒk.li/ at this stage, as students will need it to describe the photo.
- Ask students to think about why we need vegetables, fruit and plants. Elicit some ideas, e.g. we eat them, they produce oxygen, we use them to make medicines and cosmetics (e.g. shampoos), we use them to make clothes (e.g. cotton), they are decorative.
- Ask students to open their books at page 40.
- Give students a couple of minutes to look at the photograph. Ask them to describe the photo and answer the three questions.
- Students can then compare answers in pairs before you check answers with the class.
- Tell students that the themes of Unit 4 are preparing, cooking and eating food.

Suggested answers

- I can see a road with trees on either side of it.
- It's made of vegetables. The green parts are made of broccoli and the red things are probably peppers.
- The picture is very nice and interesting, but I wouldn't like to eat it. I hate broccoli.
- No, I haven't. My mum could get angry if I played with food!

Optional activity

- Ask students to look at *foodscapes* on the website of Carl Warner and choose the ones they find the most interesting. Students can share their ideas with a partner: http://www.carlwarner.com/foodscapes/.

CEFR

SKILL AREA	GOAL	EXERCISE
Listening	OVERALL LISTENING COMPREHENSION	3 p41 1–2 p48
	UNDERSTANDING INTERACTION	3–6 p48
	LISTENING TO MEDIA AND RECORDINGS	3–5 p44 1–7 p46
Reading	READING FOR INFORMATION & ARGUMENT	1–4 p42 1–3 p47 1–4 p49
Speaking	INFORMAL DISCUSSION (WITH FRIENDS)	7 p47
	INFORMATION EXCHANGE	4–5 p41 5 p42 6 p44 8 p46 6–7 p48
Writing	OVERALL WRITTEN PRODUCTION	5 p53
	REPORTS AND ESSAYS	5–7 p49
Communicative language competence	VOCABULARY RANGE	1–5 p41 4 p42 1–2 p44
	GRAMMATICAL ACCURACY	1–4 p43 1–7 p45 4–7 p47
	PHONOLOGICAL CONTROL	1 p41 4 p45 6 p48
Communication strategies	IDENTIFYING CUES AND INFERRING	4 p42 3 p49

Vocabulary Cooking verbs

Objectives

- learn cooking verbs.
- listen to someone explaining how to make a dish.
- describe a simple recipe.

Warm-up

- Books closed. Put students into pairs and ask them to talk about what they had for dinner last night.
- Students should not only explain what was in the dish that they had, but say who made it and who did the dishes.

1 🔊 **1.38** Ask students to open their books at page 41.

- Put students into pairs to match the verbs in the box with the photos.
- If you have the *Presentation Plus* software, put the pictures on the board and ask students to come up to the board in turn to match the words with the photos.
- Play the recording for students to listen, check their answers and repeat the verbs.

Answers

a boil   b fry   c grill   d roast   e grate   f chop
g slice   h mix   i bake   j spread

2 •

- Refer students to the words in the box as well as the examples.
- Check that students are able to pronounce *onion* /'ʌn.jən/, *sauce* /sɔːs/, *steak* /steɪk/ and *garlic* /'gɑːlɪk/.
- Put students into pairs and ask them to match the food items with the cooking verbs. Point out that some of the food items can be put together with more than one verb.
- Check answers.

Suggested answers

boil eggs, pasta   **fry** eggs, chicken, steak, onion, garlic
grill: bread, chicken, steak   **roast:** chicken   **grate** cheese
chop onion, garlic   **slice** bread, cake, tomatoes
mix pasta, sauce   **bake:** bread, cake   **spread** butter

Optional activity

- Put students into small groups of three.
- Ask one student to be the game master. This student should ask the other two questions, e.g. *What can we do with eggs?* The first student to give a correct answer, e.g. *Fry them!*, wins a point.
- The student with the most points at the end wins.

3 🔊 **1.39** Tell students they are going to listen to someone explaining how to make a dish.

- Before you play the recording, ask students to copy the table into their notebooks.
- Play the recording for students to complete the table by putting the words they hear in it into the correct category.
- Students can compare answers before you check answers with the whole class. Once you have checked the answers, ask students whether they would like to try the dish referred to in the recording and why/why not.

Audioscript

First slice some bread and grill it on one side. Then grate some cheese. Add salt, pepper and an egg. Mix all the ingredients together. Spread the mixture on the toast. Slice a tomato in very thin slices. Add the slices on top of the cheese and egg. Put it all back under the grill and grill for two or three minutes until the cheese starts to turn brown. Eat while it's still warm.

Answers

ingredients	cooking verbs
bread, cheese, salt, pepper, egg, tomato	slice, grill, grate, mix, spread

Your turn

4 •

- Read out the three questions.
- Put students into pairs to ask and answer the questions. Students should develop a conversation rather than simply see this as an exercise in answering the three questions quickly.

5 •

- Give students time to think of which recipes they would like to talk about. If any students to do not know any recipes, they can do some research online.
- Put students into pairs to talk about recipes and dishes.
- Ask some students to report back to the class on the recipes their partner talked about.
- To **extend** the work on the vocabulary, you could ask students to turn to the **Vocabulary bank** on page 110 and do the exercises for *Cooking verbs*.

Language note

The word *recipe* /'rɛsɪpi/ is commonly confused with *receipt* /rɪ'siːt/. The former refers to a set of instructions explaining how a dish is to be cooked, whereas the latter is a printed statement that proves that something has been paid for.

Optional activity

- Put students into pairs. Ask students to use their smartphones to research British dishes on this website: http://www.bbc.co.uk/food/cuisines/british
- Students should choose with dish they would most like to try making.
- Ask some students to report back to the class.

 Set Exercises 1, 2, 3 and 4 on page 37 of the **Workbook** for homework.
You could also ask students to do these exercises: http://learnenglishteens.britishcouncil.org/grammar-vocabulary/vocabulary-exercises/meals-and-cooking

Reading Short online texts

Objectives
- read texts about dangerous foods.
- learn words in context.
- talk about my eating habits and foods which are dangerous to eat.

Background
Fugu refers to several species of *pufferfish* (also known as *blowfish*). Pufferfish are so named for their tendency to inflate themselves to several times their normal size as a means of protection against predators.

Warm-up
- Books closed. Write *mushroom* on the board.
- Ask: *Can we eat every type of mushroom?* Explain that certain mushrooms are poisonous.
- Tell students that they are going to read about foods which can be dangerous.

1 💬 Ask students to open their books at page 42.
- Ask students to look at the photos and say what kind of food can be seen in each of them.
- Check answers. Students will find out how dangerous the food is and why in the next exercise.
- To **extend** this exercise, put students into pairs and ask them to say whether they enjoy eating onions, peanuts, fish and garlic or the dishes that contain them. Some students could then tell the class about their partner.

Answers
onions, peanuts, fish (fugu), garlic

Language note
Food is usually used as an uncountable noun, e.g. *We need to get some food for dinner* not ~~We need to get some foods for dinner~~. However, the word *foods* can be used when it means *types of food* or *dishes*, e.g. *the traditional foods of Spain.*

2 🔊 **1.40** Point out the pronunciation of *fugu* /ˈfuːguː/. Ask students to read the text and put the food referred to in order from the least to the most dangerous.
- Students can compare their answers in pairs before you check answers with the class.
- Refer students to the information in the **FACT!** box. Check that students understand that *plasma* is the part of blood that is liquid, in which red and white blood cells are suspended.

Answers
onions (can make you cry) – garlic (can burn your skin) – peanuts (can cause a very bad allergic reaction) – fugu fish (can kill you)

3 • Tell students the table is a summary of the information in the text. Show how the table is separated into three columns: food, possible dangers and advice.
- Ask students to read the text again.
- Put students into pairs to copy and complete the table.
- Check answers.

Answers
1 cry 2 a running tap 3 dogs 4 reaction 5 hospital
6 poisonous 7 specially trained fugu chef 8 burn
9 skin

Explore words in context

4 • Ask students to work alone to match the highlighted words in the text with the definitions. Help **weaker students** by giving them a translation in their own language of the highlighted words in the text.
- Check answers. You could then drill the pronunciation of the words: *toxic* /ˈtɒk.sɪ/, *allergic* /əˈlɜː.dʒɪk/, *delicacy* /ˈdel.ɪ.kə.si/, *intestines* /ɪnˈtes.tɪns/ and *severe* /sɪˈvɪər/.
- To **extend** the work on the words, find out if any students are allergic to any foods. You could also ask students to say what foods are considered to be delicacies in their country.

Answers
1 intestines 2 delicacy 3 allergic 4 toxic 5 severe

Game
- Play *Could you spell that, please?* using the words in context from Exercise 4 as well as the vocabulary from page 41.
- See **Games bank** on pages 28–29.

Your turn

5 • Refer students to the three questions.
- Put students into pairs to ask and answer them. As students may not know of any other foods which can be dangerous, encourage them to do some research online to help them answer question 3.
- Ask some students to report back to the class on what their partner said.

You can show this video as either a lead-in or a follow-up to the Language Focus 1 lesson.

▶ **Discovery** EDUCATION
4.1 Oil from goats

- Read out the title of the video. Ask students what think the video is going to be about.
- Elicit student's ideas.
- Play the video.
- Students watch it and answer the three questions.
- Then ask students if they have ever used Argan oil of if they would like to use it?
- See page 125 for further activities you can do with this video.

Suggested answers
- It's a goat.
- It's eating fruit.
- You can eat its meat or use its milk.

Language focus 1 First conditional with *if, when* and *unless*

Objectives
- learn about the use of *if, when* and *unless* in the first conditional.
- organise and talk about a special dinner for my friends.

Warm-up
- Books closed. Write the word *if* on the board and ask students if they can use the word in a sentence about the future. Most students will have learnt the first conditional before and so you should be able to elicit an example sentence.
- If students struggle to produce anything, you could put the beginning of a sentence on the board and ask students to complete it, e.g. *If I pass my exams, …*

1
- Ask students to open their books at page 43.
- Tell students that the gapped sentences are from the text on page 42.
- Ask students to copy the sentences into their notebooks and complete them. Then ask them to match each of the sentences with the meanings (a–c).
- Check answers.
- You could then remind students that the two clauses in a conditional sentence can be put in either order, e.g. *If I go to the party, I'm sure I'll have a good time.* or *I'm sure I'll have a good time if I go to the party.*
- For further information and additional exercises, students can turn to page 102 of the **Grammar reference** section.

Answers
1 **If** you are ever in Japan and want to try fugu fish for yourself, you'll have to be very careful!
2 You'll need to make sure you go to a restaurant that has a 'fugu certified' chef **unless** you want it to be your last supper!
3 **When** I go on holiday this year, I'll make sure I eat lots of garlic!
1 b 2 c 3 a

2
- Put students into pairs to do the matching exercise.
- Encourage **weaker students** to underline *if, when* and *unless* in each sentence as doing so may focus their attention on those words.
- Monitor and help as necessary.
- Check answers.

Answers
1 c 2 a 3 e 4 f 5 b 6 d

3 **1.41** Read out the information in the **Get it right!** box and then refer students to the dialogue.
- Put students into pairs and ask them to complete the dialogue using *if, when* and *unless* and the verbs in brackets.
- Play the recording for students to check their answers.

Answers
1 If 2 finish 3 'll put 4 when 5 'll put 6 unless
7 if 8 will you choose

Your turn

4
- As an introduction to the task in the **Your turn** section, you could tell students about the last special dinner you prepared for some friends.
- Tell students they are going to organise their own special dinner.
- Refer students to the three items in the list and the example sentences.
- Put students into small groups and give them time to organise their dinner. Encourage students to be as imaginative as possible with their plans for both the food and the decorations.
- Monitor while students do this task. Help with vocabulary as necessary.
- Ask one student from each group to report their special dinner to the class. Students should use *going to* when talking about their dinners, e.g. *We're going to have a special dinner next Saturday for ten of our friends. We're going to have it on the balcony of my flat. For starters we are going to have fugu prepared by a chef from Japan.*
- Once each group has told the class about its dinner, find out which dinner the class finds the most original. You could do this by referring to each group in turn and asking students to vote for it by putting their hands in the air. Count the raised hands for each group and put the totals on the board.

Set Exercises 1, 2, 3, 4 and 5 on page 38 of the **Workbook** for homework.

Vocabulary and Listening

Objectives

* learn adjectives to describe food.
* listen to a game show.
* talk about dishes I would like to try, unusual dishes and my favourite dishes.

Adjectives describing food

Warm-up

* Books closed. Write *adjectives describing food* on the board.
* Elicit adjectives used to describe reactions to the taste of food. Students might produce words like *nice, tasty* or *horrible*.

1 🔊 **1.42** Ask students to open their books at page 44.

* Put students into pairs to match the adjectives in bold with the definitions.
* Check answers.
* Play the recording for students to listen and repeat the words.
* Once you have checked answers, refer students to the use of *mmm* in sentences 2 and 5 and *yuk* in sentence 8. *Mm*, which can also be written *mmm*, is an exclamation used to express contentment, pleasure, agreement or uncertainty. How it is said depends on what is being expressed. *Yuk*, which can also be spelt *yuck*, is an exclamation to express strong disgust.

> ### Answers
> **a** sweet **b** salty **c** spicy **d** disgusting **e** delicious
> **f** bland **g** crunchy **h** slimy **i** savoury **j** bitter

> ### Language note
> The main stress in *delicious* and *disgusting* (which is on the second syllable) tends to be given very heavy emphasis in informal conversation. This is done as a means of highlighting the speaker's reaction to their perception of the taste of the food being described.

2
* Read out the question, then put students into pairs to answer it.
* Check answers. You could then ask students to name food items or dishes which are salty, spicy, etc.
* To **extend** the work on the vocabulary, you could ask students to turn to the **Vocabulary bank** on page 110 and do the exercises for *Adjectives describing food*.

> ### Answers
> a) taste: salty, spicy, bland, sweet, bitter, savoury
> b) texture: crunchy, slimy
> c) good and bad opinion: delicious, disgusting

Optional activity

* Put students into pairs to discuss the dishes and foods they like and dislike.
* Encourage students to use the adjectives from Exercise 1.
* Ask some students to report back to the class on what they learnt about their partner, e.g. *Mila thinks cheese is delicious.*

A game show

3 💬 Refer students to the photos of the dishes.
* You could then either put students into pairs to describe the dishes using the adjectives which were introduced in Exercise 1, or elicit descriptions from the class as a whole.

4 🔊 **1.43** Tell students they are going to listen to a game show in which blindfolded contestants are given mystery dishes to try. Explain that contestants are blindfolded so that their reactions to the dishes are based on taste and smell rather than sight.
* Encourage **stronger students** to note down as much as they can about what each speaker says.
* Ask some students to report their ideas to the class.

Audioscript

Turn to page 179 for the audioscript.

> ### Answers
> 3 chapulines (grasshoppers)

> ### Language note
> A *blindfold* is a piece of cloth tied around a person's eyes to deprive them of sight.

5 🔊 **1.43** Refer students to the notes. Make sure that students understand that they should circle the correct answer or complete gaps.
* Play the recording for students to do the exercise.
* Check answers.

> ### Answers
> 1 a jellyfish b Vietnam c sweet, (a bit) spicy, disgusting, slimy
> 2 a cockscombs b Italy c light, crunchy, (a bit) bland, crunchy (on the outside), (a bit) soft (on the inside)
> 3 a grasshoppers b Mexico c salty, spicy, crunchy, perfect, delicious

Your turn

6
* Refer students to the questions. Point out that *these dishes* in question 1 refers to the dishes that featured in the game show.
* Help **weaker students** by allowing the class some preparation time before they talk to a partner. There are quite a lot of questions here so it is sensible to give students some time to think about their answers. Alternatively, set a separate time limit for each question.
* Put students into pairs to ask and answer the questions.

> Set Exercises 1, 2, 3 and 4 on page 39 of the **Workbook** for homework.
> You could also ask students to read this text about unusual food around the world and to complete the accompanying exercises:
> http://learnenglishteens.britishcouncil.org/skills/reading-skills-practice/worlds-weirdest-food

Language focus 2 Second conditional with *could* and *might*

Objectives

- learn the second conditional with *could* and *might*.
- talk about disgusting and delicious food.

Warm-up

- Books closed. Elicit a first conditional sentence. Write it on the board, e.g. *If we go to the café, I will have an omelette.* Ask students if they can turn this sentence into a second conditional sentence, e.g. *If we went to the café, I would have an omelette.*
- Elicit the basic difference between these two forms, which is that the second conditional, by contrast with the first, refers to a hypothetical situation rather than a real one.

1
- Ask students to open their books at page 45.
- Tell students that the example sentences are from the listening on page 44.
- Put students into pairs to match the beginnings of the sentences with the ends. Ask students to copy the sentences into their notebooks.
- Check answers.

> ### Answers
> 1 b If I saw it on a menu, I might eat it again.
> 2 d I wouldn't eat it again if you paid me!
> 3 a Would you eat it again if you had the chance?
> 4 c I could eat that again if you offered it to me.

2
- Refer students to the words and phrases in the box.
- Put students into pairs and ask them to complete the rules using the information in the box.
- Check answers.
- For further information and additional exercises, students can turn to page 102 of the **Grammar reference** section.

> ### Answers
> 1 To form the second conditional, use *if* + **past simple** for the situation, and *would*, **_could_** or **_might_** for a possible consequence.
> 2 To form questions, use (question word) + **_would_** + subject + verb.
> 3 *If* can come at the beginning or **at the end** of the sentence/question.
> Use the second conditional to talk about situations that are **imaginary**.

3
- Complete the first sentence with the class as an example.
- Put students into pairs and ask them to complete the remaining sentences.
- Monitor while students do this task. Guide **weaker students** to the correct answers by helping them to distinguish between the different parts of the second conditional sentence.
- Check answers.

> ### Answers
> 1 could never eat; was 2 Would you like; got
> 3 had; 'd give up 4 was; might be 5 picked; 'd never eat
> 6 offered; didn't like; would you say

4
- Read out the example question.
- Ask students to use the example to help them complete the rest of the exercise. Students can work alone on this exercise.
- Check answers.

> ### Answers
> 2 What would you say if a friend asked you to lend her some money?
> 3 If you could live anywhere in the world, where would you like to live?
> 4 If you won the lottery, what would you do with the money?
> 5 What advice would you give your friend if he was worried about his exams?
> 6 If you didn't need to study this evening, what would you do instead?

Say it right!

Stress and intonation in second conditional questions

1 🔊 **1.44** Tell students they are going to learn about the use of stress and intonation.
- Play the recording for students to listen to the questions and repeat them.

2 🔊 **1.45** Play the recording for students to mark the main stresses in each of the questions.

3 🔊 **1.45** Play the recording for students to check their answers and repeat the questions.

> ### Answers
> 1 What would you **do** if you for**got** your **mum**'s **birth**day?
> 2 What would you **say** if a **friend** asked you to **lend** her some **mo**ney?
> 3 If you could **live** anywhere in the **world**, **where** would you like to **live**?
> 4 If you **won** the **lot**tery, what would you **do** with the **mo**ney?
> 5 What ad**vice** would you **give** your **friend** if he was **worr**ied about his ex**ams**?
> 6 If you **didn't need** to **stu**dy this evening, **what** would you do ins**tead?**

4 Put students into pairs and ask them to practise saying the questions with the correct stress and intonation.

5 💬 Students ask and answer the questions in Exercise 4.

Your turn

6
- Read out the information about the two lists that students have to write.
- Give students a few minutes to write their lists.

7
- Read out the example sentences and then put students into pairs to compare the lists they made in Exercise 6.

> ⊙ Set Exercises 1, 2, 3 and 4 on page 40 of the **Workbook** for homework.

Discover Culture

Fruits of the sea

Objectives

- watch a video about fishing in Japan.
- talk about seafood and food that is popular in my country.

Warm-up

- Books closed. Elicit answers to the following questions: *Have you ever eaten Japanese food? What dishes did you try? What did you think of them?*

1 💬 Ask students to open their books at page 46.
- Refer students to the photos and the words in the box.
- Put students into pairs to tell each other what they know about Japan.

2 ▶ 4.2 Tell students they are going to watch a video about Japan.
- Play the video for students to note down the topics in the box in Exercise 1 which are mentioned.
- Check answers. Encourage **stronger students** to give as much detail as they can.

Videoscript

Japan is a group of islands surrounded by water. Rich water. Water that is full of life. The sea is an important part of life in Japan. It also plays a major role in the local diet. The Japanese eat 10% of all the fish caught in the world. If the seas weren't so full of fish and seafood, the Japanese diet would be very different. They have a good reason to eat so much fish, too. The fish-based diet is one of the healthiest in the world. Life expectancy here is over eighty. It all begins here, in the seas that surround the islands. Close to the shore, you can find scallops, sea urchins, and abalone. Further out, you can find squid. Fishermen catch them at night because the squid are drawn to the shining lights of the boats. Fishing is essential to life in Japan. If fishermen didn't catch squid and other fish, the people in these coastal villages would suffer. Blue fin tuna swim in the deep waters of northern Japan. It is one of the most popular fish in all of Japan despite being one of the most expensive. It's extremely healthy and full of protein and vitamins. There's no question of Japan's love for seafood at the Tsukiji fish market in Tokyo, the world's largest fish market. Over forty thousand buyers come here every day to buy fresh fish for restaurants and supermarkets across the country. Tomorrow, it will all happen again in the seas around Japan.

Answers

geography, food, people, work

3 ▶ 4.2 Refer students to the three summaries.
- Play the video again for students to choose the best summary.
- Check answers.

Answer

2

4
- Ask students to work alone to note down which of the images in the list can be seen in the video. Students then think of three more images which appeared in the video.
- Check answers.

Answers

- the islands and seas surrounding Japan
- old people being active
- fishing boats
- tuna, squid and shellfish

5 ▶ 4.2 Refer students to the information in the box.
- Play the recording again for students to note down what this information refers to.
- Check answers.

Answers

The Japanese eat **10%** of all the fish caught in the world.
Life expectancy in Japan is over **80**.
Fishermen catch squid **at night**.
Blue fin tuna swim in the **deep waters** of northern Japan.
Over **40,000** buyers come to the Tsukiji fish market in Tokyo every day.
They buy fresh fish for **restaurants and supermarkets** across the country.

Background

Scallops and squid are *molluscs* /'mɒl.əsks/, that is, animals which are invertebrates with soft unsegmented bodies and, usually, an external shell. Snails and slugs are also molluscs.
Sea urchins are echinoderms /ɪˈkʌɪnə(ʊ)dəːms/, a type of marine invertebrate.

6 ▶ 4.2 Read out the names of the animals and check students can pronounce them: *tuna* /'tjuːnə/, *scallop* /'skɒl.əp/, *sea urchins* /siː ˈəːtʃɪn/ and *squid* /skwɪd/.
- Ask students to match the animals to the facts.
- Play the recording for students to check their answers.

Answers

1 a, b   2 c   3 d, e

Your turn

7
- Give students time to think about what they learnt by watching the video.
- Put students into pairs.
- Tell students to use the phrase *I didn't know that …* in conversation with their partner, e.g. *I didn't know that seafood was so important to the people of Japan.*
- Students tell each other about what they learnt about Japan.

8
- Refer students to the questions.
- Put students into pairs to ask and answer them.

 For homework, you could ask students to look on the Internet for a recipe for a Japanese dish.

Reading An online article

Objectives

- read an article about how what we eat is influenced by different things.
- learn prepositional phrases.
- talk about the food in my country.

Background

Mutton is the flesh of a fully-grown sheep.
The **Maoris** are the aboriginal people of New Zealand, whose way of life was affected significantly by European colonisation.
Hāngi is not only a Maori method of cooking, but also the name given to the food cooked in this way and the gathering at which this food is served.
Simit bread, a circular bread covered in sesame seeds, is a very popular snack in Istanbul, where it is sold on the streets.

Warm up

- Books closed. Choose a dish that is popular in the students' country. Ask students to say why they think this dish is popular, how it is prepared and if they know anything about the history of the dish.

1 Ask students to open their books at page 47 and look at the photos.
- If you have the *Presentation Plus* software, put the photos up on the interactive whiteboard.
- Put students into pairs to ask and answer the questions.
- Check answers.

2 🔊 **1.46** Ask students to read the article to check their answers from Exercise 1.

Answers

- buuz – dumplings with mutton, from Mongolia
- hāngi – a traditional Maori way of preparing food
- arancino – a ball of fried rice filled with a rich tomato and meat sauce, from Sicily, in southern Italy

3
- Refer students to the facts numbered 1–5, then read out the example.
- Ask students to read the article again to identify which country each fact refers to. Help **weaker students** by encouraging them to skim the text to look for key words such as *coast*, *rice*.
- Check answers. Challenge **stronger students** by asking them additional questions, e.g. *What is the most important ingredient in Mongolian food?*
- Read out the information in the **FACT!** box. Ask students why street food is popular and elicit some ideas, e.g. it can be cheap, it can be eaten quickly, food stands are often located near train and bus stations and so offer people convenience.

Fast finishers

Students can note down any information in the article which particularly surprised or interested them.

Answers

2 Mongolia 3 Italy 4 New Zealand 5 New Zealand

Explore prepositional phrases

4
- Put students into pairs to choose the correct word in each sentence. Tell students not to look into the article until they have completed the exercise.
- They should look at the article to check rather than find the answers.
- Check answers.

Answers

1 by 2 in 3 on 4 on

5
- Refer students to the gapped questions.
- Put students into pairs and ask them to complete the questions with the phrases from Exercise 4.
- To **extend** the work on the vocabulary, you could ask students to turn to the **Vocabulary bank** on page 110 and do the exercises for *Explore prepositional phrases*.

Answers

1 on the go 2 by land 3 in a number of different ways
4 on the streets

Your turn

6
- Put students into pairs to ask and answer the questions in Exercise 5.
- You could then ask students what food they tend to eat when they are on the go. If you choose to do this, you could introduce the following language:
  snack – a small amount of food eaten between meals, such as a cereal bar;
  snack on – to eat a snack, e.g. *He likes to snack on chocolate bars*;
  grab a snack / grab something – a phrase used to indicate that someone will buy a snack rather than have a meal or eat slowly, e.g. *I won't have time for lunch. I'll grab something on the way to the station*.

7
- Refer students to the questions and the example answer.
- Put students into pairs and ask them to ask and answer the questions.

Optional activity

- Put students into small groups to prepare a short presentation on food in a particular country.
- Give each group time to choose a country. Make sure that each group chooses a different country.
- Students can use their smartphones to research food in the country they choose.
- Students prepare a short presentation (on computer or using paper and pen), which should, ideally, include photos or illustrations.
- Students take it in turns to do their presentations.

Set Exercises 1, 2, 3, 4 and 5 on page 41 and Exercises 5 and 6 on page 40 of the **Workbook** for homework.

Speaking Giving instructions

Objectives
- watch teenagers talking about cooking for their family.
- listen to a description of how to cook a particular dish.
- practise giving instructions.

Warm-up
- Books closed. Put students into pairs and ask them to tell each other who does most of the cooking in their house and how often they cook at home.
- Ask some students to report back to the class on their partner.

Real talk: What would you make if you had to cook for your family for a day?

1 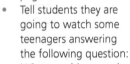 Ask students to open their books at page 48.

- Tell students they are going to watch some teenagers answering the following question:
What would you make if you had to cook for your family for a day?
- Tell students that they are going to match the words and phrases with each of the teenagers in the video.
- Play the video for students to complete the exercise.
- Check answers.

Videoscript

Narrator: What would you make if you had to cook for your family for a day?

Speaker 1: Well, I'd cook on a Saturday so I wouldn't have to get up so early! I'd make steak and eggs and maybe some pancakes – my family likes big breakfasts! And after all that, we wouldn't have to eat lunch then. Dinner would be my mum's recipe for Italian lasagne, a big green salad and plenty of garlic bread.

Speaker 2: I don't know what I'd cook for a whole day. I can only think of food for one meal! If I could choose the meal, I'd pick lunch. That's my favourite because I'm always hungry around then. I would make some delicious soup with lots of pasta and vegetables in it and some potato salad.

Speaker 3: We did cooking at school last year, so I can think of a lot of dishes. I would make some kind of rice dish, like paella or a risotto, and then a meat dish, like roast chicken or a grilled steak. I also love desserts. I would make some kind of chocolate cake or berry pie. Yum!

Speaker 4: I love eating, but I can't stand cooking, so I'd ask my brother to write a menu. I'd do the grocery shopping for him, but then he would actually do the cooking! I don't think he'd mind, especially if he chose the dishes.

Speaker 5: For a whole day? Well, I'd skip breakfast since I never eat it anyway. Then I'd just order sandwiches and pizzas for lunch and dinner.

Speaker 6: I'm a vegetarian so that would be a problem with my family since they LOVE meat! I would probably make an omelette with mushrooms, onions, spinach, cheese, and peppers. Then I'd have to cook some kind of meat on the side for them. I also like very spicy things. But they don't, so I wouldn't be able to add many spices. This would be a hard day for me.

Narrator: What would *you* make if you had to cook for your family for a day?

Answers
Speaker 1 steak, eggs, pancakes, lasagne, salad
Speaker 2 soup, pasta, vegetables, potato salad
Speaker 3 rice dish, chicken, steak, cake, berry pie
Speaker 4 nothing
Speaker 5 sandwiches, pizzas
Speaker 6 omelette, meat

---

2 Put students into pairs to ask and answer the question.

3 **1.47** Tell students they are going to listen to Josh talking to his mum.
- Read out the question.
- Play the recording.
- Students listen and answer the question.
- Check answer.

Answer
a

4 - Refer students to the phrases in the *Useful language* box.
- Students can work alone to complete the conversation using the phrases in the *Useful language* box.

5 **1.47** Play the recording for students to check their answers.

Answers
2 First of all, chop 3 Next, you 4 You need to stir it
5 Then, add 6 Finally, when

6 Ask students to work in pairs to act out the conversation in Exercise 4.
- Students can act out the conversation twice, taking a different part each time.

7 Give students time to read the recipes.
- Put students into pairs.
- Give students time to plan what they want to say.
- Students then act out their conversations using the recipes in the exercises or others that they know well.
- Monitor while students are practising their conversations. Check that they are using the phrases from the *Useful language* box.

> For homework, ask students to find out if there is a dish in their family that has been passed down through the generations. Students can then bring the recipe to the next lesson and share it with the class.

Writing Describing a local dish

Objectives

- read a description of a local dish.
- learn phrases to describe ingredients and how food is cooked and eaten.
- write a description of a traditional dish.

Background

Cornwall is a county in England, occupying the far south-west of the country. It is known for its beaches and coves. Cornwall has its own language, known as Kernowek, which is a Celtic language related to Welsh and Breton. The language is only spoken by a small number of people in Cornwall, although recent attempts at reviving it have not only led to renewed interest in the language but also in the notion of a *Cornish* identity distinct from *English*.

Warm-up

- Books closed. Ask students to say what dishes from their country are known around the world, e.g. fish and chips is associated with the United Kingdom.
- At this point, you could ask students which adjective, currently popular in English and which was introduced in Unit 1, could be used to describe fish and chips. Elicit *iconic* and write it on the board.

1
- Ask students to open their books at page 49.
- Refer students to the photo and then ask them to read the description and answer the question.
- Check answer.

Answer

Cornish pastry: thick pastry filled with steak, potato, onion and swede

2
- Ask students to read the description again.
- Put students into pairs to note down the paragraphs in the description in which the things in the list are mentioned. Point out that two things in the list are not mentioned in the description.
- Check answers.

Answers

The ingredients. 1
Where the food is from. 1
Who eats it. 2
Why people like it. 2
Where you can buy it. 3
The history of the dish. 2
How it's cooked. 1
When you eat it and *How easy or difficult it is to cook* are not in the text.

3
- Read out the information about phrases used to describe food in the *Useful language* box.
- Ask students to work alone to find further examples of such phrases in the description in Exercise 1.
- Check answers.

Answers

... **filled with** small pieces of ...
Then it's **baked in the oven**.
... but unless they are **made in** Cornwall ...

4
- Refer students to the phrases in the box.
- Complete the first sentence with the class as an example.
- Put students into pairs to complete the remaining sentences using the phrases in the box.
- Check answers.

Answers

1 served with 2 bake; in 3 filled with 4 consists of
5 made in 6 contain

Optional activity

- Put students into pairs and ask them to tell one another about their favourite meal or about a dish that their family enjoys eating together.
- Students take it in turns to describe a dish to each other using the phrases from the *Useful language* box.
- Ask some students to report back to the class on the dish their partner talked about.

 Get Writing

PLAN

5
- Students should do their planning in class. The writing can either be done in class or at home.
- Tell students they are going to write a description of a dish popular in their area or traditional dish from their country. You may want to brainstorm examples of dishes. If you choose to do this, write the names of the dishes on the board.
- Refer students back to the list in Exercise 2 and then ask them to work alone to make notes.

WRITE

6
- Tell students to use the example description as a model to follow.
- Give students ten minutes to complete the writing task. Students should write between 140 and 160 words.
- Monitor while students are writing. Help with grammar and vocabulary as necessary.

CHECK

7
- Tell students that it is very important that they check their writing in order to look for ways to improve its content, style and structure.
- Give students a few minutes to look through their descriptions and check them against the points here.
- Collect students' descriptions and mark them.

 Set Exercises 1, 2, 3, 4 and 5 on page 42 and Exercises 6, 7, 8, 9, 10 and 11 on page 43 of the **Workbook** for homework.
You could also ask students to try making their own Cornish pasty by following the recipe on this website: http://www.bbc.co.uk/food/recipes/classic_cornish_pasty_67037 They could then take a photograph of it and post it to a class blog or email or text it to other students

Unit aims

I can ...
* talk about what objects are used for and why they are useful.
* understand articles about useful and important inventions.
* talk about simple processes.
* understand a radio report about unusual inventions.
* buy a gadget.
* write an online review.

Unit contents

Vocabulary	Everyday objects
	Words in context
	Modifiers
	Communication phrases and phrasal verbs
Reading	A news article
	▶ Objects for survival
	An article
Language focus	The passive: present simple, past simple and *will*
	Relative pronouns and clauses
Listening	A radio report
Discover culture	▶ An invention that changed everything
Speaking	Buying a gadget
	▶ Real talk: What's your favourite gadget?
Pronunciation	Intonation in relative clauses
Writing	An online review
	Describing a product
CLIL	Technology: Passive houses
	▶ What a waste

Background

Food has been sold in glass bottles for centuries, while the first plastic bottles appeared in the 1940s. Their production was quite expensive and they only became more popular in the 1960s. Plastic bottles have a lot of advantages over glass bottles, e.g. they don't break easily, they are lighter and easier to transport. They have replaced glass bottles almost completely.

Be curious

* Books closed. Ask students what they do with things such as empty egg boxes, empty plastic bottles and their tops and the cardboard tubes from toilet rolls. Most students will probably say *throw them away* or *put them in the recycling bin*.
* Ask: *Is there anything else we could do with these objects?* Guide students towards the idea of adapting an object that is typically used for one purpose for another entirely different purpose, e.g. cardboard tubes from toilet rolls could be used as holders for USB cables.
* Ask students to open their books at page 52.
* Refer students to the photo and ask them to describe it.
* Give students a couple of minutes to answer the three questions. Encourage students to speculate about the object in the photo.
* Students can then compare answers in pairs before you check answers with the class.
* Tell students that the themes of Unit 5 are objects and what we use them for.

Suggested answers

* I can see a lot of empty plastic bottles.
* They could be used to make instruments, toys or games. Maybe they could be used as a building material.
* Near where I live there is a statue made out of recycled objects: old CDs, computer parts, bits of fridges and even an old bicycle.

CEFR

SKILL AREA	GOAL	EXERCISE
Listening	OVERALL LISTENING COMPREHENSION	3–4 p53
	UNDERSTANDING INTERACTION	1–6 p60
	LISTENING TO MEDIA AND RECORDINGS	1–4 p56 1–5 p58
Reading	READING FOR INFORMATION & ARGUMENT	1–5 p54 1–4 p59 1–4 p61
Speaking	INFORMAL DISCUSSION (WITH FRIENDS)	4–5 p55 6 p58
	INFORMATION EXCHANGE	6 p56 2 p58 5 p59 6–7 p60
Writing	CREATIVE WRITING	5–7 p61
Communicative language competence	VOCABULARY RANGE	1–5 p53 4–6 p56 1–4 p63
	GRAMMATICAL ACCURACY	1–5 p55 1–5 p57
	PHONOLOGICAL CONTROL	1 p53 4 p56 3 p57 6 p60
Communication strategies	IDENTIFYING CUES AND INFERRING	4 p54 4 p59

Vocabulary Everyday objects

Objectives

* learn vocabulary for everyday objects
* listen to people talking about useful objects in their lives.
* talk about the objects that are most important to me.

Warm-up

* Books closed. Write *everyday objects* on the board.
* Put students into pairs. Give students 90 seconds to write a list of objects that we use every day.
* Make this competitive by telling students the pair that comes up with the most number of everyday objects wins.
* Alternatively, as a way of introducing the idea of describing objects, put students into teams to describe a series of everyday objects (do not choose any of the ones on page 53) and ask students to put their hand up and say the word if they know it. Students win a point for each correct answer. The team with the most points at the end wins.

1 🔊 **2.01** Ask students to open their books at page 53.

* Put students into pairs to match the words with the objects in the photos. Point out that there is an element of guesswork in this exercise as only small parts of the objects are shown in the photos. Students may struggle in particular with photos b and c.
* If you have the *Presentation Plus* software, put the pictures on the board and ask students to come up to the board in turn to match the words with the photos.
* Play the recording for students to listen, check their answers and repeat the phrases.

Answers

a light bulb   b charger   c heater   d fan   e tap
f plug   g candle   h switch   i matches
j remote control

2 💬 Read out the example sentence.

* Put students into pairs.
* Ask students to say why each of the objects in Exercise 1 is important in our everyday lives.
* Check answers.

3 🔊 **2.02** Tell students they are going to listen to three people talking about the objects that are the most useful in their lives.

* Play the recording.
* Check answers.
* To **extend** this exercise, play the recording again for students to note down the reasons the people give for choosing particular items.

Audioscript

Jay: I think that's pretty easy, I mean you can't live without light or water or heat can you? So my three objects are: the light bulb because without light bulbs we can't work or study when it's dark; the tap, because it gives us clean water and clean water is probably even more important than light, and finally a heater. It's really cold in our house in winter. I really don't think we can live through the winter without a heater to keep us warm.

Kelly: Well, I agree with the tap of course, because water is really, really important. I'm not sure I agree with the light bulb. I mean you get light in other ways, can't you? With a candle for example, and I think a fan is much more important than a heater. If you're cold you can put more clothes on, but if you're hot it's really difficult to keep cool without a fan.

Huw: OK, all the things you two said are really important, but I don't think we should forget battery chargers in this day and age. I mean everything that I use for studying and communicating – my computer, my phone, my tablet – they all need recharging. If I lose or forget my charger I can't do anything!

Answers

Jay – light bulb, tap, heater
Kelly – tap, fan
Huw – (battery) charger

Game

* Play *Pictionary* using the vocabulary for everyday objects.
* See **Games bank** on pages 28–29.

Your turn

4 • Refer students to the examples.

* Ask students which of the everyday objects from Exercise 1 each of the sentences refers to, and then focus students' attention on the phrases in italics.

Answers

1 light bulbs   2 tap   3 heater   4 fan

5 • Ask students to use the phrases in italics from Exercise 4 to write about three objects from Exercise 1 that they consider to be the most important for them.

* Make sure that students understand that *important* in this context refers to how useful the object is.
* Encourage **stronger students** to write as much as they can. **Weaker students** can just write one sentence for each of the objects they choose.
* Ask some students to report back to the class on the objects their partner chose.
* To **extend** the work on the vocabulary, you could ask students to turn to the **Vocabulary bank** on page 111 and do the exercises for *Everyday objects*.

 Set Exercises 1, 2, 3 and 4 on page 47 of the **Workbook** for homework.

Reading A news article

Objectives

- read an article about an object called a *light bottle*.
- learn words in context.
- talk about alternative uses for everyday objects.

Background

The **Moser Lamp** (which is also known as a **light bottle**) was created by a Brazilian mechanic called Alfredo Moser in 2002.

Warm-up

- Books closed. Write *a light-bulb moment* on the board.
- Explain that this is a reasonably common informal phrase. Ask students if they can guess what it refers to. To help students you can draw a stick man or woman on the board with an illuminated light bulb above his or her head.
- Explain that *a light-bulb moment* is used to describe sudden realisation or inspiration, e.g. *Jack had a light-bulb moment and all at once knew how to solve the problem.*

1
- Ask students to open their books at page 54.
- Refer students to the photos and elicit answers from the class to the three questions.
- Do not confirm or reject students' ideas at this point. Students will check their ideas by reading the text in Exercise 2.

2 (2.03) Ask students to read the text to check their answers to Exercise 1.
- Refer students to the information in the **FACT!** box. To help students understand how many people this is, point out that the 400 million is more than the population of the United States and more than 50% of the population of Europe.

Answers

It's a plastic bottle, filled with water, with a black top.
It's in the roof to light the room.
It's used by people who don't have electricity in their homes.

Optional activity

- Put students into small groups and ask them to discuss the following question: *Is it the responsibility of those who have what they need in life, e.g. food, shelter, employment, to help those who do not have those things? If it is, what should people in the richer areas of the planet do every day to help those in the poorest?*
- Before students discuss the question, you may want to give them some time to note down some ideas. They can then refer to these notes in their discussions.
- Ask one member of each group to report back to the class on the discussion they had.

3
- Refer students to the gapped fact sheet. Check students remember the meaning of the adjective *rural*. (It was first seen in Unit 3 in the text about the Young Australian of the Year Award.)
- Read out the example.
- Put students into pairs and ask them to complete the fact sheet with information from the text. Help **weaker students** by guiding them to the part of the text which will help them complete the fact sheet.
- Check answers.

Answers

2 Alfredo Moser 3 Brazilian 4 electricity 5 water
6 a black top 7 hole 8 roof 9 Bangladesh
10 small businesses

Optional activity

- Ask students to use their smartphones to go online and watch Alfredo Moser's *light bottle* in action here: http://sculptthefuturefoundation.org/portfolio/my-shelter-foundation-global-lighting-project/
- Students can then share their reactions to the video with a partner. Alternatively, you can discuss their reactions with the class as a whole.

Explore words in context

4
- Refer students to definitions 1–5.
- Ask students to work alone to match the highlighted words in the article with the definitions.
- Check answers and then drill the pronunciation of the following words: *bleach* /bliːtʃ/, *specialises* /ˈspeʃ(ə)lʌɪz ɪz/ and *spread* /sprɛd/.

Answers

1 spread 2 left in the dark 3 run 4 bleach
5 specialises

Your turn

5
- Read out the example sentence and then give students time to think of any other uses for plastic bottles or other everyday objects.
- Put students into pairs to share their ideas.
- Ask some students to report back to the class on the ideas that they and their partner came up with.

You can show this video as either a lead-in or a follow-up to the Language Focus 1 lesson.

- ▶ Ask: *Have you ever spent any time at the top of a mountain in winter? Which objects are needed to survive such harsh conditions?*
- Elicit student's answers and then put students into pairs to ask and answer the questions.
- Play the video and confirm that the photo was taken in the Alps.
- Students watch it and say what they think about how little Bear needed to survive on the mountainside.
- Ask students what attracts people to experience life in extreme environments.
- See page 126 for further activities you can do with this video.

 Set Exercises 1, 2, 3, 4 and 5 on page 51 of the **Workbook** for homework.

Language focus 1
The passive: present simple, past simple and *will*

Objectives
* learn the present and past simple passive.
* learn the passive with *will*.
* talk about inventions from the past, everyday objects and future inventions.

Warm-up
* Books closed. Write the following on the board:
  1 *The MyShelter Foundation builds lots of houses.*
  2 *Lots of houses are built by the MyShelter Foundation.*
* Elicit the idea that 1 is an active sentence and 2 is passive.
* Elicit the fact that the passive is used when who or what is responsible for the action is less important to us than what it is that happens.

1
* Ask students to open their books at page 55.
* Tell students that the gapped sentences are from the text on page 54.
* Ask students to copy the sentences into their notebooks and complete them.
* Check answers.
* For further information and additional exercises, students can turn to page 103 of the **Grammar reference** section.

Answers

Present simple	
+	A small hole ¹**is cut** in the roof.
–	Moser lamps **aren't used** in the UK.
?	How much electricity **is saved** with these lamps?

Past simple	
+	Their homes **were** often **left** in the dark.
–	It ²**wasn't invented** by a famous scientist.
?	**Was** any special equipment **needed** to make it?

will	
+	The light ³**will be carried** through the water.
–	Normal light bulbs **won't be** completely **replaced** by Moser lamps.
?	**Will** Moser lamps **be used** in the new school?

1 c 2 a 3 b

Language note
The passive is most commonly used in formal written and spoken English.

2
* Read out the example sentence.
* Put students into pairs to complete the remaining sentences using the passive form of the verbs in bold. Ask them to check whether a singular or plural form of *be* is needed in each case.
* Check answers.

Answers
2 were developed   3 weren't introduced
4 are consumed   5 will be replaced   6 won't be sold

Optional activity
* Put students into pairs to write quiz questions using the past simple passive, e.g. *When was the TV invented?*
* Make different sets of pairs and ask students to do their quizzes.

3 🔊 **2.04** Ask students to describe the photos and to say what they think the objects shown in them are made from.
* Refer students to the texts.
* Choose the correct form of the verb in number 1 as an example.
* Ask students to work alone to complete the texts with the correct form of the verbs.
* Check answers. Challenge **stronger students** by asking them comprehension questions about the text, e.g. *What is special about the running shorts?*

Answers
1 are made   2 protect you   3 were used   4 helps
5 find   6 be studied   7 be displayed   8 understand
9 used

Game
* Play *The memory game* using the passive.
* See **Games bank** on pages 28–29.

Your turn

4
* Tell students they have to think of three objects to go into each of the three categories.
* Elicit the different passive forms that students will need to use in order to complete the task, e.g. *the TV was invented in the 20th century. Computers are used every day in schools and homes. Digital implants will be invented in the next 20 years.*
* While category two is simple, categories one and three are less so and will require some thought. Give students time to do some research online if necessary.

5
* Read out the example sentences.
* Put students into pairs to compare their lists and answer the questions. If students know neither when the objects were invented nor by whom, allow them to use their smartphones to look for this information online.

 Set Exercises 1, 2, 3 and 4 on page 48 of the **Workbook** for homework.

Listening and Vocabulary

Objectives
* listen to a radio report about unusual objects.
* learn and practise using modifiers.

A radio report

Warm-up
* Books closed. Ask students why they think we are attracted to buying certain objects. You could either discuss this with the class as a whole or put students into pairs to talk about it.
* Put some ideas on the board to help get students thinking: *Is it the appearance of the object that attracts us, the cost, the symbolic value of the object or the fact that everyone we know has one?*

1 💬 Ask students to open their books at page 56.
* Put students into pairs to answer the question about the objects in the photos.
* Do not check answers at this point. Students will do that in Exercise 2 by listening to the recording.

2 🔊 **2.05** Before you play the recording, put the word *stall* /stɔːl/ on the board and check that students understand that it refers to a stand at which particular goods are sold at a market or a covered area.
* Tell students they are going to listen to a reporter at a market in Brixton in London talking to stallholders (a person who owns or runs a stall) about the objects that they sell.
* Play the recording for students to check the answers that they gave in Exercise 1.
* Students can compare their answers in pairs before you check answers with the whole class.

Audioscript
Turn to page 179 for the audioscript.

> **Answer**
> **a)** reading light and heater – £250
> **b)** battery charger – £100
> **c)** fan – £5

3 🔊 **2.05** Refer students back to the objects pictured above Exercise 1, which are labelled a, b and c.
* Play the recording again for students to listen and match the objects with the sentences.
* Students can compare their answers in pairs before you check answers with the whole class.

> **Answers**
> 1 b   2 a, b   3 c   4 a   5 c   6 a

Optional activity
* Put students into pairs to share which of the three objects they would most like to own and why.
* Ask some students to report back to the class on what their partner said.

Modifiers

4 🔊 **2.06** Refer students to the words and phrases in the box. Explain that they are used in front of adjectives to modify the meaning of those adjectives, e.g. *extremely* when used in front of *tired* intensifies the expression of the speaker's tiredness. We imagine that someone who says they are *extremely tired* is even *more* tired than someone who simply says they are *tired*.
* Tell students they are going to listen to extracts from the recording in order to complete the gapped sentences with the words and phrases in the box.
* Play the recording.
* Students can compare their answers in pairs before you check answers with the class.

> **Answers**
> 2 really   3 ridiculously   4 extremely   5 kind of
> 6 much too   7 a bit   8 totally

> **Language note**
> Words such as *extremely, totally, really* and *ridiculously* tend to be used with heavy emphasis in informal conversation. Rather than rely on the words themselves to convey a sense of intensification, speakers customarily choose to emphasise the intensifying modifiers, e.g. *The new iPhone is <u>ridiculously</u> expensive.*

5 •   Ask students to look once more at the modifiers in Exercise 4.
* Students can work alone to decide what the modifiers do to the adjectives in each case, i.e. do they make them a little or a lot stronger in meaning?
* Students can compare their answers in pairs before you check answers with the class as a whole.

> **Answers**
> **a little stronger:** quite, kind of, a bit
> **a lot stronger:** much too, extremely, totally, ridiculously, really

Your turn

6 •   Read out the example sentence.
* Ask students to think of an unusual object they own and ask them to describe it using three expressions from Exercise 4.
* Put students into pairs to talk about the objects they chose to talk about.
* To **extend** the work on the vocabulary, you could ask students to turn to the **Vocabulary bank** on page 111 and do the exercises for *Modifiers*.

> Set Exercises 1, 2, 3 and 4 on page 49 of the **Workbook** for homework.
> You could also ask students to do some research online to find some more examples of objects which have two purposes. Students can then share what they find out with a partner at the beginning of the next lesson.

Objectives

- learn relative pronouns and clauses.
- practise using relative pronouns and clauses in a guessing game.

Warm-up

- Books closed. Write the following on the board:
  It's a great city. There are lots of things to do there.
- Combine the sentences, i.e. *It's a great city where there are lots of things to do.* Explain that the underlined word is a relative pronoun.

1
- Ask students to open their books at page 57.
- Tell students that the example sentences are from the listening on page 56.
- Ask students to copy the sentences into their notebooks. Put students into pairs to choose the correct options and answer the questions.
- Check answers.
- For further information and additional exercises, students can turn to page 103 of the **Grammar reference** section.

Answers

1 It's a great market **where** you can find all kinds of unusual things.
2 The heat comes from the light bulb in the middle and it's reflected by this part **which** you can see here.
3 I need something **that** I can put on my desk.
4 I wonder where the person **whose** stall it is can be.
5 They guy **who** you can see in the photo is a friend of mine.
6 I don't think the guy **that** I was talking to is going to sell a lot of battery chargers!
   a which, that   b where   c who, that   d whose

2
- Read out the information in the **Get it right!** box.
- Put students into pairs to complete the exercise.
- Point out that some words will need to be omitted from the sentences that students write. For example, in number 1, the word *here* is omitted because the word *where* provides us with the same information.
- Check answers.

Answers

2 This is the birthday present that my brother gave to me.
3 I really like the woman who we met at the market.
4 That's the man whose bike I bought last week.
5 Can you remember the name of the boy that we talked to here last week?
6 I really don't think much of the restaurant where we ate last night.

3
- Ask students to write sentences using the prompts.
- Put students into pairs to do this exercise.
- Check answers.

Answers

1 This is the person that I told / was telling you about yesterday.
2 I don't like the new teacher who has just started teaching Art.
3 My favourite market stall is the one which you can see on the left.
4 My aunt has a friend that sells handmade jewellery in the market.
5 I see that girl whose party we went to last night.
6 Over there is the shop where my brother works at weekends.

Intonation in relative clauses

1 🔊 2.07 Refer students to the sentences. Draw attention to the arrows which show either rising or falling intonation.
- Play the recording for students to listen to and repeat the sentences.

2 🔊 2.08 Play the recording for students to mark the rising and falling intonation on the stressed words in the sentences.

3 🔊 2.08 Play the recording for students to check their answers to Exercise 2 and repeat the sentences.

Answers

1 **Who's** the **per**son that you were **talk**ing to?
2 **Here** are the **tick**ets which I **got** for you.
3 **That's** the **man** who **gave** me a **lift**.
4 **That's** the ho**tel** where we **stayed** last **year**.
5 **Here** is the **char**ger that you **lent** me the other **day**.
6 **That's** the **guy** whose **stall** I **work** on at week**ends**.

4 Put students into pairs and ask them to practise saying the sentences in Exercise 2 with the correct intonation.

Game

- Play *The chain game* to practise relative pronouns and clauses.
- See **Games bank** on pages 28–29.

Your turn

4
- Give students time to write definitions. Help **weaker students** by giving them the beginning of their sentences, e.g. *She is the woman who …*
- Make sure students do not give away who or what their sentence describes, i.e. students should write *He is the computer scientist who created the World Wide Web* not *Tim Berners-Lee is the computer scientist who created the World Wide Web.*

5
- Read out the example.
- Put students into pairs to guess who or what their partner's sentences describe.

⟳ Set Exercises 1, 2, 3 and 4 on page 50 of the **Workbook** for homework.

Discover Culture

An invention that changed everything

Objectives

- watch a video about the invention of the Internet.
- talk about an invention that has revolutionised our lives.

Background

What we think of as the **Internet** gradually came into being in the 1960s and 1970s with the development of various computer network projects. It only became popular in the 1990s following the invention of the World Wide Web.

Warm-up

- Books closed.
- Write the following on the board:
  The Internet is …
  The Internet has …
- Elicit ways to finish the sentences, e.g. *The Internet is the best invention ever. The Internet has changed the world.*

1
- Ask students to open their books at page 58.
- Put students into pairs and ask them to write a definition of the Internet using the words in the box to help them. Students do not have to use the words in the box, however, and should attempt a definition that is simple and easy for someone who may never have heard of the Internet to understand.
- Elicit definitions from the class.

Suggested answer

The Internet is a global network of computers which allows people to communicate and share information with each other quickly and easily.

2 Refer students to the three questions.
- Put students into pairs to ask and answer the questions.

3 ▶ **5.2** Play the recording for students to note down how many of the devices, places and uses they discussed in Exercise 2 appear in it.

Videoscript

Narrator: The Internet! It's an amazing invention that has changed the world! The Internet is everywhere in our lives. In the early days, it was something you could only use at home or in an office. But nowadays, with wireless and mobile phone technology, we can access it wherever we go. But where did it come from, and how did it start? In the 1960s, scientists began to use computers for many things. These computers, which were big, slow, and expensive, did jobs that people couldn't. But one thing that computers couldn't do was talk to each other. So computer scientists created a network called ARPANET. This new network allowed computers to share tiny bits of information, something never quite possible before. And this was only the beginning. In 1971, one computer user sent a line of text to another user. And this was the first email!

In the 1980s and 90s, computers got smaller and cheaper. With more and more people using them, the networks got bigger, and people invented ways to share more information. Web pages, instant messaging, chat rooms: all of these were made to connect people. Those connections formed a kind of web, a world-wide web also known as 'The Internet'. And nothing was the same. Today, we use the Internet for everything: work, study, and play. The web connects us to each other and to information from around the world. And it will only grow. So, what's next for the world wide web? We asked journalist John Heilemann. He's been studying the Internet for years.

Heilemann: What I do know is the general direction of the changes that are coming for the web. Bigger, faster, more social, more pervasive, more all-consuming, more all-enveloping. Whether we like it or not, the web has taken on a life of its own. The dominoes have started their chain-reaction, with many, many more to fall.

Answers

1 desktop computers, laptops, mobile phones
2 at home, in the office, at work
3 searching for information, sharing information, sending emails, watching videos, playing games, chatting with friends

4
- Refer students to the sentences.
- Ask students to work alone to put the sentences in the order in which they appear in the video.

5 ▶ **5.2** Play the video again for students to check their answers to Exercise 4.

Answers

3 – 5 – 6 – 7 – 1 – 2 – 8 – 4

Your turn

6
- Put students into small groups.
- Students should decide on another invention that has had a revolutionary impact on human life, e.g. the wheel, the car, the television.
- Once students have decided on the invention, they make notes on it using the questions in the list to guide them.
- Students can then give a short presentation to the class.

 For homework, ask students to find out about how the invention of the World Wide Web led to an increase in the popularity of the Internet in the 1990s.

Reading An article

Objectives
- read an article about Facebook.
- learn communication phrases and phrasal verbs.
- talk about how I keep in touch with friends and family.

Background
Social networking can be traced back to the bulletin boards of the late 1970s, as well as the communities that developed on the World Wide Web in the mid 1990s. But it was not until the period 2004–2007, when social networks such as Facebook appeared, that social media began to be what it is today.

Warm up
- Books closed. Ask: *What are the most popular social networks for teenagers in your experience?*
- Elicit the names of some sites and then ask students to explain the attractions of the sites they have mentioned.

1
- Ask students to open their books at page 59.
- Refer students to the photo, the title of the article and the three possibilities for the subject matter of the article.
- Put students into pairs to choose one of the three. Remind students they should base their decision only on the photo and the title of the article.
- Elicit the answer, but do not confirm or reject it as students will check their answers in Exercise 2.

Language note
Uncool means *not fashionable* or *not desirable*.

2 🔊 **2.09** Ask students to read the article to check the answer they gave in Exercise 1.

Answer
3

3
- Refer students to sentences 1–6.
- Ask students to read the article again. Help **weaker students** by guiding them to the part of the text which will help them complete the true/false exercise.
- Check answers.
- Read out the information in the **FACT!** box. You could then ask students what they think of Facebook.

Answers
1 F (It appeared in 2004.) 2 T 3 T
4 F (Many teenagers don't want to have their parents as Facebook friends.)
5 T
6 F (The blogger isn't sure about it.)

Optional activity
- Put students into pairs.
- Students can share websites they like on their smartphones with each other, explaining why they like the site (e.g. the look of it, how easy it is to use, what you can do on it, the users of it) and how often they use it.
- Ask some students to report back to the class on their partner.

🔍 Explore communication phrases and phrasal verbs

4
- Ask students if they know of any phrases or phrasal verbs connected to the theme of communication. Students may produce phrases such as *switch on*, *log on*, *sign up* or *turn off*.
- Refer students to the highlighted words and phrases in the text.
- Ask students to work alone to match the words and phrases with the definitions.
- Help **weaker students** by giving them a translation in their own language of the highlighted words and phrases in the text.
- Check answers.
- To **extend** the work on the vocabulary, you could ask students to turn to the **Vocabulary Bank** on page 111 and do the exercises for *Explore communication phrases and phrasal verbs.*

Fast finishers
Students can write gapped sentences using the communications phrases and phrasal verbs from Exercise 4. You can then put these on the board and ask the class to complete them.

Answers
1 texting, tweeting with Twitter, making a Skype™ video call, emailing 2 kept in touch, lost touch 3 track down, catch up 4 chat

Optional activity
- Put students into pairs (A and B).
- Student A defines a communications phrase or phrasal verb from Exercise 4 for their partner to guess.
- Students swap roles and continue in this way until all the new phrases have been defined.

Your turn

5
- Tell students how you prefer to keep in touch with friends and family. Explain your choice.
- Give students a couple of minutes to order the methods of communication in the list in order of preference.
- Put students into pairs to compare their orders.
- Ask some students to report back to the class on how their partner prefers to communicate with friends and family.

 Set Exercise 5 on page 50 of the **Workbook** for homework.
You could also ask students to do a survey to find out whether the answer to the question of whether or not Facebook is uncool among their peer group is yes or no. Students can share their result of their survey at the beginning of the next lesson.

Speaking Buying a gadget

Objectives

- watch teenagers talking about their favourite gadget.
- listen to a teenager talk to a sales assistant.
- practise asking and answering questions about gadgets.

Warm-up

- Books closed. Explain the meaning of *technophile* (a person who enjoys using and is enthusiastic about technology) and *technophobe* (a person who fears, dislikes and avoids using technology).
- Ask students which of the two categories they fit into.

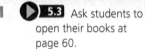 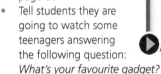

Real talk: What's your favourite gadget?

1 ▶ **5.3** Ask students to open their books at page 60.
- Tell students they are going to watch some teenagers answering the following question: *What's your favourite gadget?*
- Play the video for students to note down the gadget that each teenager most enjoys using as well as why they enjoy using it.
- Check answers.

Videoscript

Narrator: What's your favourite gadget?
Speaker 1: Probably my tablet. The new ones are designed more like big phones but I can still take it everywhere. I actually like it better than my phone because it's got a nicer camera. It's also made so you can use it outside, to take pictures in the rain or in more extreme weather.
Speaker 2: Hmmm… that's a hard question. I'm sure everyone says their phone. But not me. I don't even have a phone. I would say my miniature reading light. I share a room with my brother and since he always goes to bed early, I need my light to read. The bulb lasts forever.
Speaker 3: My phone, of course! I couldn't live without it! Could you?
Speaker 4: I like to go camping a lot, so I'd say my flashlight is my favourite gadget. It's made for long backpacking trips so it's light and compact. The best thing is that it doesn't need batteries. You just have to wind up the side handle and it turns on.
Speaker 5: I'd have to say my stress ball is my favourite gadget. Does that count as a gadget? It's made of this strange material. You can squeeze it really hard and then it just pops back into shape. I don't know why, but it always makes me feel better!
Speaker 6: My favourite gadget is my alarm clock because it's designed for people like me who don't like to get up in the morning. Basically, to turn it off, you have to throw it against the wall. I almost always wake up by the third try.
Narrator: What's *your* favourite gadget?

Suggested answers

Speaker 1: tablet – she can take it everywhere with her, it's better than a mobile phone because it's got a nicer camera
Speaker 2: miniature reading light – he shares a room with his brother who goes to bed early
Speaker 3: phone – she can't live without it
Speaker 4: flashlight – he likes going camping a lot, it doesn't need batteries
Speaker 5: stress ball – it makes him feel better
Speaker 6: alarm clock – she doesn't like waking up or getting up, it's difficult it turn it off

2 • Put students into pairs to ask and answer the question.
- Encourage students to ask additional questions and to develop a conversation.

3 **2.10** Tell students they are going to listen to Casey talking to a sales assistant.
- Read out the question.
- Play the recording.
- Students listen and answer the question.
- As the answer is only one word, encourage **stronger students** to give more information about what was said in the recording.

Answer

a smartphone

4 • Refer students to the phrases in the *Useful language* box.
- Students can in pairs to complete the conversation using the phrases in the *Useful language* box.
- Ask **stronger students** to try to complete the gaps in the conversation without looking at the phrases in box.

5 **2.10** Play the recording for students to check their answers.

Answers

2 how much memory **3** easy to use **4** Has it got a
5 What's the sound like **6** does the battery last
7 you show me

6 Ask students to work in pairs to act out the conversation in Exercise 4.
- Students can act out the conversation twice, taking a different part each time.

7 Remind students that *WiFi* is pronounced /ˈwaɪ.faɪ/.
- Give students some time to plan what they want to say.
- Students then act out their conversations.
- Monitor while students are practising their conversations. Check that they are using the phrases from the *Useful language* box.

For homework, ask students to do a survey among their friends and family to find out which gadgets are the most popular.

Writing An online review

Objectives

* read a review of a product.
* learn phrases used in reviews of products.
* write a review of a product.

Warm-up

* Books closed. Put students into pairs. Ask them to tell each other about the last technological product they bought and whether online reviews of the particular product influenced their decision to buy it.
* Ask some students to report back to the class on what their partner said.

1
* Ask students to open their books at page 61.
* Refer students to Kris's review of the headphones shown in the picture.
* Ask students to read the final sentence in the review to answer the question. You could then ask them to read the review as a whole to find the specific phrases Kris uses in her review which indicate her approval of the headphones, e.g. *they look really cool, the sound is well balanced, another good feature, great value for money* or *perfect for me*.
* Students then read the biography to check their answers.

Answer

yes

2
* Refer students to the headings in the box. Check students' understanding of *ease of use*, which means *how easy something is to use*, and the adjective *overall*, which means *in general*, e.g. *the overall winner*.
* Help students do this exercise by eliciting the sort of information you would expect to see in a sentence or paragraph entitled *design, performance,* etc.
* Ask students to read the review again.
* Put students into pairs and ask them to match the headings in the box with the different parts of the review.
* Check answers.

Answers

2 Design 3 Performance 4 Ease of use
5 Extra features 6 Overall opinion
Yes, the order of the headings is important.

3
* Read out the information about phrases used in reviews of products in the *Useful language* box.
* Check students' understanding of the phrase *comes in*, which means *available in*, e.g. *These smartphones come in five colours: red, blue, black, white and grey.*
* Ask students to work alone to find further examples of phrases used in reviews in the review in Exercise 1.
* Check answers.

Answers

They **are available** in black and red with long red cables and **look** really cool.
The headphones **come with** a travel case and a cable clip.

4
* Do the first sentence as example.
* Ask students to work alone to complete the remaining sentences using the words and phrases in the box.
* Check answers.

Fast finishers

Students can translate the words and phrases in the *Useful language* box into their own language.

Answers

1 comes in 2 available in; look 3 made of
4 come with

 # Get Writing

PLAN

5
* Students should do their planning in class. The writing can either be done in class or at home.
* Tell students they are going to write a review of a product.
* Give students a couple of minutes to choose a product to review.
* Refer students back to the headings in Exercise 2 and then ask them to work alone to make notes. If you choose to do the writing in class, encourage students to use their smartphones to look up information about the product they are going to review online.

WRITE

6
* Tell students to use Kris's review as a model to follow.
* Give students ten minutes to complete the writing task. Students should write between 140 and 160 words.
* Monitor while students are writing. Help with grammar and vocabulary as necessary.

CHECK

7
* Tell students that it is very important that they check their writing in order to look for ways to improve its content, style and structure.
* Give students a few minutes to look through their reviews and check them against the points here.
* Collect students' reviews and mark them.

 Set Exercises 1, 2, 3 and 4 on page 52 and Exercises 5, 6, 7, 8, 9, 10 and 11 on page 53 of the **Workbook** for homework.
You could also ask students to look at some English-language reviews of gadgets online and to make a note of any phrases or words which are commonly in the reviews. Students can then share these words and phrases with the class in the next lesson and you can discuss, if necessary, the meaning of any difficult ones.

6 Celebrate in style

Unit aims

I can ...

- talk about a celebration.
- understand magazine articles about special celebrations in different countries.
- use *-ing* and infinitive forms correctly.
- understand a travel programme about festivals around the world.
- make offers and requests.
- write a description of a celebration.

Unit contents

Vocabulary	Celebrations
	Verbs and prepositions
	Descriptive adjectives
	Words in context
Reading	A magazine article
	◑ Let's celebrate
	An article
Language focus	*-ing* forms
	Infinitives
	Infinitives vs. *-ing* forms
Listening	A travel programme
Discover culture	◑ Like father, like daughter
Speaking	Offers and requests
	◑ Real talk: What's the worst party you've ever been to?
Pronunciation	*to* and *too*
Writing	A description
	so or *too* + adjective
CLIL	History: 4th July celebration, USA
	◑ Reliving history

Background

Carnival is a traditional festive season which takes place at the beginning of each year, usually in February. The most famous carnival is held in Rio de Janeiro, with about two million people attending. Another important carnival takes place in Venice, where people wear elaborate masks and dress in beautiful costumes.

Be curious

- Books closed. Tell students briefly about the last party you attended or organised, e.g.: *Last Saturday it was my brother's birthday. We had a party for him. All his friends came and everyone enjoyed themselves.*
- At this point you revise the words *celebrate* and *celebration*.
- Ask students to think about the types of parties (big or small) that people organise and why, e.g. a birthday party, a wedding reception, a New Year's Eve party, a carnival party.
- Ask students to open their books at page 62.
- Give them a moment to look at the photo and then ask them to describe it briefly.
- Put students into pairs to answer the three questions.
- Check answers with the class.
- Tell students that the themes of Unit 6 are organising and enjoying different types of celebration.

Suggested answers

- The woman wearing a fancy red and gold costume is probably dancing in a street at night.
- I think this celebration is probably a carnival, possibly in Rio, because the woman is wearing a beautiful costume and she is dancing outside in the street.
- I'd like to join the carnival. The woman looks as if she is having a great time.

CEFR

SKILL AREA	GOAL	EXERCISE
Listening	OVERALL LISTENING COMPREHENSION	3 p63 1–2 p70
	UNDERSTANDING INTERACTION	3–6 p70
	LISTENING TO MEDIA AND RECORDINGS	1–3 p66 1–5 p68
Reading	READING FOR INFORMATION & ARGUMENT	1–4 p64 1–4 69 1–4 p71
Speaking	CONVERSATION	5 p68
	INFORMAL DISCUSSION (WITH FRIENDS)	5–6 p66 4 p67
	GOAL-ORIENTED COOPERATION (e.g. Repairing a car, discussing a document, organising an event)	4 p70 7–8 p70
	INFORMATION EXCHANGE	4 p63 7 p64 5 p69
Writing	CREATIVE WRITING	5–7 p71
Communicative language competence	VOCABULARY RANGE	5–6 p64 4 p66 4 p69
	GRAMMATICAL ACCURACY	1–5 p65 1–3 p67
	PHONOLOGICAL CONTROL	1 p63 3 p67 6 p70
Communication strategies	IDENTIFYING CUES AND INFERRING	4 p66 4 p69

Vocabulary Celebrations

Objectives

- learn vocabulary to describe celebrations.
- listen to people talking about different types of celebration.
- talk about the celebrations I enjoy the most.

Warm-up

- Books closed. Ask: *What are the most important events in life?*
- Elicit students' ideas and put them on the board, e.g. *births, important birthdays, weddings, leaving school, anniversaries,* etc.

Background

Prom refers to a formal dance, usually one held to celebrate the end of high school or college, to which students wear suits and dresses. Proms have long been associated with American high school culture, and feature prominently in films and TV dramas from the USA.

1 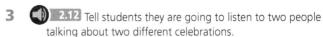 **2.11** Ask students to open their books at page 63.

- Put students into pairs to match the activities with the photos. Tell them that some expressions could describe both photos.
- If you have the *Presentation Plus* software, put the pictures on the board and ask students to come up to the board in turn to match the activities with the photos.
- Play the recording for students to listen and repeat the phrases.
- Check the answers, asking student to justify their choices.

Suggested answers

The carnival: set off fireworks, make special food
The prom: give a present
Both: put up decorations, dress up for the occasion, play music, hold a contest, have a good time

Background

The Carnival of Cultures (or 'Karneval der Kulturen' in German) is a free festival which takes place in late May or early June in Berlin. It has taken place annually since 1966 and celebrates the cultural diversity of the German capital.

2
- Refer students to the gapped text about the Carnival of Cultures.
- Ask students to read the text through once to get a general idea of its content.
- Students should then work alone to complete the text with the correct form of the phrases from Exercise 1.
- Check answers.

Answers

2 put up decorations   3 set off fireworks
4 make special food   5 give a present   6 play music
7 has a good time

Background

The festival referred to in the recording in Exercise 3 is **La Diada de Sant Jordi** (literally, *the day of St. George*), with Sant Jordi being the patron saint of Catalonia. The tradition on this day is to celebrate love.

3 **2.12** Tell students they are going to listen to two people talking about two different celebrations.

- Ask students to copy the table into their notebooks.
- Play the recording for students to complete the table with the information about the celebrations.
- Check answers.

Audioscript

Juan: There is a very special festival here in Barcelona in Spain. It's held on April 23rd and it's National Book Day. Everybody buys books and roses and gives them as presents to the people they love, or good friends. The whole town has a great time. It's really different because at this party everybody is holding a book or a rose. Some people even hold writing contests. The person who writes the best short story wins a prize.

Luana: When I was younger, I loved my birthday. I always had a cake and a party and my parents made special food for me and my friends to eat. Everybody always dressed up for the occasion in their very best clothes. But as you get older, birthdays are not as much fun as before. People still wish you a happy birthday but now it's not as important. We don't put up decorations but my mum still makes me a cake!

Answers

	Celebration	Activities
Juan	National Book Day (April 23)	buy books and roses and give them as presents; writing contests
Luana	birthday	have a cake and a party; make special food; dress up; put up decorations

Optional activity

- Put students into pairs to talk about the things they like and dislike doing when celebrating or organising celebrations.
- Encourage students to use the phrases in Exercise 1, where possible e.g. *I love giving people presents and putting up decorations, but I don't like making special food.*

Your turn

4
- Refer students to the questions.
- Put students into pairs to ask and answer the questions.
- Ask some students to report back to the class on which festivals their partner celebrates and how he or she likes to celebrate them.
- To **extend** the work on the vocabulary, you could ask students to turn to the **Vocabulary bank** on page 112 and do the exercises for *Celebrations*.

Set Exercises 1, 2, 3, 4 and 5 on page 57 of the **Workbook** for homework.

Reading A magazine article

Objectives

- read an article about proms and morps.
- learn verbs and prepositions.
- talk about school parties.

Background

See the **Background** note on page 93 above.

Warm-up

- Books closed. Ask: *What's the best party you've ever been to and why?*
- Put students into pairs to ask and answer the question.

1 💬 Ask students to open their books at page 64.
- Put students into pairs and ask them to look at the photos and describe the kind of celebrations the photos show. Students may say things such as: *The celebrations must be formal because the teenagers are wearing dressed and suits. One of the boys is playing music and everyone is wearing T-shirts.*

2 🔊 **2.13** Ask students to read the article to find out what the difference between a prom and a morp is.
- Check answers.
- Refer students to the information in the **FACT!** box. You could then ask students why people in other countries seem so keen to copy aspects of American culture.

Answer

A morp is organised by the students, so it's cheaper and more informal.

3
- Refer students to headings 1–6.
- Ask students to read the article again.
- Students can then work alone to match the headings with the paragraphs.
- Help **weaker students** with this exercise by reminding them that they should scan the article for key words, i.e. they should either look for the actual words in the headings or related words.
- Check answers.

Answers

2 E   3 A   4 F   5 C   6 B

4
- Ask students to read the text again.
- Put students into pairs to decide which sentences are true and which false. Students should correct the false sentences.
- Check answers.

Answers

1 F (Prom night is also celebrated in the UK.)
2 T   3 T   4 T
5 F (Students can party all night and carry on the next day.)
6 F (The writer says it doesn't matter if you like a prom or a morp.)

🔍 Explore verbs and prepositions

5
- Refer students to the verbs in the box.
- Ask students to find these verbs in the article (they are highlighted in bold in the text) and to note down which prepositions follow them. Point out that some of these verbs can be followed by more than one preposition (e.g. *look at, work for*), but that we're only interested in the ones used in the text).
- Check answers.

Answers

recover from   arrive at   work with   prepare for   agree on look forward to

6
- Read out the example sentence.
- Ask students to work alone to complete the remaining sentences using the correct form of the verbs in Exercise 5.
- Students can compare their answers in pairs before you check answers with the class as a whole.
- To **extend** the work on the vocabulary, you could ask students to turn to the **Vocabulary bank** on page 112 and do the exercises for *Explore verbs and prepositions*.

Answers

2 work with   3 agree on   4 recover from   5 arrived at
6 prepared ... for

💬 Your turn

7
- Refer students to the example sentences.
- Put students into pairs to ask and answer the questions.
- Encourage **stronger students** to develop conversations beyond the questions on the page by asking one another questions that arise in the course of their discussion.
- Ask some students to report back to the class on what their partner said. If you have a multicultural class, take this opportunity to discuss with the class as a whole the different types of school-leaving party that are organised in the countries that the students are from.

You can show this video as either a lead-in or a follow-up to the Language Focus 1 lesson.

▶ 6.1 Let's celebrate

- ▶ Ask: *Do you have a favourite season? Why is it your favourite?*
- Elicit student's answers and then put students into pairs to ask and answer the questions.
- Play the video.
- Students watch it and say what they learn about seasonal festivals in the video.
- Then ask students which of the festivals in the video they would like to attend.
- See page 127 for further activities you can do with this video.

 Set Exercises 1, 2, 3 and 4 on page 61 and Exercises 5 and 6 on page 58 of the **Workbook** for homework.

Language focus 1 *-ing* forms

Objectives
- learn about *-ing* forms.
- design my ideal school-leaving party.

Warm-up
- Books closed. Write the following on the board: *I enjoy celebrate my birthday*.
- Ask: *What is wrong with the sentence?*
- Elicit or introduce the correct sentence: *I enjoy celebrating my birthday*.
- Highlight the *-ing* part of the verb and tell students they are going to look at different ways the *-ing* form is used.

1
- Ask students to open their books at page 65.
- Tell students that the gapped sentences are from the text on page 64.
- Ask students to copy the sentences into their notebooks and complete them.
- Check answers.
- Students can then match the completed sentences with the rules.
- For further information and additional exercises, students can turn to page 104 of the **Grammar reference** section.

Answers
1 Teens have prom parties to celebrate **leaving** school.
2 **Hiring** DJs, organising food and reserving hotels can often cost a fortune.
3 Students might agree on **organising** a Roman theme.
1 c 2 a 3 b

2
- Refer students to the verbs in the box and read out the example sentence.
- Put students into pairs and ask them to complete the remaining sentences using the *-ing* form of the verbs in the box.
- When checking the answers to this exercise, ask students to refer to the rules in Exercise 1 and explain why each *-ing* form is needed in sentences 2–8.

Answers
2 finishing 3 Being 4 spending 5 meeting
6 shopping 7 Having 8 Thinking

3
- Ask students to look back at the completed sentences in Exercise 2. Students should decide if these sentences are true for them. If they are not, they should rewrite them so that they are.
- Put students into pairs to compare their ideas.
- Ask some students to report back to the class on what their partner said.

4
- Read out the information in the **Get it right!** box. Encourage students to learn verbs and phrases together. Prepositions are often very different between languages and so it is a good idea to learn verb and preposition combinations as complete phrases. Refer students back to the *Explore Vocabulary* section on page 64 to make this point.
- Refer students to the sentence beginnings and the example sentence.
- Ask students to work alone to complete the sentences so that they are true for them. Point out that they must use the *-ing* form of the verb.
- Put students into pairs to compare their ideas.

Fast finishers
Students can write additional sentences that are true for them using *be interested in / don't mind / spend money on* and the *-ing* form of the verb. Collect and check the sentences.

Game
- Play *Correct the sentence* using *-ing* forms.
- See **Games bank** on pages 28–29.

Your turn

5
- Put students into small groups to organise their ideal school-leaving party.
- Students decide whether the party will be formal or informal. They should also decide the following: where and when it will take place; the clothes people have to wear; the food and drink that will be served; and the music and dancing that people will enjoy. Students can also give the party a particular name.
- Ask students to present their plan for a school-leaving party to the class. Tell the groups that they are trying to convince the others that their party is the best and so they should be as persuasive as they can be.
- The class can then decide which party sounds the most fun.

 Set Exercises 1, 2, 3 and 4 on page 58 of the **Workbook** for homework.
Students could also ask their friends to describe in English their own ideal school-leaving party. Students can then share this information in small groups at the beginning of the next lesson.

Listening and Vocabulary

Objectives

- listen to a travel programme.
- learn descriptive adjectives.
- invent a festival or special event.

A travel programme

Warm-up

- Books closed. Ask: *Which is the best season in which to have a festival? Why?*
- Put students into pairs to answer the questions.
- Ask some students to report back to the class on what their partner said.

Background

The annual **International Ice and Snow Sculpture Festival** takes place in Harbin in north-east China. It starts in early January and lasts one month. Thousands of people help artists create enormous colourful sculptures of figures, animals and buildings.
The **Battle of the Oranges** food fight takes place every spring in the town of Ivrea in the north of Italy. The celebration is based on a medieval legend and involves teams throwing oranges at each other. It lasts three days.
The **Monkey Buffet Festival** is held in the Lopburi province of Thailand. The annual festival offers food and drink for thousands of monkeys in order to thank them for attracting tourists to the area.

1 🗩 Ask students to open their books at page 66.
- Put students into pairs to look at the photos and answer the questions.
- Do not check answers at this point. Students will do that in Exercise 2 by listening to the recording.

2 🔊 2.14 Tell students they are going to listen to a travel programme about the festivals in the photographs.
- Play the recording for students to check their answers to Exercise 1.

Audioscript

Turn to page 179 for the audioscript.

Answers

a Harbin, in northern China – artists make sculptures
b Ivrea in Italy – people throw oranges at each other
c Lopburi in Thailand – people offer food to monkeys

3 🔊 2.14 Refer students to statements 1–8.
- Play the recording again for students to match the festivals with the statements.
- Students can compare their answers in pairs before you play the recording again for students to check their answers.

Answers

1 a 2 b 3 c 4 b 5 c 6 a 7 b 8 a

Descriptive adjectives

4 🔊 2.15 Read out the adjectives in the box. Drill the pronunciation of these words.
- Put students into pairs to replace the words in bold in the sentences with the adjectives in the box.
- Check answers.

Answers

1 peaceful 2 crowded 3 atmospheric 4 colourful
5 stunning 6 traditional 7 scary 8 impressive

Language note

Descriptive adjectives refers to a class of adjectives, which give information about the quality of the noun being described, e.g. *a blue car*, *an angry man* or *an expensive dress*.

Your turn

5
- Ask students to work alone to think of a festival or a special event, such as the ones which feature in the recording of the travel programme.
- Give students a few minutes to make notes on their festival. They should give it a name, describe what happens, what people wear, eat and drink and how long the festival lasts.
- Monitor and help with vocabulary as necessary. Encourage students to use the adjectives from Exercise 4.

6
- Put students into small groups.
- Ask students to take it in turns to describe their festivals to each other. Students should attempt to persuade the rest of their group that theirs is the festival to attend.
- Once each student has had a turn, the group agrees on a festival to go to. You may want to suggest that each group nominated a *chairperson*, whose responsibility it will be to guide this discussion. The chairperson can then report back to the class.
- To **extend** the work on the vocabulary, you could ask students to turn to the **Vocabulary bank** on page 112 and do the exercises for *Descriptive adjectives*.

Optional activity

- Put students into small groups. Students can use their smartphones to research the following British festivals:
  1 Hogmanay in Scotland
  2 The National Eisteddfod in Wales
  3 The Edinburgh Festival
  4 The Notting Hill Carnival
  5 The Glastonbury music festival
- Give each group a different festival to research.
- Give students 5–10 minutes to find out about the festival you have allotted them.
- Students then write a short report about their festivals (saying what it is, what happens and when it happens), which they can then present to the class.

 Set Exercises 1, 2, 3 and 4 on page 59 of the **Workbook** for homework.

Language focus 2 Infinitives

Objectives
* learn about the use of infinitives.
* learn when to use infinitives and when to use *-ing* forms.
* talk about the Anime and Gaming Convention.

Warm-up
* Books closed. Write *to be, to do, to go* on the board.
* Elicit that these forms are known as *infinitives*.
* You could then ask students to write sentences with these infinitives.

1
* Ask students to open their books at page 67.
* Tell students that the example sentences are from the listening on page 66.
* Put students into pairs to copy the sentences into their notebooks and complete them with the verbs in the box.
* Check answers and then ask students to match the sentences with the rules.
* For further information and additional exercises, students can turn to page 104 of the **Grammar reference** section.

Answers
1 It's best **to see** it in the dark.
2 Go ice-swimming if you really want **to feel** the cold.
3 If you decide **to come** and see the festival for yourself, bring warm clothes.
4 It's great **to watch** them doing that.
a 1, 4 b 2, 3

2
* Refer students to the infinitive form of the verbs in the box.
* Read out the example sentence.
* Ask students to work alone to complete the remaining sentences.
* Students can compare answers in pairs before you check answers with the class as a whole.

Fast finishers
Students can write sentences about what they find easy to do and what they find difficult to do. Collect and check students' sentences.

Answers
2 to go 3 to do 4 to see 5 to have 6 to raise
7 to hold 8 to speak

Infinitives vs. *-ing* forms

Background
See the **Background** note on page 42.

3 🔊 2.16 Elicit when the infinitive is used and when the *-ing* form is used, e.g. infinitives are used after adjectives, *-ing* forms after prepositions. It will help **weaker students** complete Exercise 3 if you put these ideas on the board for them to refer to.
* Choose the correct form of the verb in number 1 as an example. Ask why *to get* is the correct choice (**Answer**: the infinitive is used after adjectives).

* Put students into pairs to complete the exercise.
* Encourage students to underline the word(s) before each gap. It will help students to focus on how the use of either the infinitive or *-ing* form is dependent upon what goes immediately before it in the sentence.
* While checking answers, ask students to give reasons for their choice of one verb form over the other.

Answers
1 to get 2 reading 3 to go 4 buying 5 to see
6 gaming 7 Dressing up 8 looking 9 to go
10 booking

Say it right!

to and *too*

1 🔊 2.17 Write *to* and *too* on the board. Tell students that they are going to learn the difference in pronunciation between *to* and *too*. Play the recording for students to listen and repeat the sentences.

2 🔊 2.18 Play the recording. Students listen to the sentences and say how *to* and *too* are pronounced.

3 🔊 2.18 Play the recording for students to check their answers to Exercise 2 and repeat the sentences.

4
* Put students into pairs and ask them to practise saying the sentences in Exercise 2 with the correct pronunciation of *to* and *too*.
* Monitor to check that students are pronouncing the words correctly.

Your turn

4
* Put students into pairs to ask and answer the questions.
* Ask some students to report back to the class on what their partner said.

> Set Exercises 1, 2, 3, 4, 5 and 6 on page 60 of the **Workbook** for homework.
> You could also ask students to write a short dialogue between two people who are organising a school-leaving party. Students should aim to include as many sentences with infinitives and *-ing* forms as they can, e.g. *Who do we want to invite? I'd like to dress up. We can't have a party without music.* Collect and check students' work in the next lesson.

Discover Culture

Like father like daughter

Objectives
- watch a video about cliff diving in Mexico.
- talk about whether I would like to try cliff diving.

Warm-up
- Books closed. Ask students to name some water sports. Write these sports on the board, e.g. *water skiing*, *diving*, *surfing*.
- Ask students if they have ever done any of these sports or if they would one day like to try them.

Background
Acapulco is a port and a resort in southern Mexico on the Pacific coast, well-known for its cliffs and beaches.

1 💬 Ask students to open their books at page 68.
- Refer students to the photos and put them into pairs to answer the question.
- Do not confirm or reject students' ideas at this point. Students will check their answers in Exercise 2.

2 ▶ 6.2 Refer students to the phrases a–c.
- Tell students they are going to watch the video to first check their answers to Exercise 1 and then decide which of the three phrases best describes the subject matter of the video.
- Check answers.

Videoscript

Narrator: This is Acapulco in Mexico. It's famous for its beaches and boating and also for its cliff divers. The tradition of cliff diving in Acapulco started in the 1920s when fishermen used to dive into the water to find their fishing lures. They soon began to challenge each other to climb higher and higher, and now the divers dive from heights of up to 30 metres! One of the most recognised cliff divers is José Luis. He's been cliff diving for 25 years, and because his entry into the water is so precise, he's called *The Knife*. For nearly 80 years, cliff diving was a tradition that involved men only until today. Now The Knife's daughter, Iris, is ready to change this tradition. She wants to be a cliff diver, just like her father.

Iris: I always wanted to be just like him. He could do different dives, and I wanted to do special dives just like him.

Narrator: Iris' mother supports her, but says:

Mother: I've told her that school is first. If she does well, we will allow her to continue to dive. If her grades begin to slip, that's the end of the diving.

Narrator: So every weekend, Iris practises.

Iris: When I'm standing 59 feet up on the cliff, I'm nervous and afraid.

Narrator: But now she is ready to dive from higher up the cliff. It's the morning of Iris' highest dive – 22 metres. The tourists are excited to see Iris perform this record-breaking jump. Iris is ready to dive. Will other female divers follow in their fathers' footsteps, like Iris? Has Iris started a whole new tradition of female cliff divers? It looks that way.

Answers
c

3 ▶ 6.2 Tell students that sentences 1–5 all refer to the video and that some are true and some false.
- Put students into pairs and ask them to correct the sentences they think are false.
- Play the video for students to check their answers.

Suggested answers
1 F (a man climbing up a cliff) 2 T
3 F (Iris's mother talking about school and education)
4 F (we can't see Iris's mother) 5 T

4 ▶ 6.2 Refer students to the incomplete sentences.
- Play the video again for students to complete the sentences. You may need to play the video twice to help **weaker students**.
- Students can compare answers in pairs before you check answers.

Answers
2 30 metres 3 80 years 4 school
5 nervous and afraid 6 22 metres

Your turn

5
- Read out the questions and then refer students to the example answers.
- Put students into pairs to ask and answer the questions.

Optional activity
- Ask students to imagine that they are cliff divers.
- Give them time to think about what they do to stay calm before they do a big dive, e.g. make their minds go blank, take several deep breaths, count to ten.
- Put students into pairs and ask them to tell each other about their ideas.

 For homework, ask students to do some research online to find out more about the extreme sport of cliff diving. They could find out where cliff diving is popular and what international championships exist. Students can share what they find out with a partner at the beginning of the next lesson.

Reading An article

Objectives
* read an article about a coming-of-age celebration in Korea.
* learn words in context.
* talk about coming-of-age festivals in my country.

Background
The phrase **coming of age** refers to the age or the occasion at which an individual is formally seen to become an adult. It is used widely, in a number of contexts, to indicate a growth of maturity, e.g. *The players who won the Under 20 World Cup with Italy are now coming of age. People who were young teens when Facebook first appeared in 2004 are now coming of age.*

Warm up
* Books closed. Write the stages of life on the board. Elicit or introduce the different stages and write them on the board, e.g. *birth, infancy, childhood, adolescence, early adulthood, middle age, old age, death.*
* Ask students why we mark transitions between these stages of our lives, e.g. in order to emphasise, in either a public or private way, that going from one stage of life to another is important and an occasion for celebration and reflection.

1  Ask students to open their books at page 69.
* Refer students to the photos.
* Put students into pairs and ask them to answer the three questions. Do not confirm or reject students' ideas at this point. Student will check their answers in Exercise 2.

2 **2.19** Ask students to read the article to check their answers from Exercise 1.

Suggested answers
These people are 20 or will be 20 before the end of the year. They're celebrating a coming-of-age day. They are wearing traditional clothes and are bowing to their parents out of respect.

3
* Refer students to sentences 1–6.
* Ask students to read the article again and then put them in pairs to choose the correct options in each of the sentences.
* Check answers.
* Read out the information in the **FACT!** box. You could then ask students what they think of the idea, prevalent in what we call *the West*, that 18 marks the beginning of adulthood. Is that age correct? Should it be older or younger?

Answers
1 has   2 watch and take part in   3 similar
4 both serious and fun   5 can   6 losing popularity

Optional activity
* Ask: *Why do you think we feel the need to celebrate particular events or days in our lives?*
* Put students into small groups to discuss their responses to this question. Ideas could include the following: to get together with friends and family; to mark special moments in life; to create memories.
* Ask one student from each group to report back to the class on the discussion their group had.

Explore words in context

4
* Refer students to the highlighted words in the article and then ask them to match those words with the definitions in 1–8.
* Students can compare their answers in pairs before you check answers with the class as a whole.
* Check that students are able to pronounce the words, particularly *aware* /əˈweə/, *pledge* /pledʒ/ and *unique* /juːˈniːk/.

Answers
1 well-liked   2 become aware of   3 snaps   4 bow
5 fears   6 unique   7 pledge   8 signifies

Your turn

5
* Refer students to the six questions.
* Give students time to read through and think about the questions. Help **weaker students** by allowing them to make some notes.
* Put students into pairs to ask and answer the questions.

Optional activity
* Refer students to the final paragraph of the article, which says that *there are fears that the traditional coming-of-age day festival is being lost in Korea.*
* Ask students if the loss of traditions is something to be sad about or whether we should accept that as cultures develop over time it is perhaps unwise to attempt to preserve everything from the past.
* Put students into small groups and ask them to discuss whether we should do things as we have always done them or should feel free to change them and adapt to new circumstances.

Speaking Offers and requests

Objectives

- watch teenagers taking about the worst party they have ever been to.
- listen to teenagers organising a birthday party.
- practise offering to do something and making requests.

Warm-up

- Books closed. Tell students about the worst party you have ever been to. It doesn't matter if you've never been to a bad one, all you need do is establish the idea, e.g. *It was my sister's 21st birthday party. Oh, it was awful! We were all in the garden. It started to rain. The tent blew over, all the food was washed away and my sister fell over and broke her arm!*

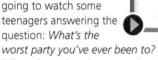

Real talk: What's the worst party you've ever been to?

1 ▶ **6.3** Ask students to open their books at page 70.
   - Tell students they are going to watch some teenagers answering the question: *What's the worst party you've ever been to?*
   - Tell students that they are going to match the teenagers in the video with the reasons in the list.
   - Play the video.
   - Students work alone to complete the exercise.
   - Check answers.

Videoscript

Narrator: What's the worst party you've ever been to?
Speaker 1: Well, that's easy. It was a party last month. Only two other people showed up. We thought it was Saturday night instead of Friday night. I don't know how that happened.
Speaker 2: Our spring dance at school. The sound system broke right at the beginning of the evening. That stopped the dancing! After that, we all just stood around hoping someone would fix it. But it never happened, and we all just went home.
Speaker 3: My own party last month. Usually, I love getting ready for parties, making the food, selecting the music, telling my friends about it. But this time, it all went wrong. In the end, I had to cancel the party.
Speaker 4: My cousin's wedding reception after her wedding. It was horrible and funny at the same time. They had this huge chocolate fountain. They wanted to let it flow all night. And it did, but then it didn't stop! There was chocolate everywhere for days.
Speaker 5: Hmm … probably this costume party I went to recently. Normally, I like dressing up, but someone told me the wrong theme. I thought it was an 'ocean' theme instead of a 'wild west' theme, so I showed up in a lobster outfit. So there I was with all of the cowboys.
Speaker 6: Probably my best friend's birthday. We planned to spend the evening at her house with a bunch of our friends, watching movies and eating pizza. But then her parents showed up and decided to stay and watch a movie with us. It just wasn't the same after that.
Narrator: What's the worst party *you've* ever been to?

Answers

Speaker 1: d   **Speaker 2:** c   **Speaker 3:** b   **Speaker 4:** f
Speaker 5: a   **Speaker 6:** e

2 - Put students into pairs to ask and answer the question.
   - Ask some students to report back to the class on their partner.

3 🔊 **2.20** Tell students they are going to listen to Helen talking to Andy.
   - Read out the question.
   - Play the recording.
   - Students listen and answer the question.
   - Check answer.

Answer

organise the music and food

4 - Refer students to the phrases in the *Useful language* box.
   - Ask students to work alone to complete the conversation using the phrases.

5 🔊 **2.20** Play the recording again for students to check their answers.

Answers

2 Shall I lend you   3 could I borrow   4 Can I help you
5 Could you ask   6 would you come

6 💬 Ask students to work in pairs to act out the conversation in Exercise 4.
   - Students can act out the conversation twice, taking a different part each time.

7 💬 Ask students to say whether the speaker in each case is offering to do something or making a request.
   - Put students into pairs and ask them to take it in turns to say and respond to sentences 1–5.

Answers

2 request   3 offer   4 offer   5 request

8 💬 Refer students to the two situations.
   - Put students into pairs.
   - Give students some time to plan what they want to say.
   - Students then act out their conversations using the two situations.
   - Monitor while students are practising their conversations. Check that they are using the phrases from the *Useful language* box.

 For homework students can read about a party and complete the exercises: http://learnenglishteens.britishcouncil.org/skills/ reading-skills-practice/facebook-party-became-riot

 # Writing A description

Objectives

- read a description of a family party.
- learn about the use of *so* and *too* with adjectives.
- write a description of a celebration.

Warm-up

- Books closed. Write *family celebrations* on the board.
- Put students into pairs and ask them to tell each other about the last big celebration their family organised. Students should answer the following questions: *What did the celebration mark? (e.g. a birthday, an anniversary) What did you do during the party? How many people came? What was the best part of the party?*
- Ask some students to report back to the class on what their partner said.

1
- Ask students to open their books at page 71.
- Refer students to the photo and then ask them to read Isabella's description and answer the question.
- Check answer.

Answer

her grandparents' 70th birthdays

2
- Refer students to the five questions.
- Ask students to read the description again.
- Put students into pairs to answer the five questions. Encourage students to make a note of which part of the description gave them their answers.
- Check answers.

Answers

1 Her grandparents were 70 last July.
2 It was in their garden.
3 They hired a big tent, made some food, and put up the decorations.
4 They had lunch and watched a film of her grandparents' lives. Her little brother played *Happy Birthday* on his guitar and everyone sang. Later they danced.
5 Yes, it was amazing.

Optional activity

- Put students into pairs and ask them to look again at Isabella's description of the birthday party that was held for her grandparents.
- Students should say what they think of the party: *Is it the type of party they would be happy to go to? Is there anything about the events that were organised that they would have changed?*

3
- Read out the information in the *Useful language* box about the difference between the meaning of *so* and *too* when those words are put before adjectives.
- Ask students to work alone to find two further examples of *so* + adjective and *too* + adjective in the description in Exercise 1.
- You could also remind students that *so* can be used to link sentences together and that an example of this can be seen in the first sentence of the text in Exercise 1: *… and last July they were seventy, so we had a party with family.* Tell students that we are not interested in this use of *so* here.
- Check answers.

Answers

The food was **so delicious**.
He was **so nervous** …
It was in their garden, because their house is **too small** …
I wanted to dance all night but I was **too tired**.

4
- Read out the example.
- Ask students to work alone to complete the sentences using *so* or *too* and the adjectives in the box.
- Students can compare their answers with a partner.
- Check answers.

Answers

2 so exciting 3 too slow 4 so cheap 5 so incredible
6 too expensive

Optional activity

- Ask students to to work in pairs and have text message conversations using *so* + adjective and *too* + adjective e.g. Student A: *Would you like to buy the new iPad?* Student B: *Yes, but they are too expensive!*
- Put students into pairs and ask them to compare their sentences.

 ## Get Writing

PLAN

5
- Students should do their planning in class. The writing can either be done in class or at home.
- Tell students they are going to write a description of a celebration.
- Refer students back to the questions in Exercise 2 and then ask them to work alone to make notes on the celebration they are going to write about.

WRITE

6
- Tell students to use the example description as a model to follow.
- Give students ten minutes to complete the writing task. Students should write between 140 and 160 words.
- Monitor while students are writing. Help with grammar and vocabulary as necessary.

CHECK

7
- Tell students that it is very important that they check their writing in order to look for ways to improve its content, style and structure.
- Give students a few minutes to look through their descriptions and check them against the points here.
- Collect students' descriptions and mark them.

 Set Exercises 1, 2, 3, 4 and 5 on page 62 and Exercises 6, 7, 8, 9, 10 and 11 on page 63 of the **Workbook** for homework.

Weird and wonderful

Unit aims

I can ...

* talk about a story I've enjoyed.
* understand a plot summary and an article about an unusual place to live.
* talk about imaginary situations in the past and give possible explanations for past events.
* understand a podcast about a local legend.
* use appropriate phrases to get more information.
* write a story.

Unit contents

Vocabulary	Story elements
	Prepositions and adverbs of movement
	Linking phrases
	Words in context
Reading	A plot summary
	● Mission, possible?
	A magazine article
Language focus	Third conditional
	must have, can't have, might/may/ could have
Listening	A podcast
Discover culture	● A lost civilisation
Speaking	Getting more information
	● Real talk: What's the biggest mistake you've ever made?
Pronunciation	Contracted forms in third conditionals
Writing	Telling a story
	Adverbs
CLIL	Biology: Extinction
	● Lions in danger

Background

A **myth** is a traditional story about gods and heroes, often one which is used to explain natural, social or historical events, and usually involving supernatural creatures, e.g. *Hercules is a character from myth*. A **legend** is also a traditional story, handed down through the generations, the source of which has never been authenticated. Characters from such stories are usually humans and the actions described have no supernatural elements.
A **knight** was a professional warrior in the Middle Ages. They had a special code of conduct in those days (chivalry). Today it's a rank of honour which in the UK is given by the monarch. The legendary King Arthur is one of the most famous knights in literature.

Be curious

* Books closed. Write *knight* /naɪt/ on the board. Drill the pronunciation of the word, pointing out the silent *k*.
* Elicit or teach the meaning of this word. Give students two minutes to write down as many words related to knights as they can, e.g. *horse, fight, war, king*.
* Make sure to revise or teach *armour* at this stage, as students will need it to describe the photo in the Students' Book.
* Ask students if they know any books or films about knights.
* Ask students to open their books at page 74.
* Give students a couple of minutes to answer the three questions about the photograph.
* Students can then compare answers in pairs before you check answers with the class.
* Tell students that the theme of Unit 7 is stories of different kinds.

Suggested answers

* I can see a knight in metal armour. There's a castle in the background.
* It comes from a legend about knights. It's probably from the Middle Ages. It could be from the UK or France.
* The knight is wearing armour to protect himself from his enemies. Maybe the country is at war.
* I enjoy these stories because they are full of adventures.

CEFR

SKILL AREA	GOAL	EXERCISE
Listening	OVERALL LISTENING COMPREHENSION	3 p75 1–2 p82
	UNDERSTANDING INTERACTION	3–6 p82
	LISTENING TO MEDIA AND RECORDINGS	1–4 p78 1–4 p80
Reading	READING FOR INFORMATION & ARGUMENT	1–3 p76 1–3 p81
Speaking	INFORMAL DISCUSSION (WITH FRIENDS)	4–5 p75 6 p76 5–6 p81
	INFORMATION EXCHANGE	5–6 p80 8 p82
Writing	CREATIVE WRITING	5–6 p78
Communicative language competence	VOCABULARY RANGE	1–5 p75 4–5 p76 4 p78 4 p81 3–4 p83
	GRAMMATICAL ACCURACY	1–5 p77 1–5 p79
	PHONOLOGICAL CONTROL	1 p75 3 p77 6–7 p82
Communication strategies	IDENTIFYING CUES AND INFERRING	4 p81
	TAKING THE FLOOR (TURNTAKING), COOPERATING, ASKING FOR CLARIFICATION, COMPENSATING, MONITORING & REPAIR	4 p82

Vocabulary Story elements

Objectives
* learn vocabulary for the elements of a story.
* listen to people talking about films.
* talk about a book I've read or a film I've seen recently.

Background
The Northern Lights is the first part of the *His Dark Materials* trilogy, a series of fantasy novels by Philip Pullman.
The Hunger Games is the first part of a trilogy of dystopian novels by Suzanne Collins.
The Chronicles of Narnia is a series of fantasy novels by C.S. Lewis.

Warm-up
* Books closed. Write the following on the board: *Which do you prefer: reading stories or watching films?*
* Put students into pairs to ask and answer the questions.
* Ask some students to report back to the class on their partner.

1 🔊 **2.21** Ask students to open their books at page 75.
* Put students into pairs to match the definitions with the elements of a story.
* Play the recording for students to listen, check their answers and repeat the words and phrases.
* Pay particular attention to the pronunciation of *villain* /ˈvɪlən/. You could explain that a *villain* may also be called the *bad guy* or the *baddie* /ˈbadi/.
* Point out that these words can be used to talk about books and films.

Answers
2 main character(s)   3 hero   4 suspense   5 villain
6 mystery   7 action   8 setting

Optional activity
* Put students into pairs (A and B).
* Student A defines a story element from Exercise 1 for their partner to guess, e.g. *This is the bad person in a story.*
* Student B says what he or she thinks the word in question is, e.g. *the villain.*
* Students swap roles and continue in this way until all the words and phrases in the box have been defined.

2 • Refer students to the description of *The Lion, the Witch and the Wardrobe*.
* Ask students to read the description and then put students into pairs to identify the different elements of a story contained within it.
* Check answers.

Suggested answers
* plot – Aslan is trying to win back his kingdom
* setting – a fantasy world
* main characters – four children
* hero – Aslan, an enormous lion
* villain – the White Witch
* suspense – the White Witch almost kills Aslan
* mystery – Aslan, by some incredible magic, comes back to life

Optional activity
* Ask students to watch a trailer on YouTube for the film version of *The Lion, the Witch and the Wardrobe*.
* Students could discuss the trailer in pairs or small groups. Did they like it? Did anything surprise them?

3 🔊 **2.22** Tell students they are going to listen to two people talking about a film they've seen recently.
* Play the recording for students to note down which four elements of a story are mentioned.
* Check answers.

Audioscript
A: I went to see *Avatar* yesterday.
B: *Avatar*? Really? At the cinema? But it's a really old film!
A: I know, but they had a special showing as part of a science-fiction festival.
B: Had you seen it before?
A: No! Can you believe it?! I really liked it. I loved the setting, that amazing planet with all those rocks and beautiful jungle, and all the incredible animals …
B: Yeah, it's really beautiful! What did you think of the plot? I thought the story was a bit obvious.
A: Yeah, me too, but the film isn't about the plot, really, is it? It's about the world not the story, and the main characters … especially the Na'vi, the blue people, and their way of life … and the human hero, Jake … he's a great character too.
B: I love the action scenes …
A: Oh yes, they are great, and the special effects are absolutely amazing!
B: I really like the whole idea behind the film too, I mean, it really makes you think …

Answers
setting, plot, main characters, action

Your turn

4 • Give students time to think of a book they've read or a film they've seen recently and make some notes on it.

5 • Put students into pairs to discuss the book or film they made notes on in Exercise 4.
* To **extend** the work on the vocabulary, you could ask students to turn to the **Vocabulary bank** on page 113 and do the exercises for *Story elements*.

 Set Exercises 1, 2, 3, 4 and 5 on page 67 of the **Workbook** for homework.
You could also ask students to find a short novel or graded reader to read. At the beginning of the next lesson, students can tell each other about the book they have started reading.

Reading A plot summary

Objectives

- read a plot summary of Ray Bradbury's *The Sound of Thunder*.
- learn prepositions of movement.
- talk about turning a story into a film.

Background

Ray Bradbury was one of the most successful writers of the 20th century. His science-fiction novels have become a central part of the genre, with *Fahrenheit 451*, a dystopian tale of a future in which the authorities burn books, being of particular note.

Warm-up

- Books closed. Write *science fiction* on the board. Ask students to define this genre of storytelling, e.g. science fiction stories are about life in an imagined future, feature technological advances, social and environmental changes, talk about life on other planets and space travel.
- Put students into pairs to talk about whether they read science fiction stories or watch science fiction films.

1   Ask students to open their books at page 76.
- Refer students to the picture and then put students into pairs to answer the questions.
- Do not confirm or reject students' ideas at this point. Students will check their ideas by reading the text in Exercise 2.

2   **2.23** Ask students to read the text to check their answers to Exercise 1.
- Students can then discuss their response to the end of the story, saying what they think happens and why. Some students will find this form of speculation easier than others. Encourage **stronger students** to go into greater detail than **weaker students**.
- Refer students to the information in the **FACT!** box. Then ask students to name some books they have enjoyed reading and why they enjoyed them.

Answers

1 A hunter travels in time and his behaviour changes the future.   2 Eckels, the main guide, some hunters   3 no

3
- Refer students to the events a–g.
- Tell students to read the plot summary again, and then put students into pairs to order the events.
- Check answers.

Answers

a – e – d – g – c – b – f

Optional activity

- Put students into small groups to write their own end to Ray Bradbury's story.
- Ask one student from each group to tell the class about the conclusion their group came up with.

Explore prepositions and adverbs of movement

4
- Write the phrase *run away* on the board. Underline *away* and elicit or explain that it refers to movement; in this case it means *at a distance from a person or place*, e.g. *The boy ran away from home.*
- Read out the example sentence and then ask students to look at how the other highlighted phrases are used in the plot summary.
- Ask students to work alone to complete the sentences with the highlighted phrases.
- Check answers and then drill the pronunciation of the following words: *float* /fləʊt/, *approach* /əˈprəʊtʃ/ and *through* /θruː/.

Answers

2 approached … through   3 floating … above
4 run back   5 stepped off   6 turned around

5
- Read out the example sentence.
- Give students time to write a description of the route they took to school on the day you do this lesson. Encourage students to use words and phrases such as *then* and *after that* in their descriptions, e.g. *I walked to the top of my street. Then I turned left and walked past the library. After that I crossed the road and walked down the hill.*
- Put students into pairs and ask them to compare their routes.
- To **extend** the work on the vocabulary, you could ask students to turn to the **Vocabulary bank** on page 113 and do the exercises for *Explore prepositions and adverbs of movement*.

Your turn

6
- Tell students they are going to think about turning the Ray Bradbury story into a film.
- Ask a student to read out the questions.
- Put students into pairs to answer the questions.
- Ask some students to report back to the class on their discussion with their partner. Does the rest of the class agree with their casting choices?

You can show this video as either a lead-in or a follow-up to the Language Focus 1 lesson.

7.1 Mission, possible?

- ▶ Ask: *What do you know about the history of space travel?*
- Elicit student's ideas. You might expect them to refer to Yuri Gagarin being the first man in space and Neil Armstrong being the first man to walk on the Moon.
- Put students into pairs to ask and answer the questions.
- Play the video.
- Then ask students if they think that there will come a time when we will all go into space routinely.
- See page 128 for further activities you can do with this video.

 Set Exercises 1, 2, 3, 4 and 5 on page 71 and Exercise 5 on page 68 of the **Workbook** for homework.

Language focus 1 Third conditional

Objectives

* learn the third conditional.
* talk about how my day yesterday might have been different.

Warm-up

* Books closed. Elicit the difference between the two conditional structures students already know: the first conditional refers to a possibility, the second conditional a hypothetical situation.

1
* Ask students to open their books at page 77.
* Tell students that the gapped sentences are from the text on page 76.
* Ask students to copy the sentences into their notebooks and complete them. Then they complete the rules.
* Check answers.
* For further information and additional exercises, students can turn to page 105 of the **Grammar reference** section.

Answers

Imaginary situation	Possible consequence
(*If* + past perfect)	(*would have* + past participle)
If Eckels ¹**had stayed** on the path,	he ²**wouldn't have killed** the butterfly.
If he ³**hadn't killed** the butterfly,	things ⁴**wouldn't have changed**.
If he ⁵**hadn't stepped** off the path,	⁶**would** the guide **have pointed** the gun at him?

* We use the third conditional to talk about imaginary situations in the ¹**past**.
* We often use the third conditionals to talk about things we ²**regret doing**.

2
* Read out the example sentence.
* Put students into pairs to complete the remaining sentences using the verb phrases from the box.
* Check answers.

Answers

2 hadn't been   3 would have changed   4 had changed
5 Would you have said   6 had talked

3
* Ask a student to read out the example.
* Ask students to work alone to write sentences in the third conditional using the prompts in brackets.
* Monitor while students do this task. Help as necessary.
* Check answers.

Answers

2 If the film hadn't been sold out, we wouldn't have gone for a burger.
3 If I had had some money, I wouldn't have gone to the bank.
4 We wouldn't have seen the man if we hadn't gone to the bank.
5 I wouldn't have bought a ticket if my friend hadn't bought one too.
6 If my friend hadn't called to ask me to go to the cinema, I wouldn't have won a million pounds!

Game

* Play *Pelmanism* to practise the third conditional.
* See **Games bank** on pages 28–29.

Say it right!

Contracted forms in third conditionals

1 🔊 **2.24** Remind students that in informal spoken and written English we use contractions (*hadn't*) rather than full forms (*had not*).
* Play the recording for students to listen to and repeat the sentences.

2 🔊 **2.25** Play the recording for students to identify the contracted forms in the sentences.
* Students can compare their answers in pairs.

3 🔊 **2.25** Play the recording for students to check their answers to Exercise 2 and repeat the sentences.

Answers

1 If my friend **hadn't** called, I**'d** have stayed at home and watched TV.
2 If the film **hadn't** been sold out, we **wouldn't** have gone for a burger.
3 If I**'d** had some money, I **wouldn't** have gone to the bank.
4 We **wouldn't** have seen the man if we **hadn't** gone to the bank.
5 I **wouldn't** have bought a ticket if my friend **hadn't** bought one too.
6 If my friend **hadn't** called to ask me to go to the cinema, I **wouldn't** have won a million pounds!

4 Put students into pairs and ask them to practise saying the sentences in Exercise 2 with the contracted forms.

Your turn

4 Ask students to write down three things that they did yesterday.

5
* Read out the example sentences.
* Help **weaker students** by modelling what you expect them to do, e.g. *Yesterday, I marked my students' homework. If I hadn't marked the homework, I'd have gone to the cinema.*
* Put students into pairs to talk about how their day might have been different had they not done what they did.

 Set Exercises 1, 2, 3 and 4 on page 68 of the **Workbook** for homework.

Listening and Vocabulary

Objectives
* listen to a podcast about the Giant's Causeway.
* learn linking phrases.
* write about legends from my country or other parts of the world.

A podcast

Background
The **Giant's Causeway** is a geological formation of columns of basalt (a volcanic rock). There is a similar rock formation in a cave on the island of Staffa in the Inner Hebrides in Scotland called *Fingal's Cave*. It was once believed that the Giant's Causeway was the end of a road made by a giant to Fingal's Cave.

Warm-up
* Books closed. Ask students to think of a place in their area noted for being particularly beautiful, e.g. a lake, a forest or a beach. Students should choose a place that they know well and have visited on several occasions.
* Put students into pairs to say why they like the place, how often they go there, and what they like to do when they go there.

1 🗨 Ask students to open their books at page 78.
* Put students into pairs to answer the question about the photo.
* Do not check answers at this point. Students will do that in Exercise 2 by listening to the recording.

2 🔊 2.26 Before you play the recording, put the word *causeway* /ˈkɔːzweɪ/ on the board. Explain that it is a raised track or road that is used to cross ground that is wet or low. Tell students that the photo shows something called the *Giant's Causeway*.
* Tell students they are going to listen to a podcast about the Giant's Causeway.
* Students listen and decide if the sentences are true or false.
* Check answers.

Audioscript
Turn to page 180 for the audioscript.

Answers
1 F (it is a natural formation)
2 F (it gives two explanations: one based on a legend and the other scientific)
3 F (the presenter prefers the first)

3 🔊 2.26 Refer students to sentences 1–8.
* Play the recording for students to choose the correct option in each of the sentences.
* Students can compare their answers in pairs before you check answers with the whole class.

Answers
1 Northern Ireland 2 12 3 Finn McCool 4 walk
5 wanted 6 dressed up like a baby boy
7 Finn was enormous 8 60

Linking phrases

4 🔊 2.27 Refer students to the words and phrases in the box. Explain that they are used to connect parts of a sentence or an idea expressed in one sentence with one expressed in another.
* The phrases are all similar to one another and it won't be immediately apparent to students how they are used. You should therefore go through each in turn. You could put an example sentence on the board and elicit a translation in the students' own language.
* Put students into pairs and ask them to complete the gapped sentences with the linking phrases.
* Play the recording again for students to check their answers.
* To **extend** the work on the vocabulary, you could ask students to turn to the **Vocabulary bank** on page 113 and do the exercises for *Linking phrases*.

Answers
2 According to 3 rather than 4 so that 5 In fact
6 In order to 7 of course 8 as a result of

Optional activity
* Put students into pairs and ask them to take it in turns to test each other on the linking phrases in Exercise 4, e.g. Student A says *rather*, Student B says *than*.
* Students can then try to put each of these linking phrases into a sentence.
* Monitor while students do this, making sure to check their sentences.

Background
The **Kraken** is a legendary sea creature that is said to live off the coast of Norway.

5 * Give students time to make a list of all the legends they know. These do not have to be from the students' own country. If students do not know any, allow them to look online for examples using their smartphones.

6 * Read out the example description of the kraken.
* Give students a few minutes to write a short text about one of the legends they made a list of in Exercise 5. Students should use the linking phrases from Exercise 4.
* Monitor while students do the writing task. Help as necessary.
* Put students into pairs to read their texts out to one another.

 Set Exercises 1, 2, 3 and 4 on page 69 of the **Workbook** for homework.
Students can also learn more about the myths and legends of Northern Ireland by looking at this website: http://www.causewaycoastandglens.com/Myths-and-Legends.T1090.aspx

Language focus 2
must have, can't have, might/may/could have

Objectives

* learn *must have, can't have* and *might/may/could have*.
* look at photos and say what must, can't, might or could have happened.

Warm-up

* Books closed. Say *Oh, no!* Then pat your pockets as if looking for your keys. Say: *I must have left my keys the café.*
* Write this sentence on the board. Underline *must have* and elicit or introduce the idea of making deductions.

1
* Ask students to open their books at page 79.
* Tell students that the example sentences are from the listening on page 78.
* Ask students to copy the sentences into their notebooks and complete them with the verbs in the box.
* If necessary, play the recording again for students to complete the sentences.
* Students can compare their answers in pairs before you check answers with the class.

> ### Answers
> 1 It's easy to believe that a giant **might have** built them.
> 2 Humans **can't have** built it either. It's just too big!
> 3 **Could a giant have** built this causeway?
> 4 He **may have** built the enormous causeway so that he could walk across the sea.
> 5 The local people say it **must have** been a giant!

2
* Refer students to the rules.
* Put students into pairs and ask them to look back at the sentences in Exercise 1 to help them complete the rules. You may wish to do this exercise with the class as a whole to help **weaker students**.
* For further information and additional exercises, students can turn to page 105 of the **Grammar reference** section.

> ### Answers
> 1 b 2 the past 3 i b ii a iii c

> ### Language note
> Point out that it is not possible to use modals of deduction for the past with the past simple form of the verb. We say *She might have gone to the café* not ~~she might went to the café~~.

3
* Read out the information in the **Get it right!** box. Point out that when we wish to refer to something that was a possibility in the past, we use *might*, *may* or *could*.
* Ask students to work alone to complete the beginnings and the ends of the sentences.
* Check answers.

> ### Fast finishers
> Students can write two sentences. One referring to something in the present, one making a deduction to make sense of it, e.g. *My brother isn't at home. He must have gone round to his friend's house.* Collect and check students' sentences.

> ### Answers
> 1 i c ii b iii a 2 i b ii a iii c

> ### Game
> * Play *Correct the sentence* to practise *must have, can't have, might/may/could have*.
> * See **Games Bank** on pages 28–29.

Your turn

4
* Refer students to the four photos and the example sentence.
* Introduce or elicit vocabulary that students will need for the exercises: *upside down, parachute jump, skydiving, gate, field, farm, uprooted tree, overturned car*.
* Ask students to work alone to write three sentences about each photograph. **Stronger students** can write more sentences than **weaker students**.
* Explain that the sentences that students write do not have to be serious. They may also be silly.

5
* Read out the example.
* Put students into pairs to compare their sentences.
* Ask some students to tell the class which of their partner's ideas they find the most probable, and which the silliest.

> ### Optional activity
> * Write a sentence on the board: *There must have been an accident.*
> * Ask students to suggest evidence for coming to such a conclusion, e.g. *There are police cars and ambulances in the street.*
> * Check that students understand the idea of linking a deduction with the evidence that led you to it.
> * Put students into pairs. Write sentences on the board in turn: *I must have upset her. He must have gone to bed very late. This room can't have been cleaned.*
> * After you have put a deduction on the board, ask students to think of evidence to support it.

 Set Exercises 1, 2, 3, 4 and 5 on page 70 of the **Workbook** for homework.
Students can investigate famous mysteries, e.g. how the pyramids were built, why the Nazca lines can only be seen from the sky, and make deductions to explain these mysteries, e.g. *The pyramids must have been built by thousands of slaves pulling and pushing stones into place.* Students can compare their sentences with a partner at the beginning of the next lesson.

Discover Culture

A lost civilisation

Objectives

- watch a video about a lost civilisation in Peru.
- talk about visiting archaeological sites or going to exhibitions of ancient artefacts.

Warm-up

- Books closed. Write *archaeology* on the board.
- Drill the pronunciation of the word: /ˌɑːkiˈɒlədʒi/.
- Introduce a definition: *archaeology is the study of history and prehistory through excavating sites and studying artefacts.*

1 💬 Ask students to open their books at page 80.
- Put students into pairs to talk about what the link between the four photos might be.

2 ▶ 7.2 Read out the two questions.
- Play the video for students to check their answers to Exercise 1 as well as answer the two questions.
- Check answers.

Videoscript

The Atacama Desert in South America is one of the hottest and driest places on Earth. It extends more than 1,000 kilometres along the Pacific coast of southern Peru and northern Chile. In the desert hills above Ilo, Peru, there are few signs of civilisation. About 15 years ago, workers from a nearby town were digging in the sand here when they found bones. Human bones. Who could have known that just below the surface were thousands of human graves containing mummies, perfectly preserved by the dry, salty sand? Archaeologists concluded that this was the home of an ancient civilisation: the Chiribaya. When they lived here, in the Ilo Valley, between 900 and 1350 AD, everything would have looked very different. At that time, there may have been as many as 30,000 people living here. But today, there are no ancient buildings or monuments, only graves. These graves hold the only clues to how the Chiribaya might have lived. Pots like these might have been used for food, or to carry water, and this ancient flute tells us that the Chiribaya must have made music. Archaeologists have found gold artefacts in some of the graves, suggesting that their owners were very rich and powerful people. Most graves contained one or two animal heads. These animals, called llamas, are still an important part of daily life in this area. The Chiribaya would have used the wool of llamas to make these beautiful hats. Some of the hats that archaeologists have found have beautiful feathers, the feathers of tropical birds. Could these feathers have come down from the Amazon Forest, so far away? With each new discovery, archaeologists learn more about this ancient civilisation, hidden for centuries beneath the dry desert sand.

Suggested answers

The photos show a grave of an old civilisation that archaeologists found in Peru. The graves in that region contain mummies and heads of llamas.
The objects show that the Chiribaya must have made music and that they were rich and powerful. Llamas were an important part of daily life. Their wool was used to make hats.

3 ▶ 7.2 Ask students to look at the information in the list a–f, which refers to different parts of the video.
- Tell students they are going to watch the video and order the information.
- Play the video.
- Check answers.

Answers

f – d – b – e – a – c

4 ▶ 7.2 Ask students to say whether number or words are needed to complete the gapped sentences.
- Play the video for students to complete the sentences.
- Check answers.

Answers

1 15   **2** 1350   **3** 30,000   **4** water   **5** rich; powerful
6 tropical birds

Your turn

5 - Elicit examples of civilisations of the past, e.g. Ancient Egypt, the Aztecs.
- Read out the two questions.
- Put students into pairs to ask and answer the questions.

6 - Ask students to look online for information about the civilisation they would like to visit.
- Students can share what they find out with the class.

Optional activity

- Put students into pairs.
- Ask students to use their smartphones to find out about famous archaeologists of the past, e.g. Gertrude Bell or Arthur Evans.
- Students should find out where the person was from, where he or she worked, what he or she discovered.
- Put pairs together to share what they find out.

➡ For homework, ask students to do some research online into archaeological sites in their country. At the beginning of the next lesson students can share what they find out with a partner.

Reading A magazine article

Objectives

- read an article about the Pueblo people.
- learn words in context.
- talk about life might have been like for the Pueblo people 1,000 years ago.

Warm up

- Books closed. Ask students to say what it is about the way people live now that is different from how people lived hundreds of years ago.
- Put students into small groups and give them a minute to come up with some ideas, e.g. we have electricity and all the associated appliances (such as fridges), hot and cold running water, central heating, etc.
- Ask one student from each group to report back to the class.

1 💬 Ask students to open their books at page 81.
- Refer students to the photos and the title of the article.
- Put students into pairs to answer the three questions.
- Do not confirm or reject students' ideas at this point. Students will check their answers in Exercise 2.

2 🔊 **2.28** Ask students to read the article to check the answers they gave in Exercise 1.
- Read out the information in the **FACT!** box. Ask students if they can name some of the tallest buildings in the United States: One World Trade Center and the Empire State Building in New York; the Trump Tower in Chicago. You could also ask students if they can name some of the tallest buildings in their country.

Answers
1 the Pueblo people, a Native American civilisation
2 from 600 to 1300 AD   3 to be safe

3 • Refer students to sentences 1–6. Explain that there is a mistake in each of the sentences and that students have to find them by looking for the correct information in the text.
- Tell students that they do not have to read the article all the way through again. They should instead scan it for information. This they can do by first identifying the key words and phrases in the sentences that they need to look for, and then scanning the text to find these words and phrases. For example, the key words in sentence 1 are *Mesa Verde National Park* and *Mexico*.
- Ask students to work alone to do the exercise. Students can compare answers in pairs before you check answers with the class as a whole.

Answers
1 The Mesa Verde National Part is in the **United States**.
2 The Pueblo people lived there for **over** 700 years.
3 The word pueblo means **village**.
4 The Balcony House is made up of **40** rooms.
5 The only door is at the **top of a 10-metre high wooden ladder**.
6 The Pueblo people used ladders and ropes **to protect themselves from enemies**.

Optional activity
- Students can use their smartphones to explore Mesa Verde National Park on Google Maps and the website of the park itself: http://www.nps.gov/meve/index.htm

 Explore words in context

4 • Refer students to the highlighted words in the article.
- Match the first highlighted word in the text with one of the definitions 1–5 as an example.
- Put students into pairs to complete the exercise.
- Check answers.

Answers
1 maze 2 canyons 3 dwellings 4 settlers 5 borders

Language note
Dwelling is a formal word for a house or place of residence and is not ordinarily used in everyday language. It tends to be used in formal contexts such as newspaper articles or documents concerning planning permission for a particular building.
Settler refers to people who go to live in a place where there are few other inhabitants.

Your turn

5 • Ask students to imagine that they lived 1,000 years ago in one of the cliff dwellings shown in the pictures.
- Give students time to think of three ways in which their lives would have been different.

6 • Put students into pairs to compare the ideas they came up with in Exercise 5. They should also discuss the question of whether there would have been advantages to living as the Pueblo people lived.
- To **extend** the work on this, ask students to investigate cave houses in other parts of the world, e.g. in southern Spain or Turkey.

➡ For homework, you could ask students to research the history of their country and find out about different groups of people who lived there and how they lived. At the beginning of the next lesson, ask some students to share what they found out with a partner.

Speaking Getting more information

Objectives

- watch teenagers talking about the biggest mistake they have ever made.
- listen to a teenager talk about a mistake she made.
- practise getting more information from someone.

Warm-up

- Books closed. Tell students about a mistake you have made. Invent the mistake if you prefer. The important thing is to introduce the idea of making mistakes.

Real talk: What's the biggest mistake you've ever made?

1 ▶ **7.3** Ask students to open their books at page 82.

- Tell students they are going to watch some teenagers answering the following question:
  What's the biggest mistake you've ever made?
- Refer students to items a–f. Play the video for students to order the mistakes.
- Check answers. Encourage **stronger students** to give as much detail as they can in their answers.

Videoscript

Narrator: What's the biggest mistake you've ever made?

Speaker 1: I've made a lot of mistakes, but I guess the biggest one was staying up all night for an exam and still failing it. If I had just gone to bed at a normal time, I would have done a lot better and maybe wouldn't have completely failed it.

Speaker 2: Probably joining the football team last year and then losing every single game. I wasn't sure about joining at all but my parents said I should. I don't even like football!

Speaker 3: That's a hard one. If I had to pick one, though, it would probably be the fact that I missed a trip with my best friend's family last summer. They invited me, but I had to do a week of summer school. It ended up being the best vacation ever. And I missed it!

Speaker 4: Not applying to a special art camp last summer. I had the application filled out and everything, but then at the last minute, I got nervous and didn't send it. Then I heard from a good friend that she got the last place. What a mistake.

Speaker 5: I don't make mistakes very often, but the one I'm sad about is not apologising to my best friend when I said something mean about her. And now we don't talk at all. If she gave me another chance, I would apologise right away and promise to be a better friend.

Speaker 6: I don't know. It depends on what you think is a mistake. Most of the mistakes I've made, I've learned from, so were they really mistakes? Maybe not.

Narrator: What's the biggest mistake *you've* ever made?

Answers

1 c   2 e   3 b   4 a   5 f   6 d

---

2 💬 Put students into pairs to ask and answer the question.
- Ask some students to report back to the class on what their partner said.

3 🔊 **2.29** Tell students they are going to listen to Dana talk to her friend Nicola about a mistake.
- Read out the question.
- Play the recording.
- Students listen and answer the question.
- Check answer.

Answer

She borrowed her mum's watch and lost it in the garden.

4
- Refer students to the phrases in the *Useful language* box.
- Students can either work alone or in pairs to complete the conversation using the phrases in the *Useful language* box.

5 🔊 **2.29** Play the recording for students to check their answers.

Answers

2 mum know   3 then what happened   4 say anything
5 That was lucky

---

6 💬 Ask students to work in pairs to act out the conversation in Exercise 4.
- Students can act out the conversation twice, taking a different part each time.

7 💬 Do the first one as an example with the class.
- Put students into pairs and ask them to take it in turns to say and respond to sentences 1–6 using the language introduced in Exercise 4.

Optional activity

- You could turn Exercise 7 into a digital activity by asking students to text and respond to the messages via a free messaging service such as WhatsApp.

---

8 💬 Read out the instructions and make sure that students understand what they have to do.
- Give students some time to plan what they want to say.
- Students then act out their conversations.
- Monitor while students are practising their conversations. Check that they are using the phrases from the *Useful language* box.

 For homework, ask students to write a short dialogue based on the one in Exercise 4. The conversation doesn't have to be about a mistake, but it should include the language that we use to get more information out of someone. Collect and check students' work in the next lesson.

 Writing Telling a story

Objectives

* read an email about an accident.
* learn about the use of adverbs.
* write a story about an event in my life.

Warm-up

* Books closed. Ask: *If something interesting happens to you, do you like to tell people about it straight away or do you usually keep it to yourself?*
* Put students into pairs to ask and answer this question.
* Ask some students to report back to the class on their partner's answer to this question.

1
* Ask students to open their books at page 83.
* Refer students to the photo and then ask them to guess the story related in Theo's email.
* Ask students to read the email and then answer the question.
* Check answer.
* You could then point out that the phrase *you'll never guess*, which is seen at the beginning of the second sentence in the email, is commonly used when introducing information that the speaker expects will be greeted with surprise, e.g. *You'll never guess what happened to me today: I won £5,000 in the lottery!*

Answer

Nick fell off his bike and hit a wall at the side of the road. He hurt his arm and his back. He broke his wrist.

2
* Refer students to the five questions.
* Ask students to read the email again.
* Students can then work alone to answer the questions.
* Check answers.

Fast finishers

Students can write about what they would do if they were in the same situation as Nick's friends in the story told in the email in Exercise 1.

Answers

1 in the country
2 Theo and his brothers (Robbie and Nick)
3 While they were cycling, a dog ran across the road right in front of them. Theo and Robbie crashed into each other. Nick fell off his bike.
4 They called their parents.
5 Their parents arrived and took Nick to hospital.

Optional activity

* Put students into small groups and ask them to tell each other whether they have ever had, or been with a friend that has had, an accident similar to one that Theo describes in his email.
* Students should provide the following information: where they were, who they were with, exactly what happened, what the outcome was.

3
* Read out the information about how adverbs are used in the *Useful language* box.
* Ask students to work alone to find further examples of adverbs used by Theo in the email in Exercise 1.
* Check answers.

Suggested answers

Obviously, we tried to stop, …
Fortunately, we were okay, …
Luckily, we had our mobiles, …
Amazingly, he only had a broken wrist.

4
* Put students into pairs and ask them to match the beginnings and ends of the sentences by joining them with the adverbs from the box.
* Check answers.

Answers

1 c They walked for a long time but eventually they arrived at the campsite.
2 e We saw the wild cats but fortunately they didn't see us.
3 b James crashed his quad bike into a tree but amazingly he didn't hurt himself.
4 a She was crying and obviously upset.
5 d We'd never bought a lottery ticket before but luckily we won £1,000!

 **Get Writing**

PLAN

5
* Students should do their planning in class. The writing can either be done in class or at home.
* Tell students they are going to write a story about an event in their life. This event doesn't have to be an accident, and doesn't even have to be a story about an unfortunate occurrence, but should be a story worth telling.
* Refer students back to the questions in Exercise 2 and then ask them to work alone to make notes.

WRITE

6
* Tell students to use Theo's story as a model to follow.
* Give students ten minutes to complete the writing task. Students should write between 140 and 160 words.
* Monitor while students are writing. Help with grammar and vocabulary as necessary.

CHECK

7
* Tell students that it is very important that they check their writing in order to look for ways to improve its content, style and structure.
* Give students a few minutes to look through their stories and check them against the points here.
* Collect students' stories and mark them.

 Set Exercises 1, 2, 3 and 4 on page 72 and Exercises 5, 6, 7, 8, 9, 10 and 11 on page 73 of the **Workbook** for homework.

Unit aims

I can ...

* talk about crimes and how serious they are.
* understand news stories about crimes and an article about unusual laws.
* report what people have said and ask for information politely.
* understand a news podcast about young heroes.
* ask questions to clarify and use appropriate phrases to confirm or deny information.
* write an online article.

Unit contents

Vocabulary	Crimes
	Words in context
	Reporting verbs
	Verb expressions
Reading	News stories
	◆ On the run
	An article
Language focus	Reported statements
	Reported questions
	Indirect questions
Listening	A news report
Discover culture	◆ Future directions
Speaking	Clarifying
	◆ Real talk: What's the biggest lie you've ever been told?
Pronunciation	Intonation in indirect questions
Writing	An online article
	Describing amounts
CLIL	ICT: Copyright
	◆ True or false

Be curious

* Books closed. Draw a basic picture of a house on the board. Ask: *What bad things can happen to the houses we live in?* Elicit some ideas, e.g. they can be damaged by rain, high winds and other weather conditions. They can be burgled. They may be partly or wholly destroyed by fire.
* Ask students to open their books at page 84.
* Give them a moment to look at the photograph and then ask them to describe it. You may need to introduce some vocabulary at this point, i.e. *on fire, firefighter, in flames, burn down.*
* Put students into pairs to answer the three questions.
* Check answers with the class.
* Tell students that the theme of Unit 8 is breaking the law.

Suggested answers

* There's a big fire and a firefighter is trying to enter the building. Maybe he wants to check that there's no one inside.
* I think it was an accident. It's possible that there was a problem with a heater or the cooker.
* Some might have wanted to destroy the building and everything that is inside. There are also some people who cannot control themselves who they feel a strong need to set fires.
* There could be people or animals inside the buildings; the firefighters would be in danger if they tried to save them. There could also be more houses next to this building.

CEFR

SKILL AREA	GOAL	EXERCISE
Listening	OVERALL LISTENING COMPREHENSION	1–2 p92
	LISTENING TO MEDIA AND RECORDINGS	4 p85 4–7 p88 1–7 p90 3–6 p92
Reading	READING FOR INFORMATION & ARGUMENT	1–3 p86 1–3 p91 1–4 p93
Speaking	INFORMAL DISCUSSION (WITH FRIENDS)	5–6 p85 5–6 p86 8 p88 7 p90 6 p91
	INFORMATION EXCHANGE	7–8 p89 7–8 p92
Writing	CREATIVE WRITING	5–7 p83
	REPORTS AND ESSAYS	5–7 p93
Communicative language competence	VOCABULARY RANGE	1–4 p85 4 p86 1–3 p88 4 p91 3–4 p93
	GRAMMATICAL ACCURACY	1–6 p87 7 p88 1–6 p89 5 p91
	PHONOLOGICAL CONTROL	1 p85 1 p88 6 p89 6 p92
Communication strategies	IDENTIFYING CUES AND INFERRING	4 p86 4 p91
	TAKING THE FLOOR (TURNTAKING), COOPERATING, ASKING FOR CLARIFICATION, COMPENSATING, MONITORING & REPAIR	4–8 p92

Vocabulary Crimes

Objectives

- learn vocabulary for different crimes.
- listen to a radio report about crimes around the world.
- talk about crime in my area.

Warm-up

- Books closed. Elicit crimes or examples of bad behaviour, e.g. cheating in an exam. Write students' ideas on the board.

1 🔊 **2.30** Ask students to open their books at page 85.
- Put students into pairs to do the matching exercise.
- Play the recording for students to check their answers and repeat the phrases
- Refer students back to the picture in h and introduce the word *graffiti* (drawings or words on a wall in a public place).

> ### Answers
> **a** kidnapping **b** mugging **c** illegal downloading
> **d** pickpocketing **e** shoplifting **f** robbery **g** arson
> **h** vandalism

2
- Complete this exercise with the class as a whole, taking care to explain the different types of crime pictured in Exercise 1.

> ### Suggested answers
> **a)** shoplifting, arson, vandalism, illegal downloading
> **b)** kidnapping **c)** mugging, pickpocketing, robbery

3
- Complete the first one with the class as an example.
- Ask students to work alone to match the two halves of the sentences.
- Check answers.

> ### Answers
> 1 b 2 e 3 a 4 c 5 d

4 🔊 **2.31** Play the recording for students to note down the five crimes that are mentioned and what the two people say about them.
- Help **weaker students** by playing the recording twice. The first time for students to write down the crimes, the second so they can note down more details about each of the crimes.
- Check answers.

Audioscript

Presenter: Today on our Crimes World Report, we look at the world's most common crimes. Damian Williams has been looking at the statistics, Damian?

Reporter: Well, the most common crimes are kind of invisible, you know…

Presenter: What do you mean?

Reporter: Well, there are lot of new crimes related to the digital age. Did you know that illegal downloading is believed to be the number one crime at the moment?

Presenter: I suppose that some people don't think of it as a crime, right?

Reporter: That's right, it's stealing somebody else's property, but some people think that film stars and musicians have enough money already…

Presenter: Yes, it's all to do with how you see it, I guess..

Reporter: It's a bit like vandalism, things like graffiti … some people call it art. As you say, it's how you see it, is it art or is it a crime?

Presenter: OK. What about other everyday crimes?

Reporter: Well, shoplifting is still very common, of course. The interesting thing is that now there are professional groups who shoplift. One person talks to the shop assistants while others rob the store.

Presenter: And then there's pickpocketing and mugging, surely very common crimes on the world's city streets?

Reporter: Yes, this can happen to anyone anywhere. Here, in London there are pickpockets everywhere but a serious mugging where you get hurt – luckily, that's rare …

Presenter: Luckily … thanks Damian.

> ### Suggested answers
> - vandalism (graffiti) – some people call it art
> - shoplifting – very common; there are professional groups who shoplift
> - pickpocketing – can happen to anyone; in London there are pickpockets everywhere
> - mugging – serious muggings are rare

Your turn

5
- Ask students to look again at the crimes in the box in Exercise 1. They should then work alone to decide which of the crimes are very serious, which quite serious and which less serious.
- Encourage students to give reasons for their decisions in the notes they make.

6
- Refer students to the questions.
- Put students into small groups to discuss the questions. They should use the notes they made in Exercise 5 to help them with question 1.
- Ask a student from each group to report back to the class on the discussion their group had.
- To **extend** the work on the vocabulary, you could ask students to turn to the **Vocabulary bank** on page 114 and do the exercises for *Crimes*.

 Set Exercises 1, 2, 3, 4 and 5 on page 77 of the Workbook for homework.
You could also ask students to choose one of the crimes in Exercise 1 and find out about when such a crime was last committed in their area. Students can share what they find out at the beginning of the next lesson.

Reading News stories

Objectives
- read an article about unsuccessful attempts at crime.
- learn words in context.
- talk about lessons that can be learnt from certain events.

Warm-up
- Books closed. Ask: *How much attention do you pay to news about crimes that have been committed? Do you read articles about crimes on websites?*
- Put students into pairs to discuss the questions.

1
- Ask students to open their books at page 86.
- Read out the captions. Explain that *cash* means *money in the form of notes and coins*. Also remind students that an *update* on Facebook refers to a change a user of that site has made to their status or some other aspect of their profile.
- Ask students to look at the photos and match them with the captions.
- Check answers.
- Ask students to guess the content of the stories each of the three captions refers to.

Answers
1 a 2 c 3 b

2 🔊 **2.32** Ask students to match the captions with the news stories.
- Check answers.
- Refer students to the information in the **FACT!** box. Ask students if there are a lot of CCTV cameras in their countries and what they think of such technology.

Answers
Photo a: the story about a thief in Toronto
The thief advertised the crime.
Photo b: the story about a man in Scotland
A police officer stole the money that the man had taken to the police station.
Photo c: the story about a man in Germany
The man forged €30 notes, which don't exist.

Language note
CCTV stands for *closed-circuit television*, which is a system of video cameras that transmit images to a limited number of televisions on a network used for surveillance by the police, etc.

3
- Refer students to sentences 1–6.
- Ask students to read the stories again.
- Put students into pairs to choose the correct options in the sentences. Help **weaker students** by telling them that sentences 1–2 refer to the first story, sentences 3–4 to the second, and sentences 5–6 to the third.
- Check answers.

Answers
1 his friends 2 before and after 3 real
4 after the event 5 dishonest 6 returned for

Explore words in context
4
- Refer students to the highlighted words in the article.
- Match the first highlighted word in the text with one of the definitions 1–6 as an example.
- Ask students to match the remaining highlighted words with the definitions.
- Check answers.

Fast finishers
Students can write one or two sentences using the words from Exercise 4. Collect and check these sentences.

Answers
1 in charge 2 register 3 fake 4 forgery, fraud
5 advertise 6 idol

Your turn

5
- Introduce students to the idea of learning a lesson from a particular event. Explain that in this context the word *lesson* refers to the things that we learn from our own experience or the experience of others.
- Read out the example sentence and then ask students to work alone to makes notes on what lessons can be learnt from the stories in Exercise 1.

6
- Refer students to the example sentences.
- Put students into pairs to discuss the ideas they made notes on in Exercise 5.
- Ask some students to report back to the class on what their partner said.

You can show this video as either a lead-in or a follow-up to the Language Focus 1 lesson.

- ● Ask: *What does the phrase 'on the run' mean?* Elicit that it refers to trying to avoid being captured by someone, usually the police.
- Put students into pairs to ask and answer the questions.
- Play the video.
- Students watch it and answer the questions.
- Check answers.

Answers
He stole chickens, horses and cars.
The police caught him and he was sent to prison.

- Then ask students why they think people commit crime.
- See page 129 for further activities you can do with this video.

 Set Exercises 1, 2, 3 and 4 on page 81 of the **Workbook** for homework.
Ask students to find more examples of 'stupid' criminals such as the Toronto thief who posted information about his criminal activities on his Facebook page. Students can share what they find out with a partner at the beginning of the next lesson.

Language focus 1 Reported statements

Objectives
* learn reported statements.
* write reported statements.

Warm-up
* Books closed. Write *reported speech* on the board. Check students understand it it is a way of reporting something someone has said, e.g. *Sarah said she was going to the park*.

1
* Ask students to open their books at page 87.
* Tell students the sentences in Exercise 1 can all be found in the article on page 86 as reported speech.
* Ask students to work alone to find the sentences in the article and copy them into their notebooks.
* Check answers.

Answers
1 … he … said … that he couldn't believe this bad luck.
2 He said that he was surprised that the police had looked at his Facebook page!
3 … he told journalists that the fake was very poor quality.
4 He said that somebody had given him the illegal note as a joke, …
5 The local police inspector said that she had never seen such a stupid crime.
6 The police officer said that he would register it.

2
* Put students into pairs.
* Tell students to use the examples of reported speech they found in the article in Exercise 1 to help them complete the rules.
* Check answers.
* For further information and additional exercises, students can turn to page 106 of the **Grammar reference** section.

Answers
When we report a conversation, …
1 the present simple changes to the **past simple**.
2 the past simple changes to the **past perfect**.
3 the present perfect changes to the **past perfect**.
4 *will* changes to *would* and *can* changes to **could**.

Language note
The rules governing reported speech are often broken in informal English. *Like* is commonly used as a means of directly reporting what someone has said and is used with the verb *be* in both the present and the past e.g. *And I'm like, 'What do you want me to about it?' and she was like 'I want you to sort it out.'*

3
* Refer students to the police officer's response to the news stories from page 86.
* Ask students to choose the correct verb forms to complete the reported version of the police officer's view.
* Check answers.

Fast finishers
Students can note down how they think the public can help the police fight crime. You could then ask students to share their ideas with the class and briefly discuss the topic.

Answers
1 were 2 found 3 would 4 had been 5 were
6 would 7 could

4
* Read out the information in the **Get it right!** box. Point out that it is not possible to say *She told she was sorry*.
* Complete the first reported statement, eliciting the changes to the grammar that are required. Write the reported statement on the board, highlighting the way the sentence has changed.
* Put students into pairs to complete the remaining sentences.
* Check answers.

Answers
1 (that) he was guilty of committing the crime
2 (that) she had stolen the money
3 (that) he had never been in trouble before
4 (that) he would never do it again
5 (that) she couldn't understand why she had done such a terrible thing
6 (that) she hadn't stolen from the old lady

Game
* Play *Guess the sentence* to practise reported speech.
* See **Games bank** on pages 28–29.

Your turn

5
* Refer students to the example and the sentence prompts.
* Give students time to write three more true and false reported statements.

6
* Put students into pairs to read their sentences out to each other. Students should guess which sentences are true and which false.

Optional activity
* Read out sentences and ask students to report them beginning with the phrase *You said…*, e.g. Student A: *I'm going to the cinema*. Student B: *You said you were going to the cinema*.
* Put students into pairs to take it in turns to say things to be reported.

 Set Exercises 1, 2, 3, 4, 5 and 6 on page 78 of the **Workbook** for homework.

Vocabulary and Listening

Objectives

- learn reporting verbs.
- listen to a news report.
- talk about which of the teenagers from the news report I think was the bravest.

Reporting verbs

Warm-up

- Books closed. Write *say* and *tell* on the board. Elicit the fact that these verbs are commonly used in reported speech. Then explain that other verbs are also used and that the focus of the first part of the lesson is on those verbs.

1 🔊 **2.33** Ask students to open their books at page 88.

- Refer students to the list of verbs in 1–8.
- Put students into pairs to match the verbs with the definitions. Students can look up the meanings of the words (as well as translations of them) in an online dictionary.
- Check answers.

> **Answers**
> 1 e 2 g 3 h 4 f 5 a 6 d 7 b 8 c

> ### Optional activity
>
> - Put students into pairs (A and B).
> - Students take it in turns to test each other on the reporting verbs.
> - Student A closes their book. Student B reads out one of the definitions from Exercise 1. Student A says what the verb is.
> - Students swap roles and continue in this way until all the verbs in Exercise 1 have been used.

2
- Ask students to work alone to choose the correct verbs in each of the sentences.
- Check answers.

> **Answers**
> 1 promised 2 admitted 3 insisted 4 suggested
> 5 decided 6 agreed 7 complained 8 explained

3
- Put students into pairs to report things they have said to other people recently, e.g. *My mum – I admitted I'd failed my Physics test*.
- Students don't have to use all the verbs, but should keep a note of the ones they do use.
- Find out if anyone in the class was able to use all eight verbs.
- To **extend** the work on the vocabulary, you could ask students to turn to the **Vocabulary bank** on page 114 and do the exercises for *Reporting verbs*.

A news report

4 💬 Refer students to the two sketches.

- Put students into pairs and ask them to say what crimes they think the sketches show.
- Check answers.

> **Suggested answers**
> **Image top left:** a robbery
> **Image top right:** a kidnapping

5 🔊 **2.34** Tell students they are going to listen to a news report about the crimes shown in the sketches in Exercise 4.

- Play the recording for students to say what the two stories of the crimes have in common.
- Check answers.

Audioscript

Turn to page 180 for the audioscript.

> **Answers**
> Both stories are about teenagers who stopped crimes.

6 🔊 **2.34** Check students are able to pronounce the words, particularly *scared* /skɛːd/, *millionaire* /mɪljəˈnɛː/, *bravery* /ˈbreɪv(ə)ri/ and *kidnapper* /ˈkɪdnæpə/.

- Point out that the words *kidnapping/kidnapper* and *bravery/brave* are related.
- Play the recording again.
- Put students into pairs to say which words belong to which story.
- Check answers.
- Students should then work in pairs to reconstruct the stories. Encourage students to write short news reports using the words in the box. Help **weaker students** by drawing their attention to the fact that news report tend to answer the following questions: *What happened? When did it happen? Where did it happen? Who was involved? How did it happen? Why did it happen?* Encourage **stronger students** to add some colour to their reports, e.g. by describing weather conditions or the mood of people in the story.

> **Answers**
> **Story 1:** scared, bravery, robber, fine
> **Story 2:** millionaire, evidence, kidnapper, reward

7 🔊 **2.34** Refer students to the gapped sentences.

- Ask students to complete the sentences with the past simple form of the reporting verbs from Exercise 1 and then note down which story the sentences are taken from.
- Play the recording for the students to check their answers.

> **Answers**
> 1 admitted 2 insisted 3 promised 4 suggested
> 5 explained
> **Story 1:** sentences 1 and 2
> **Story 2:** sentences 3, 4 and 5

> **Your turn**

8
- Read out the two questions and the example conversation.
- Point out that students will need to use third conditional sentences to answer the second question. You could help **weaker students** by modelling some example sentences, e.g. *If I'd been in that situation, I'd have used my smartphone to call the police*.
- Put students into pairs to talk about the stories that feature in the news report.
- Ask some students to report back to the class on what their partner said.

 Set Exercises 1, 2, 3 and 4 on page 79 of the **Workbook** for homework.

Language focus 2 Reported questions

Objectives
- learn reported questions and indirect questions.
- imagine a crime and roleplay a conversation about it.

Warm-up
- Books closed. Write a reported question on the board, e.g. *He asked if I liked computer games*.
- Ask students if they can say what the question is in direct speech e.g. *He asked 'Do you like computer games?'*

1
- Ask students to open their books at page 89.
- Students copy the sentences into their notebooks and complete them.
- Play the recording from page 88 for students to check.

Answers

Direct questions	Reported questions
Were you scared?	I also **asked** him if he'd been scared.
How did you catch the robber?	I asked him how he **had caught** the robber.
Why is James's evidence so important?	I asked the police why James's evidence **was** so important.

2
- Ask students to complete the rules using the examples in Exercise 1 to help them.
- For further information and additional exercises, students can turn to page 106 of the **Grammar reference** section.

Answers
1 In reported *Yes/No questions*, we use ***if***.
2 The word order is **different** in direct and reported questions.
3 The tense **changes** in reported questions.
4 Reported questions **don't have** question marks.

3
- Refer students to the example reported question.
- Put students into pairs to order the words in questions 2–5.

Answers
2 if she had been alone   3 if she had a criminal record
4 if anybody had seen her
5 why she hadn't called the police immediately.

Indirect questions

4
- Refer students to the example sentences taken from the listening on page 88.
- Ask students to copy the sentences into their notebooks.
- Play the recording again for students to complete the sentences.
- Check answers.

Answers

Direct questions	Reported questions
What did you discover there?	**Can** you tell us what you discovered there?
Give us more details about the crime, James.	James, I was **wondering if** you could give us more details about the crime.

5
- Do this exercise with the whole class.
- For further information and additional exercises, students can turn to page 106 of the **Grammar reference** section.

Answers
In indirect questions,
1 we **don't use** the auxiliary verbs *do* or *did*.
2 we **use** if in *Yes/No questions*.
3 we use the word order of a **statement**.
We use indirect questions in order to **be polite**.

6
- Read out the example.
- Put students into pairs to turn the remaining direct questions into indirect questions.

Answers
Could you tell me …
2 how old you are?   3 what happened?
4 when the robbery took place?
5 if you did anything to try to stop the robbers?
6 when the police arrived?   7 if you were frightened?
8 if anybody else saw the incident?

> **Say it right!**
>
> ### Intonation in indirect questions
> 1 🔊 **2.35** Students open their books at page 97.
>   - Play the recording for students to listen to the questions and repeat the questions.
>
> 2 🔊 **2.36** Play the recording for students to mark the rising and falling stresses in each question.
>
> 3 🔊 **2.36** Play the recording for students to check their answers and repeat the sentences.
>
> #### Answers
> 1 Could you tell me about your **fa**mily (↗), **please** (↘)?
> 2 Can you tell me how **old** (↗) you are, **please** (↘)?
> 3 Could I ask if you drive a **car** (↗), **please** (↘)?
> 4 Can I ask you to re**peat** (↗) that, **please** (↘)?
> 5 Do you know where the **toi**lets (↗) are, **please** (↘)?
>
> 4 Put students into pairs to practise saying the questions in Exercise 2 with the correct intonation.

Your turn

7
- Students should make notes, including the following information: what happened and where it happened as well as a description of the person or people involved.

8
- Put students into pairs: A and B. A are police officers and B witnesses.
- Students A ask Students B the questions in Exercise 6.
- Students swap roles.

 Set Exercises 1, 2, 3, 4 and 5 on page 80 of the **Workbook** for homework.

Discover Culture

Future directions

Objectives

- watch a video about a female police officer in China.
- talk about which jobs I think women do better than men.

Background

The **first modern police force** was the Metropolitan Police Force in London, popularly known as *the Met*.

Warm-up

- Books closed. Ask: *Why do you think people want to be police officers?*
- Elicit answers and briefly discuss the question with the class.

1 Ask students to open their books at page 90.
- Read out the two questions, put students into pairs to answer the questions.

2 ▶ 8.2 Put students into pairs to answer the question about the kinds of problems that female police officers in China might face.
- Play the video for students to check their answers.

Videoscript

Narrator: The Gansu province, in the northwest of China, is a land of ancient traditions. It was here that, 600 years ago, Chinese emperors protected their people by building the Great Wall of China. Today, people like this woman, Jolene Chu, also protect people. She is a police officer in the Gansu Province. We interviewed Jolene about her job and daily routine. She said she starts each day with a class in martial arts. All the other officers are men. We asked her if it was difficult being a female police officer.

Jolene: I may be a woman on the outside, I may appear to be very gentle, but I'm a lot tougher than I look. I'm just as capable as my male colleagues, and I've got the guts to face down hardened criminals.

Narrator: Her department reported making hundreds of arrests last year. Jolene loves her work.
She says that it was quite hard at the beginning, but now the other officers respect her and treat her as an equal. She feels she is making a contribution to society. But being a police officer is not her only job. Jolene also looks after her ageing parents. She buys and prepares all of their meals and cleans the house.

Jolene: My parents are getting old, so I do all that I can to help them. You do what you have to do.

Jolene's mother: I'm so proud of my daughter because she's so devoted to her career.

Narrator: Jolene is very successful – and a little bit different.
Many people in China's Gansu province used to think that women should get married and have children, but things are changing there, as they are everywhere.

Jolene says she sometimes worries about her future because of the different path that she has taken in life. But she believes that the choices she has made are good ones for herself, for her family and for her community. Jolene feels very positive about the future.

Suggested answers

All the other police officers are men. At first, they didn't treat her as equal.
Apart from working as a police officer, she has to look after her parents.

3
- Refer students to the list of activities a–h.
- Ask students to note down which of them they saw the police officer doing in the video.

4 ▶ 8.2 Play the video again for students to check their answers to Exercise 3.

Answers

b, d, e, f, g

5 ▶ 8.2 Ask students to work alone to choose the correct words to complete the quote.
- Play the video for students to check answers.

Answers

1 gentle   2 tougher   3 colleagues   4 guts   5 criminals

6
- Refer students to sentences 1–4.
- Tell students to change the underlined words so the sentences describe Jolene's life accurately.
- Check answers.

Answers

1 men   2 hundreds   3 proud of   4 sometimes

Your turn

7
- Read out the questions.
- Put students into pairs to ask and answer the questions.
- If appropriate, you may then want to **extend** the work on this by focusing on the third of the three questions and having a class discussion on why it is that jobs are so often divided by gender, and whether there are any jobs that men or women are more suited to doing.

> ⊙ For homework, ask students to find out about the police force in their country. They could find out the following information: when the force started, the number of police that there are, the percentage of the force that is female. Students can share what they find out with a partner at the beginning of the next lesson.

Reading An article

Objectives

- read an article about laws in different countries.
- learn verb expressions.
- give my opinion about the laws in the article.

Warm up

- Books closed. Write the phrase *the law of the land* on the board.
- Check students' understanding of the meaning of the phrase, which refers to the existing laws in a particular country, e.g. *You have to drive on the left in the UK, it's the law of the land.*

1 💬 Ask students to open their books at page 91.
- Refer students to the photos.
- Put students into pairs and ask them to answer the questions. Do not confirm or reject students' ideas at this point. Student will check their answers in Exercise 2.

Background

The Acropolis is a rock which rises up above the city of Athens, upon which an ancient citadel of many buildings was built. *Acropolis* means *summit city*.
The Odeon of Herodes Atticus is an amphitheatre located on the Acropolis. It is a popular place to watch live theatre and music.

2 🔊 **2.37** Ask students to read the travel article to check their answers from Exercise 1.

Answers

chewing gum in Singapore; it ruins the city's clean pavements
feeding the pigeons in St Mark's Square in Venice; the damage done to the ancient monuments
wearing high heels to ancient Greek sites; they can do terrible damage to the ancient stones

3
- Refer students to sentences 1–6.
- Ask students to read the article again and then put them in pairs to match the information in the sentences with Singapore, Venice or Athens.
- Check answers. Challenge **stronger students** when they give their answers to give more information than what is required to answer the question, e.g. in item 1 you would ask what the difference of opinion is about the law in question in Singapore.
- Read out the information in the **FACT!** box. Put students into small groups to come up with their own absurd law. One member of each group can then report back to the class.

Answers

1 Singapore 2 Venice 3 Singapore 4 Athens
5 Venice 6 Athens

Optional activity

- Ask students to use their smartphones to look online for more examples of absurd laws such as the one in Sarpourenx.
- Put students into pairs to share what they find.

Explore verb expressions

4
- Refer students to the highlighted words in the article.
- Ask students to work alone to match the words with the definitions.
- Check answers.

Fast finishers

Students can write a sentence using one of the expressions from Exercise 4. Collect and check students' work.

Answers

1 come into existence 2 see the point 3 dates back to
4 went ahead 5 take care 6 running out of

5
- Read out the gapped sentences 1–5.
- Ask students to work alone to complete the sentences.
- Students can compare their answers in pairs before you check answers with the class as a whole.
- To **extend** the work on the vocabulary, you could ask students to turn to the **Vocabulary bank** on page 114 and do the exercises for *Explore verb expressions*.

Answers

1 come into existence 2 running out of 3 dates back to
4 see the point 5 Take care

Your turn

6
- Read out the questions.
- Give students some time to think about their response to the questions before you put students into pairs to ask and answer the questions.
- Students could make some notes in response to the questions before they talk to a partner to help them organise their thoughts. If you choose to do this, encourage **weaker students** to write full sentences, which they can then refer to when discussing the questions with a partner.
- Ask some students to report back to the class on their partner's opinions.

 Set Exercise 6 on page 80 of the **Workbook** for homework.
You could also ask students to think of three laws that they believe should be introduced in their country. These laws should be serious rather than ridiculous. Students should give a reason for the importance they attach to the introduction of such laws. Students can share their ideas with a partner at the beginning of the next lesson.

 **Speaking** Clarifying

Objectives

- watch teenagers talking about the biggest lie they have ever been told.
- listen to a journalist interviewing a footballer.
- practise making ideas clearer and more intelligible.

Warm-up

- Books closed. Tell students a lie about yourself. This could about be your place of birth or a job someone in your family did.
- Then tell students you have told a lie rather than the truth.

Real talk: What's the biggest lie you've ever been told?

1  ▶ **8.3** Ask students to open their books at page 92.

- Tell students they are going to watch some teenagers answering the following question: *What's the biggest lie you've ever been told?*
- Play the video for students to match the person with the lie.
- Students work alone to complete the exercise.
- Check answers. Students should give as much detail as they can in their answers.

Videoscript

Narrator: What's the biggest lie you've ever been told?

Speaker 1: A classmate once told me that there was no school the next day. I went into town and my teacher saw me on her lunch break. She was not happy and I had to stay in after school every day for a week. I was so mad at my classmate.

Speaker 2: My old best friend said she couldn't come shopping with me. She was going to see her sick grandmother. I went shopping by myself instead and guess who I saw? My best friend with a whole load of other kids from my class. I found a new best friend after that!

Speaker 3: I don't know really. But once my big brother gave me a small funny-looking tomato and told me it was really delicious. I put it in my mouth all at once, but it was actually a chili pepper. It was so hot it made me cry!

Speaker 4: It was probably that awful party again when everyone pretended it was an ocean theme and I turned up dressed as a lobster. It doesn't seem like a big lie, but it really ruined the party for me and people kept saying how cute I looked, which made it even worse!

Speaker 5: My grandma always used to tell me that if you eat carrots, you'll be able to see in the dark. For years, I kept eating carrots. She also said that if I eat broccoli, it'll make my hair grow curly. Well, I can't see in the dark, I've got straight hair and I hate carrots and broccoli!

Speaker 6: A boy in my class told everyone that his cousin was Robert Pattinson from the *Twilight* movies. We all believed him and the lie just got bigger and bigger. He just laughed at us when he finally told us the truth. He'd never even seen any of his movies!

Narrator: What's the biggest lie *you've* ever been told?

Answers

a classmate   b ex-best friend   c big brother
d everyone   e granny   f classmate

2 💬 Put students into pairs to ask and answer the question.

Optional activity

- Put students into pairs to talk generally about their lives (interests, family, friends, etc.) Students should include one big lie in the conversation.
- Students then guess what the lie was.

3 🔊 **2.38** Tell students they are going to listen to an interview.

- Play the recording.
- Students listen and answer the question.
- Check answer.

Answer

He has bought a Ferrari.

4 • Refer students to the phrases in the *Useful language* box. Point out that the question *Would you like to comment on ...?* is not commonly used by people outside the media.

- Ask students to complete the conversation using the phrases in the *Useful language* box.

5 🔊 **2.38** Play the recording again for students to check their answers.

Answers

2 is it true that   3 absolutely   4 Is that right
5 are completely false   6 like to comment on
7 totally untrue

6 💬 Ask students to work in pairs to act out the conversation in Exercise 4.

7 💬 Check understanding of *pocket money*, which refers to money given to children by their parents, often on a weekly basis.

- Put students into pairs to ask and answer questions about the rumour. They should use the question *Is it true that ...?* rather than *Would you like to comment on ...?*.

8 💬 Put students into pairs. Give them time to choose which part they wish to play (actor or journalist) and plan what they want to say.

- Students act out their conversations.

 Ask students to search online to find two current rumours about celebrities. Students can share these with each other at the beginning of the next lesson.

✎ Writing An online article

Objectives

- read an article about illegal music downloads.
- learn about describing the amount of something.
- write a news report about online piracy.

Warm-up

- Books closed. Ask students how they access music, e.g. by downloading it or by buying it from a shop.
- Ask whether they ever listen to full albums or whether they prefer listening to individual songs.

1
- Ask students to open their books at page 93.
- Students read the article about illegal music downloads and answer the question.
- Check the answer and then drill the pronunciation of *piracy* /'paɪrəsi/.

> ### Answer
> It's getting better.

2
- Ask students to read the article. Students should then make notes on why illegal downloading is *so worrying*, *a bad thing* and *falling*.
- Students can compare answers in pairs before you check answers with the class as a whole.

> ### Suggested answers
> a It's so worrying because it's said to be the most common global crime.
> b It's a bad thing because music sales have fallen by more than half. It causes problems for musicians, songwriters and other industry workers.
> c It's falling because of the popularity of subscription streaming website and the closure of file-sharing sites.

3
- Read out the information in the *Useful language* box about phrases used to describe amounts. Ask students to work alone to find five examples of such phrases.
- Check answers.

> ### Answers
> **an estimated** 30 billion songs
> **more than** half
> **just under** 95 million illegal downloads
> **well over** $2.5 billion
> **up to** 75%

4
- Ask students to work alone to complete the sentences the words and phrases in the box.
- When checking answers, challenge **stronger students** by asking them to justify the answer they give.

> ### Fast finishers
> Students can write two sentences of their own using the phrases from the box in Exercise 4. Collect and check students' work.

> ### Answers
> 1 well over 2 just over 3 estimated 4 more than
> 5 approximately 6 just under

Language note

The verb *consume* was once used mostly to refer to either eating or drinking something, or using a resource, particularly something such as petrol. However, it is now has the meaning *buy and use in some way* and may refer to anything from music to TV programmes.

Optional activity

- Put students into small groups and ask them to discuss the question of film piracy. They should consider the following question: *How can it be combated and reduced?*
- Ask one student from each group to report back to the class on the ideas that their group came up with.

 Get Writing

PLAN

5
- Students should do their planning in class. The writing can either be done in class or at home.
- Tell students they are going to write a news report about film piracy.
- Put students into small groups to discuss film piracy. Encourage students to make notes on what other students say, e.g. *Marek doesn't see anything wrong with downloading films online.* These can then be used as quotes in the news report, e.g. *Marek, a seventeen-year-old student, said, "I don't think there is anything wrong with film piracy."*
- Students plan their news reports, using the information in Exercise 4 and any other information they can find by using their smartphones to look online. Students should make some notes, which they can then refer to in the following exercise.

WRITE

6
- Tell students to use the example news report as a model to follow.
- Give students ten minutes to complete the writing task. Students should write between 140 and 160 words.
- Monitor while students are writing. Help with grammar and vocabulary as necessary.

CHECK

7
- Tell students that it is very important that they check their writing in order to look for ways to improve its content, style and structure.
- Give students a few minutes to look through their descriptions and check them against the points here.
- Collect students' news reports and mark them.

> ➜ Set Exercises 1, 2, 3 and 4 on page 82 and Exercises 5, 6, 7, 8, 9, 10 and 11 on page 83 of the Workbook for homework.
> You could also ask students to read this article on online piracy: http://learnenglishteens. britishcouncil.org/magazine/entertainment/ pirated-films-it-really-worth-it

1 Milan fashion week

Summary

Have you ever been to a real fashion show? A teen blogger takes us on a tour of one of Europe's most prestigious fashion events: Milan Fashion Week. We get an inside view into the world of fashion with close ups of the beautiful outfits made by famous designers. We see the models in action as they display the latest trends on the catwalk.

Background

The most significant **fashion weeks** are those held twice a year in four cities which are commonly referred to as *fashion capitals*: Milan, Paris, New York and London.

Before you watch

1 Think about vocabulary.

- Write the word *fashion* on the board.
- Put students into pairs to brainstorm words they associate with fashion.
- Make this competitive by telling students that the pair that comes up with the most correct words wins.

Suggested answers

clothes, models, designers, design, patterns, materials, fashion shows, catwalk

Language note

The **catwalk** is the platform that models walk down during shows to display new designs. In American English it is called the *runway*.

While you watch

2 Watch without sound. Write a voice-over.

- Tell students they are going to watch a video about Milan Fashion Week.
- Play the first part of the video without sound (up to 01.20).
- Put students into groups to write a voice-over to accompany the beginning of the video.
- One member of each group can read the voice-over out to the class.
- Play the first part of the video again for students to see how their script compares to the actual one.

3 Watch and complete.

- Write the following on the board:
  1 The models were wearing so many cool new ....
  2 Maybe we'll see these .... in the shops next year!
  3 These .... are typical of Missoni.
  4 They often use bright colours and ....
  5 There were so many people working ....
  6 A few of the dresses weren't really my ....
- Play the video for students to complete the sentences.
- Check answers.

Answers

1 looks 2 designs 3 patterns 4 stripes 5 backstage
6 style

After you watch

4 Think about the statement. Discuss in groups.

- Write the following statement on the board: *Fashion creates a false image of beauty.*
- Ask students to write down some ideas in response to the statement.
- Put students into small group to discuss the statement.

At home

5 Write a review.

- Tell students that they are fashion bloggers who have recently been to fashion weeks in Paris and New York.
- Using the video about Milan to help them, students should write a review of the show, saying what they thought of the shows in each place, e.g. *Last week I was in New York for fashion week! The show was great. The place was full of people and everyone was really excited. I didn't like all the clothes on display, some were very strange, but there were some dresses for autumn that I think will be popular.*
- Collect and check students' reviews in the next lesson.

Milan fashion week

Hello, everyone! Where am I taking you today in my blog? Milan, in the north of Italy. Why Milan? Well, it's THE fashion capital of the world! And every year, Milan hosts a week of fashion shows. This year, I got the chance to see some clips from one of the shows and it looked AMAZING! The models were wearing so many cool new looks, like these, by Missoni, one of my FAVOURITE designers. Just look at these outfits! Maybe we'll see these designs in the shops next year! These patterns are typical of Missoni's designs. They often use bright colours and stripes, and they're all made in Italy. I used to think it would be cool to be a model, but it doesn't look like much fun here. Everyone has to be perfect, so there's a lot of waiting around before the show. There were so many people working backstage. It takes three hours to do the models' hair and make up! I definitely don't have the patience for that! A few of the dresses, like this one, weren't really my style. Finally, the show began. At the end of the show, all of the models walked down the catwalk together. After the show, there was a huge party with all of the models and the designers. Well, that's all for now!

2 Born to dive

Summary

What's it like to be underwater for extended periods of time? For Italian free diver Michele Rallo, being underwater with no breathing equipment is just a way of life. We see him practising off the coast of Sicily and get to witness the competition that gets him officially qualified as a professional free diver.

Before you watch

1 Brainstorm extreme sports.

- Write *extreme sports* on the board.
- Put students into small groups to think of examples of extreme sports.
- Make this competitive by telling students that the group that comes up with the most examples in 30 seconds wins.

> **Suggested answers**
>
> bungee jumping, cliff diving, ice climbing, kitesurfing, rock climbing, white water rafting

While you watch

2 Make predictions.

- Tell students they are going to watch a video about someone doing the extreme sport of free diving. Do not go into any detail as to the nature of this extreme sport.
- Ask students to make a list of things they would expect to see in the video, e.g. the sea, a swimming pool, goggles, swimming trunks, crowds of people, special diving equipment.
- Students can compare their lists in pairs.
- Play the first part of the video (up to 01.38) for students to check their answers.

3 Watch without sound.

- Turn the sound off on the video.
- Play the rest of the video (from 01.39 till the end).
- As the video plays elicit descriptions of the images from the class as a whole. Encourage students to both describe the images and to say what is happening in the story.
- Students then watch the video with the sound on to check their ideas.

After you watch

4 Discuss the questions.

- Write the following questions on the board:
  1 Why do you think people do extreme sports?
  2 Would you like to try an extreme sport? Why? Why not?
- Put students into pairs and ask them to discuss the questions. Encourage students to develop conversations by asking each other further questions.
- Ask some students to report back to the class.

At home

5 Write a description of free diving.

- Ask student to imagine that their brother or sister is a free diver. They should then write a short description of free diving, saying what they feel about what their sibling does.
- Collect and check students' descriptions in the next lesson.

Born to dive

Narrator: This is twenty-four-year-old Michele Rallo from Sicily. He has an amazing skill: he can dive forty-five metres under water on one breath of air. Michele is a free diver. Free diving means diving without any breathing equipment. Michele has been training for a long time, but he's not a professional yet. To become one, he has to dive over 50 metres in the Italian free-diving championship. But there's one problem. Michele's parents are worried about him. They have never fully understood his love for the sport and are concerned for his safety. So before the championship, Michele visits his parents to reassure them.

Mother: Do you really have to do this dive? You know it's dangerous. Really dangerous.

Michele: Fear is something you don't need. I think fear is what my mother has when she says 'Don't do this, don't do that.' But Mom doesn't understand what I do. I'm not scared because I know what I'm doing. I've never gone beyond my limits.

Narrator: On the day of the championship, there are no big crowds, only friends, the divers, and the judges. Michele uses the time to prepare himself for his dive. Michele gets the signal that it's his turn. He dives down very quickly. He has to dive over 50 metres, but he has never gone deeper than 45 metres before. It is a long wait. Over three minutes. Finally, Michele returns. He's done it! He reached 57 metres. He can now dive in professional competitions in Sicily and around the world. His dream has finally come true.

3 Insectmobile

Summary

What would an alternative to the wheel look like and how would it function? These are the questions a small group of scientists ask themselves when facing a flat tire. This launches them into a search for a new version of the wheel, and they find their ideas for their experiments in some unusual sources.

Background

The word **mobile** /ˈməʊbaɪl/ comes from the Latin *mobilis*, from the verb *movere* meaning *to move* In this use its pronunciation is /məʊˈbiːl/.

Before you watch

1 Work with a partner.

* Write the following questions on the board.
  1 What is your favourite means of transport? What are its advantages?
  2 Are there any forms of transport you do not enjoy using? What are they and why don't you like them?
* Put students into pairs to ask and answer the questions.
* You could then ask some students to report back to the class on what their partner said.

While you watch

2 Watch and complete.

* Tell students they are going to watch a video about a group of scientists trying to create a new form of transportation.
* Write the following on the board:
  1 The scientists decide to invent a .... with legs.
  2 They talk to an .... at the university.
  3 They build a .....
  4 They set up a .... for the insectmobile to travel on.
  5 The insectmobile fails the final .....
* Play the video for students to complete the sentences. Students shouldn't worry about the spelling of words. If they misspell any words, you can correct this while checking the answers.

Answers

1 vehicle 2 expert 3 prototype 4 track 5 test

3 Watch and write questions.

* Play the recording again.
* Students watch and write four questions about the video to ask their partner. Monitor while students do this task and help **weaker students** to form their questions.
* Put students into pairs to ask and answer the questions.

Suggested questions

1 What problem to the scientists have with their car?
2 Which university do they visit?
3 Which insect do they study?
4 How many tests do they do?

After you watch

4 Work in groups. Discuss the question.

* Write the following statement on the board: *What do animals do better than humans?*
* Put students into groups to discuss the question.

At home

5 Think about great inventions.

* Ask students to do some research into the greatest inventions in human history. They should choose three to make notes on.
* At the beginning of the next lesson students can tell their partner why they believe the inventions they chose are so significant.

Insectmobile

Narrator:	What happens when a bunch of scientists out on a day trip have a flat tyre? The broken wheel actually gives them some new ideas!
Man 1:	Take a look at nature!
Man 2:	There's a reason animals and insects have legs instead of wheels!
Narrator:	So, while the guys are walking home, they decide that they're going to invent a vehicle with legs. It'll be even better than the wheel! Back at the office.
Man 2:	Alright, guys, so we're gonna reinvent the wheel.
Man 3:	That sounds hard.
Narrator:	To get started, they decided to find out more. So they went to the University of California to talk to an expert.
Man:	And we know that you have a lot of experience looking at animals and insects and how they move – and I guess our first question is: How many legs should this vehicle have?
Professor:	The minimum number, I think – six would be good – because that forms a really stable platform.
Narrator:	To get a better idea, they studied a cockroach running. The professor explained how the cockroach's six legs form triangles, which are really strong and stable. The next step was to build a prototype – a test vehicle – with six legs and a passenger. After setting up the track, the guys were ready for the test. It goes well!
Man:	That's amazing! One try!
Narrator:	Next they had to design and build the *real* vehicle. Now it's time for the final test. How will their robot do? Everything is going well, until …
Man:	Nope. It's not gonna do it.
Narrator:	OK, so, they failed. But that's alright. They're going to try again.
Man:	Alright! Last leg is on. Ready to go!
Narrator:	Will they succeed this time?

4 Oil from goats

Summary

Argan oil has a mysterious origin and it has to do with goats. We travel with naturalist, Jeff Corwin, to explore the landscape of Morocco where he finds goats in trees! We learn how the relationship the goats have with their habitat and the food they find there actually creates this oil that is so beneficial to humans.

Background

Argan oil, which is made from the seeds of the argan tree in Morocco, is one of the rarest oils in the world. It is used in cosmetics and for cooking.

Before you watch

1 Talk with a partner.

- Put students into pairs to say if they know anything about how cosmetics are produced.
- Ask some students to share their idea with the class.

While you watch

2 Watch and predict.

- Tell students they are going to watch a video about the production of an oil in Morocco.
- Put students into small groups to discuss the images they would expect to see in the video.
- Ask one member of each group to report their group's ideas to the class.
- Play the video for students to find out how accurate their predictions were.

3 Watch and make notes.

- Write the following on the board:
  Taroudant goats machines Berber tribes
- Play the recording again for students to make notes on the things you wrote on the board. Encourage **stronger students** to go into as much detail as they can.
- Check answers.

> **Suggested answers**
>
> Taroudant is a place in Morocco. The area shown in the video is near there.
> Goats climb the argan trees and eat the fruit. After the fruit has passed through their body, the fruit's seeds are collected, roasted, turned into a paste and then oil.
> Nowadays the paste is made from the seeds by machines not just by hand.
> In some Berber tribes the oil is used with meat, fish and bread.

After you watch

4 Describe a product.

- Put students into groups.
- Ask students to think about a product in their country that has been made for a long time, e.g. a particular cheese or dish, an item of clothing, or a musical instrument.
- Give students time to prepare a write a description of how this product is made. Students can do some research online.
- Students can then make a short presentation to the class.

At home

5 Write about the production of argan oil.

- Tell students they are journalists who have been sent by their website or newspaper to Morocco to write about the production of argan oil in Morocco, e.g. *It was a hot day when I arrived on the outskirts of the Moroccan city of Taroudant to find goats in the trees.*
- Collect and check students' work in the next lesson.

Oil from goats

Narrator: Morocco. A country with natural beauty and strong connections between the land and the people. Today, naturalist Jeff Corwin is exploring the wildlife in the area around Taroudant. He's particularly interested in these argan trees. There's something strange about them. If you look closely, you'll see goats in the trees! They're eating the argan fruit.

Jeff: Careful there sweetheart. It's raining goats! We're about twenty kilometres from Taroudant and I've stopped to check this out. These goats, whether they know it or not, are part of a cooperative, part of a relationship. And what they do is they go up in these argan trees and they eat the fruit. This is the argan fruit right here. So how is it that this behaviour, this ability to climb this tree and eat this argan fruit positively benefits the people of this land? The goat eats the argan fruit, the argan fruit passes through the animal's body and then of course comes out the other end.

Narrator: When the seeds have passed through the goat's body, they will be roasted and made into a paste. Nowadays it's also made by machines, not just by hand. From this paste comes a delicate oil, argan oil. In certain traditional Berber tribes, the argan oil is used with foods like meat, fish and bread. Today argan oil is often used for beauty purposes, for skin and hair, and is sold around the world.

Jeff: And this is a relationship between tree, goat, and human being that has gone on for hundreds and hundreds of years.

5 Objects for survival

Summary

How well do you think you would do if you were dropped in the snowy Alps and told to survive on your own for several days? Survival expert Bear Grylls takes us on his own adventure and shows us how he manages to survive in freezing temperatures using only the simple materials he has with him.

> ### Background
> **Bear Grylls** is a British adventurer well-known in the United Kingdom as a presenter of TV programmes about survival in the wild.

Before you watch

1 Talk with a partner.

- Put students into pairs. Ask students to choose objects that they would take with them in a survival pack if they were going on an expedition in the mountains.
- Ask students to report back to the class on the items they and their partner choose.

While you watch

2 Predict and watch.

- Tell students they are going to watch a video about someone attempting to survive in the mountains in extreme cold.
- Put students into small groups to talk about which of the objects in Exercise 1 they would expect to see in the video.
- Ask one member of each group to report their group's ideas to the class.
- Play the video for students to find out how accurate their predictions were.

> ### Answers
> Bear Grylls only has a parachute, a backpack and a water bottle.

3 Order the events.

- Write the following on the board:
  1 He makes a snow cave.
  2 He ties his parachute rope around his boot.
  3 He uses his parachute as bedding.
  4 He moves down the mountain.
  5 He finds pine roots to eat.
  6 He fills his water bottle with snow.
- Ask students to work in pairs to order the events from the video.
- Play the recording again for students to check their answers.

> ### Answers
> 2 – 1 – 3 – 6 – 4 – 5

After you watch

4 Discuss survival in groups.

- Put students into groups.
- Ask students to talk about whether they would like to spend a night on an ice-cold mountainside in a snow cave and how they think they would cope in such a situation. You may need to teach the meaning of *cope*, which means *to deal effectively with a difficult situation*.

At home

5 Write a diary entry.

- Ask students to imagine that they have to spend a night alone on a freezing cold night in the Alps. They should write a diary entry about the experience, e.g. *I don't know why I'm here when I could be in bed. I'm lying in a snow cave on top of my parachute.*
- Collect and check students' work in the next lesson.

Objects for survival

Narrator: This is Bear Grylls, a survival expert. Today, he's going to show us how to survive in the mountains using only simple materials. And there he goes! Now Bear is on his own in the freezing Alps. He has to be careful not to fall through the cracks in the ice beneath the snow. His parachute rope can be used to break his fall.

Bear: Every like couple of feet I'm going to get a big bunch of it, turn it over, and make like a knot like this.

Narrator: Then he ties the knot to his shoe. His parachute is filled with snow and is used as a weight. But there's only one way to see if it will work. The hardest part is getting out! A snowstorm is coming and Bear needs to find shelter quickly. Bear will make a snow cave. The plastic from his backpack can be used to dig in the snow. Finally, he finishes the snow cave. His parachute can be used as bedding and he fills his water bottle with snow. When it melts, it'll be used for drinking water. It's morning. During the night, a lot of snow has fallen, so Bear has to dig his way out of the cave.

Bear: There is just no sign of anybody or anything for miles and miles around. And there's also no sign of anything to eat. No breakfast.

Narrator: Bear has to keep moving to find food and stay warm. He quickly moves down the mountain towards the tree line. There will be food there. In the trees, he finds pine roots to eat. Then, he builds a fire to boil water. Spruce branches can be used to make a tea that has eight times more Vitamin C than orange juice. And it tastes good! Bear has survived using very few objects. Could you do that?

6 Let's celebrate

Summary

From China to Russia, Japan to India, people have traditions and rituals that accompany the changing months. Some have festivals and others more unusual events, but all acknowledge the passage of time and the chance for renewal.

Background

Diwali is a Hindu festival celebrated in the autumn to coincide with the Hindu New Year. The word *diwali* is derived from Sanskrit meaning *row of lights*.

Chinese New Year is also known as the Spring Festival. Chinese New Year takes place in late January or early February.

Before you watch

1 Think about festivals.

- Write the following on the board: *What annual festivals do you enjoy?*
- Put students into pairs to answer the question.

While you watch

2 Watch without sound. Write a voice-over.

- Tell students they are going to watch a video about cultural celebrations around the world.
- Play the first part of the video without sound (up to 00.37).
- In groups students write a voice-over to accompany the beginning of the video.
- One member of each group can read the voice-over out to the class.
- Play the first part of the video again with sound on for students to compare their script to the actual one.

3 Watch and make notes.

- Write the following on the board:
  *firework display   to feel revitalised   cherry blossom
  Diwali   aspirations*
- Play the second part of the recording (from 00.38 till the end).
- Students watch and make notes on to explain the meaning of the words and phrases. Encourage **weaker students** to look online for help.
- Check answers.

Suggested answers

firework display – a public event at which fireworks are set off to mark an occasion; important in big cities in China
to feel revitalised – to have a new sense of vitality and life, a feeling people often have after exercise
cherry blossom – flowers on cherry trees that appear in spring; symbol of spring in Japan
Diwali – the *festival of light* that takes place in India
aspirations – things you hope to achieve

After you watch

4 Work in pairs.

- Write the following on the board: *Which of the activities from the video would you most and least like to do?*
- Put students into pairs to ask and answer the question.

At home

5 Write about festival and celebrations.

- Ask students to choose a festival or celebration that they most look forward to for each season of the year.
- Students should write a description of the events and explain why they like them.
- Collect and check students' work at the beginning of the next lesson.

Let's celebrate

Each season brings its own excitement. People all over the world enjoy celebrating the changing seasons. How do they celebrate? Enjoying time with friends and family, giving gifts or taking part in traditions, sometimes unusual. In China, winter marks the beginning of a new year. It's a time for visiting friends and family. All across China, people celebrate the New Year by lighting fireworks to bring luck for the following year. In big cities, hundreds of people are needed to make the firework display. But small parties can be a lot of fun too! In Russia, the winters are long and cold. But the people there still embrace the season by taking part in different outdoor activities. For many Russians, this includes swimming in freezing outdoor pools. Building strength in both mind and body, they feel immediately revitalised. In Japan, spring is the time of renewal. And the cherry blossom is the symbol of spring. Friends and families get together for picnicking and 'hanami' – cherry blossom watching. And when spring turns to summer, everything turns green and vibrant. It's the season of maturity and growth. It's also the season of street festivals. This elaborate festival celebrates a good rice crop. Playing instruments and watching night parades are part of the celebration. In India, autumn is a glittering, colourful and joyous time because it's Diwali, the festival of light and the beginning of a new year. Friends and family exchange gifts and enjoy each other's company. They share their hopes and aspirations for the new year, ending one season and starting the cycle over again.

7 Mission: possible?

Summary

Time travel may one day take place, but what will it take for us to be able to do it successfully? Motion sickness could be a big obstacle for humans. We see in this video how one scientist has attempted to prevent this from happening with a special invention.

Background

The word **astronaut** comes from Greek; the two parts of the word mean *star* and *sailor.*

Before you watch

1 Think about vocabulary.

- Write the following on the board:
  time travel   motion sickness   galaxy
- Put students into pairs to make notes on what the above terms mean. Encourage **weaker students** to look for ideas online.
- Check answers.

Suggested answers

time travel: the idea of travelling in time to the past or future

motion sickness: nausea caused by movement, particularly by travelling in a car, by plane, etc.

galaxy: a system of millions of stars; our own galaxy is called *the Milky Way*

While you watch

2 Watch and write a summary.

- Tell students they are going to watch a video about space travel.
- Write the following on the board:
  1 How astronauts travel to distant parts of the galaxy
  2 Scientists believe that time travel is possible
  3 How to help astronauts feel better in space
- Play the video for students to choose the best summary of the video.
- Check answers.

Answer

3

3 Watch and answer the questions.

- Write the following on the board:
  1 What do scientists regularly send to distant parts of the galaxy?
  2 When do people get motion sickness?
  3 Which country is the professor from?
  4 What has the professor invented?
  5 What does the professor's invention do?
- Play the video again.
- Check answers.

Answers

1 machines
2 when there is a difference between the movement they see and feel
3 the USA
4 special glasses
5 stops people feeling motion sickness

After you watch

4 Work in groups. Discuss the question.

- Write the following on the board: *What in the video, if anything, surprised you?*
- Put students into small groups to answer the question.

At home

5 Find out about space missions.

- Students can also find out about a mission to space from the past. They should make notes on the following: the country or countries involved; what the mission was about; how successful it was. Students can also find out about astronauts from their own country.
- Students can share what they find out with a partner at the beginning of the next lesson.

Mission: possible?

Narrator: Imagine if we could travel through time, to other parts of the galaxy. Scientists haven't mastered time travel yet, but each year technology takes us further and further into previously unknown regions. Scientists regularly send sophisticated machines to distant parts of the galaxy, but what about humans? Could humans learn how to live in space? Many astronauts suffer from motion sickness – a type of nausea. People get motion sickness when there is a difference between the movement they see and the movement they feel. Looking more closely at this issue, a professor in the US found something interesting. He studied the astronauts' experience in space and he found one who never suffered from motion sickness. He observed him carefully and discovered something unusual. The astronaut's eyes moved very quickly, as if he was seeing flashing lights. So the professor invented special glasses with flashing lights. To test the glasses, he asked two women to read a book while riding in a car. One woman wore normal, clear glasses, and the other wore the new, flashing glasses. The woman with the clear glasses soon felt sick.

Woman: I'm not feeling very well right now. Could you stop the car now, please?

Narrator: If she'd been wearing the special glasses, she probably wouldn't have experienced the motion sickness, as the other woman felt fine.
Perhaps this invention and ones like it could be the key to more exploration in space. If we had the ability to travel freely throughout the universe, how far could we go? Could we some day learn how to travel through time as well?

8 On the run

Summary

Jamey Harris is a young man who was wanted for robbery, among other crimes. In this video, we follow Jamey's footsteps as he ends up taking a wrong path in life and then questions what would have happened if he had made better choices.

Background

The phrase **on the run** means *to attempt to avoid capture, usually by the police.* People who run away from institutions are generally referred to as **runaways**, and those who go on the run from police are called **fugitives**, although the terms are used interchangeably.

Before you watch

1 Think about vocabulary.

- Write the word *crime* on the board.
- Put students into pairs and ask them to brainstorm words that they associate with crime.
- Make this competitive by telling students that the pair which comes up with the most correct words wins.

> **Suggested answers**
>
> criminal, police, police officer, theft, shoplifting, robbery, arson, jail

While you watch

2 Watch without sound.

- Tell students they are going to watch a video about a young man who goes on the run.
- Put students into pairs (A and B).
- Turn the sound off on the video.
- Student A sits with his/her back to the screen.
- Student B watches the video and describes the images.
- Students swap roles at the halfway point in the video (01.21).
- Students then watch the video with the sound on to check their ideas.

3 Watch and complete.

- Write the following on the board:
  1 Jamey is in . . . . now.
  2 His crimes started when he was a . . . . .
  3 When he was 18, he began stealing . . . . .
  4 Jamey hid in an empty building in the . . . . .
  5 His best friend and his . . . . said he was ruining his life.
  6 Jamey was visiting some . . . . when the police arrived.
- Play the video again for students to complete the sentences.
- Check answers.

> **Answers**
>
> 1 jail   2 teenager   3 cars   4 mountains   5 mother
> 6 friends

After you watch

4 Work in groups. Discuss the question.

- Write the following questions on the board: *Why do people commit crimes?*
- Put students into small groups to ask and answer the questions.

At home

5 Find out about crime.

- Ask students to do some research into the types of petty crimes (i.e. minor crimes such as theft) that are committed either in their area or in their country as a whole.
- Students can share what they find out with a partner at the beginning of the next lesson.

On the run

People in Marion County, Tennessee, in the southern United States, tell a story about a man called Jamey Harris. Jamey was known for his small crimes and is in prison now. But for years, the police couldn't catch him. Jamey's crimes began when he was a teenager. He started with stealing chickens and once, he said, he even stole a horse. It wasn't long before Jamey was stealing other things. Then, when he turned 18, he began stealing cars. His best friend told him he was ruining his life, that he should stop now and get a job, like everyone else. But Jamey had already gone too far. The local police said that Jamey Harris had to be stopped. But Jamey managed to do what he always did best – he ran. He boasted that he knew the woods better than the police did. Even the police dogs couldn't find him. After some time, the police reported that Jamey had done it again: he and some friends had stolen another car. This time, Jamey hid in an empty building in the mountains and stayed there for a few days. Jamey grew so confident that he even visited his mother one day. She told him he was ruining his life and she begged him to surrender to the police. But Jamey refused. He still believed he would never be caught. Then, just a few days later, he was visiting some friends when suddenly, the police arrived! Jamey knew that he couldn't run this time. He says now that he should have listened to his friend and his mother. He should have turned his life around when he had the chance. He'll have plenty of time to think about it now – in prison.

CLIL video activities and key

1 CLIL Trendsetters

Summary

What makes something trendy? There's no formula so businesses have to rely on trendsetters to tell them what's cool and what's not. In this video, we follow two Japanese girls who are known for their trendsetting ability and see them in action in Tokyo's most famous shopping district as they evaluate and react to various products.

> **Background**
>
> **Shibuya** is a fashionable area of Tokyo and an important shopping district.

Before you watch

1 Think about vocabulary.
- On the board write *trend* and *trendsetter*. Explain that *trend* is another word for fashion and a *trendsetter* is someone who sets a new trend.
- You could also revise some appropriate adjectives at this point such as *trendy* and *fashionable*.

While you watch

2 Watch without sound.
- Tell students they are going to watch a video about trendsetting in Tokyo.
- Play the video without sound and ask students to make notes about what the information they think will feature in the voiceover. **Weaker students** could write down ten words they think they are likely to hear in the story.
- Students compare their ideas and attempt to put the story together.
- Play the video again with the sound for students to check their ideas.

3 Watch and write questions.
- Play the recording again.
- Students watch and write four questions about the video to ask their partner. Monitor while students do this task and help **weaker students** to form their questions.
- Put students into pairs to ask and answer the questions.

> **Suggested questions**
>
> 1 Why do businesses pay attention to Saeko and Yuko?
> 2 What do the girls do with new products?
> 3 What are the girls trying out today?
> 4 What are they helping to shape?

After you watch

4 Work in groups. Think of current trends.
- Put students into small groups.
- Ask students to think of things, e.g. music, clothes, films and computer games, which are beginning to become popular with young people.
- Once students have decided on their list, ask them to think about how these things have become popular, e.g. because celebrities like them or because they had successful TV adverts.
- Ask one student from each group to share their ideas with the class.

At home

5 Think about who or what influences you to buy things.
- Ask students to choose a few objects that they have bought that mean a lot to them. These objects could be anything from an item of clothing to a technological gadget, a musical instrument or a computer game.
- Students should think about why the objects mean so much to them and why they wanted to buy the object so much. They should then decide whether they wanted it in order to be part of a current trend.
- At the beginning of the next lesson, students can compare their idea with a partner.

Trendsetters

Narrator:	How do trends start? Where do they come from and who starts them? What makes some things desirable? Who determines what will sell? And how do they become a part of popular culture? In some countries, like Japan, trends are vital. Companies are always looking forward and want to know what's coming. And that's why they watch these two girls, Saeko and Yuko. Saeko and Yuko are trendsetters. Businesses pay attention to what they do, what they wear and where they shop. In Tokyo's Shibuya district, companies know that if these girls like something they've got a product that will sell! They say, 'Sell to one girl in Shibuya and by tomorrow, you've sold to every girl in Japan.' Some businesses hire trendsetters, like Saeko and Yuko, to test new products. Today the girls are trying out a new photo booth. It takes videos instead of photos.
Girl 1:	Here it comes. Look at the hearts coming out. I think the photo booth is easier to use.
Girl 2:	We had fun though.
Narrator:	This is important information for the company. Paying attention to trendsetters makes good business sense. People like Saeko and Yuko know what they like and they know what people their age like. They are helping to shape popular culture. So what do you think is going to be the next big thing?

2 CLIL The house of the future

Summary

In this video, we see how a live-in avatar helps a family navigate basic household tasks and daily routines. We hear directly from the owners about how their life has been made easier by this addition to their family.

Background

The house of the future will contain **the Internet of things**, which refers to connecting everyday objects such as washing machines to the Internet.

Before you watch

1 Brainstorm ideas.

- Put students into small groups to think of what the house of the future will be like.
- Ask one member of each group to report their group's ideas to the class.

While you watch

2 Watch and write down the questions.

- Tell students they are going to watch a video about the house of the future.
- Ask students to watch the first part of the video (up to 00.45) and write down the questions that are asked.
- Play the first part of the video twice for students to complete this exercise.
- Encourage **stronger students** to note down all eight questions.
- **Weaker students** should write down as many as they feel able to.
- Check answers.

Answers

Can you imagine the house of the future?
What will it be like?
How will it be built?
Will houses be in cities like we know today or somewhere different?
Will your house do things for you?
Will it mow the lawn or raise the blinds?
Will it even change the music based on your mood?
What if that house already exists today?

3 Watch and make notes.

- Ask students to watch the video to make notes on all the things that Cleopatra – the name given to the technology that runs the house in the video – can do.
- Play the video from 00.46 till the end.
- Help **weaker students** by telling them there are five things to listen for.
- Check answers.

Answers

She knows who and what is inside the house.
She knows who leaves the house.
She knows who comes into the house, opens the door for them and welcomes them.
She manages the shopping, reordering items as they are needed.
She is in charge of bedtime.

After you watch

4 Think about the statement.

- Write the following statements on the board: *Computers will take all important decisions for us one day.*
- Students can write down some ideas in response to this statement.
- Put students into small groups and ask them to discuss the statements.
- Ask one member of each group to report back to the class.

At home

5 Find out about inventions for the future.

- Ask students to explore the *Internet of things* on this website: http://postscapes.com/internet-of-things-examples/
- Students can discuss the ideas on the above website in small groups at the beginning of the next lesson. Which do they like most?

The house of the future

Narrator:	Can you imagine the house of the future? What will it be like? How will it be built? Will houses be in cities like we know today or somewhere different? Will your house do things for you? Will it mow the lawn or raise the blinds? Will it even change the music based on your mood? What if that house already exists today? Meet Cleopatra. She may play a big part in the house of the future.
Cleopatra:	Nice to meet you.
Brian:	So it's kind of somewhere between a butler, a secretary, a personal assistant, and a … and a babysitter. She mostly lives on a box that we have down in our server room.
Narrator:	Cleopatra uses Radio Frequency ID technology. It allows her to know what and who is inside the house, and what's not. That includes the children.
Cleopatra:	Catherine has left the house.
Brian:	As soon as I step up to the front door, it recognises me, opens the door, welcomes me home.
Cleopatra:	Welcome home, Brian. She also manages the shopping.
Brian:	You simply scan things as you throw them away. It will automatically reorder anything that you scanned.
Narrator:	She's even in charge of bedtime.
Cleopatra:	Lights out, Zeb.
Brian:	There's so many helpful things that your house can do once it knows who you are and where you are.
Host:	If you want to add a Cleopatra to your house, it will cost around fifteen to twenty thousand bucks.
Narrator:	That's a lot of money! But if we're going to live in structures like these in the future, Cleopatra could be a necessary expense.

3 CLIL A cool experiment

Summary

An aspiring scientist asks some questions about the effect humans are having on the Earth. We learn facts about global warming and see Eric set up an experiment in which he tests out his theory.

Before you watch

1 Think about vocabulary.

- Write *science* on the board.
- Put students into small group to brainstorm words they associate with science.

> **Suggested answers**
>
> scientists, experiment, laboratory, chemistry, biology, physics

While you watch

2 Watch without sound.

- Tell students they are going to watch a video about an experiment.
- Put students into pairs (A and B).
- Student A sits with his/her back to the screen.
- Play the video without the sound.
- Student B watches the video and describes the images.
- Students swap roles at the halfway point (01.34).
- Students watch with the sound on to check their ideas.

3 Watch and answer the questions.

- Write the following on the board.
  1 What did Eric do first?
  2 What is Eric's plan?
  3 Which two gases does Eric use in the experiment?
  4 How does Eric monitor the amount of gas in each box?
  5 After how many hours does the ice begin to melt?
  6 Were the boxes containing 'greenhouse gases' warmer than the two that didn't?
- Play the recording again for students to answer the questions.
- Check answers.

> **Answers**
>
> 1 He looked at the science behind rising global temperatures.
> 2 He wants to build four greenhouses, put an ice statue in each box, fill one box with CO_2, one with methane, and two with normal air, and then record the temperatures.
> 3 CO_2 and methane
> 4 with computers
> 5 3.5 hours
> 6 yes

After you watch

4 Work in groups. Discuss the questions.

- Write the following on the board:
  1 How will global warming change life on earth?
  2 What can be done about the problem?
- Help **weaker students** by allowing them to do some research into global warming online before you put students into groups.

At home

5 Do research into weather patterns.

- Ask: *What has the weather been like in your town over the last 50 years?*
- Students will need to look for historical climate data. They can either access meteorological records online or seek information at their local library.
- Students share what they find out with the class in the next lesson.

A cool experiment

Narrator: Every year global temperatures are rising. What does this mean for our planet? Will the ice at the North and South Pole melt completely? Are we going to have more storms and floods? Eric Gustafson, an 11-year-old American scientist, wants to know why this is happening. First, he looked at the science behind it. The Earth absorbs light from the sun, which warms up the surface. Then the heat goes back into the atmosphere. Gases like CO_2 and methane absorb it and warm up our environment. These are called greenhouse gases and they are produced by guess who? Humans. How much impact do we really have on the environment? Eric has a plan. He's going to build four greenhouses, each with an ice statue. He'll fill one box with CO_2, one with methane, and two with normal air. First, they build the greenhouses, carefully and accurately. Each box must be the same. The only thing that will be different is the gas inside each box. They'll need special machines to make the ice statues. These machines are powerful and precise.

Man: Don't you just love that sound!

Narrator: But the result – four identical ice statues – is perfect for the experiment.

Man: Come on, man, what are you doing? Don't drop him!

Narrator: Now it's time to set up the experiment. Each box will receive the same amount of light. Computers will monitor the amount of gas in the boxes. Eric records the temperatures. After three and a half hours, the ice statues start to melt! And the boxes with the CO_2 and methane were one whole degree warmer. What does Eric's experiment show?

Eric: I think that this is showing that CO_2 and methane ARE major culprits for global warming.

Narrator: If greenhouse gases do this to ice, what will they do to our planet? Eric hopes to be part of the solution.

4 CLIL You are what you eat

Summary
This video takes a closer look at what is really in our food. We see how one family is able to plan their meals together and make better decisions when they are selecting food. By paying attention to nutrition labels and including more fruits and vegetables, we learn how to create a more balanced diet.

Background
Some of the information carried on **food labels in the UK**, such as weight, ingredients, shelf life and allergy information are required by law. There are special rules for products and more information might be available.

Before you watch

1 Talk about the food you eat.
- Write the following questions on the board:
  1 What did you eat yesterday?
  2 Did you think about what was in it, i.e. how much sugar, salt, etc.?
- Put students into pairs to discuss the questions.

While you watch

2 Watch and make notes.
- Tell students they are going to watch a video about food production and labelling.
- Write the following expressions on the board:
  processed food   planning meals   nutritional information pizza and burgers   fruit and vegetables   fats and proteins
- Play the recording for students to make notes on the things you wrote on the board. Encourage **stronger students** to go into as much detail as they can.
- Check answers.

3 Watch and write a one-sentence summary.
- Play the video again.
- Ask students to work in pairs to write a one-sentence summary of the content of the video. Help guide **weaker students** to a summary by asking them questions, e.g. *What was the video about? What did we see in the video?*
- Check answers.

After you watch

4 Work in groups. Discuss the question.
- Write the following question on the board: *What information in the video made you think the most about your eating habits?*
- Put students into small groups to ask and answer the question.

At home

5 Find out about information on food labels.
- Ask students to choose a couple of products at home. Is there any surprising information on the labels?
- Alternatively, students could look at the information that supermarkets provide online about the nutritional content of their products.
- Students can share what they find out with a partner in the next lesson.

You are what you eat
People say you are what you eat. But do we really know what we're eating? Technology is changing our food with some very serious results, even if cows and fruit aren't this big yet! At the moment, cows still look like this. But, now more than ever, factories are creating processed food. That is, they change it to make it last longer or taste better. By the time the food gets to the supermarket, it often has salt, sugar, preservatives, colouring and flavouring all added to make us want to eat more of it. So what can we do? Planning meals together is a good way to choose healthier food. What ingredients go into the meals you want to make? Do they have a good balance of the different food groups? When you're shopping, it's important to check for nutritional information. In the UK and the USA, most food products have to have a nutritional information label. Read labels carefully. You may be surprised. You'll soon learn to recognise what's good for you. Not too much sugar, fat, or salt. Pizza and burgers are fine once in a while, but our bodies need a lot of fruit and vegetables every day to stay healthy. The natural sugar in fruit is much healthier than processed sugar. Eating fruit is not only good for you, but its natural sugars also make it tasty. Our bodies also need other nutritional elements found in food, like milk. Milk and cheese contain fats and proteins. If the cow eats healthy, fresh grass, the milk it produces will taste better. And better tasting milk makes better tasting cheese. So, technology and nature can change the way our food tastes. And there are many ways we can learn how to eat better and stay healthy.
Remember: you are what you eat!

5 CLIL What a waste!

Summary

There is a new kind of waste affecting our planet and it's called *e-waste*. The computers and smartphones we discard have to go somewhere and they are now making an impact on our environment. This video offers suggestions as to how we can minimise the negative effect of e-waste.

Background

The terms **disposable society** or **throw-away society** are used to describe modern life, in which we buy new items rather than repair old ones.

Before you watch

1 Make a list.
- Put students into pairs and ask them to make a list of the commonest items that are thrown away in their household.
- Encourage students to think of things other than food.

2 Watch and check.
- Tell students they are going to watch the first part of a video about waste.
- Ask: *What is 'e-waste'?* Elicit students' ideas and put them on the board.
- Play the first part of the video (up to 01.13).
- Students to find out what the *e-* actually stands for.
- Check answers. Challenge **stronger students** by asking them to name some of the suggestions the people in the video came up with for what the *e-* of *e-waste* stands for.

> **Answers**
>
> electronics

3 Watch and answer the questions.
- Write the following questions on the board:
  1 How many tonnes of e-waste are generated each year?
  2 How many phones do Americans throw away in one day?
  3 How many kilos of oil are used to make one computer screen?
  4 How many litres of water are used to make one computer screen?
- Play the next section of the video (01.14 to 01.48).
- Students can answer the questions in pairs.
- Check answers.

> **Answers**
>
> 1 over two million 2 426,000 3 200 4 1,500

4 Watch and make notes.
- Ask students to make notes on the suggestions made in the video as to what can be done about e-waste.
- Play the recording (from 01.49 till the end).
- Check answers.

> **Answers**
>
> Repair computers or give them to a school.
> Recycle the waste.
> Recondition the mobiles for new owners.

After you watch

5 Work in pairs. Discuss the question.
- Write the question on the board: *What in the video, if anything, surprised you?*
- Put students into pairs to answer the question.

At home

6 Keep a 'waste' diary.
- Ask students to spend a week noting down every object they dispose of. Do they put anything in a recycling bank?
- Students can bring their completed diaries to class and discuss alternative uses for the items they discarded.

What a waste!

Narrator: What happens to the things we throw away? Even small items, like pens, are a problem. We use billions of them each year. That means thousands of kilos of rubbish from pens alone. And then there's paper. How many trees are cut down to make all the paper we use and, so often, throw away?

Nye: OK, I'll make you a copy. How many copies? OK.

Narrator: But there's a new kind of waste that's different from all of the traditional kinds of rubbish: e-waste. Scientist Bill Nye asked some people to define it.

Nye: What is e-waste?

Man 1: Um, waste… electricity that's wasted?

Woman 1: E-waste? Ecological waste or something?

Nye: Do you know what e-waste is?

Woman 2: Oh, maybe it's the economic waste. Maybe like from the economy?

Woman 3: Well, 'e' seems to be put in front of everything involving the Internet.

Man 2: Environmental waste?

Narrator: No. The 'e' in 'e-waste' is for electronics. Over two million tons of waste electronics are generated each year! Americans alone throw away 426,000 mobile phones just in one day!
E-waste is often dumped into landfill sites, where its dangerous metals create pollution.
And to make just one computer screen, we use 200 kilos of oil, 20 kilos of dangerous chemicals and 1,500 litres of water. So what do we do about it? We can repair our computers or give them to a school. If that isn't possible, there are also companies that recycle e-waste. Metal and plastic can usually be reused. Mobile phones can also be reconditioned for new owners. A reconditioned phone is much cheaper than a brand new one. So how will our environment be affected by e-waste? We can only keep it green if we take the proper steps.

6 CLIL Reliving history

Summary

Re-enactors are people who meet to recreate historical battles. With recreated footage of the early battles in US history, we see how re-enactors explore different aspects of life in a conflict, from battle gear to living conditions.

Background

There are **re-enactment groups** in many different countries re-creating battles from ancient Rome and Greece, the Middle Ages and the Second World War.

Before you watch

1 Think about dates.

* Put the following years on the board:
  2001   1941   1963   1969
* Tell students something significant in US history happened in each of the years you have written on the board.
* Put students into small groups to talk about what they think happened.
* Check answers.

> **Suggested answers**
>
> **1941:** US entered Word War II.
> **1963:** President Kennedy was assassinated.
> **1969:** Neil Armstrong became the first man to walk on the Moon.
> **2001:** New York and Washington were attacked by hijacked planes.

While you watch

2 Watch and find out.

* Tell students they are going to watch a video about American history.
* Play the first part of the video (up to 00.51).
* Ask students to note down the dates and years mentioned as well as the event those dates and years are connected to.
* Check answers.

> **Answers**
>
> 4th July 1776 – American declaration of Independence signed by 13 colonies
> 1861 – start of the American Civil War
> 1865 – end of the American Civil War

3 Watch and write questions.

* Play the second part of the video (from 00.52 till the end).
* Students watch and write four questions.
* Monitor while students do this task and help **weaker students** to form their questions.
* Students ask and answer the questions in pairs.

> **Suggested questions**
>
> 1 When did Abraham Lincoln make his speech?
> 2 How many re-enactors are there in the USA?
> 3 What do the re-enactors do before and after their battles?
> 4 Can women take part?

After you watch

4 Work in groups. Discuss the idea of re-enacting history.

* Write the following on the board: *What is re-enacting all about? Is it a hobby, a show of respect or a celebration of history?*
* Tell students these questions are asked at the end of the video.
* Put students into small groups to discuss the questions.

At home

5 Find out about the history of your country.

* Ask students to research an interesting period of their own country's history online and make some notes.
* At the beginning of the next lesson, students can tell a partner about the period they choose.

Reliving history

Narrator: The fourth of July, 1776. On this day, the United States of America was officially born. Thirteen American colonies declared their independence from Great Britain. There were many battles throughout the struggle for American independence, and today there are people who celebrate the fourth of July, not with parades and hot dogs, but with real battle gear! These people are not actors – they're re-enactors. And it's not just the American Revolution they honour with their reenactments, but also the American Civil War in 1861. This war between the north and the south went on until 1865 and over a million people died. Near the end of the war, President Abraham Lincoln made a speech on the battlefield of Gettysburg. His goal was to bring the country back together.

Lincoln: … that this nation, shall have a new birth of freedom, and that government of the people, by the people, for the people, shall not perish from the earth.

Narrator: It is the spirit of this speech that re-enactors try to recreate in their battles. There are thousands of re-enactors in the United States, and around the world. Their uniforms are specially designed to look authentic. And their weapons look very real. Attention to detail is important as they reenact what actually happened. Before and after the battle, they live like soldiers from that time. Women were not allowed to fight in the past, so they had to take on other roles. But nothing can stop them from taking on the role of a soldier now! So what is re-enacting all about? Is it a hobby, a show of respect, or a celebration of history? Ask a re-enactor!

7 CLIL Lions in danger

Summary

Recent changes in the climate and increased population have put the African lion in danger. Naturalist Jeff Corwin takes us to one of the most important lion reserves in the region. There he interviews local people about a programme helping to protect the animals.

Background

Lions are found in Africa and the northwest of India.

Before you watch

1 Brainstorm animals.

- Write *Animals from Africa* on the board.
- Put students into small groups to think of examples of animals that live in Africa.

> **Suggested answers**
>
> elephants, zebras, rhinos, leopards, buffalo, hippos, giraffes, gorillas

While you watch

2 Make predictions.

- Tell students they are going to watch a video about African lions.
- Ask students to make a list of things they would expect to see in the video, e.g. trees, hunters, lions fighting each other, lions running after other animals.
- Students can compare their lists in pairs.
- Play the video for students to check their answers.

3 Watch and make notes.

- Write the following numbers on the board:
  25,000   4 out of 5   35 million   20 to 30   2
- Play the recording again for students to make notes on the numbers you wrote on the board. Encourage **stronger students** to go into as much detail as they can.
- Check answers.

> **Answers**
>
> There are only 25,000 African lions left.
> Four out of five hunts for food that lions go on end in failure.
> Kenya's population is over 35 million.
> People used to kill 20 to 30 lions a year in this region.
> If one cow is killed by a lion, people in Samburu get two cows to replace the one that has been lost.

After you watch

4 Work in groups. Discuss the questions.

- Write the following question on the board: *What in the video, if anything, surprised you?*
- Put students into small groups to ask and answer the questions.

At home

5 Find out about endangered animals.

- Ask students to find out about animals in Africa that are endangered.
- Students should find out the following information: what the biggest threat to the animals is, the fall in numbers over the last 100 years, what is being done to save the animals in question.
- Students can share what they find out with a partner at the beginning of the next lesson.

Lions in danger

Narrator: The African lion is now in great danger. A quarter of a million lions once lived here. Now there are only 25,000. Are we humans to blame for killing the last lions of Africa? This part of Africa has not had much rain for some time. That means there are fewer animals for the lions to hunt. Four out of five hunts end in failure. But there's another reason the lions are in danger. Jeff Corwin has been working with wildlife for almost twenty years. He wants to find out why these lions are dying so fast. The wildlife here is now competing with human beings, and there are a lot more people than wildlife. Kenya's population is over 35 million and is growing rapidly every year. Jeff's going to one of Africa's most important lion reserves, a national park where wild animals have always been protected and left undisturbed. A century ago, this was all open country. Now there are farms everywhere. And with more than a quarter of a million people living just outside the park with their own animals, protection of the lions isn't always possible. As wild animals, the lions need to hunt, and when they kill the people's livestock, the *people* kill the lions. In this region of Samburu, they used to kill 20 to 30 lions a year so they could protect their animals. These days, fortunately, the way the people think is changing.

Jeff: Isn't there a programme now, in order to protect the lion?

Man: Yes.

Jeff: How does that programme work?

Man: The programme educates the community not to kill a lion because the lion has become diminished in our area now.

Jeff: It's become diminished. If one cow gets killed, the programme …

Man: The programme gives out two cattle to replace the one lost. Finding enough food is still a problem for these lions, but with programmes like these, their survival might be more possible.

8 CLIL True or false?

Summary

In today's media-rich world, how do we know whether what we see before us is real or fake? With so much information at our fingertips, it is even more important that we look more closely at what is being presented to us. This video asks these hard questions and reminds us of how important it is to look at images with a critical eye.

Before you watch

1 Work with a partner. Answer the question.

- Brainstorm places where we can get information, e.g. from social media, on the websites of media organisations, on collaborative websites, in chatrooms, in conversations with friends, etc.
- Write the following question on the board: *Where do you mostly get your information from?*
- Put students into pairs to ask and answer the question.
- Ask some students to report back to the class on what their partner said.

While you watch

2 Watch and check.

- Tell students they are going to watch a video about the idea of what is true and what is false in the digital world.
- Play the video for students to check how many of their ideas from Exercise 1 are shown in the video.
- Check answers.

> **Answers**
>
> e-reader, book, newspaper, smartphone, laptop, magazine

3 Watch and order the sentences.

- Write the following on the board:
  1 Fashion photographers are experts in manipulating images.
  2 That's where you've got control.
  3 We get so much visual information about the world now.
  4 They are controlling the message so you will buy their product.
  5 You just have to pay attention.
  6 Do we really know what we're looking at?
- Ask students to order the sentences from the video.
- Play the recording again from 01.31.
- Students can compare answers in pairs before you check answers with the class.

> **Answers**
>
> 3 – 6 – 1 – 4 – 2 – 5

After you watch

4 Work in groups. Talk about the ideas from the video.

- Ask students to note down the ideas in the video that they find the most interesting, e.g. the fact that ideas were once the preserve of experts, the idea that not everyone could read, the idea that anyone can be an expert these days, the idea of how important images have become.
- Put students into small groups to discuss these ideas.

At home

5 Write an essay.

- Write the following line from the video on the board: *The fact is that in today's world anyone can be an expert. Or so it seems.*
- Ask students to respond to this idea, offering their own view on the matter of being an expert in the world of instant digital information.
- Collect and check students' work in the next lesson.

True or false?

Narrator: Where do you get your information? And how quickly can you get it? It used to take a lot of time and money to share information with a lot of people. Books were written by experts and, if you were one of the few people who could read, you believed them. Today, with constantly changing technology, we can share information all the time, instantly. And for the first time in human history, we can create and communicate visual information, too. But who are the experts now? Do we know? The fact is that in today's world anyone can be an expert. Or so it seems. But do you believe everything you read, or see? The creator of the large Internet company, Craigslist, had this to say.

Man: What we're living through right now is the flow of power from a relatively small group of people to, in a sense, anyone who wants their little piece of power through the Net. Now, anyone can get your attention, and that matters.

Narrator: We get so much visual information about the world now, but what are those images telling us? Do we really know what we're looking at? Is what we're seeing real or fake? It's so easy now to take photos or videos and manipulate them. Fashion photographers are experts in manipulating images. They want you to believe what you're seeing in the ads they create. They are controlling the message so you will buy their product. But it's up to you to decide if the message is real or not. That's where you've got control. You don't have to be an expert. You just have to pay attention – and not believe everything you see or read.

Social Science The history of jeans

Objectives

- learn about the history of jeans.
- talk about objects and social changes in the 20th century.

Warm-up

- Books closed. Ask: *Which 20th-century objects most changed our lives?*
- Elicit answers and write them on the board.

1 💬 Ask students to open their books at page 115.
- Put students into pairs to answer the questions.

2 🔊 **1.48** Ask students to read the text.
- Put students into pairs to tell one another which facts in the text they find most surprising.

3 • Ask students to read the text again and answer the questions.
- Check answers.

Suggested answers

1 Because they were cheaper and lasted longer than other trousers.
2 By turning cowboys into heroes and making their life seem more attractive.
3 To be different from their parents.
4 More equality between classes and races.
5 It fell.

4 🔊 **1.49** Tell students they are going to listen to a teacher talking to students.
- Play the recording for students to make notes on what influenced people to wear jeans.
- Check answers.

Audioscript

Teacher: Today we are going to think again about what factors influenced who wore jeans and what this tells us about social change during the 20th century. Who can remember what we talked about yesterday?

Student 1: About when different people started wearing jeans.

Teacher: Exactly, thank you. We looked at when different social groups started wearing jeans. In the beginning only poor working-class men wore jeans, then the middle class and finally the whole world. We also looked at how factors such as the film industry influenced what people thought was acceptable. Hollywood helped to change the idea that cowboys were poor working-class men. Middle-class men liked the new image of cowboys as strong, brave and adventurous. Hollywood made it acceptable to be more like cowboys. Men's and women's roles also changed during the 20th century. The first women's jeans were introduced in 1934 but most people thought women shouldn't work outside the home. As a result they didn't think women should wear working men's clothes such as jeans either. It took another 30 years for jeans to be accepted as women's clothes. So let's see, we talked about different groups in society, about the influence of the film industry. Did we mention anything else?

Student 2: Yes, the Great Depression in America.

Teacher: Yes, well done. The economy is an important factor in social change. In times of crisis, people have to change their behaviour because they have less money. It was during this period that middle-class men started wearing jeans, perhaps because they needed to buy cheaper trousers. So by studying the history of jeans we were able to map social change in American and Europe during the 20th century. If we look at jeans today, we see how societies continue to change. Today we are worried about our planet, because of this jeans manufacturers try to protect the environment when they make jeans. Factories use less water to make jeans and farmers use fewer chemicals to grow cotton. Society continues to change and jeans continue to reflect this. Now lets open our textbooks on page …

Suggested answers

class, the film industry, the changing roles of men and women, the Great Depression, the environment

5 🔊 **1.49** Refer students to the list.
- Check understanding of the word *class*, which in this context refers to social status.
- Put students into pairs and ask them to make notes on what they remember the teacher saying about each of the items in the list.
- Play the recording for students to check their answers.

Answers

See the audioscript above.

Your turn

6 Ask students to use their smartphones to research online how the development of the items in the photos can illustrate social changes.

1.4 **Trendsetters**

See page 130 for activities you can do with this video.

Answers

- What they do, what they wear and where they shop.
- A new photo/video booth.
- It's easy to use and fun.

Technology The changing classroom

Objectives
* learn about how technology has changed the classroom.
* describe my ideal classroom.

Background
The online educational platform the **Khan Academy** was established in 2006 by former hedge-fund analyst Salman Khan.

Warm-up
* Books closed. Write the following question on the board: *How do you like to learn? What do you think the best ways are to learn?*
* Put students into pairs to discuss the questions.
* Ask some students to report their ideas to the class as a whole.

1 💬 Ask students to open their books at page 116.
* Put students into pairs and ask them to make a list of all the technology they use during a school day.

2 🔊 **1.50** Ask students to read the text about flipped classrooms to find out how many things on their lists they made in Exercise 1 appear in the text.

Suggested answers
videos, learning websites, podcasts, chat rooms, apps, mobile devices

Language note
The verb *flip* means *to turn over*.

3 💬 Ask students to read the text again and then ask them to answer the two questions.
* Check answers.

4 🔊 **1.51** Tell students they are going to listen to a student giving a presentation about learning videos.
* Play the recording for students to answer the question. Encourage **stronger students** to write down as much detail as they can.
* Check answers.

Audioscript
Today I am going to talk to you about the Khan Academy. Like many other students who need extra help, I discovered the Khan Academy when I was studying for a Maths exam. The Khan Academy is an organisation which posts educational videos online for free. It was started by one man, Sal Khan, who wanted to help his cousins with their Maths homework. Because Sal lived far away from his cousins, he started to help them using video conferencing. Eventually, as more relatives wanted his help, he posted videos on YouTube. Other students found the uploaded videos and started watching them too. Now students from all around the world use them, especially as they have been translated into many different languages. Although it started off only with Maths videos, the Khan Academy posts videos on a wide range of subjects; everything from History of Art to Physics. I use the videos when I don't understand something I'm learning in class, but it is not just students with problems who use them.

There are many home-schooled children who use them on a daily basis as an alternative to traditional schools. They are also used by teachers to help in the classroom and by parents who want to make sure they can help with their children's homework. The Khan Academy is not the only website offering educational online lessons for free, but it is one of the most well known. It uses today's technology to create a 24-hour virtual classroom and I have found it very useful.

Answer
Because sometimes she doesn't understand something she's learning in class.

5 🔊 **1.51** Play the recording again for students to complete the summary of the Khan Academy.
* Check answers.

Answers
1 all around the world   **2** many different languages
3 parents   **4** educational   **5** 24-hour

Your turn

6 • Read out the questions.
* Put students into pairs to discuss the questions. Encourage students to do some research online to help them with ideas.
* Monitor and help as necessary.
* Put sets of pairs together to present their ideal classrooms.

●Discovery EDUCATION™
2.4 The house of the future
See page 131 for activities you can do with this video.

Answers
* A butler, secretary, personal assistant and babysitter.
* To turn the lights out.
* Between 15,000 and 20,000 bucks (dollars).

 For homework, ask students to sign up to the Khan Academy and watch some of Salman Khan's videos: https://www.khanacademy.org/about

Natural Science The Archimedes' Principle

Objectives

- learn about the Archimedes' principle.
- talk about scientists and their achievements.

Background

Archimedes' principle refers to the law of buoyancy. It states that an object, when wholly or partially immersed in a fluid, is acted upon by an equal force, which is a buoyant or upward force, and which is equal to the weight of the fluid displaced by the object. The discovery of the law of buoyancy allowed Archimedes to find a way to determine whether or not the crown of the King of Syracuse was made of pure gold.

Archimedes is the subject of a popular story, concerning his discovery that the volume of fluid displaced when an object is submerged is equal to the volume of that object. The legend says Archimedes made his discovery, which led to the formulation of the principle referred to above, while taking a bath.

Syracuse is a city on the island of Sicily in Italy.

Warm-up

- Books closed. Write: *Great scientific discoveries* on the board.
- Put students into small groups and give them a couple of minutes to think of some examples of scientific discoveries, e.g. the discovery of penicillin by Alexander Fleming or the discovery of the structure of DNA by Francis Crick, James Watson and Rosalind Franklin.
- Ask one member of each group to report back to the class.

1 💬 Ask students to open their books at page 117.
- Put students into pairs and ask them to answer the questions.
- Discuss students' ideas and elicit that water is denser than air.

Background

Volume is the amount of space that an object occupies. It refers to an object in three dimensions: height, width and depth.

Mass is the measure of the amount of matter in an object, i.e. how much of something there is. Mass does not depend on gravity; wherever an object is, it will have the same mass.

Weight is a measurement of the exertion of gravity on an object. However, in everyday language **weight** and **mass** are often used synonymously.

2 🔊 **1.52** Write *Archimedes* /ˌɑːkɪˈmiːdiːz/ on the board. Drill the pronunciation.
- Elicit everything that students know about the Greek mathematician and inventor.
- Refer students to the text. Before they read the text, ask them to describe the illustrations. If possible, show the illustrations on the interactive whiteboard.
- Ask students to read the text and then put them into pairs to answer the question.
- Check answer.

Answer

He was trying to find out if the king's crown was made out of solid gold.

3
- Give students time to read the five statements.
- Ask students to read the text again and then ask them to decide whether they are true or false. Remind students to correct the false sentences.
- Students can then compare answers in pairs before you check answers with the class.

Answers

1 T
2 T
3 F (The crown and the pure gold displaced different amounts of water.)
4 F (The crown wasn't made of pure gold.)
5 F (Density is calculated by diving the weight of an object by its volume.)

Your turn

4
- Put students into pairs to talk about the scientists and their achievements.
- Monitor and help as necessary.
- Check answers.

Suggested answers

Charles Darwin: the theory of evolution
Marie Curie: the discovery of radioactivity
Galileo Galilei: the Earth's orbit around the Sun
Albert Einstein: the theory of relativity
Isaac Newton: the theory of gravity

Optional activity

- Put students into pairs to do research online into the scientific achievements referred to in Exercise 4.
- Students can then share what they find out with the class as a whole.

3.4 A cool experiment

See page 132 for activities you can do with this video.

Suggested answers

- He's 11 years old.
- The gases inside each box will be different.
- That CO_2 and methane help to cause global warming.

 For homework, ask students to find out more Archimedes and his achievements.

Technology Vertical farming

Objectives
* learn about vertical farming.
* talk about the idea of vertical farming.

Background
Vertical farming is the idea of growing crops inside high-rise buildings in cities. It was formulated in the 1990s by microbiologist Dickson Despommier.

Warm-up
* Books closed. Write the word *overpopulation* on the board.
* Explain the idea of an excessively large number of people in an area.

1 💬 Ask students to open their books at page 118.
* Put students into pairs to think of solutions to the problems in the box.

2 🔊 **1.53** Ask students to read the text and answer the question.
* Check answer.

Answers
Farmers have full control of the growing conditions in vertical farms.

3 • Put students into pairs to label the diagram.
* Check answers.

Answers
a sunlight   b water   c pots   d plants   e rack

4 🔊 **1.54** Tell students they are going to listen to a radio interview.
* Read out the question.
* Play the recording for students to answer the question.
* Check answers.

Audioscript
Presenter: Hello listeners. On *Farming Today* we are talking to farmer Dan Parkhurst, but he isn't a typical farmer because he never needs to get his hands dirty! Dan owns a vertical farm. Can you explain to us why you started the vertical farm, Dan?

Dan: Yes. A few years ago I found out that a factory was going to be knocked down. So I decided to try and save the building and see if I could use it for something else. Something that would bring life back into the city, create jobs and give something back to the people who live close to the factory; to the community. I wanted something that would help the city, not make it dirtier or more polluted. I heard about vertical farming and it seemed perfect; a clean farm in the middle of the city.

Presenter: But it must be difficult to grow fruit and vegetables in an old factory.

Dan: No, not at all. It's the perfect space to grow plants – the factory building has lots of windows so there's plenty of light and we don't have to worry about the weather because we control both the temperature and the amount of water the plants receive. Another thing the factory offers is a great location. It is close to lots of restaurants and shops that buy the vegetables, so the food doesn't travel long distances in lorries or aeroplanes. This is obviously much better for the environment but it also reduces costs so it's cheaper for the customers too. On Sundays we even open a market and people can come to the factory and buy their vegetables directly from us. Our customers often comment that the vegetables taste great because they are so fresh.

Presenter: That's great Dan, it sounds like you are an important part of the community.

Dan: Yes, we try to be. We sell our vegetables locally and we employ local people too.

Presenter: Well thank you Dan for explaining a little bit about your vertical farm and how it is helping both the planet and your local community. Good luck with this wonderful project.

Dan: Thank you.

Suggested answers
It is environmentally friendly and it's good for the local community.

5 🔊 **1.54** Read out the questions.
* Play the recording again for students to answer the questions.
* Check answers.

Answers
1 It would have been knocked down.
2 It is close to lots of restaurants and shops.
3 He sells them sell locally.

Your turn

6 • Read out the information.
* Put students into pairs to talk about vertical farming.

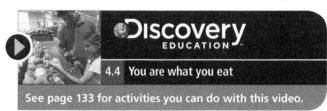

●DISCOVERY EDUCATION™
4.4 You are what you eat
See page 133 for activities you can do with this video.

Suggested answers
* To make it taste better or last longer.
* the nutritional information
* the natural sugar in it

Technology Passive houses

Objectives
- learn about passive houses.
- talk about different types of houses.

Background
Passive house is a translation of the German *passivhaus*.
The first passive house was built in Germany in 1990.

Warm-up
- Books closed. Write *eco-friendly* on the board. Check students understand the meaning of the word.
- Elicit examples of how we can be eco-friendly.

1 💬 Ask students to open their books at page 119.
- Put students into pairs to ask and answer the questions.

2 🔊 **2.39** Ask students to read the article about passive houses.
- Put students into pairs to answer the question.
- Check answer.

Answer
They are designed for both climates.

3
- Refer students to the diagram.
- Put students into pairs and ask them to label the diagram.
- Check answers.

Answers
a summer sun **b** low roof **c** winter sun **d** thick walls
e good quality windows

4 🔊 **2.40** Tell students they are going to listen to a conversation between two friends.
- Read out the question.
- Play the recording.
- Check answer.

Audioscript
Tom: Hi Simon, how was your holiday?
Simon: It was fine thanks. I went to my grandma's house just like I do every year. How was yours?
Tom: It was great. We stayed in an amazing passive house.
Simon: A passive house? What's that?
Tom: They're houses designed so they don't need any artificial heating. They're heated naturally by the sun.
Simon: But you went to Norway didn't you, there's not much sun there.
Tom: No, but that's the beauty of it, they're so well designed they don't need much sun. One of the amazing things was the floor, it was concrete, which sounds horrible but it wasn't. The sun shone on it during the day and heated it up then it released the heat at night and kept the house warm. It was always warm in the house.
Simon: I wish my grandma's house was like that. It's such an old house that, even with central heating, it is difficult to heat.
Tom: Yes, I can imagine. The other thing I liked was that, with such big windows, the house was always bright and sunny. In the evenings, we didn't need to put any lights on until the sun had almost disappeared.

Simon: Well my grandma's house is a typical old village house with such small windows that on cloudy days we sometimes have to put lights on in the middle of the day. What else did you like?
Tom: I liked how much space there was. It wasn't a very big house but because it was all very open inside, with very little furniture, it felt big. The owner told us that you can't put a lot of furniture in passive houses because they block the sun and stop the floor from heating up.
Simon: Then there's no chance of my grandma living in a passive house, her house is full of furniture.
Tom: Well during this holiday I really learned a lot about houses and I have decided I definitely want to stay in a passive house next year too.
Simon: I think maybe I'll come with you next year, what do you think?

Answers
The passive house sounds more comfortable.

5 🔊 **2.40** Refer students to the table, which shows the differences between the two houses described in the recording.
- Play the recording again.
- Ask students to work in pairs to complete the table.
- Check answers.

Answers
1 sun **2** cold **3** big **4** bright, sunny **5** a lot

Your turn

6
- Read out the question.
- Put students into pairs to discuss their ideas.

5.4 What a waste

See page 134 for activities you can do with this video.

Answers
- electronic waste, such as computers, mobile phones
- into landfills
- repairing computers, donating them to schools, re-using phones or recycling computer parts

 For homework, students could investigate passive housing in their country or area. They can share what they find out with a partner at the beginning of the next lesson.

History 4th July celebration, USA

Objectives

- learn about Independence Day in the USA.
- talk about re-enacting historical events.

Background

A **pilgrim** is a person who goes to a place that is sacred to them due to the beliefs they hold.

The **Pilgrim Fathers** is the name given to a group that fled religious persecution in England and went on to found the colony of Plymouth in the north-east of the United States in 1620.

Warm-up

- Books closed. Write *the USA* on the board.
- Give students a minute to write down everything that comes to mind when they think of the United States of America, e.g. places, people, its history, etc.
- Put students into small groups and ask them to compare the ideas they wrote down.

1 💬 Ask students to open their books at page 120.
- Refer students to the timeline for early American history.
- Put students into pairs to answer the questions.
- Check answers, focusing in particular on any other events of early American history that students know something about.

2 🔊 **2.41** Ask students to read the travel guide.
- Read out the two questions.
- Elicit the answers to the questions.

Answers

The Declaration of Independence was signed on this day in 1776.
The Declaration of Independence is read out by actors in typical 18th century clothes.

Optional activity

Ask students to use their smartphones to access online maps of the 13 British colonies along the east coast of what is now the USA.

3 • Give students time to read the four questions.
- Ask students to read the travel guide again and answer the questions.
- Students can then compare answers in pairs before you check answers with the class.

Answers

1 1776 2 Great Britain 3 1783
4 life, liberty and the pursuit of happiness

Optional activity

- Draw students' attention to the most famous phrases from the American Declaration of Independence, which are referred to in the final paragraph of the text in Exercise 2.
- Check that students understand that the verb *pursue* /pəˈsjuː/ means, in this context, try to get or achieve something.
- Ask: *What does it mean that people have the right to 'life, liberty and the pursuit of happiness'? What do you think 'pursuing happiness' actually means? How can people 'pursue happiness'?*
- Either discuss these questions with the class or put students into groups to discuss them.

Your turn

4 • Read out the three questions.
- Put students into pairs to answer the questions. Encourage students to use these questions as a means of developing a conversation about the idea of re-enacting history.

6.4 **Reliving history**

See page 135 for activities you can do with this video.

Answers

- the American Civil War
- To look real.
- Yes, they play the role of soldiers in re-enactment battles.

 For homework, ask students to research one event in American history. This event can be from the recent or the distant past. Students can share information with a partner at the beginning of the next lesson.

Biology Extinction

Objectives
* learn about how the honeybee is at risk of extinction.
* design a poster informing people about the risk of extinction to the honeybee.

Warm-up
* Books closed. Write the following question on the board:
How would you describe the relationship between human beings and the other animals that live on the planet? Do we need other animals?
* Elicit students' ideas.

1 💬 Ask students to open their books at page 121.
* Put students into pairs and ask them to look at the photo and answer the questions.
* Tell students that they should try to express what they want to say even if they don't know some words.

> ### Answers
> 1 collecting pollen   2 by pollinating the flowers

2 🔊 **2.42** Ask students to read the text about the bees and ask the question.
* Check answers.

> ### Suggested answers
> They don't have enough food. Diseases and chemicals kill them.

3 * Ask students to work alone to match the highlighted words in the article with the definitions 1–6.
* Check answers.

> ### Answers
> 1 mites   2 extinction   3 hive   4 pollination
> 5 hibernation   6 pollinators

4 🔊 **2.43** Tell students they are going to listen to Lisa taking to her father about bees.
* Play the recording for students to note down what it is that Lisa wants her father to do.
* Check answers.

Audioscript
Dad: Hi Lisa, How was school today?
Lisa: It was good, thanks. In science we were learning about bees. They are amazing. Did you know that if all the bees die, half of the fruit and vegetables in the supermarkets will disappear?
Dad: That would be terrible.
Lisa: Yes, it would. But it's hard to imagine they could really disappear. A queen bee can live for five years and lay up to 2,500 eggs a day.
Dad: Wow, that's a lot of babies!
Lisa: Yes, and that is happening all over the world, because bees live on every continent except Antarctica. Bees really look after themselves well too. They make two or three times more honey than they really need. So it just doesn't seem fair that such a successful and helpful insect is at risk of extinction.

Dad: No, you're right. Is there anything we can do to help?
Lisa: Yes, our teacher said there are lots of things we can do to help save the bees.
Dad: Oh really? What kind of things?
Lisa: Well as they need more flowers to feed on, we could plant more flowers in the garden. We would have to stop using chemicals in the garden though because the chemicals that gardeners and farmers use are part of the reason why the bees are dying. And actually we should try to buy food that has been grown without chemicals so that farmers stop using chemicals too.
Dad: They're great ideas, Lisa.
Lisa: We could buy honey from local beekeepers, but I looked on the Internet and there aren't any beekeepers around here. So Dad, what I think we really should do is become beekeepers and keep our own hives. What do you think? It would be great.
Dad: Hmm, let me think about it.

> ### Answers
> She wants him to help save the bees by planting more flowers in the garden, not using chemicals, buying food grown without chemicals and keeping their own hives.

5 🔊 **2.43** Refer students to the fact file.
* Play the recording again for students to copy and complete it.

> ### Answers
> 1 five years   2 up to 2,500
> 3 on all continents except Antarctica
> 4 two or three times the amount they need

Your turn

6 * Put students into pairs.
* Give students time to do some research online about what might be done to help save the bees.
* Students should then design a poster to inform people about the risk of bees becoming extinct.
* Display students' posters on the classroom wall.

 Discovery EDUCATION

7.4 Lions in danger

See page 136 for activities you can do with this video.

> ### Answers
> * 25,000
> * drought and competition with humans
> * two

> For homework, ask students to find out about other animals threatened with extinction. Students can share what they find out with a partner at the beginning of the next lesson.

ICT Copyright

Objectives
* learn about copyright law.
* talk about recording films in the cinema, copying and selling CDs and copying information from the Internet.

Background
The first **copyright law** in the UK was passed in 1709. It was called the *Statute of Queen Anne* and was introduced as a means of regulating the book trade. In recent years the Internet has transformed conceptions of the ownership of information. Arguments about who should own what continue, with some claiming that accessing material online is acceptable, while others declaring that it is against the law.

Warm-up
* Books closed. Write the following question on the board: *Who owns a piece of music, a book, an e-book, a film or a video game?*
* Elicit students' ideas, e.g. the person who created it, the production company responsible for the development and release of the product, nobody.

1 💬 Ask students to open their books at page 122.
* Put students into pairs to ask and answer the questions.
* Ask some students to report back to the class on what their partner said.

2 🔊 **2.44** Draw the copyright symbol on the board: ©.
* Ask students to read the first paragraph in the text as an introduction to the idea of copyright.
* Read out the question in Exercise 2, then ask students to read the rest of the text to find the answer.
* Check the answer.

> ### Answer
> no

3 • Refer students to sentences 1–5.
* Tell students that some of the sentences are true and some false.
* Ask students to read the text again for them to decide whether the sentences are true or false. Students should correct the false sentences.
* Students can compare answers in pairs before you check answers with the whole class.

> ### Answers
> 1 T
> 2 F (A piece of work may be protected under the copyright law even without the copyright symbol.)
> 3 F (Copyright law prevents people from giving copies.)
> 4 T 5 T

Your turn

4 • Put students into pairs to discuss the questions.
* Ask some students to report back to the class on what their partner said.

Optional activity
* Introduce the idea of *royalties*. A **royalty payment** refers to the percentage of revenue from sales that an author, musician, theatrical performer, etc., receives. They are commonly referred to as **royalties**.
* Tell students that this is how musicians, novelists, stand-up comedians, etc., get paid for much of what they do.
* Write the following statement on the board: *We should not have to pay for cultural content. It should all be freely available.*
* Put students into small groups to decide whether they agree or disagree with the statement.
* Ask one student from each group to report back to the class on the discussion their group had.

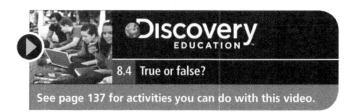

8.4 True or false?

See page 137 for activities you can do with this video.

Answers
* Anyone can be an expert today.
* fashion photographers
* We have to decide if the messages we receive are real or true. We have to pay attention and not believe everything we see and read.

 For homework ask students to do some research into the *copyleft movement* and forms of licensing work such as *Creative Commons*. Students can discuss the ideas behind these responses to traditional forms of copyright in the next lesson either in pairs or in small groups.

Project

A presentation

Objectives
- look at a presentation about Stephen Sutton.
- plan a presentation about a famous young person I admire.
- give a presentation to the class.

Preparation
- Bring card, a pair of scissors and a glue stick for each group.

Background
Stephen Sutton (1994–2014) was a teenager from England who developed cancer at the age of 15 and died from it at the age of 19. Before his death, he raised millions of pounds for the Teenage Cancer Trust charity, becoming well-known both in the UK and in other countries.

Warm-up
- Books closed. Revise the meaning of the verb *inspire*, which students learnt in Unit 3.
- On the board write: *inspiration* /ˌɪnspɪˈreɪʃ(ə)n/.
- Check that students both understand and are able to pronounce the words. Elicit that it is someone or something that inspires others to do things, e.g. *Ronaldo is a great inspiration to young footballers around the world*.
- Put students into pairs and ask them to talk briefly about people that inspire them. The people students talk about do not have to be famous.
- Ask some students to report back to the class on what their partner said.

Language note
Stephen and **Steven** are variant spellings of the same name. They are both pronounced /ˈstiːv(ə)n/.

Look

1
- Ask students to open their books at page 123.
- Ask students to look at the slides of a presentation about Stephen Sutton. Check that students understand that a *slide* refers to a single page of a presentation which is viewed on a screen.
- Read out the two questions and give students time to read the information and answer the questions.
- Students can compare answers in pairs before you check answers with the class.

Suggested answers
1 No, he was diagnosed with cancer at the age of 15 and died aged 19.
2 He dedicated his life to raising money for teenage cancer sufferers and raised almost £5 million.

2
- Ask the class the following questions: *Do you give presentations at your school? Do you enjoy listening to presentations? What do you think makes a presentation interesting?*
- Elicit answers to the questions from the class as a whole.
- Refer students to sentences 1–10 and then put students into pairs.
- Give students a few minutes to decide which of the sentences describe how to give a good presentation.
- Check answers. Ask students to justify the choices they made.

Suggested answers
3, 4, 5, 7, 9, 10

Prepare

3
- If you have a large class, you may want to put students into small groups rather than pairs, or else too much time will be taken up with listening to presentations. If you have a small class, put students into pairs.
- Give students time to choose a famous young person that they admire.
- Students can look on the Internet to find out about this person's background and main achievements. They should also look for photos of this person as well as any interesting quotations that he or she is associated with.
- On this last point, encourage students to see that saying *You've got to work hard to achieve your goals* is obvious rather than interesting. Explain that any quotations they choose to use in their presentations should in some way be memorable.

4
- Give students sufficient time to prepare their presentations. Students can either use a software programme such as PowerPoint or big pieces of card.
- Monitor and help as necessary.

Present

5
- Ask students to take it in turns to give their presentations to the class. Make sure that both students in each pair (or all students in the group) give part of the presentation.
- At the end of each presentation, the pair or group can ask the class questions on what has been presented to them to see how much they can remember of what they have heard.
- The class then decides which famous young person's achievements are the most impressive.

 Ask students to research online to find examples of other people who have raised a lot of money for charity. Students can share what they find out with a partner at the beginning of the next lesson.

Project

An advertisement

Objectives
- look at an advertisement for Strolleradio.
- plan an advertisement about an invention that never become popular.

Preparation
- Bring card, a pair of scissors and a glue stick for each group.

Warm-up
- Books closed. Ask: *What information does an advertisement for a product usually include?*
- Elicit answers to the question and write them on the board, e.g. the name and price of a product, the name of the manufacturer of the product, a tag line.

Look

Background
Despite certain differences in these forms of baby transportation, in general, the words **stroller**, **pushchair** and **buggy** are used interchangeably in the UK to refer to folding or collapsible chairs on wheels which are suitable for both babies and young children. **Pram** refers to the more traditional four-wheeled carriage in which the baby lies flat.

1
- Ask students to open their books at page 124.
- Read out the three questions. Give students some time to look at the advertisement and to read the information. Encourage them to answer the questions.
- Students can compare answers in pairs before you check answers with the class.

Suggested answers
1 Strolleradio
2 It's a stroller with a radio. It keeps babies entertained and educated.
3 No. The picture makes it look like a joke. The product doesn't look real.

2
- Put students into pairs and ask them to look at the advertisement again and answer questions 1–4.
- Check answers.

Suggested answers
1 It promises your baby will be entertained and educated. He/She will never be bored again.
2 six
3 in short phrases
4 availability, claims to what the product will produce (entertainment and lack of boredom), the product is new

Prepare

3
- On the board write: *Inventions that never became popular.*
- Ask students if they can think of any examples. Elicit these examples and write them on the board.
- Tell students they are going to produce an advertisement for an invention that never become popular.
- Read out the information about what students have to include in their advertisements.
- Put students into pairs and give them time to do some research online. You could direct **weaker students** to: http://www.viralnova.com/cool-old-inventions/
- Give students sufficient time to prepare their advertisements. Students can either use computers or card to produce their advertisements.
- Monitor and help as necessary.

Present

4
- Ask students to display their advertisements in the class.
- Students should read all of their advertisements and then come up with a list of three that they would like to have.
- Ask some students to tell the class about their top three. The students you invite to read their top three out to the class should be asked to account for their choices.

Optional activity
- Ask students to work alone to write a list of five inventions that became incredibly popular and which we could not imagine living without.
- Put students into small groups to consider the question of why it is that those inventions became popular. You could guide students in this discussion by putting the following questions on the board: *Why is it that some inventions become popular? Do we buy new things because we need them or do we buy them because they have become fashionable?*
- Give students a few minutes to discuss these questions.
- Ask some students to report back to the class on the discussion they had in their group.

 For homework, ask students to make a list of three successful products. This could be anything from a vacuum cleaner to a smartphone. Students should then write a list of reasons to explain the success of the product. Students can share this information with other students in small groups at the beginning of the next lesson.

Project

A comic strip

Objectives
- read a comic strip about online theft.
- create a comic strip about a crime.

Preparation
- Bring A3 paper, a pair of scissors and a glue stick for each pair.

Warm-up
- Books closed. Ask students how government departments, health services, police services, etc., can get particular information to the public, e.g. by putting information on the radio, on websites, on TV and in newspapers; by producing leaflets which can be posted through people's letterboxes; by producing billboards to display in the street.
- You could then ask students what they think is the most effective way of warning the public about a particular danger, e.g. catching the flu in winter. Elicit students' ideas and write these ideas on the board.

Look

1
- Ask students to open their books at page 125.
- Give students some time to look at the comic strip.
- Refer students to sentences 1–3. Put students into pairs to choose the correct option in each case.
- Check answers.

> #### Answers
> **1** theft **2** simple **3** will

2
- Ask students to work alone to complete the sentences about how to write a comic strip by choosing either *do* or *don't* in each case.
- Students can compare their answers in pairs before you check answers with the class as a whole. Ask students to justify the choices they made.

> #### Answers
> **1** Don't **2** Do **3** Do **4** Don't

> #### Language note
> In addition to its use as an auxiliary verb used to form questions and negatives, *do* is used to add emphasis, e.g. *I do love sunsets.*

Prepare

3
- Revise common crimes with the class, e.g. *theft, robbery, burglary, shoplifting, vandalism*. Tell students they are going to create a comic strip to warn people of the dangers of certain crimes. Encourage students to avoid choosing a crime, such as arson, that it difficult to come up with suitable advice about.
- Read out the information about what students have to include in their comic strips.
- Put students into pairs and give them time to choose the crime they want to warn about.
- Give out the materials students need (card, pairs of scissors glue sticks) and give students sufficient time to produce the sketch of their comic strips.
- Monitor and help as necessary.
- Once students have finished their comic strips, ask them to swap them with another pair to check.
- Give students some time to produce a final version of their comic strip.

Present

4
- Ask students to display their comic strips in the class.
- Students should read all of the comic strips to find out whether they understand the warning in each case. If they do not understand the warning in a particular comic strip, they should seek out the pair who produced the comic strip and ask for further explanation.
- With the class as a whole, discuss the crimes that the comic strips were about.
- If appropriate, you could find out if any of the students have ever been victims of these crimes, as well as talk about ways of preventing the crimes from taking place.

> #### Optional activity
> - Ask students to use their smartphones to look at some examples of real crime-prevention leaflets produced by the police.
> - Alternatively, you could show them examples available at: http://www.westmercia.police.uk/about-us/publications-and-consultation/crime-prevention-leaflets.html
> - You can then put students into pairs or small groups to discuss the leaflets. Do students think the leaflets are effective? Why? What would they change about them and why?

 Ask students to look in local newspapers, shops or in the streets of their town and city, for examples of notices, posters or leaflets regarding crime prevention. Students can take a photos of anything they see and show them to a partner at the beginning of the next lesson.

Reviews key

Review 1 and 2

Vocabulary

1

2 stripy   3 flat   4 silk   5 cool   6 baggy   7 flowery   8 fitted

2

2 by   3 on   4 with   5 of   6 with   7 of

3

2 b   3 a   4 d   5 c   6 f

4

2 together   3 up   4 on   5 up   6 on   7 on

Explore vocabulary

5

2 driver   3 corner   4 number   5 strings   6 show

6

2 success   3 flexible   4 correct   5 challenges   6 passionate

Language focus

1

2 didn't use to   3 used to   4 would   5 use   6 did   7 didn't use to   8 Did they use to   9 would   10 would

2

2 hadn't finished   3 rang   4 had forgotten   5 had arranged   6 ran   7 took   8 had started   9 didn't let

3

2 ourselves   3 himself   4 each other   5 themselves   6 myself   7 itself   8 herself

4

2 haven't sent   3 have you been going   4 've/have learned   5 've been listening   6 haven't heard

Language builder

5

2 b   3 a   4 c   5 a   6 c   7 a   8 b   9 b   10 c   11 c

Speaking

6

1 d   2 a   3 b   4 e   5 c

Review 3 and 4

Vocabulary

1

2 form   3 course   4 exam   5 experience   6 job   7 fees

2

2 developed   3 become   4 millionaire   5 made   6 supports   7 won   8 award   9 break

3

2 Chop   3 Boil   4 Roast   5 Mix   6 Fry   7 Spread   8 Slice

4

2 bland   3 slimy   4 bitter   5 slimy   6 sweet   7 sweet   8 sweet

Explore vocabulary

5

2 take … time   3 take … advice   4 taking up   5 take place

6

1 in   2 on   3 by   4 on

Language focus

1

2 'm going to see   3 starts   4 'm meeting   5 'm catching   6 'm going to have   7 Are you going   8 'm doing   9 starts   10 ends

2

2 Everyone will be watching the ceremony on TV.
3 I'm sure Emma will will first prize.
4 Winning £10,000 is going to make a huge difference to her life.
5 She won't have to worry about money anymore.
6 She might leave school and start her own restaurant.

3

2 'll want   3 like   4 'll love   5 're   6 'll prefer   7 'll get   8 don't   9 'll need   10 want

4

2 f   3 a   4 c   5 d   6 e

Language builder

5

2 b   3 a   4 c   5 b   6 c   7 a   8 b   9 a   10 b   11 b   12 a   13 b   14 c

Speaking

6

2 That's   3 Next   4 Then   5 When   6 shall   7 best

Reviews key

Review 5 and 6

Vocabulary

1
2 light bulb 3 remote control 4 tap 5 switch 6 heater

2
2 ridiculously 3 extremely 4 kind of 5 much too 6 totally

3
2 a 3 b 4 g 5 c 6 e 7 d 8 f

4
2 crowded 3 scary 4 colourful 5 impressive 6 stunning
7 peaceful

Explore vocabulary

5
2 keep 3 Skype™ 4 tweeting 5 texting 6 email 7 track

6
2 for 3 with 4 on 5 at 6 from

Language focus

1
2 were replaced 3 aren't used 4 are thrown 5 is recycled
6 will be awarded 7 will be given

2
2 This is the shop where I bought my clock.
3 My dad has a friend who/that collects old radios.
4 Is this the machine which/that is used to play old records?
5 This is the film which/that I told you about.
6 Where is the boy whose book I borrowed?

3
2 singing 3 playing 4 putting 5 becoming 6 studying
7 doing 8 having

4
2 organising 3 to make 4 to find 5 Dressing up
6 to design 7 visiting

Language builder

5
2 c 3 b 4 c 5 d 6 b 7 a 8 d 9 d 10 c
11 a 12 c

6
1 b 2 d 3 e 4 c 5 a

Review 7 and 8

Vocabulary

1
2 setting 3 main characters 4 hero 5 mystery 6 action

2
2 In order to 3 so that 4 Of course, 5 Rather than
6 then again,

3
2 c 3 a 4 e 5 f 6 d

4
2 complain 3 admit 4 explain 5 decide 6 suggest
7 agree 8 insist

Explore vocabulary

5
2 around 3 through 4 above 5 back 6 off

6
1 date back 2 came into existence 3 see the point
4 take care 5 go ahead

Language focus

1
2 If you had studied, you wouldn't have failed the test.
3 I'd have answered the phone if I had been at home.
4 He wouldn't have been late for school if he hadn't missed the bus.
5 Tim would have gone to the party if he hadn't had a cold.

2
2 Sally could have won the lottery.
3 Julie may have been sick yesterday.
4 Simon can't have studied very hard.
5 Sue must have passed her driving test.
6 Tom might have crashed his bike.

3
2 (that) there had been a robbery.
3 (that) the robbers had taken all the money.
4 (that) he'd go and call the police.
5 (that) he could describe one of the robbers.

4
1 She asked him where he was from.
2 They asked me if I had seen anything.
3 Could you tell us what your address is?
4 He asked if there had been any noise.
5 Do you know where the safe is?

Language builder

5
2 a 3 b 4 d 5 a 6 c 7 a 8 b 9 b 10 a

Speaking

6
1 know 2 true 3 false 4 lucky 5 anything

Grammar reference key

Unit 1

1

She used to have pink hair.
She didn't use to like gardening.
She used to shock people.
She didn't use to bake cakes.
She used to break the rules.
She didn't use to follow the rules.

2

She wouldn't wear long dresses.
She would shock people.
She would break the rules.
She wouldn't bake cakes.
She wouldn't follow the rules.

3

2 had gone   3 hadn't remembered   4 hadn't met
5 hadn't won   6 had missed

4

2 Had you saved some money? Yes, I had.
3 Had she brought her skateboard? No, she hadn't.
4 Where had they been? They had been shopping.
5 Had you heard of that book? No, I hadn't.
6 What had the dog eaten? It had eaten my shoes!

Unit 2

1

2 each other   3 itself   4 each other   5 herself   6 yourself

2

2 has been   3 haven't studied   4 have you had   5 haven't seen
6 have watched

3

2 Where have you been going for French lessons?
   I've been going to a language school near the library.
3 Have you been watching his video blogs?
   Yes, I've been watching them since the beginning.
4 Who has been teaching her?
   A family friend has been teaching her.
5 How long have they been seeing each other?
   They've been seeing each other for about two months.

Unit 3

1

2 are going   3 are you going   4 starts   5 're meeting
6 we're going to

2

2 e   3 a   4 f   5 b   6 d

3

2 won't be using   3 will be driving   4 will be eating
5 won't be watching   6 Will we be uploading

Unit 4

1

2 may/might ask   3 promise   4 'll check   5 won't finish

2

2 If she asked me to be a volunteer, I might ~~to~~ say yes.
3 He~~'ll~~ **'d** make a fortune if he started selling his paintings.
4 If you ~~cook~~ **cooked** steak, I wouldn't eat it.
5 Could you walk to school if you ~~would move~~ **moved** house?

Unit 5

1

2 weren't sold   3 was developed   4 weren't invented
5 is made   6 are eaten   7 aren't called   8 are enjoyed

2

2 won't be worn   3 will be built   4 won't be flown
5 will be elected

3

2 whose   3 which/that   4 which/that   5 where   6 who/that

4

2 The woman ~~whose~~ **who is** wearing a blue top in my aunt.
3 I first saw it on a blog ~~what~~ **which/that** I follow.
4 The invention that ~~it~~ changed the world was the wheel.
5 I called the brother of the guy ~~who~~ **whose** mobile I found.
6 One thing which she told me ~~it~~ was very interesting.

Grammar reference key

Unit 6

1

2 Shopping 3 Seeing 4 worrying 5 Waiting

2

2 getting 3 playing 4 watching 5 dressing up

3

2 seeing 3 remembering 4 buying 5 selling

4

2 to win 3 to hear 4 to go 5 to finish

5

2 to make 3 to go 4 to spend 5 to study

Unit 7

1

2 wouldn't have been; had taken
3 would have missed; hadn't checked
4 had caught; wouldn't have arrived
5 wouldn't have gone; hadn't recommended
6 had had; would have studied

2

2 must have 3 can't have 4 might have 5 may have

3

2 I could have left them at home.
3 She can't have heard.
4 They may have gone home.
5 Someone might have lost it.

Unit 8

1

2 have caught the criminals.
3 can help you look after your cousin.
4 'll call him/you after 5 o'clock.
5 loves listening to music.

2

2 asked Simon how long he would be in Italy for.
3 asked Joe how much money they had stolen.
4 asked me if I could tell him my password.
5 asked me what I wanted for my birthday.

3

2 Can you tell us where ~~is~~ the market **is**?
3 Excuse me, do you know what time ~~it~~ **the film** starts ~~the film~~?
4 I was wondering ~~that~~ **if** you could help me.
5 Can I ask you how long ~~did~~ you ~~wait~~ **waited** there?

Vocabulary Bank key

Unit 1

Explore compound nouns

1

guitar band   motor industry   street corners   style changes
taxi fare   telephone box

2

guitar string, guitar music
motor show, motor vehicle
street art, street fashion
style icon, style consultant
taxi cab, taxi driver
telephone call, telephone number

Unit 2

Explore word building

1

The column on the left is nouns.
The column on the right is adjectives.

2

1 respectable, respected, respectful
2 trusted, trusting
3 difficulty

Phrasal verbs (learning and socialising)

2

bring together   count on   get on with   give up   look up to
pass on   set up   sign up

Unit 3

Explore expressions with *take*

2

1 seriously
2 pleasure in
3 to

Achievements

2

become a millionaire
break records
develop a project
do voluntary work
make a fortune
start a business
support the community
win awards

Unit 4

Explore prepositional phrases

1

by	in	on
surrounded	different ways	the go
		the streets

2

by	in	on
5 o'clock	10 minutes	depends
influenced	danger	fire
walk	New Zealand	the menu
	your country	

3

influenced by   walk by   in New Zealand   depends on

Unit 5

Everyday objects

1

* need electricity? charger, fan, heater, light bulb
* need batteries? remote control
* give light? candle, light bulb, matches

Explore communication phrases and phrasal verbs

2

keep

Unit 6

Explore verbs and prepositions

2

agree on
arrive at
look forward to
prepare for
recover from
work with

3

Suggested answers
agree with sb
arrive in London
look after sb
work at a hospital

Vocabulary Bank key

Unit 7

Story elements

1

- people in a story? hero, main character(s), villain
- where the story takes place and what happens? action, plot, setting
- the type of story it is? mystery, suspense

Explore prepositions of movement

2

approach through
float above
run back
step off
turn around
turn towards

3

1 out of   2 along   3 over   4 across   5 up   6 away   7 back

Workbook key

Starter Unit

1 2 decided 3 was concentrating 4 wasn't looking 5 fell 6 were walking 7 saw 8 called 9 arrived 10 was trying 11 told 12 were pulling 13 noticed 14 was still holding

2 2 Which 3 Why 4 Who 5 How 6 When 7 What
2 f 3 a 4 b 5 g 6 c 7 d

3 2 worried 3 terrifying 4 boring 5 exciting 6 tired

4 2 look round 3 chill out 4 find out 5 set off 6 come back

5

w	a	s	t	e	s	k	l
o	v	a	z	a	w	o	e
b	i	v	c	r	i	p	a
a	r	e	d	s	t	u	v
n	e	j	l	h	c	o	e
d	d	r	q	u	h	m	a
t	u	r	n	d	o	w	n
o	c	t	a	p	f	u	n
n	e	x	t	h	f	f	o

6 2 switches off 3 turn down 4 reduce 5 left 6 waste

7 2 set off 3 didn't take off 4 was 5 arrived 6 Have you been 7 have spent 8 have made 9 has decided 10 went 11 stayed 12 have booked

8 2 make 3 do 4 make 5 do 6 make 7 make 8 do

9 2 yet; already 3 yet 4 already/just; yet 5 still; just

10 2 gallery 3 sculpture 4 exhibition 5 microphone 6 portrait

11 2 When does the safari start?
3 What animals can we see there?
4 Which airport does the flight go from?
5 How did she get to the safari park?
6 Have you seen any lions yet?

12 1 object 2 subject 3 object 4 'I saw Luis.' 5 subject 6 'Luis saw me.'

13 2 went 3 happened 4 did you stay 5 did you eat 6 did you do 7 did you like 8 speaks

14 **Across:** 4 safari 7 trekking 8 sailing 9 exchange
Down: 2 climbing 3 see 6 down 5 skiing 6 theme park

15 2 never 3 since 4 ever 5 for 6 since 7 never 8 ever

16 2 Have you ever met a famous person?
3 How long have you lived in this flat?
4 Have you (ever) visited this gallery (before)?
5 Has she been here for a long time?
6 How long has he been playing the guitar?

17 2 pen-knife 3 sleeping bag 4 first aid kit 5 contact lenses 6 water bottle

Unit 1

Vocabulary

1 2 shoes 3 shirt 4 jacket 5 jeans 6 T-shirt 7 skirt 8 jumper 9 coat 10 scarf

2 2 stripy 3 fitted 4 leather 5 baggy 6 silk 7 cool 8 flowery 9 denim 10 tight

3 1 stripy; denim 2 Annie; flowery; flat 3 Leo; baggy 4 Nicola; fitted, silk 5 Alexis; tight; cool

4 2 baggy 3 jumpers 4 stripy 5 shoes 6 leather 7 shirts 8 jeans

Language focus 1

1 1 habits 2 infinitive 3 *used to* 4 actions state

2 2 did you use to have 3 used to spend 4 used to sit 5 didn't use to listen 6 used to be 7 used to like 8 used to buy

3 3 would spend 4 would sit 5 wouldn't listen 8 would buy

4 2 both 3 used to have 4 Did your mum use to be 5 both 6 didn't use to have 7 both 8 both 9 used to look 10 used to look like

Listening and vocabulary

1 The presenter says she's against uniforms.

Audioscript

Tonight's discussion topic isn't new, but a lot of young people have strong feelings about it: school uniforms. Nowadays many countries in the world have uniforms but just as many countries don't! In Germany, where pupils don't wear uniforms, a government minister recently suggested that they should be introduced, and this started a national debate. So what are the arguments?

People in favour of uniforms say that they make pupils feel proud of their school, and create a feeling of everyone working together as a team. In a uniform, rich and poor look the same, and no one has to think about what clothes to wear every morning. Also, no one can wear the latest fashion or a particular cool style, so pupils can focus on studying, instead of worrying about how they look.

People who disagree say that uniforms are often expensive and uncomfortable. And because teenagers grow so fast, they may need new clothes every few months. One ex-secondary school headmaster told me that he's against uniforms because when pupils break the rules, teachers have to spend time monitoring and punishing them, when they should be concentrating on teaching. He also thinks fitted blazers, white shirts and ties are not practical for many school activities like science and art: anything not done at a desk. He also says that no one has shown that wearing a school uniform improves learning or behaviour anywhere in the world.

But does it depend on what uniform? I remember at my school we used to wear a stripy jacket, blouse and tie, a long skirt and flat shoes. I hated it! At least now girls can wear trousers, and many schools have introduced polo shirts and jumpers for boys and girls instead of shirts and ties. That kind of uniform is definitely better.

Personally, I'm against uniforms. Do you agree? Are you happy with your school policy? What is your uniform if you have one? Ring us with your opinion, or if you prefer, send us an email. Our number is …

Workbook key

2   **2** many   **3** many   **4** Germany   **5** proud   **6** same
  7 studying   **8** expensive   **9** grow   **10** teaching
  11 practical   **12** learning   **13** trousers   **14** better
  15 ring

3   **2** f   **3** g   **4** h   **5** a   **6** e   **7** b   **8** d

4   **2** happy with   **3** afraid of   **4** keen on / interested in
  5 excited about   **6** interested in / keen on   **7** proud of
  8 disappointed by

Language focus 2

1   **1** had   **2** before   **3** past simple

2   **2** hadn't been   **3** Had they changed   **4** hadn't made
  5 had left   **6** had you played

3   **2** had changed   **3** had grown   **4** had worn   **5** looked
  6 had been   **7** arrived   **8** had joined

4   **2** didn't have   **3** went   **4** had sold   **5** felt   **6** got
  7 had   **8** was   **9** hadn't said   **10** had seen
  11 had bought

6   **2** street art   **3** guitar music   **4** motor industry
  5 telephone box   **6** taxi driver

Reading

1   famous actors; comic artists; young people; science-fiction writers

2   **1** awards   **2** geeks   **3** wander round
  4 non-profit organisation   **5** disguise

3   **1** a   **2** b   **3** a   **4** b

4   **2** (comic) geeks   **3** Comic-Con   **4** comic fans
  5 a (huge) three-day international convention
  6 visitors to Comic-Con   **7** educational sessions and talks
  8 Comic-Con   **9** costumes of comic book characters
  10 Daniel Radcliffe

Writing

1   They've been together since 1961. / They've been together for
  over 50 years.

2   **2** California   **3** surf   **4** *Good Vibrations*   **5** thirty-six/36
  6 tours

3   **2** After   **3** During   **4** Over   **5** as   **6** in

4   **2** Although   **3** during   **4** over   **5** After   **6** as

5   **2** one of the biggest   **3** one of the most popular
  4 one of the richest   **5** one of the most interesting

6   **2** He has **now** sold over 20 million copies of his latest album.
  3 They are **still** touring today after 30 years.
  4 She **also** sang many of her songs in French.
  5 They were one of the most successful bands **ever**.

7   Sentence 4

8   information about the members of the band   ✓
  their recent work   ✓
  the number of number one hits   ✓
  some of their most famous lyrics   ✗
  the number of records they have sold   ✓
  problems the band had in their career   ✗
  when and where they formed   ✓
  the name of a well-known album or single   ✓
  the names of bands that they have influenced   ✗

Review

1   **2** a flowery dress   **3** a baggy jumper   **4** flat shoes
  5 a leather jacket   **6** a denim skirt

2   **2** of   **3** by   **4** of   **5** by   **6** about   **7** on   **8** in

3   **2** would travel   **3** wouldn't see   **4** Did your mum use to be
  5 didn't use to like   **6** would attend   **7** Did you use to go
  8 used to have   **9** would stay   **10** used to love

4   **2** I hadn't seen Melanie in a dress before she wore one to
  the party.   **3** After he'd bought the shoes, he went home.
  4 We hadn't been there long when it started to rain.
  5 They decided to wait until they had finished their homework.
  6 Had the concert started when you got there?

5   **2** made   **3** just; still   **4** never   **5** since
  6 were trekking; fell; broke   **7** yet
  8 does the new school year start   **9** Did you use to
  10 had lived   **11** Have you been; went; was

6   **2** a   **3** c   **4** b   **5** c   **6** a   **7** a   **8** c   **9** b   **10** b
  11 c

7   **2** these shoes   **3** the changing rooms   **4** suits you
  5 look great   **6** don't fit

Get it right!

1   **2** use to   **3** use to   **4** used to   **5** used to   **6** use to
  7 use to   **8** used to

2   **2** correct   **3** Sarah saw that Julian ~~forgot~~ **had forgotten**
  his keys.   **4** We had to walk to school because our dad ~~was~~
  had sold the car.   **5** She was happy because she **had** always
  wanted to meet him.   **6** correct   **7** They ~~ate~~ **had eaten**
  all the pizza before we ~~had~~ arrived.   **8** The dog was afraid
  because it ~~was~~ **had** heard fireworks.

3   **2** I bought a dress from the new cloth**es** shop in my town.
  3 I'm not interested in cloth**es** and I don't like shopping.
  4 correct   **5** You should ~~use~~ **wear** old clothes because we're
  going to paint my bedroom.   **6** correct   **7** My sister always
  wears ~~a~~ fashionable clothes.   **8** People usually wear traditional
  cloth**es** for weddings.

Unit 2

Vocabulary

1

i	e	a	s	y	g	o	i	n	g	h	t
m	p	r	e	d	s	u	b	a	n	a	a
p	a	l	s	e	t	y	p	e	i	r	l
a	s	m	o	t	i	v	a	t	e	d	s
t	s	r	w	e	a	s	h	c	i	w	o
i	i	o	n	r	s	h	y	s	t	o	c
e	o	p	v	m	s	e	n	t	e	r	i
n	n	s	a	i	v	a	r	m	k	a
t	a	l	e	n	t	e	d	i	r	i	b
n	t	u	s	e	a	w	o	c	i	n	l
d	e	d	y	d	r	i	c	t	y	g	e

2   **2** impatient   **3** talented   **4** easy-going   **5** strict
  6 sociable   **7** hard-working   **8** shy   **9** passionate
  10 determined

Workbook key

3   2 talented   3 easy-going   4 hard-working
    5 motivated/determined   6 impatient

4   2 sociable   3 passionate   4 strict   5 impatient
    6 hard-working   7 talented   8 determined / motivated

Language focus 1

1

Singular

I	you	he	she	it
myself	yourself	*himself*	herself	itself

Plural

we	you	they
ourselves	yourselves	themselves

2   2 herself   3 ourselves   4 themselves   5 itself
    6 yourselves   7 himself   8 yourself

3   1 himself   2 each other

4   2 yourselves   3 himself   4 each other   5 herself
    6 each other

5   2 ourselves   3 himself   4 myself   5 each other
    6 each other   7 themselves   8 each other

7   2 passionate   3 flexibility   4 happiness   5 challenging
    6 successful

Listening and vocabulary

1 c

Audioscript

Presenter: Our guest today is sprinter Errol Dixon. Errol, you're an unusual athlete. Can you explain what you do?

Errol: Yes, I'm a guide runner. I've run with several different athletes since I started, and at the moment I run with Liz Stevens. She went blind when she was a teenager, so I'm her 'eyes' in a race. She's a 100m and 200m sprinter, but there are guide runners for longer races too.

Presenter: How does it work, then?

Errol: Well, we need to practise together a lot. We had to train ourselves to run the same distance with every step, at the same time. We hold a guide rope in our hands to stay together, so we have to move our arms at the same time too. Liz is talented, dedicated and really fast. It's hard work for me!

Presenter: I imagine! Do you have to run at exactly the same speed?

Errol: Yes, that's really important, we have to concentrate.

Presenter: Do you talk to each other during the race?

Errol: We talk at the start when I help her put her hands behind the line, but when you're sprinting it's difficult to talk. Luckily the 100m race is straight, so we just run for the finish line! In the 200m there's a bend in the track, so I tell her when to change direction.

Presenter: Why did you sign up to be a guide runner?

Errol: Well, everyone in my family is passionate about athletics. My uncle was a guide runner at the Paralympic Games in Beijing, and he passed on the techniques to me. Liz and I have run together for three years now, we're the same age and we get on well. We hope to run in the next Paralympic Games.

Presenter: Do the blind runner and the guide runner both get a gold medal?

Errol: If they win, yes, they do. The first time that happened was at London 2012, actually. I think if you're a team, you *should* both get a medal.

Presenter: Absolutely! Errol, thank you, and good luck to you and Liz in your next race!

2   2 b   3 b   4 a   5 a   6 a   7 b   8 b

3   2 sign up   3 look up to   4 pass on   5 count on
    6 get on with   7 give up   8 bring together

4   2 pass on   3 get on with   4 set up; sign up   5 give up
    6 bring together   7 look up to

Language focus 2

1   1 past   2 how many

2   2 She's won a lot of competitions.   3 We've made three cakes for the party.   4 How many times have they been there?   5 I've sent 100 texts this week.   6 How many people has he invited to the birthday party?

3   1 hasn't   2 long we have been doing something
    3 continue

4   2 's/has been practising   3 have/'ve been working
    4 have been looking   5 've/have been going
    6 has/'s been running

5   2 I've been doing charity work every Saturday for two years.
    3 I've/We've been doing parachute jumps and quizzes.
    4 I've/We've organised four parachute jumps so far.
    5 It's been helping groups of children all over the country.
    6 The charity has helped thousands of children.

6   2 How long have you been coming to this school?
    3 Have you been learning English for a long time?
    4 How many times have you looked at your mobile phone today?

Reading

1 b

2   1 tolerant   2 made fun of   3 moderators   4 bullying
    5 weird

3

Appearance	Personality	Interests	Behaviour
fat, big nose, make-up	weird, annoying	singing, theatre	funny laugh

4   2 2011   3 Lady Gaga and her mother Cynthia
    4 for people to accept differences and individuality
    5 safety   6 skills   7 opportunities   8 online/cyber-
    9 social media   10 young   11 schools   12 communities

Writing

1   To thank her for her help since she has moved to Dublin.

2   2 They used to live in the same neighbourhood in Liverpool.
    3 To sign up for lots of after-school activities.   4 She's learning Irish and the guitar.
    5 They talk to each other on Skype™ and send messages.
    6 She's finding it easier and has made a few friends.

3   2 felt   3 find   4 feeling   5 finding

4   (possible answers)
    2 I felt a little shy when I first came to this school.
    3 I found Maths very difficult at the beginning.
    4 I felt determined to get on with my new friends.
    5 I sometimes find meeting new people quite hard.
    6 I always feel motivated to try new things.

Workbook key

5 2 Meeting new people after school is always easier for you.
3 Bringing all my friends together was a wonderful experience.
4 Going to swimming classes with you has been great fun.
5 Writing a diary has been very useful (for me).

6 2 motivating 3 worried 4 confusing 5 depressed
6 amazing

7 Sentence 3

8 1 why she's writing
2 how she felt about the changes in her life
3/4 what she's doing to solve her problems
4/3 how her friend helped her
5 how her life has changed
6 say thank you

Review

1 2 e 3 a 4 f 5 d 6 c

2 2 give up 3 pass on 4 set up 5 bring together
6 sign up

3 2 yourselves 3 yourself 4 myself 5 himself
6 each other

4 2 How many text messages have you sent today?
3 They've won several awards for their charity work.
4 I haven't had any exams this month.
5 How many times has she been to the youth club?
6 He's helped a lot of people with problems.

5 2 've/have you been coming 3 hasn't been going
4 've/have been making 5 's/has been helping
6 Have (you) been giving

6 2 's been going 3 have you had 4 haven't sold
5 've been picking 6 have they been helping

7 2 c 3 b 4 a 5 c 6 c 7 b 8 b 9 c 10 b
11 b 12 c

8 2 a 3 b 4 b 5 c 6 b 7 b 8 c 9 c 10 a

9 A: What's up Pam? You don't look very happy.
B: I've had another argument with my mum.
A: Oh, you poor thing! What was it about?
B: She says I use my phone too much, and she doesn't want to pay for it.
A: Look, I'm sure she'll calm down soon. She always does.
B: Well, she doesn't realise how important my phone is. I'd be lost without it!
A: I know what you mean. Look, you don't need to worry. Just don't use your phone much if she's there. She'll soon forget.
B: Yes, I suppose you're right. That's what happened last time!
A: Right! I'm sure it will be fine. Now, how can I make you feel better? Shall we go to the sports centre?

Get it right!

1 2 herself 3 himself 4 ourselves 5 themselves
6 yourself

2 ... I advise you to take the train ...; Another piece of advice ...; ... and my advice is that ...; ... an important piece of advices is that ...; ... send you some more advices.

3 2 talltented 3 hard-working 4 sociable 5 impatient
6 easy-going 7 strickt

Unit 3
Vocabulary

1 2 d 3 g 4 b 5 i 6 f 7 h 8 e 9 c

2 2 (course) fees 3 application form 4 entrance 5 courses
6 path

3 2 part-time 3 work 4 career/job 5 training
6 experience 7 degree 8 application form

Language focus 1

1 2 starts 3 is going to do 4 take 5 is going
6 aren't going 7 I'm going to study 8 does school finish

2 2 'm going 3 'm not going to do 4 'm going to relax
5 is/are taking 6 starts 7 ends 8 'm going to work
9 'm going to play

3 2 takes 3 is participating 4 is ... going to prepare
5 's going 6 's going to practise 7 's not going to get
8 'm going to study

5 2 advice 3 up 4 the exams 5 time

Listening and vocabulary

1 writing, stage acting, university course

Audioscript

Journalist: Sarah, why haven't we seen you in films recently?
Sarah: Oh, I stopped making films when I was 13.
Journalist: Goodness! Why?
Sarah: Well, I started acting when I was five, and made my first film at six. I was lucky to be in some successful films with Hollywood stars, I even won awards! It was exciting at first and I had a great time, but it was like a game, really. After a while I got bored with it. I wanted to go to school and make friends with kids my own age, not hang around on film sets with adults and study with tutors. So I decided to give it up and go to high school in my home town.
Journalist: Did you plan to go back to acting?
Sarah: At first I wasn't sure. Film producers would still send me scripts to read, so it was a possibility. Then I realised I was actually much happier as a normal person doing normal things. I don't think being famous is for me, and I never wanted to make a fortune. So I always said no. I'm not going to go back to films, although I may try acting in the theatre.
Journalist: Now you've just published your first novel at 18. What is it about?
Sarah: It's about a group of teenagers who are a bit lost. They just don't know what they want to do in life, or how they feel about the world. I suppose it's about what it's like growing up in the twenty-first century.
Journalist: Is it autobiographical?
Sarah: No, not really. I think I've always known what I wanted to do and luckily I've always been able to do it.
Journalist: So what are your plans now?
Sarah: Well, in the fall I'm going to university in New York. I plan to continue writing novels, and I might act in student productions if I can. I haven't done much acting since Hollywood!
Journalist: Wow! You'll be busy. Well, I'm sorry I won't be seeing you in any more films, but I wish you great success.
Sarah: Thanks.

2 2 F 3 T 4 T 5 T 6 F 7 F 8 F 9 T 10 F

3 2 records 3 awards 4 community 5 millionaire
6 project 7 voluntary work 8 fortune

Workbook key

4   **2** become (a multi-)millionaire   **3** do (any) voluntary work
   4 start (an online) business   **5** developed (the) project
   6 made a fortune   **7** supports (poor children in) the community
   8 won (a Hero) award

Language focus 2

1   **2** may/might have   **3** is/'s going to break   **4** will/'ll be
   5 is/'s going to finish   **6** may/might win; won't be
   7 aren't going to make   **8** will/'ll get

2   **1** *be*; *-ing*; 2 predictions   **3** state

3   **2** 'll be making   **3** will be working   **4** won't be living
   5 Will (you) be staying   **6** 'll be doing

4   **2** c   **3** a   **4** f   **5** d   **6** e

5   **2** 'll be winning   **3** 'll provide   **4** might take   **5** may decide
   6 won't stay

Reading

1   Angela: d   Santiago: c   Charley: a

2   **1** essential   **2** ambition   **3** talks   **4** turns   **5** cure

3   **2** Angela   **3** Angela and Charley   **4** Santiago   **5** Charley
   6 Santiago and Charley   **7** Angela   **8** Santiago and Charley
   9 Santiago   **10** Santiago

4   **1** Charley   **2** Angela   **3** Santiago   **4** Charley   **5** Santiago
   6 Angela

Writing

1   The author disagrees with the opinion.

2   2, 3, 5

3   **2** Firstly,   **3** Although   **4** In addition,   **5** whereas
   6 In conclusion,

4   **2** In addition   **3** Although   **4** whereas   **5** However
   6 In conclusion

5   **2** Many   **3** Lots   **4** a few   **5** All   **6** Some

6   **2** think   **3** doing   **4** left   **5** studying

7   **2** believe   **3** far   **4** Personally   **5** view

8   **1** b   **2** d   **3** a   **4** c

Review

1   **2** work experience   **3** course fees   **4** entrance exam
   5 career path   **6** part-time job

2   **2** a fortune   **3** a millionaire   **4** the community   **5** a project
   6 awards

3   **2** starts   **3** does his train get; arrives
   4 Are you going; 'm going to try

4   **2** 're not going to   **3** will   **4** might   **5** 're going to   **6** 'll

5   **2** They won't be making a fortune with that crazy idea!
   3 He will be starring in Hollywood films in a year or two.
   4 She will be starting her own company in a couple of years.
   5 Will people be buying this product in five years' time?

6   **2** a   **3** b   **4** c   **5** a   **6** c   **7** a   **8** b   **9** a   **10** c

7   **2** a   **3** b   **4** c   **5** b   **6** c   **7** b   **8** c

8   **2** think the best way is   **3** How shall we decide
   4 I was thinking of   **5** what kind of thing   **6** I'd rather
   7 that's a good idea

Get it right!

1   **2** get   **3** are going   **4** are you   **5** study   **6** spend
   7 is he   **8** travel

2   **2** My brother will be successful in the future.
   3 I'm sure you'll enjoy your new job.
   4 If it rains, we'll have lunch at my house.
   5 They'll meet us at the station at 4 o'clock.
   6 I promise you that you won't forget your visit.

3   **2** work   **3** job   **4** course   **5** job   **6** job; career

Unit 4

Vocabulary

1   **2** spread   **3** fry   **4** boil   **5** slice   **6** roast   **7** grill   **8** mix
   9 bake   **10** grate

2   **2** mix; milkshake   **3** chop onions   **4** roasts potatoes
   5 fry; chicken   **6** spread; jam   **7** grill cheese   **8** boils eggs
   9 bake apples   **10** grate chocolate

3   **2** Slice   **3** spread   **4** grate   **5** Bake   **6** Boil   **7** chop
   8 mix   **9** boil   **10** fry   **11** spread   **12** bake   **13** grill

Language focus 1

1   **2** Unless   **3** if   **4** Unless   **5** When   **6** if

2   **2** The chips will burn unless you fry them gently.
   3 If Paula cooks tonight, she'll make spaghetti again.
   4 Will you help me with the recipe when I cook supper
     tonight?
   5 Unless they remember to buy more bread we won't have
     enough.
   6 If he slices the tomatoes with that knife, he'll cut his finger.

3   **2** don't understand   **3** when   **4** might be   **5** eat
   6 When   **7** 'll ask   **8** Unless   **9** brings

4   **2** 'll have   **3** won't get   **4** if   **5** eat   **6** 'll protect
   7 unless   **8** contains   **9** when/if   **10** 'll find   **11** when/if
   12 won't have

Listening and vocabulary

1   **2** delicious   **3** savoury   **4** bitter   **5** sweet   **6** disgusting
   7 crunchy   **8** bland   **9** slimy   **10** spicy

2   **2** slimy   **3** bland   **4** savoury; sweet   **5** delicious
   6 crunchy   **7** bitter   **8** salty

3   He ate three of the world's hottest chillies.

Audioscript

Presenter: On the programme today is Matt Sanchez, a chef from
     Los Angeles. Matt you're famous for your spicy barbecue
     sauces. How did that start?
Matt: Ten years ago I visited the Fiery Foods Festival in
     Albuquerque, New Mexico. It's dedicated to hot, spicy food,
     especially the chilli pepper. You can find hundreds of chilli-
     flavoured products, like sweets, chocolate, nuts or cheese,
     and many different kinds of sauces and oils to go with a
     barbecue. It was fantastic! I've been going there ever since!
Presenter: Are all chillies hot?

Workbook key

Matt: Well, some are much hotter than others, but it depends how sensitive your tongue is. I was born in Mexico, where the chilli pepper comes from, so I've eaten hot food since I was a child. My mum even used to give us chilli sweets! Anyway, about a hundred years ago, a man called Wilbur Scoville created a system to tell how hot a chilli is, with a special heat unit. He called it the Scoville Heat Unit, after himself. The average chilli is about five thousand Scoville heat units, but if you chop a chilli into small pieces and throw away the seeds, it won't be so hot.

Presenter: And the hottest chillies?

Matt: Well, at the last Fiery Foods Festival, I discovered the Carolina Reaper, which is officially the hottest chilli in the world, at over two million units!!

Presenter: Wow, did you try it?

Matt: Yes! If you had the chance, wouldn't you? I wanted to see if I could eat something that hot, so I agreed to participate in a competition to eat three Carolina Reapers in the shortest time possible!

Presenter: Goodness! Can you prepare for that?

Matt: People say that eating bananas or boiled potatoes, and drinking milk before you start is a good idea, but I didn't have time. I ate my peppers quite slowly, but I finished them all. The winner was amazing, though. He managed to eat all three in just nine seconds!

Presenter: That *is* fast! Did you drink a lot of water afterwards?

Matt: Oh no! Water doesn't help at all. The best thing to take away the burning sensation is ice cream. If it isn't chilli-flavoured, that is!

4   2 ten years   3 chilli   4 Mexico; chilli sweets
  5 how hot chillies are   6 two million
  7 three; shortest time
  8 bananas; potatoes; milk   9 nine seconds
  10 ice cream

Language focus 2

1   1 imaginary   2 past simple; *would, could* or *might*   3 *would*
  4 can

2   2 e   3 a   4 f   5 c   6 d

3   2 If I was/were (very) hungry, I might eat something.
  3 If she knew how to cook, she might make lunch.
  4 He wouldn't eat goat's cheese unless he had no choice.
  5 If there was/were a pizza delivery service, we could order one.

4   2 would do   3 could ask   4 asked   5 would have
  6 wouldn't be   7 stopped   8 might be   9 would like
  10 prepared   11 did   12 could discover

5   2 in   3 by   4 on

6   2 in many different ways   3 on the go   4 surrounded by

Reading

1   No

2   1 disposable   2 tasty   3 floats away   4 seasoning
  5 sprinkle

3   2 Because astronauts are from different countries and like different things.   3 So they can choose tastes they like before they go into space.   4 Because in microgravity food is quite bland / blander than it is on Earth.   5 Normal salt and pepper would float and could damage the space station or get in an astronaut's eyes or nose.

4   2 eight   3 first day   4 on Earth   5 drinks   6 packaging
  7 stays fresh   8 of the packet   9 with water   10 heated up
  11 drinks   12 fridge

Writing

1   The weather in Ireland is often cold and wet so a hot stew is good food to keep you warm.

2   2 The other ingredients are carrots and onions.
  3 Nobody knows who invented it.
  4 You might find stews with beef, sausages or fish.
  5 They used to make it over a fire.
  6 You can eat it in pubs and restaurants all around Ireland.

3   2 contains   3 served   4 made

4   2 e   3 d   4 a   5 f   6 c

5   2 be   3 is   4 was   5 were

6   2 usually   3 used to   4 used to   5 usually

7   Sentence 5

8   2 how to cook the dish   3 what the ingredients are
  4 who invented it   5 why it's so popular
  6 how people cooked the dish in the past
  7 where you can eat or buy it   8 a recommendation

Review

1   2 mix   3 grate   4 Boil   5 chop   6 boil   7 Slice
  8 spread

2   2 sweet   3 disgusting   4 bland   5 slimy   6 savoury
  7 delicious   8 crunchy   9 bitter   10 spicy

3   2 Unless you want to do it yourself, I'll make the birthday cake.
  3 I'll put the food in the oven when your friends arrive for the party.
  4 You won't be able to eat it all unless I help you.
  5 I'll ring you when I get home from the restaurant.
  6 If she eats any more crisps, she might not want any supper.

4   2 had   3 needed   4 could cook   5 'd feel   6 didn't like
  7 passed   8 'd look   9 went   10 might open   11 owned
  12 could get   13 became   14 would appear
  15 couldn't do   16 had

5   2 b   3 c   4 b   5 b   6 a   7 b   8 a   9 a   10 b
  11 c   12 a

6   2 a   3 b   4 c   5 a   6 c   7 b   8 b

7   2 first of all, chop   3 Next, you   4 need to stir
  5 then, add   6 Finally, when

Get it right!

1   2 What **would** you ~~will~~ cook if you could cook anything you wanted?   3 correct   4 The coffee would be less bitter if you ~~would~~ added more sugar to it.   5 If you ~~would eat~~ **ate** a poisonous mushroom, you ~~will~~ **would** be very ill.
  6 Would you eat fugu fish if it ~~will be~~ **was** on the menu?

2   2 on; in   3 in   4 on   5 in   6 in

3   2 dishes   3 dishes   4 food   5 meals   6 food

Workbook key

Unit 5

Vocabulary

1 **Across:** 4 candle 5 switch 7 light 9 remote 10 tap
11 bulb
Down: 1 fans 2 matches 3 heater 4 charger 6 plug
8 control

2 2 fans 3 remote control 4 candles 5 tap 6 matches

3 2 chargers 3 light bulbs 4 plug 5 switch 6 taps
7 heater

Language focus 1

1 2 isn't cooled 3 were sold 4 wasn't invented
5 will be shown 6 won't be used

2 2 was followed 3 was released 4 said 5 went
6 were played 7 was seen 8 was developed 9 spend
10 are played 11 will be designed 12 will find

3 2 were invented; weren't manufactured
3 are sold; aren't needed 4 didn't use
5 won't be delivered; will be tested 6 was made; is used

4 2 was injured 3 was flown 4 was ordered by
5 were filmed 6 is finished 7 is edited 8 are added
9 will be released by 10 will be held

Listening and vocabulary

1 b

Audioscript

Wayne: Hi Andy! When are you off to college? You start soon, don't
you? Are you all ready?
Andy: Yeah, I'm off in a couple of weeks. I'm really excited, and an
amazing thing has happened!
Wayne: Oh yeah? What's that?
Andy: Well, my mum wanted me to tidy away all the toys I've got in
my bedroom before I go.
Wayne: Toys? What sort of toys?
Andy: Transformers, mostly. I started to collect Transformers when
I was about 7. You know, the ones that can change from a
robot into a car, or an insect into an action figure.
Wayne: Yeah, I remember them. I had a few too.
Andy: Well, for a few years I was totally obsessed with them and
bought as many as I could with my pocket money. Every
birthday I asked for money to buy more. I even had a book
where I wrote down every one I had and what I needed to get
next. Friends started giving me theirs when they got bored
with them, and my uncle gave me a lot that *he* was given
when he was little. In the end I had a big collection.
Wayne: How many have you got, then?
Andy: Over 500. Some of them are older than me, too! Anyway,
Mum suggested I put them all away before I go to college. If I
leave them out, they'll need to be cleaned and she says she's
not going to do it. Anyway, I thought about it, and I decided
that I'm a bit old for all those toys now. I was really into them
once but not anymore. And the collection's much too big.
It takes up most of the space in my room. So I went on the
Internet to see if I could sell them and guess what?
Wayne: What?
Andy: They're really popular and some of them are worth quite a bit
of money. So I've advertised them on a specialist website, and
someone who runs a collectors' shop is keen on buying them. I
may be able to sell them for several thousand dollars!
Wayne: Wow! That's amazing.
Andy: I know! It's hard to believe people are that interested. Why
don't you look for yours?
Wayne: Yes, I will!

2 2 b 3 c 4 a 5 a 6 a and c 7 b 8 b

3 2 b 3 a 4 b

4 2 ridiculously 3 totally 4 much 5 bit 6 really 7 kind
8 extremely

Language focus 2

1 2 where 3 whose 4 which/that 5 who/that 6 where
7 which/that 8 whose

2 2 This is the house where I stayed.
3 That's Xavier, the boy who/that I did the exchange with.
4 That's Emil, the little brother whose bedroom I shared.
5 That's Serge, the brother who/that Xavier shares/shared a
room with.
6 These are the pancakes which/that we ate for breakfast every
day.
7 These are the neighbours whose swimming pool we used
while I was there.
8 This is the café where we went to play pool.

3 2 That is the restaurant where we had lunch.
3 They're the people who/that won the lottery.
4 She's the neighbour whose car was stolen.
5 Those are the jeans which/that I bought yesterday.
6 I love the shop where I buy cheap video games.
7 Liam is the boy who/that I sold my old games console to.
8 Those are the people whose cat is missing.

5 2 email 3 texting 4 chatting 5 lost touch
6 track down 7 catch up 8 keep in touch 9 tweet
10 Skype™

Reading

1 clockwork

2 1 waterproof 2 wind 3 clamp 4 handle
5 eco-friendly

3 2 couldn't use/didn't have electricity 3 rechargeable batteries
4 want to use less electricity

4 2 MP 3 BL 4 MP 5 T 6 BL

Writing

1 You can send and receive messages and emails, use social
media, monitor your heart rate, check the time and make and
receive calls.

2 2 F – It can last for up to a week. 3 T 4 T
5 F – It is totally waterproof. 6 T

3 2 looks 3 made of 4 can also use it 5 comes with
6 come in

4 2 The pink phone looks very cool. 3 The camera is only
available in black. 4 The screen is made of plastic.
5 You can also use it to make phone calls.
6 The tablet comes with several apps.

5 2 e 3 b 4 a 5 d 6 c

6 2 big enough 3 too expensive 4 long enough
5 too weak 6 too short

7 2 The design looks amazing. 3 The phone has a very
large screen. 4 The remote control is incredibly easy to use.
5 The range of colours is spectacularly good.
6 It's a perfect size.

Workbook key

8
name of the product	✓
colours available	✓
functions – what it does	✓
price	✗
personal opinion	✓
comparison with other products	✗
options or accessories	✓
features – special things about it	✓

Review

1 2 d 3 h 4 a 5 i 6 j 7 c 8 b 9 f 10 e

2 2 much too 3 quite 4 extremely 5 a bit 6 really
7 kind of 8 totally

3 2 was invented 3 is sold 4 are found 5 are produced
6 won't be needed 7 will be replaced

4 2 Xavi is the boy whose dad used to work with my dad years
ago.
3 Yesterday we visited the museum where Edison's first light
bulbs are displayed.
4 This is the guitar which/that he made himself at the age of
16!
5 Is that the man who/that helped you the other day?
6 I think that's the girl whose bag you found this morning.

5 2 a 3 c 4 d 5 a 6 d 7 b 8 c 9 b

6 2 b 3 a 4 a 5 c 6 a 7 b 8 b 9 c 10 c

7 2 Is it easy 3 how much memory 4 What's (the sound) like
5 How long does (the battery) last 6 Could you show

Get it right!

1 2 will be made 3 will be spent 4 will be seen
5 will be created 6 will be carried

2 give – gave – given; leave – left – left; sell – sold – sold; make –
made – made; find – found – found; show – showed – shown;
see – saw – seen; spend – spent – spent

3 2 There is a park in the city which ~~it~~ is very clean and quiet.
3 There are a lot of drivers who ~~they~~ do not know how to drive
very well.
4 I got the part-time job in London ~~what~~ **which/that** I wanted.
5 I've moved to a new house which ~~it's~~ **is** a bit bigger.
6 correct
7 That is the girl who I told you about ~~her~~.
8 I'm looking for a man who ~~he~~ left his mobile phone in
the café.

4 2 Don't touch the light bulb! It's extrem**e**ly hot.
3 Mobile phone chargers can be qui**e**t**e** expensive.
4 correct
5 The light in a bottle is a total**l**y unique invention.

Unit 6

Vocabulary

1

verbs

g	o	p	l	a	y
i	b	d	o	v	e
v	h	r	s	e	t
e	a	e	t	h	k
m	v	s	w	o	p
d	e	s	t	l	u
m	a	k	e	d	x
s	a	d	p	u	t

nouns

s	t	e	p	l	a	d	y	z
p	i	q	r	o	y	e	n	o
i	m	p	e	r	f	c	u	p
b	e	n	s	f	m	o	c	h
f	i	r	e	w	o	r	k	s
i	n	u	n	o	t	a	c	p
c	o	n	t	e	s	t	u	f
t	u	s	x	b	r	i	j	o
o	c	c	a	s	i	o	n	o
x	k	r	m	h	s	n	o	d
t	m	u	s	i	c	s	h	l

2 2 make special food 3 give a present / hold a contest
4 set off fireworks 5 have a good time
6 dress up for the occasion 7 put up decorations
8 give a present / hold a contest

3 2 play (your favourite) music 3 give (them) a present
4 make special food 5 put up decorations
6 have a good time

4 2 play (popular) music 3 dress up for the occasion
4 food (is) made 5 hold (another popular) contest
6 has a good time 7 fireworks (are) set off

Language focus 1

1 1 nouns 2 prepositions 3 verbs

2 2 watching: Rule 3 3 passing: Rule 3 4 dancing: Rule 1
5 putting: Rule 3 6 making: Rule 2 7 Choosing: Rule 1
8 celebrating: Rule 2

3 2 You can't organise a big party without having a few
problems.
3 My mum really enjoys going to weddings.
4 Wearing special clothes makes me feel uncomfortable.
5 You must practise making a speech before the awards
ceremony.
6 I'm not very good at singing or dancing.
7 Some people can't stand being in a large crowd at a concert.
8 The best thing about going to the festival is seeing the
fireworks.

Workbook key

5 2 e 3 f 4 a 5 b 6 d

6 2 working with 3 agree on 4 recover from 5 prepare for 6 looking forward to

Listening and vocabulary

1 clearing up and booking bands

Audioscript

Presenter: Today I'm talking to Emma Roberts, who organises one of the biggest music festivals in Britain on a farm in England. Emma, how long have you been organising the festival?

Emma: Five years. I have a great time!

Presenter: This year's festival has just finished. How many people attended?

Emma: About 110,000.

Presenter: Wow! So when do you start preparing for next year's festival?

Emma: Well, first we have to clear up this year's! Most people camp, so it gets really messy. It takes weeks to get rid of the rubbish. We have some tents to hire, but most people bring their own tent. Then at the end of the festival they often just leave it, especially if it's wet. So volunteers take down all the tents, and the ones we don't want we give to charity. We also have to take down four stages, and all the facilities, like showers, toilets, backstage rooms for the bands, food tents, stalls and exhibitions. The festival is the size of a small town, so clearing it all up takes about six weeks.

Presenter: What else do you do?

Emma: The most important thing is booking the bands. The festival is over three days, so we need a big line-up, including several really popular acts, the headliners, to finish each night. Organising those bands often starts years before, because the really big groups organise their concert schedules a year or more in advance.

Presenter: I'd no idea it was like that! So you know some of next year's names now?

Emma: Er, yes. We've already booked three headliners for next year, and quite a few other bands and musicians too, but I can't announce the names yet.

Presenter: Oh, well, never mind! How do you decide which artists to get?

Emma: Well, we include rock, pop, indie, dance and folk, so I ask music journalists and DJs for suggestions, and I go to concerts. Many fans send me emails, too. And often artists themselves ask to play! New and old bands all want to be seen here. The only problem is when bands split up before the festival. That happens every year!

Presenter: Well … Emma, thanks for chatting, and good luck with next year's festival!

2 2 T 3 F 4 T 5 F 6 T 7 F 8 T 9 F 10 F

3 2 crowded 3 stunning 4 scary 5 impressive 6 traditional 7 peaceful 8 colourful

4 2 peaceful 3 impressive 4 crowded 5 colourful 6 traditional 7 atmospheric

Language focus 2

1 1 adjectives 2 verbs

2 2 to organise: Rule 1 3 to practise: Rule 1 4 to go: Rule 2 5 to wear: Rule 2 6 to be: Rule 1

3 2 to celebrate 3 to agree 4 to go 5 to visit 6 to think 7 to have 8 to tell 9 to take 10 to find

4 2 to get; to pay 3 singing 4 Putting 5 to see 6 to come 7 to celebrate; having 8 to being

5 2 having 3 asking 4 to do 5 to help 6 to worry 7 to guess 8 doing 9 going 10 having 11 finishing

Reading

1 New York City: 4, 6; Rio de Janeiro: 1, 3; Edinburgh: 2, 5

2 1 banned 2 illuminated 3 in aid of 4 see in 5 take your pick

3 2 E 3 R 4 NY 5 E 6 R 7 NY 8 R

Writing

1 It was for a class in their last year at school and all the classmates went.

2 2 Their parents made the food.
3 She thought it was funny to see her classmates dressed for a party.
4 Because she thought the video was very sad.
5 She told them not to make too much noise.
6 Because she was tired.

3 2 so 3 too 4 too 5 so 6 too

4 2 too 3 too 4 so 5 too

5 You don't need *that* in sentences 2, 3 and 5.

6 2 then 3 After 4 then 5 after 6 Then

7 2 e 3 c 4 a 5 d

8 2 where the celebration was 3 the arrangements they made 4 the food 5 what they did 6 how she felt at the end

Review

1 2 f 3 e 4 a 5 b 6 d

2 2 atmospheric 3 crowded 4 peaceful 5 traditional 6 colourful

3 2 getting 3 Studying; celebrating 4 swimming 5 cooking, chopping

4 2 to provide 3 to dance 4 to organise 5 to remember 6 to make 7 to organise 8 to set up 9 to earn 10 to think

5 2 to have 3 to talk 4 thinking 5 to organise 6 to help 7 preparing 8 having

6 2 c 3 b 4 a 5 a 6 b 7 c 8 a 9 c 10 b

7 2 c 3 b 4 a 5 b 6 c 7 b 8 a 9 c 10 b

8 2 Can I help you make your costume? 3 I'll help you if you like.
4 Could you ask your parents to drive us there?
5 Shall I lend you a pair of baggy trousers?
6 Could I borrow your pirate hat?

Get it right!

1 2 at 3 on 4 at 5 in 6 in 7 about

2 2 said 3 tried 4 paying 5 playing 6 enjoying

3 2 to come 3 to do 4 helping 5 to go 6 visiting 7 swimming; try

Workbook key

Unit 7
Vocabulary

1

Crossword:
- 3 across: suspense
- 6 across: villain
- 7 across: action
- 8 across: mystery
- 1 down: setting
- 2 down: hero
- 4 down: characters
- 5 down: plot

2 2 action 3 characters 4 plot 5 mystery 6 setting

3 2 e 3 d 4 c 5 a 6 f

4 2 mystery 3 characters 4 hero 5 plot 6 suspense
7 villains 8 action

Language focus 1

1 1 past perfect; *have*; past participle 2 past 3 regret

2 2 e 3 a 4 f 5 c 6 d

3 2 Would JK Rowling have become a millionaire if Harry Potter
had sold fewer copies?
3 If Edward's family hadn't saved Bella, vampires would have
killed her.
4 Tris would have died if Four hadn't rescued her.
5 If Hazel hadn't met Gus, she wouldn't have visited
Amsterdam.
6 Katniss wouldn't have volunteered for the Hunger Games if
her sister's name hadn't been picked.

4 2 If our neighbour hadn't said Byrony Lake was lovely, we
wouldn't have gone there.
3 If we hadn't hired a rowing boat, my mother wouldn't have
lost her ring in the water.
4 If we hadn't all liked Byrony Lake, we wouldn't have gone
there again a few weeks later.
5 If we hadn't taken our fishing rods, we wouldn't have caught
five fish.
6 If we hadn't cooked them for supper, Dad wouldn't have
found Mum's ring inside his fish!

5 2 around 3 back 4 towards 5 above 6 through

Listening and vocabulary

1 1 c 2 d 3 a 4 b

Audioscript

Today our unexplained mystery comes from Peru, in South America. High
up in the Peruvian desert, 400 kilometres south of Lima, is a strange sight.
It's called the Nazca lines, hundreds of strange symbols made with long
white lines.

The most mysterious thing about the Nazca lines is that on the ground
it's impossible to see the shapes they make. In order to see what they
represent, you have to look at them from above. So, although a Peruvian
archaeologist discovered them in 1927, it wasn't until planes flew over the
desert for the first time, in the 1930s, that all the weird and wonderful
shapes became visible. The lines are an incredible collection of gigantic
animals, birds, fish, insects, geometric shapes and strange symbols. Among
approximately 900 figures there's a spider, a monkey, a pelican, a killer
whale, and a shark, as well as humans, trees and plants, all in an area 80
kilometres long. The largest figures are over 200 metres wide.
Of course, once people realised what the lines were, they started to
investigate their origins. According to experts, they were created by the
local Nazca culture between 400 and 650 AD. The lines were made by
removing the small reddish stones on the surface of the desert to uncover
the white sand beneath. They've existed unchanged for at least 1,500
years as a result of the dry, windless desert climate and because few people
ever go there. The Nazca probably made some of the shapes by using
wooden poles to keep the long lines so straight.
But what they were for is still a mystery. One theory suggested the lines
were designed so that aliens could land. However, the surface of the desert
is too soft for spaceships to land on, and this theory doesn't explain all the
different shapes. Another suggestion was that the lines were connected
to studying the planets, the stars and the night sky, but there is no real
evidence for that. Other theories are that the lines show underground
canals, or have some other religious significance like asking their gods to
bring water. We'll probably never know, but the Nazca lines became a
UNESCO World Heritage Site in 1994, and so will continue to amaze us all
for hundreds of years.

2 2 b 3 c 4 a 5 b 6 c 7 a

3 2 alternative 3 true 4 said 5 cause 6 obvious
7 why 8 wanted

4 2 As a result of 3 Rather than 4 In fact 5 in order to
6 so that 7 Of course 8 Then again

Language focus 2

1 1 *have* + past participle 2 *must* 3 *might*, *may* and *could*
4 *can't*

2 2 must 3 could 4 might 5 can't 6 may

3 2 The thief must have switched it off.
3 It may have been too heavy.
4 It could have happened on Friday or Saturday.
5 He can't have worn gloves.
6 He must have dropped it.
7 It can't have been very difficult.
8 He might have hidden it or he could have sold it.

4 2 can't have transported 3 must have been
4 might/may/could have had 5 might/may/could have buried
6 might/may/could have used

Reading

1 fantasy; short stories

2 1 out loud 2 publisher 3 make a deal 4 futuristic
5 rejection letters

3

Name	Anna Caltabiano
Age	17
Family	only child; mother Japanese, father Italian-American
Place of birth	Hong Kong
Home	Palo Alto, California
Education	Chinese school, Hong Kong; USA
Hobbies	reading, writing
Books	*All That Is Red*, *The Seventh Miss Hatfield*

Workbook key

4 2 Anna would stay at home and write a novel instead of going to summer camp.

3 She draws pictures of her ideas first, then she writes dialogue in phone texts to herself.

4 Young people growing up who don't know what side they are on.

5 She published the book herself.

Writing

1 The branch of a tree almost fell on her and her parents when they went for a walk on a windy day.

2 2 b 3 d 4 g 5 a 6 c 7 e

3 2 immediately 3 obviously 4 luckily 5 Amazingly
6 fortunately 7 Eventually

4 2 Luckily/Fortunately/Amazingly 3 Eventually 4 Obviously
5 Amazingly/Suddenly/Eventually

5 2 e 3 b 4 a 5 c

6 2 lucky 3 suddenly 4 loud 5 quietly 6 amazing

7 2 could have hurt 3 could have lost 4 could have missed
5 could have broken

8

background information	✓
descriptive adjectives	✓
adverbs	✓
a variety of past tenses	✓
what happened in the end	✓
what people said	✓

Review

1 2 villain 3 suspense 4 main characters 5 heroes
6 setting 7 plot 8 mystery

2 2 Of course 3 as a result of 4 In order to 5 In fact
6 According to 7 rather than 8 then again

3 2 If he hadn't stolen the chicken, his owner wouldn't have shouted at him.

3 If he had run in the other direction, he wouldn't have gone into the zoo.

4 The tigers would have eaten him if he had run into their cage.

5 If I had seen the cat and the bear together, I would have been amazed.

6 I wouldn't have believed the story if there hadn't been a photo.

4 2 might/may/could have been 3 can't have been
4 must have been 5 might/may/could have made
6 can't have realised

5 2 d 3 c 4 b 5 a 6 b 7 c 8 a 9 b 10 b 11 c

6 2 b 3 a 4 b 5 b 6 a 7 c 8 a

7 A: I nearly got into big trouble yesterday.

B: Really – why was that?

A: Well, I borrowed my sister's bicycle to go to the shop.

B: Does she let you borrow it?

A: No! So I didn't ask her. Anyway, I was only in the shop for a minute, but when I came out, the bike was gone.

B: Oh no! So then what happened?

A: Well, I decided to walk back through the park, and I found her bike by the lake!

B: Wow! That was lucky!

A: I know! Extremely lucky! I rode home quickly before anything else happened.

B: Did your sister find out?

A: No, I didn't tell her. If she'd found out, she'd have been really angry!

Get it right!

1 2 If she **had** arrived later, it would have been impossible to save her life.

3 The book would have been better if the hero ~~wouldn't have~~ **hadn't** died.

4 correct

5 I **would have** missed my friends if I had gone on holiday with my parents.

6 If they ~~would have~~ **had** known the film was so exciting, they would have gone to see it.

7 We wouldn't have found the house if you ~~didn't~~ **hadn't** sent us a map.

2 … someone have ~~leave~~ **left** the gate …; He can't **have** jumped over the gate.; … he might have ~~go~~ **gone** under it?; Someone must **have** opened the gate.; He might ~~has~~ **have** hidden somewhere …; … my mum might have ~~came~~ **come** home …; He can't have ~~go~~ **gone** far!

3 2 so that 3 so that 4 so that 5 in order 6 In order to
7 in order

Unit 8

Vocabulary

1 2 kidnapping 3 robbery 4 vandalism
5 illegal downloading 6 arson 7 shoplifting 8 mugging

2 2 shoplifting 3 vandalism 4 illegal downloading
5 mugging 6 pickpocketing 7 arson 8 kidnapping

3 2 pickpocketing 3 arson 4 mugging 5 shoplifting
6 illegal downloading 7 robbery 8 vandalism

4 2 Pickpocketing 3 mugging 4 illegal downloading
5 robbery 6 arson 7 vandalism

Language focus 1

1 1 say; tell 2 tell; say

2 2 told 3 said 4 told 5 said 6 tell 7 told

3 2 had run; hadn't caught 3 couldn't stop; would help
4 had reported 5 had broken 6 weren't

4 2 I didn't steal / haven't stolen any sweets.
3 I have / 've got my little brother with me.
4 He put the sweets in my bag. 5 I'll put them back.
6 I can pay for them.

5 2 he lived 3 he'd seen 4 he'd seen it 5 it was
6 he didn't know 7 a man had got out
8 he couldn't remember 9 he would ask 10 she came

Listening and vocabulary

1 2 promise 3 agree 4 explain 5 decide 6 admit
7 insist 8 complain

2 2 promised 3 decided 4 complained 5 insisted
6 agreed 7 admitted 8 suggested

3 b

Workbook key

Audioscript

Olga: This is an interesting article. There's a new scheme starting here next year called restorative justice.

Justin: Restorative justice? What's that?

Olga: Well, it says here it's when the victim of a crime and the offender, the person who committed it, have an official meeting to talk about it called a conference. It's all organised carefully.

Justin: And what happens at the conference?

Olga: Well, apparently, victims and offenders can tell their stories. The idea is that the victim explains to the criminal how the crime made him or her feel, and the harmful effect it has had on their life. And the offender explains why they did it, and has a chance to say they're sorry for what they did.

Justin: It sounds a bit weird to me. If I'd been the victim of a mugging, for example, I wouldn't want to see the mugger again, would you? It would be quite scary!

Olga: Maybe at first, yes, but actually, wouldn't you like to tell them exactly what you thought of them? And try to make them feel guilty about what they did to you? I think I would!

Justin: Maybe, I suppose.

Olga: Right! It must be a good thing for the offender to realise the harm they caused. And also, at the conference they can agree on something the offender could do to repair the damage, like giving back money they stole or doing voluntary work in the community – painting or cleaning and stuff like that. In the article it says that in New Zealand they did a survey of people who'd gone through the process, and 77% of the victims said it made them feel better.

Justin: Mmm. I'm still not sure, though. What if I didn't want to meet them?

Olga: You wouldn't have to. Restorative justice is a voluntary process. A meeting only happens if the victim and the offender both agree to it. And, before they can take part, offenders must admit responsibility for the offence, and that it was wrong. The other thing it says here is that in New Zealand, where they've been doing this for a long time, offenders who've met the victim like this are 25% less likely to commit another crime. So that's positive, isn't it?

Justin: Definitely!

4 **2** victims; offenders / criminals **3** conference **4** how the crime; life / lives **5** they did it; apologise / say sorry **6** weird; scared **7** give back / pay back / return; voluntary **8** made them feel better / helped (them) **9** (a) voluntary (process); agrees **10** less likely

Language focus 2

1 **1** ask **2** if **3** change; isn't; subject; verb; don't use; don't put

2 **2** if I had noticed anyone following me.
3 if I could describe the man. **4** what kind of phone it was.
5 if I had a tracker app on my phone.
6 what the man had said. **7** if I had seen anyone else.
8 where she could contact me.

3 **1** tell; was **2** if **3** statement; verb; don't use

4 **2** if I could ask you a few questions.
3 what the man looked like?
4 how much there was in the wallet?
5 if you had seen the man before?
6 why you didn't call the police then.
7 where you got off the bus?
8 what time it was?

6 **2** come into existence **3** take care **4** see the point
5 go ahead **6** run out of

Reading

1 the stolen things; the robbers' names; some fingerprints; a broken window

2 **1** sleuth **2** denied **3** forced entry **4** turned out
5 investigative skills

3 **2** d **3** b **4** f **5** j **6** h **7** k **8** c **9** l **10** i **11** g
12 a

Writing

1 In a school/student newspaper.

2 **2** T **3** T **4** F – A few of them complain about the noise.
5 T

3 **2** three **3** thirds **4** about **5** just

4 **2** Just under 70% of students at our school recycle.
3 Approximately 50 people in the school think it's wrong to download illegally. **4** Just over 50% half of the students in our survey have downloaded music from the Internet.
5 About 40 students were at the demonstration.
6 Well under ten students have been robbed.

5 **2** Illegal downloading has risen in the last decade.
3 The size of our class has gone up in the last five years.
4 Many shops have opened in this area recently.
5 A lot of small businesses have closed this year.

6 **2** Everyone **3** All the students **4** Every **5** wants

7 **2** Can anyone explain this situation? **3** Do young people still pay for online content? **4** Why have cinema audiences decreased recently? **5** What is the real situation for young people nowadays?

8 A 3 B 1 C 4 D 2

Review

1 **2** pickpocketing **3** vandalism **4** arson **5** robbery

2 **2** agree **3** explained **4** suggest **5** decided

3 **2** he watched a lot of detective drama on TV. **3** she could remember the number of his car. **4** they hadn't downloaded many songs illegally. **5** they would catch the person who had attacked him.

4 **2** when I had last seen him **3** if he was in trouble
4 if I had noticed **5** what I could remember
6 why last Tuesday was important **7** if I would look at
8 if I recognised

5 **2** if I need a degree to become a CSI? **3** if I have to be a police officer? **4** how long all that takes. **5** what else I need?
6 why you are interested in this career?

6 **2** a **3** c **4** d **5** a **6** d **7** b **8** a **9** a **10** c

7 **2** a **3** a **4** c **5** b **6** c **7** b **8** a

8 **2** Is that right **3** must be joking **4** like to comment on
5 They're totally untrue **6** rumours are completely false
7 absolutely

Get it right!

1 … I shouldn't have ~~said~~ **told** a lie …; … they would ~~tell~~ **say** I couldn't go …; … he ~~said~~ **told** my mum that …; When my mum ~~told~~ **said** what she had heard …; If I ~~say~~ **tell** them that I lied …

2 **2** My teacher asked me if ~~have I~~ **had** any plans for the summer holidays. **3** I asked my parents ~~could I~~ **if I could** go to the party. **4** correct **5** My teacher asked me why ~~am I~~ **I am** always late for lessons. **6** My mum and dad asked ~~to~~ me where ~~was I~~ **I had been** last night.

3 **2** a **3** a **4** commit **5** crime **6** crime

Speaking extra key

Unit 1

1 1 Mum was crazy about pop music.
2 My parents weren't that into music.
3 I guess they liked disco.
4 My grandparents were into the Beatles.
5 My parents were both really into Michael Jackson.
6 They were into punk music and everything that went with it.

2 They are brother and sister.

3 1 about   2 changing   3 fit   4 size   5 looks   6 suits

Audioscript

Girl: So, you've got a pair of jeans. Let's find a cool T-shirt for you.
Boy: How about this one? It's got a bit green L on the front!
Girl: Yeah, L for 'loser'.
Boy: Hey! Come on, you're supposed to be helping me!
Girl: Here, try this one.
Boy: OK, where are the changing rooms?
Girl: Over there. And try this one as well.
Boy: So what do you think?
Girl: Well, it doesn't fit very well. It's too small for you.
Boy: But it's M – medium. It's my size.
Girl: Have you put on weight?
Boy: Very funny.
Girl: Sorry, but it looks a bit tight.
Boy: I'll try the other one on.
Girl: OK, that's better. You look great in that one.
Boy: Do you think so? Do you think this colour suits me?
Girl: Red? Of course … it goes with your red hair!
Boy: This is the last time I go shopping with my sister!

4 1 shoes, don't, fit   2 don't, think, suits
3 don't, good, dress   4 coat, not, size   5 not, sure

5 It's the same dress that Sue is going to wear to Sophie's party.

6 1 how about   2 suit you   3 Where are the changing rooms
4 You look great   5 your size   6 fit very well

Audioscript

Amy: Right, Sue, how about this dress for Sophie's party? I like the stripes.
Sue: Yeah, it's a nice dress. But stripy clothes don't suit you.
Amy: Yeah, you're right and it's a bit short, isn't it?
Sue: Hey, look at this one. It's denim but it's a lovely colour.
Amy: OK, I think I'll try it on. Where are the changing rooms?
Sue: They're over there. I'll be there in a minute. … So, let's see you.
Amy: OK, here's the denim dress. What do you think?
Sue: Wow! You look great!
Amy: Do you think? I think it's too small.
Sue: No, it's definitely your size. Not too big here not too small there!
Amy: Hold on, I've got another one.
Sue: Err … no, that doesn't fit very well. It's really baggy.
Amy: What do you mean? It's perfect!
Sue: Yes, you're right. It's perfect. But Amy … it's the same dress I'm going to wear to Sophie's party. Sorry.

Unit 2

1 1 little   2 through   3 difficult   4 come   5 helps
6 easier

2 Jo has to play a difficult piano piece tomorrow.

3 1 up   2 poor   3 down   4 mean   5 worry   6 fine
7 better

Audioscript

Tim: What's up, Jo?
Jo: I told my dad I wanted to give up piano lessons and now he's angry with me.
Tim: Oh, you poor thing! Why is he angry?
Jo: Well, you know my dad … he's so passionate about music.
Tim: Well, I'm sure he'll calm down soon. Why do you want to give up?
Jo: I don't know … it's just that we've got all these exams and I'm trying to study every day and I have piano lessons twice a week. And Chinese classes and hockey at the weekend.
Tim: I know what you mean. It's really hard to do everything!
Jo: And I have to practise this really difficult piece on the piano. I just don't think I'm very talented when it comes to music.
Tim: Of course you are. You don't need to worry. You're so hard-working. I'm sure you'll learn it.
Jo: But I have to play the whole thing tomorrow.
Tim: I'm sure it'll be fine. Just keep practising. So, how can I make you feel better?
Jo: Can you listen to me play it and tell me … honestly … what you think?
Tim: Of course, go on then.

4 All the sentences go down.

5 It got changed with Lewis' guitar.

6 1 what's up   2 it'll be fine   3 You poor thing   4 calm
down soon   5 How can I   6 what you mean   7 don't need
to worry

Audioscript

Dylan: Lewis, you *have* to help me!
Lewis: OK, Dylan, what's up?
Dylan: Remember the other night at my house when I borrowed my brother's guitar?
Lewis: Yes, isn't it funny that I have the same guitar as your brother?
Dylan: Well, now there's a hole in the back of the guitar. He's really angry!
Lewis: Well, I'm sure it'll be fine. I've got a hole in my guitar but it doesn't matter really … That's funny, I can't find it now.
Dylan: But now he won't lend me his guitar.
Lewis: You poor thing. Do you want to borrow mine?
Dylan: Great thanks. But what about my brother?
Lewis: Oh, I'm sure he'll calm down soon.
Dylan: Yes, but he really loves that guitar.
Lewis: How can I make you feel better?
Dylan: I don't know … I hate it when I can't talk to my brother.
Lewis: I know what you mean. It's awful.
Dylan: But how did I make a hole in the guitar?
Lewis: You don't need to worry. He'll soon realise that … Hold on. This isn't my guitar. Look, the strings are different!
Dylan: That's my brother's guitar!
Lewis: And he has my guitar … the one with the hole!

Unit 3

1 1 c   2 e   3 a   4 d   5 b

2 They are trying to decide what to buy their mum for her birthday.

3 1 need   2 thinking   3 rather   4 suggest   5 idea
6 shall   7 way

Speaking extra key

Audioscript

Girl: So what are we going to buy Mum for her birthday?
Boy: Do we have to decide now? I'm in the middle of level 37 of this game!
Girl: Level 37? Wow! Anyway, yes, we need to decide quickly because her birthday is next Saturday.
Boy: OK, well, I was thinking of a nice silk scarf or a bag, something like that.
Girl: But she's got lots of bags and I think Dad was going to buy her a really expensive one. I think I'd rather buy her something really different – what about a ride in a fast car, like a Ferrari or a Lamborghini? You know she loves cars.
Boy: But isn't that really expensive?
Girl: It's not that expensive, and I think Gran and Granddad would help us.
Boy: Well, if they're going to help us, why don't we give her something really nice?
Girl: What kind of thing do you suggest?
Boy: What about a weekend away in a nice hotel?
Girl: Yes, that's a good idea, too.
Boy: Sometimes I have good ideas, you know!
Girl: So how shall we decide?
Boy: Hmm … good question. Hold on, I think the best way is to ask Mum – she's always good at choosing presents for people.
Girl: Yeah, but the present is for her!!!
Boy: Oh, yeah!!

4
2 That's a good idea.
3 Personally, I'd rather go on a holiday.
4 I think the best way is to ask someone.
5 What kind of thing do you suggest?

5   They are going to talk about different career possibilities in the future.

6   1 I was thinking of   2 I'd rather   3 That's a good idea
4 we need to decide   5 do you suggest   6 How shall we decide   7 I think the best way

Audioscript

Oliver: So, we have to make a presentation to the class and we haven't even thought about what we're going to talk about.
Emily: I *have* thought about it. I was thinking of doing a presentation about interesting celebrations around the world.
Oliver: I think Conor and Natalie are going to do that. Personally, I'd rather talk about some different career possibilities in the future. We talked about it one day in social science class.
Emily: Oh yeah! That's a good idea, too. But do you think it'll be easy to find information?
Oliver: Yes, actually, I've already done a bit of research and there's loads of stuff on the Internet.
Emily: OK, great. So we need to decide who does what. Someone has to write the presentation.
Oliver: And we should probably include some pictures.
Emily: OK, what kind of pictures do you suggest?
Oliver: Hmm … I don't know. We can decide that when the time comes. How shall we decide who does what, then?
Emily: I think the best way is for me to let you start and when it's ready I'll make the presentation.
Oliver: Ha ha. So I do all the work?
Emily: Of course.

Unit 4

1   1 get up   2 choose   3 dishes   4 stand   5 skip
6 vegetarian

2   They are making a cake.

3   1 thing   2 first   3 Next   4 stir   5 Then   6 Finally

Audioscript

Cerys: So, are you going to help me or not?
Sarah: Yes, of course. What do we need?
Cerys: OK, the first thing to do is get the ingredients. We'll need eggs, flour and sugar …
Sarah: … and butter and yoghurt from the fridge. Right. What's next?
Cerys: So, first of all, put the sugar and butter into a bowl and mix them together.
Sarah: OK, that's done. What now?
Cerys: Now break the eggs and mix those in.
Sarah: Yuk, it looks a bit slimy now.
Cerys: Well, you haven't finished yet. Next, you add the yoghurt. You need to stir it a lot.
Sarah: If I had a machine, this would be easier.
Cerys: Then all you do now is start mixing in the flour.
Sarah: Mmm … that's delicious.
Cerys: Finally, when you've finished mixing it, put it in here and spread it out.
Sarah: Mmm … OK, hold on, just a little bit more.
Cerys: Come on. If you don't put it in the oven to bake now, you'll have nothing left!!

4   The voice goes up in 1–3 and then down in 4 as this is the final instruction.

5   They are making burgers.

6   1 first thing to do   2 Then all I have to do   3 first of all I mix
4 mix it well   5 Next, I put in   6 Finally

Audioscript

Jamie: So, do you remember how we made them the last time?
Paolo: Yes, of course I remember. It was really easy.
Jamie: Good, because you're going to make them this time. So what's first?
Paolo: Erm … the first thing to do is to chop some onions and to fry them a little bit.
Jamie: Yes, that's right. Then what?
Paolo: Then all I have to do is to mix the other ingredients together.
Jamie: OK, so what are the other ingredients?
Paolo: Erm … minced meat, of course. And …
Jamie: … bread. Well, breadcrumbs. And one other thing.
Paolo: Eggs. So, first of all I mix the minced meat, the bread and the eggs together.
Jamie: That's right. You need to mix it well. Use your hands.
Paolo: Next, I put in the fried onions.
Jamie: Yes. Don't forget to add salt and pepper.
Paolo: Finally, when the mix is ready, I make some balls of meat and hit them with my hand to make them flat.

Unit 5

1   1 e   2 c   3 a   4 d   5 b

2   The shop assistant doesn't know how to use the tablet.

3   1 tell   2 much   3 Has   4 long   5 like   6 show   7 use

Audioscript

Susie: Excuse me, can you tell me about this tablet?
Shop assistant: Yes, of course.
Susie: How much memory has it got?
Shop assistant: This one is just 16 gigabytes … no 8, sorry … but you can add extra memory because it has a USB port just here… no here on the other side … I think.
Susie: Has it got a good camera?
Shop assistant: Yes, it has actually. This one has a 10-megapixel camera. Or is it 8?
Susie: And how long does the battery last?
Shop assistant: About 10 hours of constant use.
Susie: What's the sound like?
Shop assistant: Well, the good thing about this tablet is that the speakers are at the front. … just here … err, somewhere …

Speaking extra key

Susie: OK. Could you show me how it works?
Shop assistant: Yes, of course. Just a moment …
Susie: Is it easy to use?
Shop assistant: Oh yes, just press this button to start. Oh, no, sorry. It's this button here. … No that's the volume. … Err, James, can you help us … sorry about this

4 1 up 2 down 3 down 4 up 5 up 6 up

5 Because it's too expensive.

6 1 can you tell me about 2 How much memory 3 how long does the battery 4 what's (the operating system) like 5 Has it got 6 is it expensive 7 show me another one

Audioscript

Isabelle: Excuse me, do you work here?
Shop assistant: Yes, I do. How can I help you?
Isabelle: Well, I'm looking for a good laptop.
Shop assistant: OK, well, we have lots. What kind were you looking for?
Isabelle: Well, I don't really know … I don't know much about computers. What about this one here, can you tell me about this one?
Shop assistant: Yes, this is the new XG 950, it's very fast.
Isabelle: How much memory has it got? I'm only really going to use it for work and to connect to the Internet.
Shop assistant: It's got 1 terabyte. That should be more than enough, I expect.
Isabelle: I'll need to use it when I'm travelling, so how long does the battery last?
Shop assistant: It depends on exactly what you're doing, but about ten hours.
Isabelle: And what's the operating system like? Is it easy to use?
Shop assistant: Yes, it's very easy to use, don't worry.
Isabelle: Has it got USB ports? I'll need to connect my camera and MP3 player.
Shop assistant: Yes, there are two here and one here on the other side.
Isabelle: And … is it expensive?
Shop assistant: Well, this one is $899.
Isabelle: Oh, could you show me another one? Maybe a bit cheaper?
Shop assistant: Yes, of course. Now, how much were you thinking of spending?

Unit 6

1 1 showed 2 broke 3 went 4 funny 5 outfit 6 parents

2 They are going to buy the present at the shopping centre.

3 1 help 2 borrow 3 Would 4 shall 5 ask 6 'll

Audioscript

Josh: Oh, I almost forgot, it's my dad's birthday tomorrow. I haven't got him a present.
Leo: Don't worry, you've got lots of time. What are you going to give him?
Josh: I've no idea. I was going to buy him a shirt.
Leo: Can I help you to choose one? I love shopping for clothes!
Josh: Great. Let's look on the Internet first. Could I borrow your tablet?
Leo: Here you are.
Josh: Would you come to the shopping centre with me later?
Leo: OK, shall I ask my mum to drive us there?
Josh: That would be brilliant. Could you ask her to pick us up later as well?
Leo: Sure. Come on, I'll help you find a nice shirt online first if you like.
Josh: OK. Do you know any good websites?

4 1 I'll help you if you like.
2 Shall I lend you my bike?
3 Could I borrow your laptop?
4 Could you ask your sister to come?
5 Can I help you with the decorations?
6 Would you come to the shopping centre with me?

5 They are going to study history together.

6 1 Could I borrow 2 if you like 3 can I help you 4 Shall I ask 5 Would you come 6 Could you ask

Audioscript

Ana: Hi Milly. Could I borrow your Portuguese dictionary?
Milly: Yeah, sure. What are you doing?
Ana: I'm writing to my pen pal, but I don't know what to say.
Milly: I'll help you if you like.
Ana: No, it's OK. I think I'll leave it until tomorrow. I have to study history for a test.
Milly: Well, can I help you to study for the test?
Ana: Great. You're really good at history.
Milly: Well, I like it. Shall I ask you some questions about the chapter?
Ana: That's a good idea. But let me study it first. Would you come to my house later?
Milly: Sure. Could you ask your mum to make some of her delicious pancakes?
Ana: I'm afraid not. She's away on a business trip.
Milly: Oh no … well, if your mum's not around, I'm not going to your house.
Ana: What? So you're not going to help me with my history?
Milly: Of course I am, I'm only joking!

Unit 7

1 1 e 2 c 3 b 4 f 5 a 6 d

2 It was down the side of the sofa.

3 1 that 2 know 3 anything 4 then 5 lucky

Audioscript

Ellen: Oh, what's this … Is this a new phone?
Omar: You've found it! I've been looking for that all afternoon. If I'd lost it, I'd have been in big trouble. My dad's lent it to me.
Ellen: Really – why is that?
Omar: Well, he's let me borrow it so that I can call him after the concert tonight. But, you'll never guess what I did earlier …
Ellen: What?
Omar: I dropped it down the stairs!
Ellen: No! Does your dad know?
Omar: Yes, he does. He was there! In fact, it hit him on the head.
Ellen: Did he say anything?
Omar: Of course. He was really angry.
Ellen: Oh no! So then what happened?
Omar: Well … I switched it on and it still worked.
Ellen: That was lucky!
Omar: So, Dad told me to put it in a safe place, and I did, but I forgot where I'd put it! It must have slipped down the side of the sofa.
Ellen: Why didn't you just call it?
Omar: Oh, yeah. That's a good idea! Why didn't I think of that?

4 1 really, why, that 2 that, lucky 3 mum, know 4 no, then, happened 5 say

5 They got a big black mark on them.

6 1 why was that 2 then what happened 3 she say anything 4 did your mum 5 That was lucky

Speaking extra key

Audioscript

Lucy:	Wow! I love those trainers.
Ruby:	Oh, thanks. I only bought them last week. But they almost got me into a lot of trouble.
Lucy:	Really – why was that?
Ruby:	Well, the first day I put them on, right, I was running and I fell and there was a big black mark across the left shoe! The first day … !
Lucy:	Oh no! So then what happened?
Ruby:	Well, when I got home, I went into the kitchen and started to clean them. And then my mum walked in.
Lucy:	Did she say anything?
Ruby:	Yes, she said 'I'm glad to see you're looking after those new trainers'!!
Lucy:	So did your mum not know?
Ruby:	No, she didn't!! She thought I was just cleaning them.
Lucy:	And where's the big black mark?
Ruby:	Oh, I cleaned it off … it was actually very easy.
Lucy:	Wow! That was lucky!

Unit 8

1 1 d 2 f 3 b 4 c 5 a 6 e

2 Because he is in a famous band and was a student at her school.

3 1 right 2 false 3 comment 4 totally 5 true
6 joking 7 absolutely

Audioscript

Stella:	So, thanks for the interview for your old school magazine, Jeff.
Jeff:	It's my pleasure.
Stella:	So we've heard that you're going to leave the band. Is that right?
Jeff:	Look, these rumours are completely false. I love being with the band. We've been on tour for the last year, travelling all around the world, and we're all really tired, so we're on a break.
Stella:	Yes, but people are saying that you don't get on well with Andy, the singer. Would you like to comment on that?
Jeff:	Sure. Look all these stories about us not getting on … they're totally untrue. I've known Andy since we were at the primary school just down the road from this school.
Stella:	And is it true that you don't want Andy to come to your wedding?
Jeff:	You must be joking! Andy is coming to my wedding – of course he is. He's my best friend!
Stella:	OK, last question … are you really going to marry a girl you met at this school?
Jeff:	Yes, absolutely. Daisy and I were at this school together for six years!

4 1 completely 2 totally 3 absolutely 4 really

5 He would introduce a school uniform.

6 1 You must be joking 2 Is it true that 3 is completely false
4 Is that right 5 it's totally untrue
6 would you like to comment 7 Yes, absolutely

Audioscript

Student:	So, Mr Jackman. Thank you for letting us interview you for the student website.
Head teacher:	You're welcome.
Student:	Now, we've heard that you sometimes sleep at the school in your office.
Head teacher:	You must be joking! No, I go home every night, believe me.
Student:	OK. There are some other rumours going around, too. Is it true that a TV station is coming to the school?
Head teacher:	What? A TV station? Here? I'm afraid that rumour is completely false.
Student:	Well, we heard that they're going to make a reality TV programme about life in the school. Is that right?
Head teacher:	Well, I think it would be a great idea. But no, it's totally untrue, sorry.
Student:	And would you like to comment on the rumour that you want to introduce a school uniform next year?
Head teacher:	Yes, absolutely! That is true. It would make everyone's life so much easier if they wore the same clothes.

Language focus extra key

Starter Unit

1 1 was playing; found 2 didn't hear; was chatting
3 were fishing; caught 4 didn't see; was talking
5 didn't go; was raining

2 2 went 3 cycled 4 ate 5 began 6 started
7 haven't been 8 have made 9 have joined
10 haven't had

3 2 just 3 still 4 yet 5 yet 6 already

4 2 is he 3 Were they 4 did you 5 Are you

5 2 sings the best 3 did they watch 4 watched them play
5 makes you happy

6 2 since 3 for 4 ever 5 since 6 never

7 2 How long has he lived in London? 3 Have they taken their
test yet? 4 Have you ever been to Hawaii?
5 Where has she been for her holiday?

Unit 1

1 2 Did you use to have 3 X 4 did you use to live
5 didn't use to have 6 would sit 7 wouldn't eat 8 X

2 2 would 3 used to 4 Did (you) use to 5 would
6 wouldn't 7 did (you) use to 8 didn't use to
9 would 10 would

3 2 Had (you) heard; saw 3 were, had missed
4 was; hadn't invited 5 passed; had taken
6 had played; became 7 had (you) written; published
8 went; hadn't tried 9 Had (they) climbed; went
10 had (she) lived; met

4 2 had never been 3 had always wanted 4 had had
5 got 6 was 7 had never seen 8 hadn't brought
9 had arrived 10 had set 11 stayed 12 danced

Unit 2

1 2 myself 3 ourselves 4 yourself/yourselves 5 himself
6 each other 7 itself 8 themselves 9 each other
10 herself

2 2 ourselves 3 us 4 myself 5 it 6 myself
7 themselves 8 them 9 you 10 each other

3 2 haven't had 3 Have (you) heard 4 've seen
5 've played 6 have (you) won 7 haven't seen
8 has been 9 Has (Jason) finished 10 has (only) read

4 2 Has (Suzanna) been studying 3 have been playing
4 have (they) been going 5 have (you) been walking
6 have been calling 7 Have (you) been reading
8 have been taking 9 has been visiting
10 has been collecting

Unit 3

1 A 1, 3, 8, 10 B 4, 6, 9 C 2, 5, 7

2 2 're visiting 3 're staying 4 're taking 5 leaves
6 arrives 7 'm going to learn 8 'm going to apply
9 starts 10 takes

3 2 might need 3 will pass 4 might break
5 are going to miss 6 might give 7 may lend
8 will become

4 2 How will we be spending our free time?
3 Where will people be going on holiday?
4 What fashions will we be wearing?
5 Will children be going to school?
6 What type of food will people be eating?

5 2 People won't be reading books anymore.
3 Spaceships will be taking people to Mars for their holidays.
4 We'll be designing our own clothes on computers.
5 No, they won't. Children will be doing all their classes online.
6 Restaurants will be serving seaweed instead of vegetables.

Unit 4

1 2 make; 'll cook 3 when; add 4 unless; eat
5 'll make; arrive 6 eat; won't 7 might make; if
8 hurry; might get

2 A 2 b, 3 a, 4 a B 1 a, 2 b, 3 a, 4 c C 1 a, 2 c, 3 c, 4 c

3 2 Martin could go cycling in the park if he didn't have so much
homework.
3 If we weren't so busy, we might go to the beach this
weekend.
4 Sam and Christy wouldn't ask for help unless they really
needed it.
5 If someone gave me a free ticket to any country, I'd go to
Australia.
6 I wouldn't eat raw fish unless it was in a Japanese restaurant.

4 2 How often would you argue if you shared a bedroom?
3 How would you feel if he didn't talk to you?
4 What would you like to (be able to) do if you could have any
superpower?
5 Where would you go if you could fly?
6 Who would you choose if you could meet any film star?

Unit 5

1 2 developed 3 are sent 4 were transmitted
5 Will (radio waves) be used 6 took 7 isn't used
8 was discovered 9 are prevented 10 will be treated

2 2 Certificates were signed by merchants promising to pay a
certain amount of money.
3 The paper money was called 'flying money' because it flew
away so easily.
4 Paper money wasn't introduced by European countries until
more than 500 years later.
5 The first bank note was printed by a Swedish bank in 1661.
6 Today, bank notes are used all over the world.
7 Many payments are also made using digital systems.
8 In the future, physical money will be replaced by digital
money.
9 Coins and notes won't be used anymore.
10 They'll only be found in museums and in history books.

3 2 that 3 whose 4 which 5 where 6 which
7 where 8 whose

4 2 f 3 d 4 e 5 g 6 b 7 h 8 c

Language focus extra key

Unit 6

1 2 dressing 3 dancing 4 chatting 5 Making 6 trying
7 helping 8 standing 9 looking 10 Worrying
11 going 12 buying 13 Walking 14 saying

2 2 Simon invited me to dance with him.
3 We were amazed to get free concert tickets.
4 We agreed to watch the fireworks tonight.
5 My friend asked us to go to a party.
6 It was difficult to talk because of the noise.
7 We were ready to leave ten minutes ago.
8 Which dress did you decide to wear?

3 a 5 b 2 c 4 d 7 e 1 f 3 g 6

4 2 dressing 3 designing 4 planning 5 organising
6 Finding 7 to lend 8 to get 9 to do 10 to invite
11 asking 12 having

Unit 7

1 2 He wouldn't have fallen into the lake if he hadn't stepped off the path.
3 If she hadn't left her phone in the car, she would have called the police.
4 We would have bought some food if we had brought some money.
5 If you hadn't made so much noise, you wouldn't have woken the neighbours.
6 He wouldn't have broken the window if he had been more careful.

2 2 would have believed; hadn't taken
3 hadn't woken; wouldn't have seen
4 wouldn't have lost; had been
5 wouldn't have found; hadn't had
6 would you have done; had seen
7 Would you have gone; had heard
8 would he have escaped; hadn't followed

3 2 He can't have studied much.
3 They might/may/could have missed the bus.
4 It must have been his birthday.
5 You can't have seen it yet.
6 They must have had a party.

4 2 might/may/could have gone 3 might/may/could have put
4 must have left 5 can't have gone
6 might/could (they) have taken
7 might/may/could have decided 8 must have felt

Unit 8

1 2 lives/lived 3 had seen 4 had looked 5 hadn't seen
6 didn't want 7 thought 8 couldn't remember
9 would call 10 saw

2 2 (that) he had seen the film a week before
3 (that) she wasn't sure what time she would finish work that evening
4 hadn't seen the film yet but (that) the reviews had been very good
5 would call me the next day
6 couldn't come to the concert

3 2 where I had been that morning at 10 am
3 if I had heard any unusual noises
4 what had happened
5 if there had been a crime
6 where the robbery / it had taken place
7 if I had spoken to any neighbours that day
8 if I would get in touch if I heard any information

4 2 what your address is?
3 what you saw?
4 who called the police?
5 if you saw the car number plate.
6 if you noticed their appearance?
7 where you work?
8 if you could come with us to the police station.

Workbook audioscript

Track 1 Unit 1 page 9

Tonight's discussion topic isn't new, but a lot of young people have strong feelings about it: school uniforms. Nowadays many countries in the world have uniforms but just as many countries don't! In Germany, where pupils don't wear uniforms, a government minister recently suggested that they should be introduced, and this started a national debate. So what are the arguments?

People in favour of uniforms say that they make pupils feel proud of their school, and create a feeling of everyone working together as a team. In a uniform, rich and poor look the same, and no one has to think about what clothes to wear every morning. Also, no one can wear the latest fashion or a particular cool style, so pupils can focus on studying, instead of worrying about how they look.

People who disagree say that uniforms are often expensive and uncomfortable. And because teenagers grow so fast, they may need new clothes every few months. One ex-secondary school headmaster told me that he's against uniforms because when pupils break the rules, teachers have to spend time monitoring and punishing them, when they should be concentrating on teaching. He also thinks fitted blazers, white shirts and ties are not practical for many school activities like science and art: anything not done at a desk. He also says that no one has shown that wearing a school uniform improves learning or behaviour anywhere in the world.

But does it depend on what uniform? I remember at my school we used to wear a stripy jacket, blouse and tie, a long skirt and flat shoes. I hated it! At least now girls can wear trousers, and many schools have introduced polo shirts and jumpers for boys and girls instead of shirts and ties. That kind of uniform is definitely better.

Personally, I'm against uniforms. Do you agree? Are you happy with your school policy? What is your uniform if you have one? Ring us with your opinion, or if you prefer, send us an email. Our number is …

Track 2 Unit 2 page 19

Presenter: Our guest today is sprinter Errol Dixon. Errol, you're an unusual athlete. Can you explain what you do?

Errol: Yes, I'm a guide runner. I've run with several different athletes since I started, and at the moment I run with Liz Stevens. She went blind when she was a teenager, so I'm her 'eyes' in a race. She's a 100m and 200m sprinter, but there are guide runners for longer races too.

Presenter: How does it work, then?

Errol: Well, we need to practise together a lot. We had to train ourselves to run the same distance with every step, at the same time. We hold a guide rope in our hands to stay together, so we have to move our arms at the same time too. Liz is talented, dedicated and really fast. It's hard work for me!

Presenter: I imagine! Do you have to run at exactly the same speed?

Errol: Yes, that's really important, we have to concentrate.

Presenter: Do you talk to each other during the race?

Errol: We talk at the start when I help her put her hands behind the line, but when you're sprinting it's difficult to talk. Luckily the 100m race is straight, so we just run for the finish line! In the 200m there's a bend in the track, so I tell her when to change direction.

Presenter: Why did you sign up to be a guide runner?

Errol: Well, everyone in my family is passionate about athletics. My uncle was a guide runner at the Paralympic Games in Beijing, and he passed on the techniques to me. Liz and I have run together for three years now, we're the same age and we get on well. We hope to run in the next Paralympic Games.

Presenter: Do the blind runner and the guide runner both get a gold medal?

Errol: If they win, yes, they do. The first time that happened was at London 2012, actually. I think if you're a team, you *should* both get a medal.

Presenter: Absolutely! Errol, thank you, and good luck to you and Liz in your next race!

Track 3 Unit 3 page 29

Journalist: Sarah, why haven't we seen you in films recently?
Sarah: Oh, I stopped making films when I was 13.
Journalist: Goodness! Why?
Sarah: Well, I started acting when I was five, and made my first film at six. I was lucky to be in some successful films with Hollywood stars, I even won awards! It was exciting at first and I had a great time, but it was like a game, really. After a while I got bored with it. I wanted to go to school and make friends with kids my own age, not hang around on film sets with adults and study with tutors. So I decided to give it up and go to high school in my home town.
Journalist: Did you plan to go back to acting?
Sarah: At first I wasn't sure. Film producers would still send me scripts to read, so it was a possibility. Then I realised I was actually much happier as a normal person doing normal things. I don't think being famous is for me, and I never wanted to make a fortune. So I always said no. I'm not going to go back to films, although I may try acting in the theatre.
Journalist: Now you've just published your first novel at 18. What is it about?
Sarah: It's about a group of teenagers who are a bit lost. They just don't know what they want to do in life, or how they feel about the world. I suppose it's about what it's like growing up in the twenty-first century.
Journalist: Is it autobiographical?
Sarah: No, not really. I think I've always known what I wanted to do and luckily I've always been able to do it.
Journalist: So what are your plans now?
Sarah: Well, in the fall I'm going to university in New York. I plan to continue writing novels, and I might act in student productions if I can. I haven't done much acting since Hollywood!
Journalist: Wow! You'll be busy. Well, I'm sorry I won't be seeing you in any more films, but I wish you great success.
Sarah: Thanks.

Track 4 Unit 4 page 39

Presenter: On the programme today is Matt Sanchez, a chef from Los Angeles. Matt you're famous for your spicy barbecue sauces. How did that start?
Matt: Ten years ago I visited the Fiery Foods Festival in Albuquerque, New Mexico. It's dedicated to hot, spicy food, especially the chilli pepper. You can find hundreds of chilli-flavoured products, like sweets, chocolate, nuts or cheese, and many different kinds of sauces and oils to go with a barbecue. It was fantastic! I've been going there ever since!
Presenter: Are all chillies hot?
Matt: Well, some are much hotter than others, but it depends how sensitive your tongue is. I was born in Mexico, where the chilli pepper comes from, so I've eaten hot food since I was a child. My mum even used to give us chilli sweets! Anyway, about a hundred years ago, a man called Wilbur Scoville created a system to tell how hot a chilli is, with a special heat unit. He called it the Scoville Heat Unit, after himself. The average chilli is about five thousand Scoville heat units, but if you chop a chilli into small pieces and throw away the seeds, it won't be so hot.
Presenter: And the hottest chillies?
Matt: Well, at the last Fiery Foods Festival, I discovered the Carolina Reaper, which is officially the hottest chilli in the world, at over two million units!!
Presenter: Wow, did you try it?
Matt: Yes! If you had the chance, wouldn't you? I wanted to see if I could eat something that hot, so I agreed to participate in a competition to eat three Carolina Reapers in the shortest time possible!
Presenter: Goodness! Can you prepare for that?

Workbook audioscript

Matt: People say that eating bananas or boiled potatoes, and drinking milk before you start is a good idea, but I didn't have time. I ate my peppers quite slowly, but I finished them all. The winner was amazing, though. He managed to eat all three in just nine seconds!

Presenter: That *is* fast! Did you drink a lot of water afterwards?

Matt: Oh no! Water doesn't help at all. The best thing to take away the burning sensation is ice cream. If it isn't chilli-flavoured, that is!

Track 5 Unit 5 page 49

Wayne: Hi Andy! When are you off to college? You start soon, don't you? Are you all ready?

Andy: Yeah, I'm off in a couple of weeks. I'm really excited, and an amazing thing has happened!

Wayne: Oh yeah? What's that?

Andy: Well, my mum wanted me to tidy away all the toys I've got in my bedroom before I go.

Wayne: Toys? What sort of toys?

Andy: Transformers, mostly. I started to collect Transformers when I was about seven. You know, the ones that can change from a robot into a car, or an insect into an action figure.

Wayne: Yeah, I remember them. I had a few too.

Andy: Well, for a few years I was totally obsessed with them and bought as many as I could with my pocket money. Every birthday I asked for money to buy more. I even had a book where I wrote down every one I had and what I needed to get next. Friends started giving me theirs when they got bored with them, and my uncle gave me a lot that *he* was given when he was little. In the end I had a big collection.

Wayne: How many have you got, then?

Andy: Over 500. Some of them are older than me, too! Anyway, Mum suggested I put them all away before I go to college. If I leave them out, they'll need to be cleaned and she says she's not going to do it. Anyway, I thought about it, and I decided that I'm a bit old for all those toys now. I was really into them once but not any more. And the collection's much too big. It takes up most of the space in my room. So I went on the Internet to see if I could sell them and guess what?

Wayne: What?

Andy: They're really popular and some of them are worth quite a bit of money. So I've advertised them on a specialist website, and someone who runs a collectors' shop is keen on buying them. I may be able to sell them for several thousand dollars!

Wayne: Wow! That's amazing.

Andy: I know! It's hard to believe people are that interested. Why don't you look for yours?

Wayne: Yes, I will!

Track 6 Unit 6 page 59

Presenter: Today I'm talking to Emma Roberts, who organises one of the biggest music festivals in Britain on a farm in England. Emma, how long have you been organising the festival?

Emma: Five years. I have a great time!

Presenter: This year's festival has just finished. How many people attended?

Emma: About 110,000.

Presenter: Wow! So when do you start preparing for next year's festival?

Emma: Well, first we have to clear up this year's! Most people camp, so it gets really messy. It takes weeks to get rid of the rubbish. We have some tents to hire, but most people bring their own tent. Then at the end of the festival they often just leave it, especially if it's wet. So volunteers take down all the tents, and the ones we don't want we give to charity. We also have to take down four stages, and all the facilities, like showers, toilets, backstage rooms for the bands, food tents, stalls and exhibitions. The festival is the size of a small town, so clearing it all up takes about six weeks.

Presenter: What else do you do?

Emma: The most important thing is booking the bands. The festival is over three days, so we need a big line-up, including several really popular acts, the headliners, to finish each night. Organising those bands often starts years before, because the really big groups organise their concert schedules a year or more in advance.

Presenter: I'd no idea it was like that! So you know some of next year's names now?

Emma: Er, yes. We've already booked three headliners for next year, and quite a few other bands and musicians too, but I can't announce the names yet.

Presenter: Oh, well, never mind! How do you decide which artists to get?

Emma: Well, we include rock, pop, indie, dance and folk, so I ask music journalists and DJs for suggestions, and I go to concerts. Many fans send me emails, too. And often artists themselves ask to play! New and old bands all want to be seen here. The only problem is when bands split up before the festival. That happens every year!

Presenter: Well … Emma, thanks for chatting, and good luck with next year's festival!

Track 7 Unit 7 page 69

Today our unexplained mystery comes from Peru, in South America. High up in the Peruvian desert, 400 kilometres south of Lima, is a strange sight. It's called the Nazca lines, hundreds of strange symbols made with long white lines.

The most mysterious thing about the Nazca lines is that on the ground it's impossible to see the shapes they make. In order to see what they represent, you have to look at them from above. So, although a Peruvian archaeologist discovered them in 1927, it wasn't until planes flew over the desert for the first time, in the 1930s, that all the weird and wonderful shapes became visible. The lines are an incredible collection of gigantic animals, birds, fish, insects, geometric shapes and strange symbols. Among approximately 900 figures there's a spider, a monkey, a pelican, a killer whale, and a shark, as well as humans, trees and plants, all in an area 80 kilometres long. The largest figures are over 200 metres wide.

Of course, once people realised what the lines were, they started to investigate their origins. According to experts, they were created by the local Nazca culture between 400 and 650 AD. The lines were made by removing the small reddish stones on the surface of the desert to uncover the white sand beneath. They've existed unchanged for at least 1,500 years as a result of the dry, windless desert climate and because few people ever go there. The Nazca probably made some of the shapes by using wooden poles to keep the long lines so straight.

But what they were for is still a mystery. One theory suggested the lines were designed so that aliens could land. However, the surface of the desert is too soft for spaceships to land on, and this theory doesn't explain all the different shapes. Another suggestion was that the lines were connected to studying the planets, the stars and the night sky, but there is no real evidence for that. Other theories are that the lines show underground canals, or have some other religious significance like asking their gods to bring water. We'll probably never know, but the Nazca lines became a UNESCO World Heritage Site in 1994, and so will continue to amaze us all for hundreds of years.

Track 8 Unit 8 page 79

Olga: This is an interesting article. There's a new scheme starting here next year called restorative justice.

Justin: Restorative justice? What's that?

Olga: Well, it says here it's when the victim of a crime and the offender, the person who committed it, have an official meeting to talk about it called a conference. It's all organised carefully.

Justin: And what happens at the conference?

Olga: Well, apparently, victims and offenders can tell their stories. The idea is that the victim explains to the criminal how the crime made him or her feel, and the harmful effect it has had on their life. And the offender explains why they did it, and has a chance to say they're sorry for what they did.

Justin: It sounds a bit weird to me. If I'd been the victim of a mugging, for example, I wouldn't want to see the mugger again, would you? It would be quite scary!

Workbook audioscript

Olga: Maybe at first, yes, but actually, wouldn't you like to tell them exactly what you thought of them? And try to make them feel guilty about what they did to you? I think I would!

Justin: Maybe, I suppose.

Olga: Right! It must be a good thing for the offender to realise the harm they caused. And also, at the conference they can agree on something the offender could do to repair the damage, like giving back money they stole or doing voluntary work in the community – painting or cleaning and stuff like that. In the article it says that in New Zealand they did a survey of people who'd gone through the process, and 77% of the victims said it made them feel better.

Justin: Mmm. I'm still not sure, though. What if I didn't want to meet them?

Olga: You wouldn't have to. Restorative justice is a voluntary process. A meeting only happens if the victim and the offender both agree to it. And, before they can take part, offenders must admit responsibility for the offence, and that it was wrong. The other thing it says here is that in New Zealand, where they've been doing this for a long time, offenders who've met the victim like this are 25% less likely to commit another crime. So that's positive, isn't it?

Justin: Definitely!

Track 9 Speaking extra page 87 Exercise 2

Girl: So, you've got a pair of jeans. Let's find a cool T-shirt for you.

Boy: How about this one? It's got a bit green L on the front!

Girl: Yeah, L for 'loser'.

Boy: Hey! Come on, you're supposed to be helping me!

Girl: Here, try this one.

Boy: OK, where are the changing rooms?

Girl: Over there. And try this one as well.

Boy: So what do you think?

Girl: Well, it doesn't fit very well. It's too small for you.

Boy: But it's M – medium. It's my size.

Girl: Have you put on weight?

Boy: Very funny.

Girl: Sorry, but it looks a bit tight.

Boy: I'll try the other one on.

Girl: OK, that's better. You look great in that one.

Boy: Do you think so? Do you think this colour suits me?

Girl: Red? Of course … it goes with your red hair!

Boy: This is the last time I go shopping with my sister!

Track 10 Speaking extra page 87 Exercise 4

1 These shoes don't fit me.
2 I don't think it suits you.
3 You don't look good in that dress.
4 This coat is not my size.
5 I'm not so sure.

Track 11 Speaking extra page 87 Exercise 5

Amy: Right, Sue, how about this dress for Sophie's party? I like the stripes.

Sue: Yeah, it's a nice dress. But stripy clothes don't suit you.

Amy: Yeah, you're right and it's a bit short, isn't it?

Sue: Hey, look at this one. It's denim but it's a lovely colour.

Amy: OK, I think I'll try it on. Where are the changing rooms?

Sue: They're over there. I'll be there in a minute. … So, let's see you.

Amy: OK, here's the denim dress. What do you think?

Sue: Wow! You look great!

Amy: Do you think? I think it's too small.

Sue: No, it's definitely your size. Not too big here not too small there!

Amy: Hold on, I've got another one.

Sue: Err … no, that doesn't fit very well. It's really baggy.

Amy: What do you mean? It's perfect!

Sue: Yes, you're right. It's perfect. But Amy … it's the same dress I'm going to wear to Sophie's party. Sorry.

Track 12 Speaking extra page 88 Exercise 2

Tim: What's up, Jo?

Jo: I told my dad I wanted to give up piano lessons and now he's angry with me.

Tim: Oh, you poor thing! Why is he angry?

Jo: Well, you know my dad … he's so passionate about music.

Tim: Well, I'm sure he'll calm down soon. Why do you want to give up?

Jo: I don't know … it's just that we've got all these exams and I'm trying to study every day and I have piano lessons twice a week. And Chinese classes and hockey at the weekend.

Tim: I know what you mean. It's really hard to do everything!

Jo: And I have to practise this really difficult piece on the piano. I just don't think I'm very talented when it comes to music.

Tim: Of course you are. You don't need to worry. You're so hard-working. I'm sure you'll learn it.

Jo: But I have to play the whole thing tomorrow.

Tim: I'm sure it'll be fine. Just keep practising. So, how can I make you feel better?

Jo: Can you listen to me play it and tell me … honestly … what you think?

Tim: Of course, go on then.

Track 13 Speaking extra page 88 Exercise 4

1 I'm sure it'll be fine.
2 You don't need to worry.
3 I know what you mean.
4 I'm sure she'll calm down soon.
5 Oh! You poor thing.

Track 14 Speaking extra page 88 Exercise 5

Dylan: Lewis, you *have* to help me!

Lewis: OK, Dylan, what's up?

Dylan: Remember the other night at my house when I borrowed my brother's guitar?

Lewis: Yes, isn't it funny that I have the same guitar as your brother?

Dylan: Well, now there's a hole in the back of the guitar. He's really angry!

Lewis: Well, I'm sure it'll be fine. I've got a hole in my guitar but it doesn't matter really. … That's funny, I can't find it now.

Dylan: But now he won't lend me his guitar.

Lewis: You poor thing. Do you want to borrow mine?

Dylan: Great thanks. But what about my brother?

Lewis: Oh, I'm sure he'll calm down soon.

Dylan: Yes, but he really loves that guitar.

Lewis: How can I make you feel better?

Dylan: I don't know … I hate it when I can't talk to my brother.

Lewis: I know what you mean. It's awful.

Dylan: But how did I make a hole in the guitar?

Lewis: You don't need to worry. He'll soon realise that … Hold on. This isn't my guitar. Look, the strings are different!

Dylan: That's my brother's guitar!

Lewis: And he has my guitar … the one with the hole!

Track 15 Speaking extra page 89 Exercise 2

Girl: So what are we going to buy Mum for her birthday?

Boy: Do we have to decide now? I'm in the middle of level 37 of this game!

Girl: Level 37? Wow! Anyway, yes, we need to decide quickly because her birthday is next Saturday.

Boy: OK, well, I was thinking of a nice silk scarf or a bag, something like that.

Girl: But she's got lots of bags and I think Dad was going to buy her a really expensive one. I think I'd rather buy her something really different – what about a ride in a fast car, like a Ferrari or a Lamborghini? You know she loves cars.

Boy: But isn't that really expensive?

Girl: It's not that expensive, and I think Gran and Granddad would help us.

Boy: Well, if they're going to help us, why don't we give her something really nice?

Girl: What kind of thing do you suggest?

Boy: What about a weekend away in a nice hotel?

Girl: Yes, that's a good idea, too.

Workbook audioscript

Boy: Sometimes I have good ideas, you know!
Girl: So how shall we decide?
Boy: Hmm … good question. Hold on, I think the best way is to ask Mum – she's always good at choosing presents for people.
Girl: Yeah, but the present is for her!!!
Boy: Oh, yeah!!

Track 16 Speaking extra page 89 Exercise 4

1 I was thinking of buying her a scarf.
2 That's a good idea.
3 Personally, I'd rather go on a holiday.
4 I think the best way is to ask someone.
5 What kind of thing do you suggest?

Track 17 Speaking extra page 89 Exercise 5

Oliver: So, we have to make a presentation to the class and we haven't even thought about what we're going to talk about.
Emily: I *have* thought about it. I was thinking of doing a presentation about interesting celebrations around the world.
Oliver: I think Conor and Natalie are going to do that. Personally, I'd rather talk about some different career possibilities in the future. We talked about it one day in social science class.
Emily: Oh yeah! That's a good idea, too. But do you think it'll be easy to find information?
Oliver: Yes, actually, I've already done a bit of research and there's loads of stuff on the Internet.
Emily: OK, great. So we need to decide who does what. Someone has to write the presentation.
Oliver: And we should probably include some pictures.
Emily: OK, what kind of pictures do you suggest?
Oliver: Hmm … I don't know. We can decide that when the time comes. How shall we decide who does what, then?
Emily: I think the best way is for me to let you start and when it's ready I'll make the presentation.
Oliver: Ha ha. So I do all the work?
Emily: Of course.

Track 18 Speaking extra page 90 Exercise 2

Cerys: So, are you going to help me or not?
Sarah: Yes, of course. What do we need?
Cerys: OK, the first thing to do is get the ingredients. We'll need eggs, flour and sugar …
Sarah: … and butter and yoghurt from the fridge. Right. What's next?
Cerys: So, first of all, put the sugar and butter into a bowl and mix them together.
Sarah: OK, that's done. What now?
Cerys: Now break the eggs and mix those in.
Sarah: Yuk, it looks a bit slimy now.
Cerys: Well, you haven't finished yet. Next, you add the yoghurt. You need to stir it a lot.
Sarah: If I had a machine, this would be easier.
Cerys: Then all you do now is start mixing in the flour.
Sarah: Mmm … that's delicious.
Cerys: Finally, when you've finished mixing it, put it in here and spread it out.
Sarah: Mmm … OK, hold on, just a little bit more.
Cerys: Come on. If you don't put it in the oven to bake now, you'll have nothing left!!

Track 19 Speaking extra page 90 Exercise 4

1 First of all, mix the ingredients together.
2 Then, put it in the fridge for about ten minutes.
3 Next, you spread the mix out in here.
4 Finally, put it in the oven for 20 minutes.

Track 20 Speaking extra page 90 Exercise 5

Jamie: So, do you remember how we made them the last time?
Paolo: Yes, of course I remember. It was really easy.
Jamie: Good, because you're going to make them this time. So what's first?
Paolo: Erm … the first thing to do is to chop some onions and to fry them a little bit.

Jamie: Yes, that's right. Then what?
Paolo: Then all I have to do is to mix the other ingredients together.
Jamie: OK, so what are the other ingredients?
Paolo: Erm … minced meat, of course. And …
Jamie: … bread. Well, breadcrumbs. And one other thing.
Paolo: Eggs. So, first of all I mix the minced meat, the bread and the eggs together.
Jamie: That's right. You need to mix it well. Use your hands.
Paolo: Next, I put in the fried onions.
Jamie: Yes. Don't forget to add salt and pepper.
Paolo: Finally, when the mix is ready, I make some balls of meat and hit them with my hand to make them flat.

Track 21 Speaking extra page 91 Exercise 2

Susie: Excuse me, can you tell me about this tablet?
Shop assistant: Yes, of course.
Susie: How much memory has it got?
Shop assistant: This one is just 16 gigabytes … no eight, sorry … but you can add extra memory because it has a USB port just here… no here on the other side … I think.
Susie: Has it got a good camera?
Shop assistant: Yes, it has actually. This one has a ten-megapixel camera. Or is it eight?
Susie: And how long does the battery last?
Shop assistant: About ten hours of constant use.
Susie: What's the sound like?
Shop assistant: Well, the good thing about this tablet is that the speakers are at the front. … just here … err, somewhere …
Susie: OK. Could you show me how it works?
Shop assistant: Yes, of course. Just a moment …
Susie: Is it easy to use?
Shop assistant: Oh yes, just press this button to start. Oh, no, sorry. It's this button here. … No that's the volume. … Err, James, can you help us … sorry about this

Track 22 Speaking extra page 91 Exercise 4

1 Could you show me this tablet?
2 How much memory has it got?
3 What's the camera like?
4 Can you tell me about this smartphone?
5 Is it difficult to use?
6 Has it got speakers?

Track 23 Speaking extra 5 page 91 Exercise 5

Isabelle: Excuse me, do you work here?
Shop assistant: Yes, I do. How can I help you?
Isabelle: Well, I'm looking for a good laptop.
Shop assistant: OK, well, we have lots. What kind were you looking for?
Isabelle: Well, I don't really know … I don't know much about computers. What about this one here, can you tell me about this one?
Shop assistant: Yes, this is the new XG 950, it's very fast.
Isabelle: How much memory has it got? I'm only really going to use it for work and to connect to the Internet.
Shop assistant: It's got one terabyte. That should be more than enough, I expect.
Isabelle: I'll need to use it when I'm travelling, so how long does the battery last?
Shop assistant: It depends on exactly what you're doing, but about ten hours.
Isabelle: And what's the operating system like? Is it easy to use?
Shop assistant: Yes, it's very easy to use, don't worry.
Isabelle: Has it got USB ports? I'll need to connect my camera and MP3 player.
Shop assistant: Yes, there are two here and one here on the other side.
Isabelle: And … is it expensive?
Shop assistant: Well, this one is $899.
Isabelle: Oh, could you show me another one? Maybe a bit cheaper?
Shop assistant: Yes, of course. Now, how much were you thinking of spending?

Workbook audioscript

Track 24 Speaking extra page 92 Exercise 2

Josh: Oh, I almost forgot, it's my dad's birthday tomorrow. I haven't got him a present.

Leo: Don't worry, you've got lots of time. What are you going to give him?

Josh: I've no idea. I was going to buy him a shirt.

Leo: Can I help you to choose one? I love shopping for clothes!

Josh: Great. Let's look on the Internet first. Could I borrow your tablet?

Leo: Here you are.

Josh: Would you come to the shopping centre with me later?

Leo: OK, shall I ask my mum to drive us there?

Josh: That would be brilliant. Could you ask her to pick us up later as well?

Leo: Sure. Come on, I'll help you find a nice shirt online first if you like.

Josh: OK. Do you know any good websites?

Track 25 Speaking extra page 92 Exercise 4

1 I'll help you if you like.
2 Shall I lend you my bike?
3 Could I borrow your laptop?
4 Could you ask your sister to come?
5 Can I help you with the decorations?
6 Would you come to the shopping centre with me?

Track 26 Speaking extra page 92 Exercise 5

Ana: Hi Milly. Could I borrow your Portuguese dictionary?

Milly: Yeah, sure. What are you doing?

Ana: I'm writing to my pen pal, but I don't know what to say.

Milly: I'll help you if you like.

Ana: No, it's OK. I think I'll leave it until tomorrow. I have to study history for a test.

Milly: Well, can I help you to study for the test?

Ana: Great. You're really good at history.

Milly: Well, I like it. Shall I ask you some questions about the chapter?

Ana: That's a good idea. But let me study it first. Would you come to my house later?

Milly: Sure. Could you ask your mum to make some of her delicious pancakes?

Ana: I'm afraid not. She's away on a business trip.

Milly: Oh no ... well, if your mum's not around, I'm not going to your house.

Ana: What? So you're not going to help me with my history?

Milly: Of course I am, I'm only joking!

Track 27 Speaking extra page 93 Exercise 2

Ellen: Oh, what's this ... ? Is this a new phone?

Omar: You've found it! I've been looking for that all afternoon. If I'd lost it, I'd have been in big trouble. My dad's lent it to me.

Ellen: Really – why is that?

Omar: Well, he's let me borrow it so that I can call him after the concert tonight. But, you'll never guess what I did earlier ...

Ellen: What?

Omar: I dropped it down the stairs!

Ellen: No! Does your dad know?

Omar: Yes, he does. He was there! In fact, it hit him on the head.

Ellen: Did he say anything?

Omar: Of course. He was really angry.

Ellen: Oh no! So then what happened?

Omar: Well ... I switched it on and it still worked.

Ellen: That was lucky!

Omar: So, Dad told me to put it in a safe place, and I did, but I forgot where I'd put it! It must have slipped down the side of the sofa.

Ellen: Why didn't you just call it?

Omar: Oh, yeah. That's a good idea! Why didn't I think of that?

Track 28 Speaking extra page 93 Exercise 4

1 Really – why was that?
2 That was lucky!
3 Did your mum know?
4 Oh no! So then what happened?
5 Did she say anything?

Track 29 Speaking extra page 93 Exercise 5

Lucy: Wow! I love those trainers.

Ruby: Oh, thanks. I only bought them last week. But they almost got me into a lot of trouble.

Lucy: Really – why was that?

Ruby: Well, the first day I put them on, right, I was running and I fell and there was a big black mark across the left shoe! The first day ... !

Lucy: Oh no! So then what happened?

Ruby: Well, when I got home, I went into the kitchen and started to clean them. And then my mum walked in.

Lucy: Did she say anything?

Ruby: Yes, she said 'I'm glad to see you're looking after those new trainers.'!!

Lucy: So did your mum not know?

Ruby: No, she didn't!! She thought I was just cleaning them.

Lucy: And where's the big black mark?

Ruby: Oh, I cleaned it off ... it was actually very easy.

Lucy: Wow! That was lucky!

Track 30 Speaking extra page 94 Exercise 2

Stella: So, thanks for the interview for your old school magazine, Jeff.

Jeff: It's my pleasure.

Stella: So we've heard that you're going to leave the band. Is that right?

Jeff: Look, these rumours are completely false. I love being with the band. We've been on tour for the last year, travelling all around the world, and we're all really tired, so we're on a break.

Stella: Yes, but people are saying that you don't get on well with Andy, the singer. Would you like to comment on that?

Jeff: Sure. Look all these stories about us not getting on ... they're totally untrue. I've known Andy since we were at the primary school just down the road from this school.

Stella: And is it true that you don't want Andy to come to your wedding?

Jeff: You must be joking! Andy is coming to my wedding – of course he is. He's my best friend!

Stella: OK, last question ... are you really going to marry a girl you met at this school?

Jeff: Yes, absolutely. Daisy and I were at this school together for six years!

Track 31 Speaking extra page 94 Exercise 4

1 These rumours are completely false.
2 They're totally untrue.
3 Yes, absolutely.
4 That is a really interesting story.

Track 32 Speaking extra page 94 Exercise 5

Student: So, Mr Jackman. Thank you for letting us interview you for the student website.

Head teacher: You're welcome.

Student: Now, we've heard that you sometimes sleep at the school in your office.

Head teacher: You must be joking! No, I go home every night, believe me.

Student: OK. There are some other rumours going around, too. Is it true that a TV station is coming to the school?

Head teacher: What? A TV station? Here? I'm afraid that rumour is completely false.

Student: Well, we heard that they're going to make a reality TV programme about life in the school. Is that right?

Head teacher: Well, I think it would be a great idea. But no, it's totally untrue, sorry.

Student: And would you like to comment on the rumour that you want to introduce a school uniform next year?

Head teacher: Yes, absolutely! That is true. It would make everyone's life so much easier if they wore the same clothes.

Student's Book audioscript

Track 1.05 Starter page 5 Exercise 3

Interviewer: We are here with All for One, the popular band that play *all* their own instruments. When are you playing tonight?

Tony: We go on stage at about eight o'clock, yes?

Simon: Yes, that's right.

Interviewer: How did you all meet?

John: We met at an arts festival – Simon and Tony were buskers … isn't that right, Simon?

Simon: … yes, I play the guitar and the piano and Tony plays the violin and the guitar. We were both playing guitars at the festival though.

John: … and I was doing an art class on graffiti! I saw Simon and Tony playing and asked if I could join them – I love singing.

Interviewer: Who writes all the songs you play?

Simon: We all put ideas together to write the songs.

Interviewer: When was your first concert?

John: Hmm. It was about two years ago, but we've never played in a concert hall like this one.

Interviewer: What other instruments can you play?

Tony: I'm learning to play the piano – Simon is teaching me!

Interviewer: What do you do in your free time?

Simon: We go to see other bands, play football … the usual things!

John: I do acting classes – I'd like to act on stage too.

Interviewer: What other music do you like?

Tony: We all like classical music as well as pop, rock …

Interviewer: Where are you going after you finish here?

Simon: We're going to get something to eat and meet our families.

Interviewer: Great! Well thanks for your time guys!

Track 1.11 Unit 1 page 12 Exercise 2

Interviewer: Today in the studio is 16-year-old David Richardson, the star of Haversham Drama school's new production, based on the famous 1980s movie, *Back to the Future*. The play opened at the New Theatre last week. So, David, what's it all about?

David: Well, the film first came out in 1985 and it was really famous at the time.

Interviewer: Had you seen it before you started on the production, David?

David: No, I hadn't seen it. But when I watched it, I loved it and I was really excited about working on the show.

Interviewer: What's the story?

David: In the film, a teenager, Marty McFly, travels back in time to the 1950s and meets his parents when they were teenagers. The film is thirty years old this year. Our show is a celebration of that anniversary.

Interviewer: Is the show different from the movie?

David: Well, yes, we've written a new script and made a few changes. In the movie, Marty travels back from 1985 to 1955. In our show, he travels from 2015 to 1985 …

Interviewer: I like that … thirty years after the film … very nice. And is the focus on life in the 1980s?

David: Yes. I'm fascinated by that side of the show – my parents were teenagers in the 1980s, they talk about how life was different, but I hadn't really thought about it before, what teenagers were interested in then, the clothes they used to wear, the technology they had in those days … the show really brings it to life.

Interviewer: And was life very different?

David: Lots of things were the same, teenagers were keen on the same things, like music, computer games, spending time with friends – but the technology was so different! No Internet, no text messages, no touchscreens. Marty's mum had never seen a mobile phone!

Interviewer: It sounds like fun, but some people have been a little disappointed by the show. They say it isn't as good as the movie …

David: You can't please everybody … we're really happy with it and proud of all our hard work. You should see it and tell us what you think. We aren't afraid of criticism you know!

Interviewer: I certainly will! And if anyone else is interested, the play is on at the …

Track 1.22 Unit 2 page 22 Exercise 3

Interviewer: Our report today comes from a secondary school in Nottingham, where a special project is bringing together students and older people. Jake, tell me about your project, how does it work?

Jake: Well, we've had five meetings since September and we've been meeting once a week here in the school. We help older people learn how to use computers and smartphones and things. It's been a great success so far. More and more people are signing up every week.

Interviewer: What do you do exactly?

Jake: Well, some people want to know about social networks. Others want to understand more about their mobile phones. We sit with them and help them.

Interviewer: Is it difficult?

Jake: It was at the beginning. I've learned a lot of things since we started. We need to be really patient. We don't want them to think it's too difficult and give up. We need to explain things really carefully. It feels good to help people and to know that they trust us and you know, look up to us in a way.

Interviewer: Mabel, you've been coming to classes for three weeks. What have you learned?

Mabel: Well, I've learned how to share photos on my phone. It's such a great way to stay in touch with my family. I've set up a Facebook page too. We haven't looked at online shopping yet, that's what we're doing today. I can buy food from the local supermarket on the Internet and then they bring it to my door! It's fantastic!

Interviewer: And do you get on with your teachers?

Mabel: These kids are great. From the very beginning they've been so kind. I know it can be difficult! We older people are a bit slow sometimes, but they're really good at passing on their knowledge to us a bit at a time and we can always count on them to explain things simply and patiently.

Interviewer: Thanks to both of you for showing us that you're never too old to learn … and never too young to teach!

Track 1.31 Unit 3 page 34 Exercise 2

Male: Welcome back, everybody. We're continuing our look at today's papers. Glenda, there's a report here in the Globe on the girl who's known as 'the flip-flop sensation', Madison Nicole Robinson, better known as Madison Nicole. Did you see that?

Female: Yes, it's on the front page of all the local papers, it's going to be today's top story.

Male: So, she's become a millionaire because she set up a flip-flop business…

Female: OK, but you're probably thinking what's so special about her flip-flops?

Male: Yeah … well, it's funny - it says here that she doesn't actually design flip-flops but FishFlops®…

Female: Exactly! Flip-flops with fish on them… the amazing thing is that she had the idea when she was only eight!

Male: But it says that she started the business when she was 13, right?

Female: That's right and she sold 60,000 pairs in her first year.

Male: She also learned how to do the business side too, she knows about shopping and pricing and everything. I mean, she's developed the project herself. All of it!

Student's Book audioscript

Female: She clearly has a real business mind, because she's made a fortune! 60,000 pairs ... at $25 a pair! She might become the richest teenager in the States, I don't know…

Male: That's true, but the good thing is that according to the article, she also helps charities. Did you see that? She gave away 10,000 pairs of FishFlops® to people in need, she gets celebrities to sign them and donates them as well ... and she does voluntary work in the community.

Female: Wow, now that's great to help other people in that way.

Male: Absolutely. I'm sure she'll be winning awards for her business idea soon.

Female: I think she should try for 'The Young Business Person of the Year', don't you?

Male: Yes, she should, I'm sure she'll win!

Female: Yes, I bet she's going to go on to great things, she'll be breaking business records in the future, I don't think this will be the last we hear of Madison Nicole!

Male: Yes, and meanwhile her FishFlops® will be the latest fashion. I bet you everybody will be wearing them on the beach this summer.

Track 1.43 Unit 4 page 44 Exercise 4

Presenter: So, here we are for today's blind taste test. Our contestants today are Dale, Josie and Kirstin. Are you ready?

Contestants: Yes!

Presenter: So, here's the first dish – ready, steady, taste! … Right, you can look now. So, Dale, what did you think?

Dale: Well it certainly tastes better than it looks! It's interesting – sweet … and a bit spicy.

Presenter: Would you eat it again if you had the chance?

Dale: Yes, if I saw it on a menu, I might eat it again.

Presenter: Great - Josie?

Josie: I'm sorry, I think it's totally disgusting! … the texture … It's really slimy. I wouldn't eat it again if you paid me!

Kirstin: I agree. I really don't like the texture.

Presenter: What do you think it is?

Kirstin: Some sort of fish?

Presenter: Yes, that's right! Jellyfish.

Contestants: Jellyfish!!

Presenter: Yes, jellyfish salad is common in a lot of Asian countries. This recipe is Vietnamese. OK contestants, ready for the second dish?

Contestants: Yes.

Presenter: Ready, steady, taste! … OK, forks down. Take a look. Kirstin, what did you think of that?

Kirstin: Much better, they're light and crunchy. I could eat that again if you offered it to me.

Josie: I'm not so sure. It was a bit bland.

Presenter: Dale?

Dale: Sorry, not really a big fan, they're crunchy on the outside but a bit soft on the inside …

Presenter: Any ideas what it might be?

Dale: Ears maybe?

Presenter: Not far off! They're cockscombs, fried cockscombs, you know the little red things on the top of a male chicken's head – an Italian dish.

Kirstin: Really?? Ugh … I don't like them anymore!

Presenter: So, the last dish. Ready, steady, taste! … OK, you can look now …

Josie: Oh wow, are they what I think they are?

Kirstin: Grasshoppers?

Presenter: Yes.

Dale: Wow! They're really nice! Salty, spicy, crunchy. Perfect!

Josie: Definitely my favourite.

Kirstin: It's amazing. They're delicious! Where can you get them?

Presenter: Well, they're called chapulines and they're a Mexican dish. You can eat them in a taco, on toast, or just on their own like chips! So, thank you Dale, Josie and Kirstin. Chapulines are definitely the winner of our taste test today!

Track 2.05 Unit 5 page 56 Exercise 2

Reporter: Hello, today I'm in Brixton market in south London. It's a great market where you can find all kinds of unusual things. What a wonderful stall! What's this? … A light?

Stallholder 1: Yes, a reading light and heater at the same time.

Reporter: Really? That's quite unusual.

Stallholder 1: Well, it's quite old – a lot of early electric heaters were used as lights. The heat comes from the light bulb in the middle and it's reflected by this part which you can see here.

Reporter: That's really hot! I need something that I can put on my desk to keep me warm in winter! How much is it?

Stallholder 1: £250.

Reporter: £250? … Err … not today … thank you …. Wow, that was ridiculously expensive! Ah, what's this? I wonder where the person whose stall it is can be? Ah – hello.

Stallholder 2: Hello!

Reporter: So, what are you selling? They're very beautiful, but what are they?

Stallholder 2: They're designed to help save energy at home, but they look extremely stylish, too.

Reporter: What's that? The one that I can see on the shelf behind you. It looks like a tree …

Stallholder 2: It's a battery charger - the leaves are tiny solar panels which take energy from the sunlight and then you plug in your phone here, in the base.

Reporter: Wow, that's really useful… How much is it?

Stallholder 2: Well … the guy who you can see in the photo, he's the guy who makes them and he's a friend of mine, he gave it to me for just £100 …

Reporter: Hmm … OK … thank you … Goodbye! They *are* kind of pretty, but they're much too expensive! I can get a solar-charger that costs a lot less money than that! I don't think the woman that I was just talking to is going to sell a lot of battery chargers! Ah this stall looks a bit better – everything for £5! Hi!

Stallholder 3: Hi.

Reporter: What's this?

Stallholder 3: A fan! The blades, the parts that turn, are inside, so it's totally safe to use. The air comes out here. Try it!

Reporter: Wow! Amazing! And I love the colours too! Are they really only £5?

Stallholder 3: Yes, the woman that I got them from gave them to me for a great price!

Reporter: Can I have two, please? One pink and one blue.

Stallholder 3: Here you are miss … have a good day!

Reporter: You too! My niece and nephew will love these!

Track 2.14 Unit 6 page 66 Exercise 2

Presenter: Hi, welcome to *Round The World*. Today we're going back to our archive of the weird and wonderful. Back in January, Carolyn was in northern China …

Carolyn: Hi - today is the fifth of January and Harbin is filled with hundreds of ice statues. They're really stunning. Some people make buildings too – huge cities of ice. Hundreds of thousands of people are here to enjoy the impressive artwork. Personally, I think it's best to see it in the dark, when the statues are lit up with colourful lights. It's really atmospheric! You can even go ice-swimming if you really want to feel the cold! If you decide to come and see the festival for yourself, remember to bring warm clothes, it's just too cold otherwise!

Presenter: A month later, we heard from Parisa in Italy.

Parisa: Greetings from Ivrea! This peaceful Italian town looks totally different at the moment. It's for the famous Battle of the Oranges. The people of the town dress up in traditional costumes and throw more than a million oranges during a crazy battle! You wouldn't normally expect to see so many people in a small town like this, but there are more than a hundred thousand people here right now! The streets are really crowded and the fighting can get quite scary at times … still at least oranges smell nice!

Student's Book audioscript

Presenter: Finally, you remember a month ago we heard from Charlene in Thailand … She told us about another food festival…

Charlene: Today is a special day in Lopburi. In November every year, people hold a special food festival for the three thousand monkeys who live near here. It all starts at ten in the morning with singing and dancing. Then the monkeys are invited to come down out of the trees and the fun begins. It doesn't take them very long to eat the mountain of sticky rice, fruit salad and egg dessert. You really have to see this if you get the chance. It's very noisy and it's very messy! But it's great to watch them doing that! It's fantastic fun!

Presenter: Sounds like a lot of fun. Well, I really hope you've enjoyed hearing about those festivals again… until next time!

Track 2.26 Unit 7 page 78 Exercise 2

The Giant's Causeway looks like an image from a computer game, but it's real! These amazing geometrical rock columns lead down from the north-east coast of Northern Ireland in a series of giant steps. The tallest columns are over 12 metres high and the steps go down into the sea. You look at these perfect symmetrical shapes and you think, this can't have formed naturally! But, then again, humans can't have built it either. It's just too big!

The local people say it must have been a giant! According to local legends, long, long ago, giants lived in the Celtic lands of Ireland and Scotland. One of these giants, the Irish giant, Finn McCool, wanted to cross the Irish Sea to Scotland to meet and fight another giant, the Scottish giant Benandonner. But Finn didn't like water, so, they say that rather than swim across, he may have built an enormous causeway so that he could walk across the sea. In fact, 70 miles away, on the west coast of Scotland, similar steps lead out of the sea and back to land. So, could a giant have built this causeway just to stop his feet from getting wet?

When Finn saw Benandonner, he realised the Scottish giant was much bigger than him and he couldn't possibly beat him in a fight. He ran back to his wife who had a great idea. In order to trick Benandonner, she dressed Finn up as a baby. The Scottish giant crossed the causeway and when he saw the enormous baby, he must have been absolutely terrified. If the baby was this big, how big was his father? Benandonner ran back across the rocks, never to return! Looking now at these incredible rocks, it's easy to believe that a giant might have built them.

But, of course, there is another explanation. Scientists say that the causeway exists as a result of a series of violent volcanic eruptions more than 60 million years ago. The eruptions pushed columns of hot lava – liquid rock – into the air through the cold water. As the lava passed through the water, it turned to rock and formed these incredible columns we see today.

Which explanation do you prefer? Giants or nature? I think I prefer the first.

Track 2.34 Unit 8 page 88 Exercise 5

Anchor: Welcome to our summary of Florida local news. Today, we have two stories of teenage heroes who stopped very different crimes this week. Tracy, can you tell us what you discovered there?

Tracy: Sure I can, Ted! The first story took place in Tampa. Thirteen-year-old Ralph Black came home from school and found a robber in the living room. Earlier, I asked him what it had felt like when he saw the robber and I also asked him if he'd been scared. He admitted that he'd been a little scared!

Ralph: Well, I walked in and there was this guy – a total stranger – standing in the middle of the room! He saw me and ran straight out the door. I don't know why but I decided to follow him … all the way to the library!

Tracy: And this is what he said when I asked him how he had caught the robber.

Ralph: It was weird. Nobody wanted to help me at first. The police only arrested the man at the library after I insisted that he was a robber.

Tracy: Thanks to Ralph's bravery, the family got their property back and the robber received a fine.

Anchor: Thanks, Tracy – the second crime took place in Jacksonville. Here, James Clyde a 15-year-old at Mountfields High School, gave police the information they needed to rescue a young millionaire. Now, I believe that James himself is there with you Tracey?

Tracy: Yes, he's here with me. So James, I was wondering if you could give us more details about the crime.

James: Sure … well I had just got off the school bus when I saw this businesswoman get stopped by two men and pushed into the back of a red car. I remembered the car really well and that was important. The police promised me I'd receive a big reward for help in finding the kidnappers, so I really tried my best to remember every detail.

Anchor: Well done, young man! So, what happened to that mysterious millionaire, Tracy?

Tracy: Well, she suggested that she and James met to thank him in person! She told me that because the crime was so serious, the kidnappers were sent to prison for twenty years. I asked the police why James's evidence was so important and they explained that it was a very detailed description. James – you love everything about cars and that's why you described it so well!

James: I guess that's right, yes… it was lucky!

Anchor: Well, thanks James and thanks Tracey for the reports, Florida can be proud of its teens today!

Your notes

Your notes

Your notes

Thanks and acknowledgements

The authors and publishers acknowledge the following sources of copyright material and are grateful for the permissions granted. While every effort has been made, it has not always been possible to identify the sources of all the material used, or to trace all copyright holders. If any omissions are brought to our notice, we will be happy to include the appropriate acknowledgements on reprinting.

p. 6: Student's Book Cover: Getty Images/Philippe Marion; Student's Book p. 62: (B/G) Getty Images/Paul Grebliunas; Student's Book p. 63: (L) Alamy/Paul Springett C, (R) Getty Images/RubberBall Productions; p.7: Student's Book Cover: Getty Images/Philippe Marion; p.8: Student's Book p. 62: (B/G) Getty Images/Paul Grebliunas; Student's Book p. 63: (L) Alamy/Paul Springett C; (R) Getty Images/RubberBall Productions; p. 8: Student's Book p. 64: (TL) Alamy/©Robert Slade/ Manor Photography, (CL) Getty Images/iStockphoto/3bugsmom; Student's Book p. 65: (TL) Getty Images/Jutta Klee; p. 9: Student's Book p. 66: (BL) Alamy/©FocusChina, (BR) Shutterstock/Paolo Bona; Student's Book p. 67: (BL) Alamy/©ZUMA Press, Inc., (CR) Alamy/©Piero Cruciatti; Student's Book p. 68: (T) Alamy/©All Canada Photos, (TR) Alamy/©Robert Fried; Student's Book p. 69: (B) Getty Images/Chung Sung-Jun, (CR) Getty Images/Chung Sung-Jun; p. 10: Student's Book p. 70: (CR) Getty Images/Stefano Gilera/Cultura; (BR) Corbis/Barry Lewis; p. 71: (TR) Getty Images/Hugh Threlfall; Student's Book p. 72: (1) Alamy/©Chris Howes/Wild Places Photography, (2) Alamy/©keith morris, (3) Shutterstock/Andy Dean Photography, (4) Getty Images/David Sacks, (5) Getty Images/iStockphoto/8213erika, (6) Alamy/©Kumar Sriskandan, (7) Alamy/©Ian Lamond, (8) Getty Images/Peter DaSilva, (BR) Getty Images/Jupiterimages; Student's Book p. 73: (T) Getty Images/verdateo; p.11: Student's Book p. 120: (CR) Getty Images/The Washington Post; p.11: Student's Book p. 112: (TL) Alamy/©Paul Springett C, (TR) Getty Images/RubberBall Productions; p. 12: Workbook p. 57: (CR) Corbis/BEAWIHARTA/ Reuters; Workbook p. 59: (T) Alamy/©Suzanne Long, (B) Getty Images/Scott Campbell/Contributor; Workbook p. 60: (B) Getty Images/Henglein and Steets, Workbook p. 61: (1) Corbis/Ricardo Azoury, (2) Getty Images/Jeff J Mitchell, (3) Getty Images/Buda Mendes/LatinContent, (4) Getty Images/Anna Bryukhanova, (5) Getty Images/Jeff J Mitchell, (6) Alamy/©Richard Levine; p. 62: (T) Alamy/©Image Broker; p. 13: Workbook p. 64: (T) Alamy/©Tetra Images; Workbook p. 65: (B) Alamy/©J.R. Bale; Workbook p. 92: (B) Alamy/©IanDagnall Computing; p. 16: Student's Book p. 69: (B) Getty Images/Chung Sung-Jun, (CR) Getty Images/Chung Sung-Jun.

Front cover photography by Getty Images/Philippe Marion.

The publishers would like to thank the following Illustrators:

Q2A Media Services inc.: p. 9: Student Book p.68 & 69: p.11: Student Book p. 124.

All video stills by kind permission of:

Discovery Communications, LLC 2015: p. 6: Student's Book Cover, Student's Book p. 62 (1, 2, 4); p. 7: Student's Book Cover; p. 8: Student's Book p. 62 (1, 2, 4); p. 8: Student's Book p. 65 (1); p. 9: Student's Book p. 68 (1); p.11: Student's Book p. 120: (1); p. 14: Workbook p. 94: (1); Cambridge University Press: p. 6: Student's Book p. 62 (3); p. 8: Student's Book p. 62 (3); p. 10: Student's Book p. 70; p. 15: Workbook p. 100 (1).

The authors and publishers would like to thank:
Bartosz Michalowski and Tanya Whatling for their editorial work
Claire Dembry and Julia Harrison for their work on the Corpus and CEFR
Ben Goldstein, Ceri Jones, Vicki Anderson, Ruth Appleton, Diane Nicholls and Joanna Herbert
for their contributions to the Introduction

The authors and publishers are grateful to the following contributors:
emc design ltd: concept design
emc design ltd: text design and layouts
emc design ltd: cover design